THE OIL AND GAS LEASE IN CANADA

JOHN BISHOP BALLEM

The Oil and Gas Lease
in Canada

UNIVERSITY OF TORONTO PRESS

©University of Toronto Press 1973
Toronto and Buffalo

Printed in Canada
ISBN 0-8020-1879-3
Microfiche ISBN 0-8020-0218-8
LC 72-75734

CONTENTS

Preface

The oil and gas lease is an intricate legal document designed to establish and regulate the position of lessor and lessee over minerals lurking thousands of feet below the surface, minerals which are migratory in nature and whose very existence is highly problematical. The current form of lease is the product of more than a century of evolution, most of which took place in a foreign country. In the last twenty years the lease has been heavily battered by Canadian courts and has been subjected to much patching and makeshift repairs.

This book is essentially an enquiry into the present state of the oil and gas lease in Canada and how well it discharges the function of governing the relationship between mineral owner and mineral explorer-producer. I have examined every clause that is normally encountered and have attempted to explain the role each is designed to fill and to analyse the suitability of its present wording. I think it will become apparent that the lease: (a) contains hazards to the lessee (the dogged determination of oil companies to continue with the lethal 'unless' type of drilling clause is explicable only in terms of a corporate death-wish); (b) has provisions which are undeservedly onerous to the lessor and others which are a source of frustration and irritation to him; and (c) has many variations in wording among the various forms, although every lease has the same purpose, so that documents which appear to the layman as generally similar may yield radically different results. In addition, new techniques and procedures as well as legislation have created areas which are not adequately covered by present forms.

In the light of these conclusions, I feel that we now have had sufficient experience and jurisprudence in Canada to devise a document which would remove the hazards to the lessee, improve the position of the lessor, and generally provide a framework within which the minerals could be developed in a reasonable and equitable fashion. Supported by this belief, I have ventured to prepare a model form of lease which I hope achieves these objectives.

Throughout I have tried to keep in mind not only the requirements of lawyers and law students, but also those of professional landmen who deal with leases every day. The landman's work requires a thorough understanding of the lease. It is hoped that this discussion of the lease and the manner in which the individual clauses operate may prove helpful in reaching this understanding.

As legal documents go, the oil and gas lease is a phenomenon. A substantial body of case law has been constructed around it, to the extent that it may be considered a separate branch of the law. It has forced the re-examination and, in some cases, the re-definition of some basic legal concepts. It still contains unanswered questions and problems that remain to be solved. Add to this the fact that it frequently covers resources of astronomical value and one can see why lawyers who work with the lease regard it as a fascinating and challenging instrument. It is in this spirit that I have approached the lease in the following pages.

PART ONE

FUNCTION AND LEGAL CATEGORIZATION
OF THE OIL AND GAS LEASE

1
Function and history of the oil and gas lease

An oil and gas lease is a jumbled collection of rights, grants, concessions, and obligations between the owner of minerals and the would-be developer of them. The exploration for these substances is a costly and risky enterprise and one that the average owner of minerals has neither the inclination nor the financial resources to undertake. Unless the landowner happens to be a huge corporation, such as a railroad, with sufficient resources to run the risk of exploration for oil, he will be happy to delegate the chore to an oil company. This can be achieved by an outright sale of the mineral rights, but such a procedure has little to recommend it from the point of view of either party. The mineral developer could not afford to build up a very substantial land spread if it was forced to pay the fee simple rate, while the mineral owner would be ill advised to dispose of all his rights in the minerals and thus lose the chance of participating in the benefits of a discovery.

The lease approach is the one which best meets the requirements of both parties. It grants to the lessee a lesser interest than an outright fee simple conveyance, but in its modern form confers a sufficient grant and term to permit the operator to remove the minerals if discovered. It protects the interest of the mineral owner by imposing certain time limitations within which the operator must explore the lands or lose the lease, and it preserves for the owner a continuing interest in the minerals by reserving a royalty.

There have been many influences at work in the development of the current form of the oil and gas lease. There is the nature of the right itself, which is much more than that granted under the conventional 'lease' since the mineral lessee must have the right to remove minerals if the grant is to be effective. The physical characteristics of the substances have also had a substantial effect upon the evolution of the oil and gas lease form. The substances are migratory and are free to move from point to point within the confines of a reservoir. In the earliest American cases, the courts seemed to view these minerals as flowing in underground rivers and this colourful, if inaccurate, concept clearly affected some of the formative jurisprudence.[1] As late as 1921 a Texas court had this impression of what took place underground: '... they are supposed to percolate restlessly about under the surface of the earth, even as the birds fly from field to field and the beasts roam from forest to forest ...'[2] Oil and gas do not flow of their own volition in underground streams, but they are capable of moving within the pool if the reservoir balance is disturbed. Thus, if a well commences production, the reservoir pressure in the vicinity of the bore will be altered and these fluid and gaseous hydrocarbons will move towards the lowered pressure. Any document which attempts to deal with such substances must reflect their migratory nature.

HISTORY OF EARLY JURISPRUDENCE

The lease form which we use today is the result of nearly a century and a quarter of evolution and judicial interpretation.

The lessee under an oil and gas lease has one of the most insecure tenures known to the common law. The slightest misstep may detonate one of many booby traps (all placed by the lessee) which will terminate the grant. The interpretation of the courts led to further complexities as the lessee attempted to shore up its position. The result is a document 'containing language notable for its ambiguity.'[3] There is a polite controversy as to whether the first oil well was drilled in Canada or in the United States.[4] The honour seems to belong to a well dug near Petrolia in the Province of Ontario in 1858. This preceded by one year the Titusville, Pennsylvania, well which is generally recognized as having initiated the modern oil industry in North America. Regardless of which well came first, the major development of the industry took place in the United States and it was in that country that the lease form developed its present shape and content. It was the search for salt, that fundamental of life, that led to the establishment of the petroleum industry in America. The need for salt had set in motion the development of techniques and equipment, notably cable drilling rigs, for digging artesian

---

1 Moses, *The Evolution and Development of the Oil and Gas Lease*, Second Annual Institute on Oil and Gas Law, 1
2 *Medina Oil Development Co. v Murphy*, 233 s.w. 333, 335 (Texas Civ. App. 1921)
3 *Canadian Fina Oil Limited v Paschke* (1957) 21 w.w.r. 260, Porter JA, 261
4 *Dusters and Gushers* (1968), 13

wells to produce salt water. The procedures and equipment were adapted to drilling for oil.

The salt industry had evolved a form of lease since the owners of the land were seldom in a position to test their salt-bearing potential. It was common for the owners to grant to others the right to explore and produce in return for a portion of any salt which might be obtained. This type of document was one which could be readily adapted to drilling for oil. American legal writers usually quote the following document as being the first oil lease agreement ever recorded:

Agreed, this fourth day of July, 1853, with J.D. Angier, of Cherrytree township, in the county of Venango, Pa., that he shall repair up and keep in order, the old oil spring on land in said Cherrytree township, or dig and make new springs, and the expense to be deducted out of the proceeds of the oil, and the balance if any, to be equally divided, the one half to J.D. Angier and the other half to Brewer, Watson & Co. for the full term of five years from this date. If profitable.

(signed) Brewer, Watson & Co.,
J.D. Angier.[5]

This elementary form of lease included a number of fundamentals of the modern form, namely the requirement of drilling, 'dig and make new springs'; the designation of a fixed term and the recovery of expenses with a sharing of any resulting profits. It differs from the present approach in that it did not provide for a cash payment for the granting of the right and it terminated at the end of the fixed term regardless of whether or not there was production.

Termination of a lease at the expiration of the defined term could work a very substantial hardship on the lessee who had brought the lands into production. The first solution to this problem was the creation of very prolonged primary terms, some indeed containing a grant of the rights and privileges 'for ever.' By 1875 the industry had accumulated a fair body of experience and individual operators began to amass large-scale holdings of land. This led to less emphasis on immediate drilling, with the lessor being compensated for the delay by monetary payments and the development of a flexible grant that would return the rights to the owner at the end of a fixed period unless there was production. The typical term or *habendum* clause, developed in the final quarter of the nineteenth century, is virtually identical with that commonly in use today and provides that the lessee shall hold the lands for a determined period and for so long thereafter as oil or gas shall be produced therefrom.

5 Moses, *supra* n. 1, 6–7; Walker, 'Defects and ambiguities in oil and gas leases' (1950), 28 *Tex. L. Rev.* 895

Between 1875 and the close of the century the basic ingredients had been developed and were contained in the common form of lease. These ingredients were: (a) payment of a bonus consideration for granting of the rights; (b) a provision for a fixed period of time after which the lease would terminate unless there was production; (c) the reservation of a royalty to the lessor; and (d) a provision under which the lessee could defer a commitment to drill by a monetary payment to the lessor, with the primary term acting as a final limit beyond which the drilling obligations could no longer be postponed.

EARLY CANADIAN FORMS

Exploratory operations in Ontario led to the development of some rudimentary forms which appear to have been based on agricultural leases. The earliest types demised a specified area of land 'for the purpose of prospecting for oil' and 'for the purpose of digging and boring for oil,' with very little else in the way of provisions.[6] There was considerable oil activity in the Province of Alberta in the decades following the Dingman well discovery in 1914, but there was no consistency in the type of lease used. Each was an individual contract, some being no more than a few paragraphs that fell far short of delineating the rights between the parties while other more sophisticated operators used versions of the forms that had developed south of the border. The development of these early Canadian forms is largely irrelevant to the present-day Canadian lease, since a particular type of American lease was imported into this country and quickly gained wide acceptance. The American form was of a type generally described as Producers 88. It is essential to know its background in order to understand the modern Canadian form.

DEVELOPMENT OF PRODUCERS 88

One hundred years ago a compromise had been worked out between the lessor's desire for immediate drilling and the lessee's wish to have the right to postpone the costly operations. A balance was struck through a clause which provided that, if the lessee did not drill immediately, the lessor would be compensated by the payment of a sum of money. This, in turn, led to a provision whereunder the lessee would either commence drilling within a specified period 'or pay the lessor.' To avoid an accumulation of periodic payments the lease granted the lessor the right to surrender.

6 Lewis, 'The Canadian petroleum and natural gas lease' (1952), 30 *Can. Bar Rev.* 965, 968

The Oklahoma Supreme Court interpreted such a clause in *Brown* v *Wilson*[7] and held that, since the lease was voidable at the option of the lessee by surrender, it must be likewise voidable by the lessor.

Obviously this finding caused great consternation in the oil industry. The view that a right of surrender could not be unilateral was subsequently rejected by later Oklahoma decisions.[8] In the meantime, however, oil attorneys had devised a new form to avoid the holding in the *Brown* v *Wilson* case and this form became known as Producers 88. The new form circumvented *Brown* v *Wilson* by eliminating the surrender clause and by substituting for the 'or' clause an 'unless' form under which the lessee did not promise to either drill or pay rentals. The new form resulted in an automatic termination of the lease if the lessee had not drilled by the required time 'unless' it elected to make the payment. As is pointed out by Walker, the new type of lease met with popular approval and prior to 1920 had spread throughout Oklahoma, Kansas, and Texas. It was accepted so widely that landowners frequently insisted upon only the Producers 88 being used. It is not surprising that the designation Producers 88, which had originally been nothing more than the printer's means of identifying the form for his own purposes, began to appear on a great number of leases, some of which bore little or no resemblance to the original document. In subsequent years many revisions were made and the new forms were often described as Producers 88 Revised. The basic Producers 88 document contained an 'unless' type of drilling clause, a fixed primary term with provision for continuance in the event of production and a cash bonus for granting of the lease. It was this form that was imported into Canada.

LEDUC

The oil and gas industry may be said to have been carried on in Canada on a sporadic and localized basis ever since 1858, the year of the Petrolia well.[9]

---

7 (1916) 160 P 94

8 *Northwestern Oil & Gas Co.* v *Branine* (1918) 175 P 533; *Rich* v *Doneghey* (1918) 177 P 86. The details surrounding the drafting of the Producers 88 form are set forth by Walker, *supra* n. 5, 896–7.

9 For a fascinating account of the 1914 oil boom that followed the Turner Valley discovery, see Gray, *The Great Canadian Oil Patch* (1970); *Dusters and Gushers*, *supra* n. 4. In the years following 1858, exploration gradually shifted west to the western Canadian sedimentary basin. The first commercial gas field in western Canada was the Medicine Hat field drilled in 1901. Turner Valley, which was discovered in 1913, was the first substantial producer. In the years intervening between Turner Valley and Leduc in 1947 exploration was largely haphazard and sporadic.

But it was the discovery of the Leduc field, near the city of Edmonton, announced by Imperial Oil Limited in early 1947 which gave it the necessary impetus and economic muscle to grow into the giant it is today. The Leduc discovery sparked some highly organized and extensive land plays. The casual approach to mineral leasing, where each lease was typed up on an individual basis, was no longer appropriate. Efficiency demanded a standardized form and one, moreover, that could be completed by the land agent in the field.

In June 1947 as a preparatory step in a major land acquisition project, Imperial assembled a group of experts to prepare an acceptable form of lease. This group included an independent American lease broker, representatives of an American-affiliated oil company and some local lawyers and landmen. The American experts brought with them a form of the Producers 88 lease.

This form was adapted for Canadian use by including the appropriate affidavits of execution, affidavits or consents and acknowledgment required under the provincial Dower or Homestead Acts, and was reworked to the extent that the drilling covenant, for some reason which remains obscure, was made a proviso to the granting clause rather than a separate and distinct covenant. The lease was then printed on both sides of two folded sheets which made it mechanically easy for the field landman to slip it into his typewriter and fill in the blanks. The form was numbered 23620 and has been revised on several occasions in the intervening years as a result of interpretations placed by the courts upon the language. It remains the closest thing we have in Canada to a standardized lease and is used, sometimes with minor variations, by the majority of mineral leasing companies and by printing firms which publish lease forms.

THE FREEHOLD LEASE IN CANADA

The importance of the oil and gas lease is by no means uniform throughout Canada. Privately owned minerals are the exception rather than the rule. Some provinces have vested or revested by legislative *fiat* all oil and gas in the Crown.[10] In most other provinces the division of mineral rights as between

10 Oil and Natural Gas Act, R.S.N.B. (1952) c 162, s 2; The Petroleum and Natural Gas Act, R.S.N.S. (1967) c 228, s 2; The Oil, Natural Gas and Minerals Act, S.P.E.I. (1957) c 24, s 27. The New Brunswick Act is typical of those of the other Maritime provinces and reads as follows: '2. All oil and natural gas are hereby declared to be, and to have been at all times prior hereto, property separate from the soil and vested in the Crown in the right of the province.'

Newfoundland has also provided for the vesting of petroleum in the Crown, Petroleum Natural Gas Act (1965), S.N. (1965) c 56, although there are some

private individuals and the Crown depends on the point of time at which the Crown began to withhold mineral rights in granting patents of the surface. In Quebec, 1880 is the critical year.[11]

There is no statutory cut-off in Ontario and the normal rule of conveyancing applies, so that if the minerals are reserved such reservation is to be found in the original grant. The policy followed by the government of Ontario with respect to land grants is to reserve or except mines and minerals where the land is granted for resort or agricultural purposes.[12]

In what are now the provinces of Manitoba, Saskatchewan, and Alberta, the lands at the time of the major migration of homesteaders were under the control of the federal government. Originally homesteader grants included mines and minerals, but by order-in-council passed in 1887 the government of Canada provided for the reservation to the Crown of all mines and minerals from patents which had not already been made by October 31 of that year. This, however, applied only to lands west of the third meridian, which is at the approximate east–west centre point of what is now the province of Saskatchewan. Mines and minerals in lands lying to the east of the third meridian were reserved from Crown patents after the year 1889. The mineral rights so retained by the federal Crown were ultimately transferred to the individual provinces to place them in a position of equality with the older provinces which had retained their mineral rights upon entry into Confederation.[13]

Those homesteaders who took out land grants from the Hudson's Bay Company received title to mines and minerals until 1908, when the Company began to reserve mines and minerals to itself. Similarly, those who acquired

exceptions to this: '(3) Privately owned petroleum. – Subsection (2) does not apply to petroleum or any right, title or interest therein which, before the date of the enactment of this Act, was expressly assured to any person other than Her Majesty in right of the province by a statute of the province which is not repealed or by a valid and subsisting deed, lease, license or other instrument made under or pursuant to or ratified by any statute of the province.'

11 Mining Act, s.q. 1965, c 34, s 5–10

12 The confusion and uncertainty that had been created by a lack of a uniform practice in dealing with minerals under land grants was removed by statute (now R.S.O. 1970, c 380, s 63) which declared void any reservations in letters patent issued before May 6, 1913, subject to certain prior existing mining rights. Mines and minerals in lands patented after May 6, 1913, are to pass to patentee unless expressly reserved. S 62 provides that mines and minerals under lands granted for agricultural purposes are reserved after April 1, 1957.

13 Alberta Natural Resource Act 1930 (Can), c 3, 1930 (Alta) c 21; Manitoba Natural Resources Act 1930 (Can), c 29, 1930 (Man), c 30; Saskatchewan Natural Resources Act 1930 (Can), c 41, 1930 (Sask) 87. See also, La Forest, *Natural Resources and Public Property Under the Canadian Constitution* (1969), cs 2 & 3

land from the Canadian Pacific Railway received title to mines and minerals until 1902.[14]

Since the settlement of western Canada by homesteaders proceeded from east to west, there are more privately held mineral rights in the eastern portions. For example, Lewis & Thompson estimate that approximately 75 per cent of the mineral rights in the southwestern part of the Province of Manitoba, where conditions are most suited to oil and gas discovery, is privately owned. On the other hand, only 10 per cent of the mineral rights within Alberta is in private hands, and that figure includes substantial holdings by both the Hudson's Bay Company and the Canadian Pacific Railway Company.[15] In British Columbia the percentage is even smaller, and such privately owned minerals as exist are in those portions of the province where there have been no substantial discoveries to date.

In the light of the current pattern of mineral holdings and the presence of oil and gas, the lease is of importance in Ontario, Manitoba, Saskatchewan, and Alberta. In the event of future discoveries it could become significant in British Columbia, Quebec, and Newfoundland.[16] The lease, however, cannot be disregarded by lawyers in other provinces as mineral owners are migratory and their title moves with them. Thus it often happens that a lawyer, whose practice is far removed from the field of oil and gas, is called upon for his views of that strange document known as the oil and gas lease.

14 See Lewis & Thompson, *Canadian Oil and Gas,* § 27
15 Ibid, § 29
16 Mineral rights outside the boundaries of the individual provinces appear to be vested in the federal government although the ultimate disposition of the off-shore rights remains a matter of negotiation between the federal and certain provincial governments. See *Re Off-Shore Mineral Rights of British Columbia* [1967] S.C.R. 792, where the Supreme Court held that Canada, and not the littoral province, owned the mineral rights of the seabed and sub-soil seaward from the ordinary low-water mark. See also *Statement by the Prime Minister on Off-Shore Mineral Rights in the House of Commons*, March 4, 1969. In any event it is clear that there can be no freehold mineral rights outside presently existing provincial boundaries.

2
Legal category of the oil and gas lease

One of the more engaging characteristics of the oil and gas lease is that under the common law it is not a lease at all. The conventional lease contemplates merely the use of property and the return of it to the lessor at the end of the term in a virtually unchanged state. The rights granted under an oil and gas lease are of an entirely different order and nature since the lessee, in order to enjoy the grant, must have the right to possess and remove the minerals.

The most commonly quoted judicial definition of a mining lease is that of Lord Cairns in *Gowan* v *Christie*[1] as follows: 'Not in reality a lease at all in the same sense in which we speak of an agricultural lease ... What we call a mineral lease is really when properly considered a sale out and out of a portion of land. It is a liberty given to a particular individual for a specific length of time to go into and under the land and to get certain things there if he can find them and to take them away just as if he had bought so much of the soil.'

PROFIT À PRENDRE

The Supreme Court of Canada has characterized the oil and gas lease as a *profit à prendre*, which, simply put, means the right to take something from the soil of another. This judicial definition was arrived at in the case of *Berkheiser* v *Berkheiser*.[2] In this case the court had to decide whether the grant of a petroleum and natural gas lease amounted to an ademption. An ademption occurs whenever a testator, having made a specific devise of land,

1 (1873), L.R. 2 Sc. & Div. 273, 284   2 [1957] S.C.R. 387, 7 D.L.R. (2d) 721

subsequently conveys or sells it to a third party. This act by the testator deprives the specific devisee of its benefits and diverts the proceeds from the sale or conveyance into the residue of the estate. The principle behind ademption is that the subsequent disposition of the property by the testator acts as a revocation of the will.[3] In the *Berkheiser* pattern, the testator in 1947 devised to the appellant a quarter section of land in Saskatchewan. Four years later the testator entered into an oil and gas lease with an oil company. In 1953 he died and sometime subsequent to that event the petroleum and natural gas lease was surrendered by the lessee. The respondents, who were the residuary beneficiaries under the testator's will, argued that the granting by the testator of an oil and gas lease subsequent to the execution of the will amounted to an ademption. The lower courts, the case then being known as *In Re Sykes*,[4] held that the granting of an oil and gas lease was an out and out sale, or agreement for sale, of minerals *in situ* and therefore an ademption had occurred.

The Supreme Court evaluated the terms of the lease as follows:

What as a practical matter is sought by such a lessor is the undertaking of the lessee to explore for discovery and in the event of success to proceed with production to its exhaustion. Neither presence nor absence of the minerals was here known, and initial task was to verify the existence or non-existence of the one or the other. The fugitive nature of each is now well known; a large pool of either, underlying many surface titles, may in large measure be drained off through wells sunk in one of them; tapping the reservoir against such abstraction may, then, become an urgent necessity of the owner.

In that situation the notion of ownership *in situ* is not the likely thing to be suggested to the mind of any person interested because primarily of the difficulty of the factual conception itself. The proprietary interest becomes real only when the substance is under control, when it has been piped, brought to the surface and stored. Any step or operation short of that mastery is still in the stage of capture.[5]

Rand J held that an instrument creating such a right was a *profit à prendre* and that under such instruments the title to the substances as part of the land remains in the owner and upon it is imposed the incorporeal right which the termination of the lease extinguishes. The title having remained in the original owner, there could be no ademption.

---

3 *In Re Dawsett* v *Meakin* [1901] 1 Ch. D 398; *Blake* v *Blake*, 1880 1 Ch. D 481
4 (1955) 16 W.W.R. 172 (Sask.); 16 W.W.R. 459 (Sask. C.A.). I commented on this decision before it reached the Supreme Court of Canada: Ballem, *Pitfalls in the Categorization of Petroleum Leases* (1956) 2 U.B.C. Legal Notes 329
5 *Supra* n. 2, S.C.R. 391

NOT VOID FOR UNCERTAINTY OF TERM

One effect of characterizing an oil and gas lease as a *profit à prendre* has been to defeat attacks based on uncertainty of term. It is impossible to predict how long the substances may be taken from lands covered by a lease; since the lease continues in force by its own terms until production ceases, it has been argued that a lease is void for uncertainty of term. This issue was raised in *Crommie* v *California Standard Company*.[6] The court applied the *Berkheiser ratio* that such a lease was really a *profit à prendre* for an uncertain term and therefore could not be struck down on that basis.

CONTRACT FOR SALE OF PROPERTY AND REAL ESTATE

The judicial categorization of a lease as a *profit à prendre* does not prevent it from fitting into other legal pigeon-holes under different circumstances. In the Supreme Court of Canada decision of *McColl-Frontenac* v *Hamilton*,[7] decided prior to *Berkheiser*, an oil and gas lease was held to be 'a contract for the sale of property' sufficient to bring it within the provisions of section 91 of the Alberta Dower Act. In the *McColl* case there was a defect in the dower affidavit in that the wife had not executed it apart from her husband as required by the statute. Section 91 is a curative provision to the effect that when any woman has executed a contract for the sale of property and the consideration has been totally or partly performed by the purchaser and in the absence of fraud, she shall be deemed to have consented to the sale. The Supreme Court applied the definition of Lord Cairns in *Gowan* v *Christie* wherein the mineral lease was treated as being a sale out and out of a portion of land to find that the instrument came within the definition in the Dower Act. It is clear from the judgment of Estey J that he regarded even a *profit à prendre* as being a sale of property within the meaning of the Act, so that a *profit à prendre* can also be 'a contract for the sale of property.'

A lease, although legally a *profit à prendre* has been held by the Saskatch-ewan Court of Appeal to be a 'disposition' within the meaning of section 9 of the Infants Act. Thus, the court could order the leasing of minerals in which an infant had an interest. The lease is a disposition of at least a part of the contingent interest of the infant.[8]

Mines and minerals comprise part of a testator's real estate and a lease of

---

6 (1962) 38 w.w.r. 447 (Alta.)
7 [1953] 1 s.c.r. 127, 1 d.l.r. 721, 5 w.w.r. (n.s.) 1
8 *Re Thomas Estate* (1958) 24 w.w.r. 125 (Sask. c.a.). This case antedated the 1960 amendment to the Devolution of Real Property Act. An application under that Act would now be effective.

those minerals is an incorporeal hereditament which runs with the land. The rental payable under such a lease is to be dealt with as being 'the proceeds realized from any sale of any real estate.'[9]

An oil and gas lease is a sufficient interest in land to entitle the lessee to redeem a mortgage on the land, but the granting of such a lease does not offend against a covenant in an agreement for sale which prohibited any assignment by the purchaser unless it was approved in writing by the vendor.[10] A lease is real estate within the meaning of the Alberta Real Estate Agents Licencing Act, which prohibits the bringing of an action for commission or remuneration for services in connection with a trade in real estate unless the person bringing the action was licensed as an agent under the Act. Accordingly, a lease 'broker' not licensed as a real estate agent could not bring an action for commission resulting from a transaction in oil and gas leases.[11]

A lease, however, is not 'land' within the meaning of the Alberta Judicature Act. *Sharon Co. Ltd.* v *British American Oil Company Limited*[12] involved an ingenious defence against an action to enforce an agreement to purchase two petroleum and natural gas leases. The purchaser who had elected not to complete the transaction relied, inter alia, upon the Judicature Act[13] which reads: '34.(17) In an action brought upon a mortgage of land, whether legal or equitable, or upon an agreement for the sale of land, the right of the mortgagee or vendor thereunder is restricted to the land to which the mortgage or agreement relates and foreclosure of the mortgage or cancellation of the agreement for sale, as the case may be, ...' If 'an agreement for the sale of land' could apply to an agreement to sell the petroleum and natural gas leases, then the vendor would be without remedy other than cancellation of the transaction. The Judicature Act did not contain a definition of 'land,' but the purchaser argued that the definition of 'land' as contained in the Land Titles Act should be adopted since the two pieces of legislation were in *pari materia*, that is, they dealt with the same subject matter.[14] The definition of 'land' in the latter Act specifically included 'mines, minerals and quarries thereon or thereunder lying or being.' The Alberta Court of Appeal held that the two Acts were not in *pari materia* because the

---

9 *Re Cleveland Estate* (1963) 41 w.w.r. 193 (Sask.)
10 *Gallagher* v *Gallagher and Freeholders Oil Company Limited* (1962–63) 40 w.w.r. 35; *Andrusiak* v *Sitko* (1953), 62 Man. r 117, 8 w.w.r. (n.s.) 449
11 *Arkansas Fuel & Minerals Ltd.* v *Dome Petroleum Ltd. and Provo Gas Producers Limited* (1966) 54 w.w.r. 494
12 (1964) 48 w.w.r. 347
13 r.s.a. 1970, c 193
14 Maxwell on *Interpretation of Statutes*, Eleventh Edition, 34, 35

scope and purpose of the Acts were not similar since the particular section of the Judicature Act was really to protect debtors and had been founded in times of economic depression.

An action to terminate a sub-lease of an oil and gas lease is not a proceeding to recover possession of land within the meaning of a Rule of Court that permits such a proceeding to be commenced by originating notice.[15]

SOMETIMES A LEASE

A *profit à prendre* can also be a lease. This paradox involves two cases and one legislative enactment. In *Re Heier Estate*[16] the Saskatchewan Court of Appeal was faced with an application for approval of a petroleum and natural gas lease granted by the executors of the estate. The application was made under Section 15 of the Devolution of Real Property Act[17] which then read as follows: '15.(1) The personal representative may, from time to time, subject to the provisions of any will affecting the property; (a) lease the real property or any part thereof for any term not exceeding one year; (b) lease the real property or any part thereof with the approval of the court, for a longer term.' The court held that it could not approve the instrument under the above section since 'the so called lease here under review is a sale of a portion of the land in the form of petroleum and natural gas with liberty to enter upon the lands mentioned in the instrument for the purpose of searching for and severing and carrying away the petroleum and natural gas within, upon or under the said lands. The application is made under Section 15 of the Devolution of Real Property Act for the approval of a lease and as the instrument is not a lease the application must be dismissed.'

In 1956 Alberta enacted the Land Titles Clarification Act[18] which provides:

2. It is hereby declared that the term 'lease' as used in The Land Titles Act and any Act for which The Land Titles Act was substituted includes, and shall be deemed to have included, an agreement whereby an owner of any estate or interest in any minerals within, upon or under any land for which a certificate of title has been granted under The Land Titles Act or any Act for which The Land Titles Act was substituted, demises or grants or purports to demise or grant to another person a right to take or remove any such minerals for a term certain or

15 *Stockford and Jackson* v *Willow Creek Holding Company Limited* [1938]
     3 w.w.r. 260
16 (1952–53) 7 w.w.r. (n.s.) 385
17 r.s.s. 1940, c 108   18 r.s.a. 1970, c 199

for a term certain coupled with a right thereafter to remove any such minerals so long as the same are being produced from the land within, upon or under which such minerals are situate.

Professor Thompson writes that it is generally believed that the section was passed so that oil and gas leases could be registered under the Land Titles Act. Financial institutions lending money on the security of leases desired a means whereby their interest could appear on the register.[19]

The issue in the second case, a decision of the Supreme Court of Canada, was identical with that in the *Heier* case, but in *Hayes* v *Mayhood*[20] an Alberta executrix was involved and the Land Titles Clarification Act had been passed. In the *Hayes* case the testator died in 1938 and his executrix granted an oil lease to an oil company in 1957 with the approval of the court made pursuant to that section in the Alberta Devolution of Real Property Act which corresponds to the Saskatchewan section quoted above. The lease was challenged on the ground that court approval could not be obtained since an oil and gas lease was not a lease within the meaning of the Devolution of Real Property Act. The appellant relied upon the *Berkheiser* characterization of a mineral lease as a *profit à prendre* and also referred to the decision of the Saskatchewan Court of Appeal in the *Heier* estate. The Supreme Court of Canada, however, found that the Land Titles Clarification Act had the effect of bringing a mineral lease within the applicable section of the Alberta Devolution of Real Property Act. This result was achieved despite the fact that the Land Titles Clarification Act referred only to 'the term "lease" as used in the Land Titles Act.'

Martland J imported the statutory interpretation into the Devolution of Real Property Act, noting that, while the word 'lease' was not defined in the Act, it must have been intended to include in its application leases of real property under the Land Titles Act. The learned judge also observed, as a sort of second ground for his finding, that, if the meaning of the word 'lease' in the Devolution of Real Property Act was ambiguous, then under the rules of statutory interpretation the definition in the subsequent Act, the Land Titles Clarification Act, could be looked at to see the proper construction applicable to the earlier statute. This rule applies where both statutes are in *pari materia*. Martland J held the two statutes to be in *pari materia* since both had provisions relating to real property in the province of Alberta.

19 Thompson, 'The nature of the oil and gas lease – A statutory Definition' (1960), 1 *Alta. L. Rev.* 463
20 [1959] S.C.R. 568; 18 D.L.R. (2d) 497

Hence the subsequent definition of the word 'lease' in the Land Titles Clarification Act could be applied to the Devolution of Real Property Act.

Insofar as Alberta is concerned, the decision in *Hayes* v *Mayhood* could have far reaching implications. It would seem that it is a sufficient ground to hold the word 'lease' to be ambiguous (a necessary condition for the application of the *pari materia* rule) if there is no definition of it in the particular statute. Accordingly, any Alberta statute which deals with leases and does not contain a definition of 'lease' may apply to the oil and gas lease. This means that Alberta statute law covering ordinary leases of property may be considered as applying to oil and gas leases. Without attempting to catalogue all such statutes, Professor Thompson lists the Landlord's Rights on Bankruptcy Act,[21] the Limitation of Actions Act,[22] the Seizures Act,[23] the Judicature Act,[24] and those English statutes of pre-1870 origin dealing with real property law which are deemed to have been imported into the province.

That the Alberta Legislature is alive to this hazard is shown in the Landlord and Tenant Act.[25] This Act was passed in 1964, well after *Hayes* v *Mayhood*. Section 2 of the Act provides as follows: 'This Act does not apply to minerals held separately from the surface of land or any dealings in minerals.'

In the absence of any legislation such as the Land Titles Clarification Act, both the *Berkheiser* and *In Re Heier* decisions remain undisturbed by *Hayes* v *Mayhood*. In those provinces which do not have the equivalent of the Land Titles Clarification Act it would seem impossible for an executor of an estate to grant an oil and gas lease unless so empowered by specific legislation. In Saskatchewan the problem has been overcome by the enactment of an amendment to the Devolution of Real Property Act[26] which includes a new subsection authorizing the executor, with the approval of the court, 'to lease, grant a *profit à prendre* in respect of or otherwise deal with or dispose of mines and minerals or sand and gravel forming part of the real property.' This permits the granting of a lease without the side effects of *Hayes* v *Mayhood*.

Manitoba has followed the example of Saskatchewan and has amended the Devolution Act by including a specific authorization to the personal representative to grant mineral leases subject to the approval of the court

21 R.S.A. 1970, c 201
22 R.S.A. 1970, c 209   23 R.S.A. 1970, c 338
24 R.S.A. 1970, c 193   25 R.S.A. 1970, c 232
26 s.s. 1960, c 8 (subsequently embodied in Devolution of Real Property Act R.S.S. 1965, c 125)

under certain circumstances:[27] '21A(1) Subject to subsection (2), a personal representative in whom the mines and minerals in, on or under land are vested under this Act may grant, or join in, or consent to, grants of, rights and licences to search for, mine for, drill for, take, win or gain in remove, the minerals or any specified mineral by instrument commonly called a "lease" or otherwise.'

APPLICATION OF LANDLORD AND TENANT LAW

The extent to which the ordinary law of landlord and tenant applies to an oil and gas lease, if at all, remains unclear. In a 1947 decision of the Saskatchewan King's Bench, *Kendall* v *Smith and Northern Royalties Limited*,[28] the court expressed the view that it was doubtful whether the statutory or common law of landlord and tenant should be applied to a contract such as an oil and gas lease, but nonetheless applied such law on the basis that the courts of Alberta, where the documents were most common, have for some years been applying the law of landlord and tenant in establishing the rights of the parties to such contract.[29] The application of the law was further justified by the assumption of the parties that it did apply to their contract. In this instance the lessor has proceeded under the Saskatchewan Landlord and Tenant Act by serving notices to quit, there being no provision for re-entry in the unusual form of lease involved. The court was prepared to assume that such procedures apply to an oil and gas lease, but went on, for other reasons, to hold that the contract had not terminated.

A decade later, the Manitoba Court of Appeal held, again on the basis of *Berkheiser*, that an oil and gas lease, being a *profit à prendre* did not create the relation of landlord and tenant and the common law rights and liabilities arising out of such relationships could not apply, at least insofar as the right of re-entry for breach of condition or covenant is concerned.[30] This latter view appears to be more in line with present-day approach.

The legal categorization of the lease does not alter the fact that it is essentially a contract embodying detailed terms and provisions. Its status as a *profit à prendre*, an interest in land, is of vital import in determining the applicability of certain statutes. The fact that in some of its aspects it partakes of a landlord–tenant relationship may allow the importation of some concepts and techniques from that area of the law, such as the use of a notice to quit,

27 R.S.M. 1970, c D 70
28 [1947] 2 W.W.R. 609
29 The learned trial judge did not cite any authorities for this proposition
30 *Langlois* v *Canadian Superior Oil* (1957–58) 23 W.W.R. 401

the apportionment of a royalty as rent,[31] or possibly the right to distrain for payments due under the lease. Nonetheless, the express terms of the document itself must play the decisive role in ascertaining the rights and obligations of the parties to each other.

31 *Re Dawson and Bell* [1946] 1 D.L.R. 327. For a detailed discussion of this case, see that portion of the text dealing with royalties, *infra*.

PART TWO
ENTERING INTO THE LEASE

3
Negotiations for and capacity to grant a lease

The typical acquisition procedure begins with a decision by an oil company to move into a particular area. Land titles in the land registry office are searched to ascertain the registered owner of the mineral rights. The owner, as disclosed by the register, is then contacted by an employee of the company or by an independent leasing agent acting on its behalf. (The independent agent is often referred to by the apt, if not altogether flattering, sobriquet 'lease hound'). The employee or agent usually will have qualified as a commissioner for oaths so that he may take the required affidavits or acknowledgments where permitted by statute.[1] He will have with him the form of lease currently used by the oil company. The lease will, almost invariably, be in printed form covering both sides of two legal-size folded sheets.

EXECUTION

In the eyes of the prospective lessor the bonus consideration to be paid for the granting of the lease undoubtedly will loom as the single most important factor. Once the dollar figure has been agreed upon, whether at the first or

---

1 The Saskatchewan Homesteads Act specifically disqualifies a person from taking an acknowledgment of a wife when such person, his employer, partner, or clerk has prepared the document in question or is otherwise interested in the transaction involved. This language would appear to be sufficiently broad to disqualify a land agent who negotiates the lease and would certainly disqualify him if he filled in any of the blanks. The Homesteads Act R.S.S. 1965, c 118, s 3. If the disposition includes minerals, Manitoba restricts its eligible officials to lawyers and notaries public, The Dower Act, R.S.M. 1970, c D 100 s 9.

subsequent meetings, the other terms of the lease will be discussed. In an attempt to head off later attacks on the lease, it is the universal practice of all professional landmen to review each clause with the lessor. Any remaining blanks, such as the depository for payments under the lease, are completed and the lessor then executes the lease. This is done by signing the document in front of a witness who may be, and frequently is, the land agent himself, and such witness, then or later, swears the affidavit of execution. There will, or should be, a wafer seal affixed opposite the signature of the lessor. The dower or homestead formalities are completed, whether by way of consent and acknowledgment of the spouse, or by affidavit of the lessor.

On rare occasions, if the person acquiring the lease also happens to be a principal of the lessee company, the lease may be executed by it at the same time. Usually, however, the agent takes with him the lease for subsequent execution by the lessee, sometimes leaving an extra copy of the unsigned lease with the lessor, more often not.

PAYMENT

At this stage of the proceedings the lessee would not have made an exhaustive investigation of the lessor's title and any charges or prior claims that might be registered against it. Nor would the lessee have been able to protect its position by registration of the new lease or a caveat. Consequently, the lessor will be advised that the lease is subject to title and to registration of the lessee's interest. Payment of the bonus consideration is postponed until this has been accomplished with sometimes a definite understanding as to the time period within which payment must be made. More frequently, however, the undertaking as to time within which payment must be made is left quite indefinite. Most land agents now appear to have adopted the practice of leaving at least a token cash payment, presumably to avoid a total failure of consideration. In addition, the agent may give the lessor a bank draft for the full amount conditional upon title approval.

CAPACITY

The fact that an oil and gas lease involves an interest in land, that there is an aspect of title as well as contract, complicates the question as to when and how a lease comes into existence and who may grant it. The ideal mineral lessor would: (a) be the registered owner of the mineral rights free of any lien or encumbrance, (b) have attained his full age of majority, (c) be single, (d) be of sound mind. Such a paragon has full capacity to enter into a lease. Any variation from this model, however, will create its own special problems.

REGISTERED OWNER

A lease taken in good faith from a registered owner remains valid even if the title of that registered owner is subsequently upset. The new owner takes subject to the lease.[2]

MAJORITY

Under the common law a person does not become fully responsible for his deeds and actions and fully able to bind himself by contract until he has attained the age of twenty-one years. This age limit has been reduced in most of the jurisdictions with which we are concerned.[3] British Columbia and Saskatchewan have selected nineteen years as the legislative majority, while Alberta, Manitoba, and Ontario have reduced it to eighteen. Upon attaining his majority, whether it be twenty-one or less, the mineral owner may dispose of his rights. While he remains an infant, however, he does not have this power. Provincial legislation offers a way in which an infant's mineral rights can be dealt with, provided certain safeguards are observed.[4] The Saskatchewan legislation is a typical example of the procedure which must be followed; Section 9 sets forth the tests that are to be applied and the authority that is to be obtained.

Where an infant owns or has an interest in a parcel of land and a sale, lease or other disposition of the same or a part thereof is necessary or proper for his maintenance or education, or his interest requires or will be substantially promoted by such disposition, the Court of Queen's Bench may order the sale, lease or other disposition to be made under the direction of the Court or one of its officers, or by the guardian of the infant, or by a person appointed for the purpose, or by the infant, in such manner and with such restrictions as it deems expedient.

The above section refers to 'disposition,' which has been held sufficiently wide to include a petroleum and natural gas lease.[5] Most provincial legislation

---

2 *Henderson* v *Montreal Trust Company* (1954) 11 w.w.r. (N.S.) 289 (Alta.); affirmed although this specific point not dealt with (1955) 14 w.w.r. 210 (C.A.).
3 The Age of Majority Act, s.b.c. 1970, c 2; The Age of Majority Act, s.a. 1971, c 1; The Coming of Age Act, 1970, s.s. 1970, c 8; The Age of Majority Act, s.m. 1970, c 91
4 The Infants Act r.s.a. 1970, c 185; The Infants Act r.s.s. 1965 c 342; The Infants Act r.s.o. 1970, c 222; The Infants Act r.s.b.c. 1960, c 193; Child Welfare Act r.s.m. 1970, c c80
5 *Re Thomas Estate* (1958) 24 w.w.r. 125. See *ante* ch. 2

contains the identical reference, so it would appear that a lease may be validly granted where the minerals are owned by an infant if the required procedure is followed.[6]

The grounds on which a lease may be approved by the court are cast in very wide and generalized terms. The test is what 'is necessary or proper for his maintenance or education, or his interest requires or will be substantially promoted' by the granting of the lease. *In re Bonner Estate*[7] the application was brought by the administratrix of the estate holding the lands as trustee for four minors. The official guardian had consented to the lease and those of the four infants who were over the age of fourteen years[8] had also consented. The court reviewed the terms of the lease, noting that the bonus seemed reasonable since there was no production of petroleum or natural gas in the immediate area, that the delay rental was at the usual annual rate of $1.00 per acre and the royalty of 12½ per cent was also standard. The court, holding that the interest of the infants would be substantially promoted by the proposed disposition of the substances, approved the application and directed the administratrix to complete the lease.

The same judge refused approval in a subsequent application *In re Crumley Estate*.[9] Section 11 of the Saskatchewan Infants Act provides that the application for the order approving the disposition shall be made in the name of the infant by his next friend or guardian. In the *Crumley* case the lease had actually been signed by the executor some two years before the application was brought. The application was not made by the guardian or next friend but by the oil company lessee. The infant had never consented to the granting of the lease and was seventeen years of age at the time of the application. The official guardian also opposed the application. In the interval between the time the executor signed the lease and the making of the application there had been an intensive search for oil and gas in the general area of the lands. The bonus and delay rentals payable under the lease as signed were considerably less than the same rates offered at the time of the applica-

---

6 British Columbia does not refer to a 'disposition,' but in section 13(1) of the B.C. Infants Act the Supreme Court is authorized to direct the leasing of land owned by the infant for various purposes including 'the working of mines.' This could be interpreted as including the right to make mineral leases, which, in turn, could be extended to include oil and gas leases.

7 (1953) 8 w.w.r. (n.s.) 140

8 A requirement under the Saskatchewan Act, s 11, presumably in acknowledgment of increasing maturity. The consent of a reluctant minor may be dispensed with by order of the court.

9 (1953–54) 10 w.w.r. (n.s.) 284

tion. It was contended by the applicant that the court must consider the circumstances in the light of the conditions at the time that the lease was made. The court dismissed the application, seemingly on a number of grounds, including that it was not brought by the proper party, the wishes of the infant at the age of seventeen should not lightly be disregarded, the official guardian opposed the application, and there was no evidence that the disposition was in the interest of the infant. In fact, the court looked at the circumstances existing at the time of the application, this being the appropriate time as the transaction could not be complete or binding until the approval of the court was obtained, and held that the proposed disposition was definitely not in the interest of the infant.

Saskatchewan, but not the other provinces, dispenses with the approval of the court if the official guardian consents to the disposition of the property and, (a) the value does not exceed $5,000.00 or (b) where one or more infants own not more than an undivided one third share in a parcel of land and the owners of the remaining shares desire to sell or otherwise dispose of the land. In view of the fluctuations in the value of mineral rights it would seem that one would rely on the exemption under (a) at one's peril. Under proper circumstances, however, the second exception is workable.

PERSONAL REPRESENTATIVES

The effect of provincial legislation concerning the real property of deceased persons is to vest such property in the personal representative of the deceased. The personal representative holds the property as trustee for the persons by law beneficially entitled thereto and ultimately is required to convey the real property to such persons. The difficulties encountered by the personal representatives of a deceased mineral owner in granting a valid lease were described in some detail in chapter 2. In those provinces in which the granting of freehold leases is most common, the matter has been dealt with by specific legislation.[10] In the remaining provinces, including British Columbia and Ontario, the capacity of a personal representative to grant a valid lease is doubtful. In those provinces it would seem that no lease could be entered into during the interval between the death of the original mineral owner and the registration of a new title in the name of the heirs.

10 The Devolution of Real Property Act R.S.S. 1965, c 125 s. 15(c); The Devolution of Estates Act R.S.M. 1970, c D 70; Alberta has accomplished the same result by a combination of the Land Titles Clarification Act R.S.A. 1970, c 199 and *Hayes* v *Mayhood* [1959] S.C.R. 568; 18 D.L.R. (2d) 497. See discussion *ante* ch. 2

INCAPACITATED PERSONS

There are two problem areas in dealing with persons whose ability to contract is affected by mental infirmity. First, there is the question of how to obtain a lease where the mineral owner has been officially certified as mentally incapacitated, and secondly, the possibility that a lease granted by an owner not officially certified later might be upset on the grounds that he lacked contracting capacity through mental infirmity.

Once a person has been declared incapacitated, provincial legislation provides that the affairs of such person are to be administered by a committee. The legislation also provides that the committee have certain powers to deal with the property of such person.[11] In some instances, notably in Saskatchewan and Ontario, the question of mineral leases is specifically dealt with and the committee with the requisite order from the court is empowered to grant leases of minerals. In British Columbia the same result would appear to be achieved by Section 16 which grants to the committee all the rights, privileges, and powers with regard to the mental patient's estate as he himself would have had.

In those provinces, however, where the applicable legislation has not been revised to deal specifically with mineral leases, there may be a void. In Alberta the relevant act confers power upon the court to authorize and direct the committee to, among other things, 'grant leases of property.' The act defines 'lease' as: 'means lease with or without an option to the lessee of purchasing.' This definition on its face would not include a mineral lease which has been categorized as a *profit à prendre*. Furthermore, the fact that there is a definition of 'lease' would appear to exclude the *pari materia* approach used in *Hayes v Mayhood* since the existence of a definition theoretically should remove the necessary element of ambiguity.[12]

The legislative procedures, where they exist, offer a clear-cut route by which a mineral lease may be validly obtained from a person who has been declared to be mentally incapacitated. Dealing with a mineral owner who, while not subject to a judicial determination of incompetency, nonetheless betrays signs of imbalance can be both hazardous and unpredictable. The capacity of the lessor may be attacked and, if the attack is successful, the lease will be treated as voidable.

11 The Mentally Incapacitated Persons Act R.S.A. 1970, c 232; The Lunacy Act R.S.S. 1965, c 846; The Administration of Estates of Mentally Disordered Persons Act R.S.S. 1965, c 347; The Patients Estate Act S.B.C. 1962, c 44; The Mental Incompetency Act R.S.O. 1970, c 271; The Mental Health Act R.S.M. 1970, c M110
12 For a discussion of the approach used in this case, see *ante* ch. 2

The principles that govern in a situation of this type were laid down in *Fyckes* v *Chisholm*[13] as follows: 'The contract of a lunatic or person mentally incapable of managing his affairs if not *per se* void, but only voidable on its being shown that the other party had knowledge, actual or constructive, of such lunacy or mental incapacity, failing which such contract, if fair and bona fide, is binding.' Not only must the signing party be established as being incapacitated, but there must be knowledge on the part of the other party to the contract. The knowledge may be either actual or constructive; a party may not avoid knowledge by mere failure to make proper enquiries. The existence of such knowledge is always a question of fact but there are certain guidelines which were well summarized in *Jones* v *Gordon*.[14]

My Lords, the law upon the subject is clear, and in full accordance with sound policy and commonsense. It is thus stated in a work of very high authority: 'A wilful and fraudulent absence of inquiry into the circumstances, when they are known to be such as to invite inquiry, will (if a jury think that the abstinence from inquiry arose from a suspicion or belief that inquiry would disclose a vice in the bills) amount to general or implied notice.'[15]

In *Hunt* v *Texaco Exploration Company*[16] the lessee had been negotiating sporadically for about six years with the lessor in an attempt to obtain a lease, always without success. There was evidence that the lessor, who was at the advanced age of 80 years, suffered from cerebral sclerosis and that his mental condition had deteriorated progressively over a period of years. Two other agents who had attempted to negotiate an oil and gas lease with the lessor testified that they considered him to be mentally incapacitated and so abandoned their efforts to close a transaction with him. Prior to the signing of the lease, there had been an adjudication under which the lessor was found incapable of handling his own affairs, but because of the difficulty of raising the required bond, the committee was not appointed until after the execution of the lease. The action to have the lease set aside on the ground of incapacity of the lessor was brought by the committee.

The trial judge analysed the evidence, including the testimony of the two land agents and the fact that the lessee had known the lessor for several years during which time the lessor had consistently refused to make any deals with him. This analysis led to the finding that the lessee must have been aware of the incapacity of the man with whom he was dealing. The lease was therefore set aside.

---

13 (1911) 19 o.w.r. 977
15 Passage quoted is from Byles on *Bills*, 119

14 (1877) 2 a.c. 616
16 (1955) 14 w.w.r. 449

DOWER AND CURTESY

Under the English common law the wife had a right on her husband's death to have a life estate on one third of the lands he owned at death or had owned since marriage. The right only vested upon the husband's death, but a wife nevertheless had an inchoate interest in the husband's real property during his lifetime. That interest could not be alienated or interfered with by the husband without the wife's consent.[17] Similarly, a husband had a life estate on certain property owned by the wife at the time of her death. This estate was known as curtesy and was subject to his having issue by her born alive and capable of inheriting the property.[18] In the course of years there were many refinements as to what type of property and estate was subject to dower or curtesy and as to the requirements that must be fulfilled before the estates vested. Fortunately, we need not concern ourselves with these fine distinctions since our only enquiry is the restriction or limitation that these ancient rights place upon the granting of an oil and gas lease by a mineral owner.

Dower and curtesy, being part of the existing law of England, were imported by operation of law into the provinces and territories of Canada, except Quebec.

THE WESTERN PROVINCES

Both these marital estates have been eliminated in western Canada. In what is now Alberta and Saskatchewan, the Territories Real Property Act passed in 1886, which established a Torrens system of land title registration, did away with these two survivors of feudalism. They were abolished in Manitoba in 1885, while British Columbia did not remove them until 1925.[19]

The total disappearance of dower rights created hardships and pressure to protect the interest of the wife. These were well described in a passage from *Overland* v *Himelford*:[20]

---

17 *Freedman* v *Mason* (1956) 4 D.L.R. (2d) 576; Anger and Honsberger, *Canadian Law of Real Property* (1959), 51–2
18 Ibid, 82
19 See Bowker, *Reform of the Law of Dower in Alberta* (1955–61) 1 *Alta. L. Rev.* 501; the present-day form of the legislation abolishing these estates is to be found; Transfer and Descent of Land Act R.S.A. 1970, c 368; The Administration Act R.S.B.C. 1960, c 3; The Law of Property Act R.S.M. 1970, c L90; The Devolution of Real Property Act R.S.S. 1965, c 125; The Intestate Succession Act R.S.S. 1965, c 126
20 [1920] 2 W.W.R. 481

Previous to the year 1915, the people of this province had experienced a land boom, particularly in the cities and towns, with all its attendant speculation. The wives in Alberta said, in effect, to the Legislature, where this speculation affects our homes we want it stopped. We have a home in the morning but it is sold or mortgaged at night. Our husbands may deal with their lands as they please subject only to their duty of providing us with a home which shall be placed beyond the risk of their speculation. These representations resulted in legislation in 1915 called The Married Woman's Home Protection Act, ch. 4. The name of this Act is very suggestive, although it created no right of property in the wife. It gave her only a right of filing a caveat which forthwith clouded the title, and prevented the husband from dealing with the land, in so far as registration was required, from the moment the caveat was lodged.

The three prairie provinces, Alberta and Saskatchewan in 1915, and Manitoba in 1918, responded to this pressure by enacting legislation protecting the family's rights to the homestead. In British Columbia the absence of dower persisted from 1925 until homestead protection legislation was passed in 1948.

While these provincial enactments are referred to interchangeably as relating to dower or homestead rights, they are really homestead acts and are based upon the homestead laws that were developed in many state jurisdictions in the United States. These laws protected the family homestead by restricting the right of the owner to dispose or encumber it, granting the wife or family a life estate in it after the owner's death and making it exempt from seizure or sale under execution.[21]

There is a general similarity in purpose and structure among the western legislation dealing with dower and homestead rights, but there is also a considerable variation as to the procedures and forms that are to be followed. Consequently, when dealing with leases in each province, it is essential to scrutinize the appropriate legislation to determine that the precise requirements have been met. The main areas of concern, if not the details of compliance, are common to all the legislation.

APPLICATION OF DOWER OR HOMESTEAD TO OIL AND GAS LEASES

The various provincial acts, in effect, prohibit a disposition of the homestead without the consent of the wife. The language used in describing what is

21 This latter feature is achieved in western Canada by separate enactments, see,
for example, Homesteads Act R.S.B.C. 1960, c 175; Exemption Act R.S.A. 1970, c 129

prohibited, whether it be a 'disposition' or 'transfer any interest in land,' is certainly broad enough to include the granting of an oil and gas lease, which is both an interest in land and a disposition. The Alberta legislation expressly applies dower to mines and minerals contained in a homestead, but this does not appear necessary. British Columbia, as will be noted later, requires the added element of registration before the homestead law applies.

DEFINITION OF HOMESTEAD

The three prairie provinces impose an area limitation on the homestead. In a city, town, or village, the limitation will be the parcel of land on which the dwelling place is located up to a certain number of lots. In rural areas, much more relevant to oil and gas leases, the limitation is based on acreage. In Alberta and Saskatchewan the limitation is 160 acres, while in Manitoba it is 320 acres.

If lands are involved in addition to the homestead, i.e. if an oil and gas lease covered 320 acres in Alberta or Saskatchewan, the transaction could not be enforced as against the homestead portion, nor could damages be recovered from the owner for failure to perform an agreement to sell the homestead. The Supreme Court of Canada reasons that if damages were assessed against the husband by reason of his wife's refusal to consent to a disposition of the homestead, then, since the fortunes of husband and wife are intertwined, there would be an element of compulsion on the part of the wife to so consent.[22] With respect to the remaining portion of the lands, the court has jurisdiction to either grant specific performance of the transaction, or damages in lieu thereof.[23] Applying this to an oil and gas situation, there is a possibility that the lessee could obtain specific performance of the lease against that portion of the lands not included in the homestead.

Whether a given parcel of land does or does not constitute the homestead usually is self-evident from the facts. Occasionally, however, there may arise a situation where the circumstances of the transaction or of the parties themselves may create doubt as to the applicability of the act. In *Anderson* v *Reid*[24] the land originally had been acquired by the plaintiff and his wife from the Soldier Settlement Board but his agreement for sale was subsequently cancelled owing to default. He continued in possession under yearly leases until the lands were put up for sale by public tender. The Board assured him that he would be given prior consideration when the tenders were reviewed. In order to submit a bid he raised money from the defendant and the arrange-

22 *McKenzie et al.* v *Hiscock et al.* (1968) 65 D.L.R. (2d) 123 (S.C.C.)
23 Ibid
24 (1957) 21 W.W.R. 186

ment between them was that the money would be advanced not by way of loan, but solely on the condition that the defendant would obtain absolute title. The plaintiff would be allowed to continue living on the land until it was required by the defendant. The plaintiff's bid was accepted and the defendant advanced the purchase price. In order to complete the transaction the plaintiff executed a transfer of the land to the defendant but plaintiff's wife did not consent to it. The two transfers, from the Board to the plaintiff and from the plaintiff to the defendant were registered only one minute apart. The court held that the Homesteads Act did not apply because the transfer given by the plaintiff husband did not convey or transfer any equitable interest in the land but was necessary merely for the completion of the proposed transaction.

The Manitoba Court of Appeal dealt with homestead and a single person in *Langan* v *Ducharme*.[25] Langan, a widower, owned and occupied a house. He then married the plaintiff who was a widow and moved into her home. The plaintiff wife did not on any occasion reside at the home owned by her husband. Some months after the marriage, Langan transferred his own house to the defendant and himself as joint tenants. The plaintiff wife did not give a consent under the Dower Act and Langan's affidavit on the transfer stated that no part of the land was or ever had been his homestead within the meaning of the act. Langan then left the plaintiff and moved back to his former home at a time which the court found to be subsequent to the execution of the transfer. The court held that at the time of the marriage Langan's home was not a 'homestead' within the purpose and object of the Act and that in fact the homestead of the marriage was the plaintiff's residence. It also adopted the words of Kilgour J in *National Trust Co.* v *Greenguard*:[26] 'Although in some contexts a man may be said to have several homes, in my opinion, the essential scheme of the statute under consideration excludes the possibility of more than one home at a time.'

The court expressly refrained from dealing with some other points which were raised but were not necessary for the disposition of the appeal. The questions which remained open were:

Whether if a *married* owner occupies a dwelling house as his or her home, the other spouse never living in the house, it is a 'homestead' within the meaning of the Dower Act; whether if the spouses each own a dwelling house and both houses are during the marriage occupied by the owner as the home (with or without the other spouse) there could be two 'homesteads' within the meaning of the act, with each spouse having dower rights in the 'homestead' of the other;

25 (1957) 22 w.w.r. 126   26 [1929] 3 w.w.r. 363, 366

whether a house owned by one spouse can be the 'homestead' of both spouses or whether it can be the 'homestead' only of the owner, the other spouse having rights therein as provided by the Dower Act?

RIGHT OF THE HUSBAND IN HOMESTEAD

The four western provinces wiped the slate clean of dower and curtesy and replaced it with specific legislation. Two of the provinces, Manitoba and Alberta, granted the husband a claim against the homestead of the wife, while the other two have confined the homestead rights to the wife. Manitoba achieved this result by a specific provision granting the husband, where the wife owns the homestead, the same rights as she would have where he was the registered owner. Alberta, in its Dower Act, uses words such as 'married person' and 'spouse,' which are applicable equally to both husband and wife. British Columbia and Saskatchewan have confined their homestead legislation to granting the wife rights with respect thereto. For the purposes of our discussion of dower rights any reference to 'wife' or to the feminine gender should be deemed to include the husband, where appropriate, in all references to Alberta and Manitoba legislation.

EFFECT OF LEASE WHERE CONSENT OF WIFE NOT OBTAINED

Dower and homestead rights are an anomaly in the Torrens land registry system. This system, which prevails in Alberta, Saskatchewan, British Columbia, and in Manitoba and Ontario with some admixture of the old registry system, is based upon the indefeasibility of the register. The main feature of the Torrens system has been described:

The object is to save persons dealing with registered proprietors from the trouble and expense of going behind the register, in order to investigate the history of their author's title, and to satisfy themselves of its validity. That end is accomplished by providing that everyone who purchases, in *bona fide* and for value, from a registered proprietor and enters his deed of transfer on the register shall thereby acquire an indefeasible right, notwithstanding the infirmity of his author's title.[27]

With the exception of British Columbia, dower rights are invisible. They do not appear on the register and there is nothing against the title to show

27 *Gibbs* v *Messer* [1891] A.C. 248

whether the lands in question are subject to any such claim. British Columbia has circumvented this aspect by structuring its legislation so that the existence of dower rights depends on an entry made on the register. If the register does not disclose this entry, then the wife's right to dower is defeated. While this undoubtedly contributes to the certainty of a registered title, it has some obvious drawbacks in that the wife may not know of the requirement to file or may be reluctant to do so since such action may introduce an arm's length aspect into the marriage relationship. In the other provinces, the purchaser must always seek out and deal with dower rights.

The conflict between dower and the Torrens system has led to some uncertainty as to the precise status of a disposition of the homestead where the consent of the wife has not been obtained. The British Columbia legislation makes such a disposition 'null and void for all purposes,' and Manitoba provides that such a disposition shall be 'invalid and ineffective.' This language would seem to establish that in those provinces at least such a disposition would be totally unenforceable and would give rise to no rights against the homestead.

Alberta and Saskatchewan follow a somewhat different route in protecting the homestead rights. Saskatchewan requires that every disposition or encumbrance of the homestead shall be signed by the wife. Alberta prohibits a married person from disposing of the homestead unless the spouse consents in writing and makes a married person who so disposes guilty of a summary conviction offence. The Alberta legislation also provides that where a married person makes a disposition without the consent of the spouse which results in a registration of title in the name of another person, that title is valid and the spouse's rights are for damages equivalent to one half of the money paid for the property. This does not apply to oil and gas leases which do not result in a new title.[28] Apart from this, neither province specifies the legal status of a disposition without the required consent. Two decisions of the Supreme Court of Canada appear to hold that a defective disposition is totally unenforceable in these provinces. *Meduk* v *Soja*[29] involved the Alberta Dower Act and an agreement for sale of a house in Edmonton which was owned by the wife and was the homestead of the couple. (Remember that in Alberta the husband also has dower rights.) Her husband did not consent to the

28 For a full discussion of the various versions of Alberta legislation and the development of the present act, see Bowker, *supra* n. 19, 502–8
29 [1958] s.c.r. 167; consent of the spouse must be obtained even when the agreement is only a preliminary agreement. In *Rose* v *Dever* [1972] 2 w.w.r. 431 the Manitoba Court of Appeal held that where a married man signed a standard real estate form of offer to purchase, which did not contain the consent of the wife, the document was unenforceable.

agreement. He was asked by the real estate agent in the presence of the prospective purchasers whether he would sign the agreement, but declined on the ground that the property belonged to his wife and she could do what she wanted with it. It was obvious from the evidence that both the vendors and the purchasers were unaware that the provisions of the Dower Act applied to the transaction. The purchasers moved into possession of the premises and there was evidence that the husband assisted in turning over possession to them and even suggested that the deal be postponed until the listing with the real estate agency had expired so as to avoid payment of commission. Since it was an agreement for sale only, no new title had been created under the Torrens system. Some two months after the purchasers had moved in, the vendor wife commenced proceedings to obtain possession on the grounds that the spouse had not consented to the disposition. Cartwright J said 'the making of the agreement by her without the consent in writing of her spouse was expressly forbidden by section 3(1) of the Act and unless John Meduk did consent in writing, *her acceptance was ineffective to form a contract*' (italics mine).

The Saskatchewan Homesteads Act was subsequently reviewed by the Supreme Court on the same point. In *McKenzie* v *Hiscock*[30] the court interpreted *Meduk* v *Soja* as establishing that without the required consent there could be no enforceable contract. While the latter case dealt with the Alberta legislation which differs in some respects from that of Saskatchewan, it was clear that the court applied the same principles and also considered a previous decision of the Saskatchewan courts which, dealing with an earlier form of the Homesteads Act, held that the assent of the husband alone to an agreement of sale respecting the homestead is 'an ineffectual assent.'[31]

Despite the fact that the Alberta and Saskatchewan legislation does not expressly make such a disposition null and void, the current weight of judicial opinion is that a defective disposition, not creating a new registered title, will be so considered.

CONSENT AND ACKNOWLEDGMENT

All of the acts require the written consent of the spouse to a disposition of the homestead. Manitoba provides that the consent may be embodied in or endorsed upon the actual disposition or may be by a separate document. British Columbia provides that the consent may be embodied in or endorsed upon the instrument and also that the execution by the wife of any disposition

---

30 *Supra* n. 22
31 *Halldorson* v *Holizki* [1919] 1 w.w.r. 472; affirmed 47 d.l.r. 613

by itself constitutes the necessary consent. Alberta and Saskatchewan are more particular as to the affixing of the consent and require that the disposition shall contain, or have annexed to, or endorsed, or written thereon, the form of declaration by the wife that she has executed the same for the purposes of relinquishing her rights in the homestead. If the form of declaration is contained in the instrument, the signature of the spouse to the instrument will also be a sufficient signature to the consent. If, however, the consent is annexed to the instrument, the spouse must sign both the consent and the instrument.

The distinction between 'contained in' and 'annexed to' caused much judicial soul searching in *Reynolds* v *Ackerman*.[32] The lease in this case did not follow the normal printed form, but consisted of two pages of typewriting, with both the consent and certificate of acknowledgment appearing on another page attached to the lease. Both the form of consent and the certificate of acknowledgment were properly completed by the wife, but she had not signed the lease itself.

The neat point at issue was whether the consent should be considered as 'annexed to the instrument' or 'contained in the instrument.' If the latter, then the signature of the spouse to the consent form would be sufficient. It would be otherwise, however, if the consent was merely annexed to the instrument, since under those conditions both documents required the signature of the spouse. The judge concluded that, because the consent was on a separate sheet, it must be considered as having been annexed to the instrument rather than forming part of it. This conclusion was reached with reluctance, the court rather wistfully declaring that if the consent had been placed on the front of page one, or somewhere on page two, or even on the back of page two, it would have been considered as having been contained in the instrument. In the result the lease was declared invalid.

CERTIFICATE OF ACKNOWLEDGMENT

A consenting spouse must also acknowledge that she is aware of the nature of the disposition and of the protection offered by the homestead legislation and that the consent was given free of compulsion. To fortify the latter requirement, the legislation uniformly requires that this acknowledgment be taken separate and apart from the disposing spouse. Each province has its own form of acknowledgment which must be strictly complied with, but the foregoing represents the purpose of such a precaution. The legislation also

32 (1960) 32 w.w.r. 289 (Alta.); (Judgment actually rendered November 27, 1953, but the decision was not reported until 1960)

lists the officials who are authorized to take the certificate. British Columbia and Alberta include any person so authorized under the respective Land Titles or Land Registry Acts. These are judges, court and land registry registrars, notaries public, magistrates, justices of the peace, down to and including commissioners for the taking of affidavits. The other two provinces are more selective. Manitoba requires that where the disposition is with respect to a mineral interest, the acknowledgment must be made before a barrister-at-law or a notary public. Saskatchewan does not include commissioners in its list of acceptable officials and excludes any person from taking an acknowledgment of the wife when that person, his employer, partner or a clerk has prepared the document in question or is otherwise interested in the transaction involved.

The requirement that the acknowledgment be taken apart from the other married partner has given rise to a substantial amount of litigation and has overthrown a number of otherwise valid documents. In *Brown* v *Prairie Leaseholds Ltd.*[33] the evidence accepted by the court established that, when the wife signed the form of acknowledgment, she did so in a room where her husband was moving in and out, dressing the children in snow-suits to go to a Christmas party. There was no evidence of any compulsion on the part of the husband and it was clear that the wife understood the nature of the document and signed of her own free will and volition. It was held nonetheless that the requirement that the acknowledgment be made apart from her husband was mandatory: 'the plain intendment of the phrase in my opinion is that husband and wife should be separated from each other so that it would not be possible for him to hear anything she might be saying or anything that might be said to her, and so that he cannot see whether she is signing her name or whether she is not signing it.'[34]

In *Reddick* v *Pearson*[35] the defendant husband leased the petroleum and natural gas rights under the homestead and the defendant wife, although not described as a party to the lease, signed at the foot of the document below her husband's signature. Various payments were made under the lease and sometime after its execution the lessee sent the defendants a typewritten acknowledgment in the form prescribed by the Act. The defendants took it to the home of a commissioner for oaths who read it silently, the defendant wife signed it, and then the commissioner signed it. The husband was present in the room and at the table where the signing was done. It was then returned to the lessee and attached to the lease. McLaurin J found that public policy

33 (1953) 9 w.w.r. (n.s.) 577 (Man.) affirmed without written reasons (1954)
   12 w.w.r. (n.s.) 464 (c.a.)
34 (1953) 9 w.w.r. (n.s.) 594   35 [1948] 2 w.w.r. 1144

required a strict compliance with the terms of the Dower Act: 'I have arrived at the conclusion that under this Act a stage has been reached where by reason of considerations of public policy it is imperative that the wife's consent to any disposition be given in accordance with the requirements of sec. 7 and that her hearty concurrence otherwise with this transaction does not estop her or her husband from invoking the Act to nullify the lease.'[36]

In *Friess* v *Imperial Oil Limited*[37] the male plaintiff lived on a half-section of land as purchaser under an agreement for sale, one quarter-section of the land was the homestead. An agent of the defendant company met with the plaintiff and negotiated an oil and gas lease. At this time the plaintiff's wife was ill and the declaration and acknowledgment were not taken, nor was she examined apart from her husband. At the request of the agent the fourteen-year-old daughter of the plaintiffs signed her mother's name to the declaration and a justice of the peace completed the required certificate. For a number of years the delay rental payments were made and accepted; then an action was brought to set aside the lease on the grounds of non-compliance with the Homesteads Act. The lease was held to be null and void with respect to the homestead, although still binding with respect to the other quarter-section.

DISPENSING WITH CONSENT

Each act contains machinery whereby the requirement of consent may be dispensed with. The approval or direction of the court is required in each instance and there is some variation among the provinces as to the grounds on which such an order may be obtained. British Columbia provides that it may be obtained where the husband and wife are living apart or where the wife has not lived within the province since the marriage, or her whereabouts are unknown, or she is mentally incompetent, or the consent has been unreasonably withheld. The grounds in Manitoba obtain when the parties have been living apart for six months or more or the spouse is mentally incompetent. Alberta allows the dispensation when the parties are living apart, where the spouse has not lived within the province since the marriage, where the whereabouts of the spouse are unknown, where there are two or more

36 Ibid, 1147. Bowker suggests that this case may have been overruled by *McColl-Frontenac Oil Co.* v *Hamilton* [1953] 1 s.c.r. 127, 1 d.l.r. 721. The latter case applied a curative provision to cure a defect in the acknowledgment and, presumably, the same route was available to the court in the *Reddick* case. In the absence of any observation on the curative provision from the court in the *Reddick* decision this must retain conjecture. In any event, since the clause no longer exists in Alberta, the *Reddick* decision is good law
37 (1954) 12 w.w.r. (N.s.) 151

homesteads, or where the spouse is a mentally incompetent person. Saskatchewan injects a note of morality by providing that the order may be obtained where the wife of the owner is living apart from her husband 'under circumstances disentitling her to alimony,' or is of unsound mind.

The dispensing power in an earlier form of the Manitoba Dower Act was reviewed by the Court of Appeal in *Monchamp* v *Monchamp*.[38] At that time the requirement was that the wife had been living apart from the husband for two years or more. The period has now been shortened to six months, but the wording 'living apart' has been retained. In the *Monchamp* situation the husband had previously obtained an order to dispense with the consent of the wife since the parties had been living apart for more than the required period of time. The order provided that one-third of the purchase price was to be held in trust pending the disposition of a then existing divorce action. The husband subsequently obtained a divorce and applied to have the monies paid out to him. There was evidence that the wife had separated from her husband because of his cruelty. The court held that, where a separation had been caused by the cruelty of the husband, the wife should not be deprived of her dower rights. The same approach was applied in *Hall* v *Neff*,[39] the court interpreting another provision of the Manitoba Act which disentitled the wife from any right under the Act where she had left her husband, 'with the intention of living separate and apart from him.' In this case the widow had been living separate and apart from her husband under a separation agreement, and upon his death she claimed an interest in a dwelling house which her husband had purchased some six years after the parties had separated. The court held that the section which deprived a widow of her dower rights where she had left her husband with the intention of living separate and apart could not apply where the parties had separated by agreement. Under those conditions the wife could not be said to have left or abandoned him. Both cases quoted with approval an earlier decision of the Manitoba Court of Appeal:[40]

What the legislature had in view in enacting this section was that if the wife, on her own initiative, elects to abandon or desert her husband, she shall then be taken to have forfeited her rights in his property, but if she lives apart from her husband under an agreement between them she surely cannot be said to have left or abandoned him within the meaning of the section. What might be regarded as a proper penalty for the wife's desertion of her husband would, where the husband agrees and consents to her leaving and living apart from him, be a manifest

38 (1953) 8 w.w.r. (n.s.) 366
39 (1953) 8 w.w.r. (n.s.) 380 (Man.)   40 *In re Linius* [1923] 1 w.w.r. 272

act of injustice, which the legislature never intended, and, where the wife is compelled by the acts and conducts of the husband to leave, and live apart from him, the injustice would be still more glaring. I am of the opinion, therefore, that this case does not come within sec. 20 and the widow is, consequently, entitled to her share in her late husband's estate under the provisions of the Dower Act.

This line of reasoning is still applicable to the approach taken in Saskatchewan where the consent may be obtained only if the wife has left under conditions disentitling her to alimony. In the other provinces the requirement is merely that the parties be living apart. Undoubtedly, the circumstances would have some bearing on the conditions in the order regarding the manner of payment of the purchase price or holding a portion in trust for the wife's claim.

AFFIDAVITS

All of the jurisdictions, save British Columbia, provide an alternative to the consent of the spouse under certain conditions. The owner may make an affidavit that he is not married or that the land in question is not his homestead.[41] This procedure has no place under the British Columbia scheme which depends upon actual registration of the homestead before it becomes operative.

JOINT OWNERSHIP

The Alberta Act contains a specific exception to dower where the married person is a joint tenant, tenant-in-common, or owner of a partial interest in the land with a person or persons other than the spouse. Under these conditions the act does not apply. In a sense this clause may be regarded as an extension of the common-law dower position which held that dower could not apply to a joint tenancy, but the wife was entitled to her dower rights where the land was held as a tenant-in-common since there was a separate and divided title in the latter instance. The other western provinces do not contain this exception and it would seem that the particular requirements of the relevant acts must be complied with, although one would not expect to encounter many instances where a homestead would be owned jointly with a third party.

41 Once again there is some variation in the precise form and wording of this affidavit among the various provinces, but the effect is the same. Manitoba requires an additional affidavit by the grantee that, when the wife consents, the consenting woman is in fact his wife.

CURATIVE PROVISIONS

With the exception of Alberta, the western provinces have some form of curative provision embodied in the act. The clause in the British Columbia act is virtually identical with one contained in a former version of the Alberta Dower Act. The Alberta provision was considered by the Supreme Court of Canada in *McColl Frontenac Oil Company* v *Hamilton*,[42] which involved an oil and gas lease. The defect in this particular case was that the acknowledgment of the wife's consent was made in the presence of her husband. The lessee relied upon the curative provision then present in the Alberta Act: '9.(1) When any woman has executed a contract for the sale of property, or joined in execution thereof with her husband, or given her consent in writing to the execution thereof, and the consideration under the contract has been totally or partly performed by the purchaser, she shall, in the absence of fraud on the part of the purchaser, be deemed to have consented to the sale, in accordance with the provisions of this Act.' The court held that the granting of an oil and gas lease came within 'sale of property' and applied the clause to uphold the lease.

This provision was removed from the Alberta Act in 1948,[43] but the British Columbia Act contains a similar clause, although the reference to 'sale of property' has been changed to 'sale of the homestead.' Bowker queries whether this language would cover an oil lease. The point is a nice one and in the absence of any authority must remain open.

Both the Saskatchewan and Manitoba curative provisions are basically the same. They provide that no person acquiring an interest under the instrument shall be bound to make enquiry as to the truthfulness of the facts alleged in the affidavit or in the certificate of acknowledgment, and upon delivery of such instrument it will become valid and binding, except for fraud. The acts also define what constitutes fraud as knowledge on the part of the person taking under the instrument that the land is in fact the homestead and that the person making the disposition has a wife who is not a party to the document. If fraud is present, the wife can have the new certificate of title cancelled. The curative provisions in both Saskatchewan and Manitoba undoubtedly will cover most instances and protect the purchaser. They cover both affidavits by the grantor that the land was not the homestead and acknowledgments by a consenting spouse.

A false affidavit was involved in *Prudential Trust Co. Ltd.* v *Olson*[44] wherein the grantor swore that the lands were not his homestead, although

---

42 *Supra* n. 36
43 Dower Act 1948 S.A., c 7   44 [1960] S.C.R. 227

in fact they were. There were two subsequent assignments of the lease; Canadian Williston was the lessee at the time the action was brought. The Supreme Court of Canada held that the curative provision applied to protect a *bona fide* purchaser for value and there was no evidence that Canadian Williston had any knowledge of the fact that the lands had included the grantor's homestead; nor was there any evidence that the original agent who took the lease had any such knowledge.

In *Farmers Mutual Petroleum* v *Jackson*[45] the farmer transferred his mineral rights. The document was obtained by an agent of the plaintiff company at the farmhouse. The farmer completed an affidavit that the land was not his homestead, although in fact it was. Apparently the grantor felt that the reference to homestead in the affidavit meant taken and 'homesteaded' under the Dominion Lands Act. The trial judge found that the agent knew, or should have known, that the land was the defendant's homestead and therefore the agent's principal could not rely on the protection of the curative provision.

The majority of the cases involved a defect in the wife's consent. In *Lavoi* v *Marchildon*[46] the action was brought for specific performance of an agreement for sale. The defence relied upon the fact that the person who took the wife's acknowledgment had also typed in a clause which was inserted into the agreement and thus was disqualified. The Saskatchewan trial court found that both the plaintiff and his wife fully understood the nature of the transaction, but that subsequent developments had made them unwilling to proceed with the sale. Offended by such a use of the act the court declared that to permit the defendant to escape his obligations by setting up his wife's rights under the Homesteads Act would be unconscionable and would be using the act as an instrument to further unconscionable dealing. The curative provision was applied to make the agreement 'valid and binding.' Since the wife was a party to the document, the exception to this clause could not be invoked.

The curative provision came to the rescue of an assignee of the original lessee in *Bonkowski* v *Rose and Cordillera Petroleum Limited*.[47] At the time of granting the lease the wife was willing to join and she signed the prescribed forms. On the evidence, however, she not only signed the certificate in the presence of her husband, but also never appeared before the justice of the peace who signed the form. The document appeared perfectly regular. The lessee's interest in the lease was subsequently assigned to the defendant Cordillera whose agent testified that, following his normal practice, he would

45 (1956) 19 w.w.r. 625
46 (1953) 8 w.w.r. (n.s.) 366   47 (1955) 16 w.w.r. 481

have examined the form of consent and acknowledgment and, on the basis of such examination, concluded that the requirements of the act had been met. The lease was upheld on the basis that it was the intent of the curative provision to protect a purchaser who relies on facts stated in the certificate. This decision is significant in that there can be no doubt that the agent who originally took the lease had knowledge of the deficiency. Nonetheless, a *bona fide* subsequent purchaser can rely on a certificate which has no patent defect.

The *Bonkowski* decision was applied in *Kuball* v *Prudential Trust Company and Canadian Williston Minerals Limited,*[48] where the same defect occurred in that the wife had not appeared before the justice of the peace who completed the certificate. The Supreme Court of Canada expressly approved the *Bonkowski ratio* in *Prudential Trust Co. Ltd.* v *Forseth.*[49] The document in the *Forseth* situation was actually a transfer of an undivided one-half interest in the mineral rights, but was referred to as a lease in both the form of consent and certificate of acknowledgment. Martland J held that the essential requirements of the Homesteads Act are 'that the wife shall sign the instrument; that, on separate examination by a proper officer, she shall acknowledge that she understands her rights to the homestead and signs the instrument of her own free will and consent, without compulsion by her husband, and that she has executed it for the purpose of relinquishing her rights in the homestead.' It was the view of the court that the inaccuracy of the description of the documents in the true form was not material to the circumstances of the case. It would appear from the foregoing passage that such a misdescription would not have been fatal even as between the original parties. The *Bonkowski* case was referred to and its finding that the object of the curative section is to give a transferee in good faith protection where there has been a *prima facie* compliance with the act was approved.

ONTARIO

Ontario has retained a common-law right to dower as modified, limited, and extended by legislation.[50] The Ontario Dower Act[51] contains some of the most stunningly anachronistic language still to be found in Canadian statute books.[52]

---

48 (1957) 21 w.w.r. 273 (Sask.)
49 [1960] s.c.r. 210; 30 w.w.r. 241, 21 d.l.r. (2d) 587 (s.c.c.)
50 Anger & Honsberger, n. 17, 52
51 r.s.o. 1970, c 135 (originally enacted in 1834, 4 Wm. iv, c 1)
52 Regard, for example: '1. A wife, on the death of her husband may tarry in his

Since the Ontario act basically preserves the common-law dower, the right accrues only to the wife. If the wife has not lived within the province since marriage, the Act takes away her right. There is no limitation as to homestead since the wife's inchoate life estate attaches to all the husband's real property.

Barring dower

If a wife is willing to bar her dower, she does so by joining in the execution of the instrument. There are no elaborate precautions involving acknowledgments such as we find in the western Canadian legislation.

The Registry Act[53] provides that where a deed, conveyance ... , lease ... , is made by a man and no person joins as his wife, such document shall not be registered unless there is made on, or securely attached to it, an affidavit by him deposing that the man was married, unmarried, divorced, or a widower. Thus, the wife's position is protected by prohibition against registration unless her position is established by affidavit.

Effect of wife's failure to bar dower

In Ontario the wife's refusal to join in a conveyance already executed by the husband appears to grant the purchaser two optional courses of action. The wife cannot be compelled to execute a bar of dower. On the other hand, the purchaser cannot be compelled to accept a deed without a bar of dower. He may, however, terminate the contract, or bring an action for specific performance which will be granted if he is willing to accept the land subject to dower. If the purchaser elects to seek specific performance, he is entitled to ask the court to direct that a portion of the purchase price be paid into court to indemnify him against any future claim by the wife.[54] The *Freedman* case applied to a conventional sale and purchase of real property, but there would appear to be no obstacle to utilizing the same approach in the case of an oil and gas lease. The lessee, confronted with a refusal on the part of the wife to join in the lease, could very well seek specific performance. The future contingent interest of the wife could be protected by a deposit of one-third of the bonus consideration to be followed by a like disposition of any royalties that might accrue in the event of production.

chief house for 40 days after his death, ...' '8. Where a wife willingly leaves her husband and goes away and continues with her adulterer, she is barred evermore of her action to demand her dower that she ought to have of her husband's land, unless her husband willingly and without coercion is reconciled to her and suffers her to dwell with him, in which case she is restored to her action.'

53 R.S.O 1970, c 409 s 42 (6)
54 *Freedman* v *Mason, supra* n. 17

ESTOPPEL

The doctrine of estoppel[55] has on occasion been advanced in an attempt to cure a dower defect that lies outside the scope of the curative provisions. In the light of the cases decided to date the chances of success appear remote. The Supreme Court has expressly stated that the possibility of avoiding a statutory requirement by estoppel is at least questionable.[56]

55 For a full discussion on the elements of estoppel and when it may be invoked, see Part v: Involuntary Termination, *infra*
56 *B.A. Oil Company* v *Kos* (1964) 46 w.w.r. 141, 149, 42 2 d.l.r. (2d) 426, 433

4
Formation of the lease

Even if the lessee is blessed with a lessor having full capacity to contract and successfully navigates the shoals of dower and homestead, the lease may yet founder. The negotiations and resulting documentation still must add up to a binding, enforceable agreement between the parties. In addition to its other attributes the lease is an agreement and needs to pass all the tests that determine the existence of a valid contract.

CONTRACT

There are as many definitions of contract as there are text writers. All, however, agree that a valid contract must have the following elements: (a) an intention to be bound; the parties must intend that their obligations each to the other are enforceable and that any failure to perform will involve legal consequences; there must be a binding offer, properly accepted; (b) a consideration or price to be paid for the promises or undertakings; (c) an understanding between the parties as to the subject matter of the contract.[1]

In the case of a lease it is not enough, however, that the arrangement between the parties include all the foregoing ingredients. Because a lease is an interest in land, due respect also must be paid to the ancient canons of real property law.

STATUTE OF FRAUDS

In 1677 the Imperial Parliament passed an act 'for prevention of many fraudulent practices commonly endeavoured to be upheld by perjury and

---

1 See Chitty on *Contracts* (23rd ed.) (1969) vol. 1, 2

subornation of perjury.' The Statute of Frauds sought to achieve this objective by providing that, with respect to certain classes of contracts, no action could be brought unless the agreement, or some memorandum or note thereof, was in writing and signed by the party to be charged, or by his agent. There are several categories of agreements covered by the Statute; oil and gas leases fall within those relating to the sale of land.

Despite its great age and several centuries of severe criticism, the Statute is alive and well in Canada. Some provinces have passed their own legislative version of it,[2] while in others it flourishes through the migration of English common law to the colonies.[3] The Statute does not purport to affect the validity of those contracts which are subject to it. It does, however, make them unavailable as grounds for an action unless they are in writing or there is some written memorandum of their terms. In the eyes of a litigant with an unenforceable contract, this may well appear to be a distinction without a difference.

Gordon v *Connors*[4] established that the Statute applies to oil and gas leases: 'There is an additional reason, in my opinion, for refusing to regard the landmen's lease as part of the option. The contract is one that must be in writing under the Statute of Frauds.'[5] In view of the express inclusion of interest in lands in the Statute, together with the judicial categorization of the lease, it is hard to conceive any other result.

The courts have been generous in defining what comprises a note or memorandum, and undoubtedly this has avoided many hardships that otherwise would have been created by operation of the Statute. The memorandum will be enforced if it contains the essential particulars, namely, a description of the parties, the property and the price.[6] The memorandum must, however, contain all the essential features; thus, where verbal evidence of a contract established that payment of a portion of the purchase price was to be deferred for a year, a written receipt which did not contain that term could not meet the statutory requirements.[7]

Canadian Williston Minerals Ltd. v *Forseth and Imperial Oil Limited*[8] is

2 Statute of Frauds, R.S.B.C. 1960, c 369; R.S.O. 1970, c 444
3 See Cote, 'The Introduction of English Law Into Alberta' (1962–4), 2–3 *Alta. L. Rev.* 262
4 (1953) 8 W.W.R. (N.S.) 145 (Alta. C.A.) affirmed [1953] 2 S.C.R. 127 (The Supreme Court of Canada did not deal with the issue of the applicability of the Statute of Frauds)
5 Ibid, 153
6 *Petroleum Engineering Company Limited* v *Clark and Elliott* (1952) 5 W.W.R. (N.S.) 119 (Sask. C.A.)
7 *Lesiuk* v *Schneider* [1917] 2 W.W.R. 747 (Alta.)
8 (1962) 33 D.L.R. (2d) 72 (Sask. C.A.)

an example of how far the courts will reach, when so motivated by the equities, to find a memorandum that will satisfy the requirements of the Statute. This case was a follow-up to *Prudential Trust Co. and Canadian Williston Minerals Ltd.* v *Forseth*,[9] where Forseth unsuccessfully attacked an agreement under which he was required to assign one half of his mineral rights. Despite the judicial determination, he subsequently refused to assign the minerals or to account for the one half share of the royalties accruing under the Imperial lease. The assignee sued for specific performance and the owner defended on the basis of the Statute of Frauds. There had been some earlier litigation in which Forseth sued one, Benson, who had negotiated the assignment as agent of Prudential. The statement of claim in that action recited that an offer of $100.00 had been made to Forseth by Benson for an option to take a petroleum and natural gas lease, and that the offer had been accepted and the assignment completed. Additionally, in the action where the assignment was upheld by the Supreme Court, the statement of claim issued by Forseth embodied the full text of the assignment, together with the offer of $100.00 pursuant to which it was made. These pleadings were filed as exhibits and made part of the record in the subsequent case. Both the trial judge and the Saskatchewan Court of Appeal held that the pleadings provided a sufficient memorandum to meet the statutory requirements. The earlier statement of claim was 'not to be viewed as a pleading but as a memorandum.'

The judicial disposition to find that almost any sort of written note, receipt, or memorandum will satisfy the Statute can only go so far. There has to be at least something in writing and it must contain the essential terms. It is well known that a lease embodies numerous terms and involves many complicated points and issues that require agreement between the parties. Hence, the Statute of Frauds when applied to an oil and gas lease will prove difficult to satisfy with anything short of a fully detailed document signed by the lessor. In other words, the only note or memorandum that one can say with confidence will satisfy the Statute is an oil and gas lease itself.

SEAL

The following passage is very short but it has caused more than its share of consternation to oil lawyers. (The reference to 'this decision' is to the *Berkheiser* case):

This decision, and the decisions referred to therein, and the other cases I have read, justify me in saying that the document I have to construe – and I am here

9 [1960] s.c.r. 210, (1959) 21 d.l.r. (2d) 587: see discussion, *infra*

confining my remarks to a document in such terms – is not a lease but is a grant of a *profit à prendre* which is itself an interest in land and an incorporeal hereditament. As an incorporeal hereditament it can be created only by grant, that is by a document under seal.[10]

There is nothing ambiguous or revolutionary in this statement. The grant under an oil and gas lease is required under the common law to be made by deed.[11] A deed requires a seal; 'No writing without a seal can be a deed.'[12]

What constitutes a seal

While the principle that a deed requires sealing remains intact, there has been a constant erosion of the strict requirements of the seal itself. The act of sealing a document is an ancient one dating back to the period before the ability to write became a common accomplishment. Originally a seal had to be of wax impressed on the document and bearing an impression sufficient to identify the owner. Now, however, no wax, wafer, or other adhesive substance is required; anything attached to the document, or a physical impression or perforation may be a valid seal if the executing party intended to adopt it as such.[13]

In *Bell & Black* it was held that a circle made by a pen with the word 'seal' written inside was sufficient. An impression upon a paper without wax or any other extraneous substance can be a seal.[14] The real test is whether the impression was made for the purpose of sealing. Indeed, even if no mark or impression appears but the testamentary and attestation clauses state that the document was sealed, there may be a presumption that a seal was affixed. The presumption, however, must be buttressed by some corroborative evidence. The presence of a mark, or possibly some dried adhesive indicating that a seal was once affixed, might be sufficient corroboration.

The essential requirement is that the party signing the document adopt whatever impression there may be as his seal. Strictly speaking this is a subjective test and could lead to some interesting situations where a lease is concerned. The usual practice of the lessee is to affix a red wafer seal before presenting the document for signing by the lessor. Rarely would the existence or significance of the seal be pointed out to the lessor. The mere fact that the seal was affixed prior to execution is sufficient under the test laid down in

10 *Langlois* v *Canadian Superior Oil of California Ltd.* (1957–8) 23 w.w.r. 401, 407
11 Chitty, *supra* n. 1, 9
12 Sheppard's *Touchstone of Common Assurances*, 56
13 *Re Bell & Black* (1882) 1 o.r. 125; Anger and Honsberger, *Canadian Law of Real Property*, 560
14 *Foster* v *Geddes* (1856) 14 u.c.q.b. 239

Stromdale & Ball v *Burdon*:[15] 'If a party signs a document bearing wax or wafer or other indication of a seal, with the intention of executing the document as a deed, that is sufficient adoption or recognition of the seal to amount to due execution as a deed.'

This case was decided in 1951, which makes it dazzlingly modern in terms of the law relating to the sealing of documents, and reflects the judicial distaste for this relic of the dark ages. Today it is sufficient if the party intends the document to be a deed. A lessor signing an oil and gas lease certainly intends the document to be a deed, thus any seal impressed prior to his act of signing would be deemed to have been adopted by him. This would not follow, however, where the seal is added, as sometimes happens, by the lessee or his agent after the lessor has signed the document. The matter then becomes one of evidence as to the point in time at which the seal was affixed. The fact that the lease contains a reference to 'signed, sealed and delivered' and that the witness in his affidavit of execution deposes that he saw the lessor 'sign, seal and execute' is *prima facie* evidence that the seal was affixed before execution. If, however, a lessor could persuade the court that the seal was not there when he signed it the lease could not be upheld.

DELIVERY

Another ancient, but still surviving, formality is the requirement of delivery; 'A conveyance, though signed and sealed, does not take effect until it is delivered.'[16] Once again the requirements have been whittled away, and today any act or words of the party which show that he intended to deliver the deed as an instrument binding on him is sufficient, even though he may not part with actual possession. The act of delivery should be relatively easy to establish under the circumstances of most oil and gas transactions since the lease is usually handed over by the lessor to the other party for execution. In addition, there is a recital that it has been delivered, and this should be sufficient even if the lessor kept the document in his own possession.

COMPLETION OF THE CONTRACT

The precise legal status of the parties in the interregnum between execution by the lessor and receipt by him of a copy signed by the lessee is an intriguing question. There are several possibilities: (a) is there a completed contract

15 [1951] 2 T.L.R. 1192
16 Anger and Honsberger, *supra* n. 13, 562: *Styles* v *Wardle* (1825) 107 E.R. 1297;
   Dillabaugh v *McLeod* (1910) 16 W.L.R. 149 (Sask.)

subject only to the deficiency that the lessor could not sue on it by reason of the Statute of Frauds? (b) is the execution and delivery by the lessor merely an offer which must be accepted by the lessee before it becomes effective? (c) does it, in effect, create an option which can be withdrawn by the lessor prior to acceptance?

One thing at least seems clear. Like any other contract, an oil and gas lease must include the element of an offer duly accepted. Sometimes there may be a question as to whether the offer emanates from the lessor when he signs the lease, or whether from the lessee when it offers to lease the rights for a specified consideration. Assuming for the moment that the offer is created when the lessor signs the lease and gives it to the lessee or its agent, then the normal rules of offer and acceptance apply. An offer, unless it is stated to be open for only a limited period, can be accepted at any time prior to revocation. There must be some overt act on the part of the offeree to indicate his acceptance; it is not enough that he has made up his mind to accept the offer; he has to do something which the law will treat as a communication for the acceptance to the other party. Sometimes the precise manner of communication is prescribed, but more often the parties are silent as to this point. The law has long ago decided, arbitrarily, but also on a balance of convenience, that, if the parties can be said to have contemplated the use of the mails as a means of communication of the acceptance, then the acceptance is effective the moment it is mailed.[17] Such acceptance is effective even if the letter or other communication is delayed or lost and never received by the offeror.[18]

There remains the question as to whether the parties contemplated the use of the mails for communication of acceptance. If the offer itself had been mailed, there could be no question that they so intended. When it comes to a lease, however, it is quite common for it to be handed personally from the lessor to the lessee or its agent. Even under these circumstances, mailing of an executed copy of the lease by the lessee should be good communication of acceptance since, according to ordinary commercial usage, the lessee could reasonably be expected to return an executed copy through the mails.[19]

The offeror who wishes to withdraw his offer cannot rely on the mere act of mailing. The revocation must be actually communicated to the offeree before it becomes effective. If acceptance of the offer has been mailed by the offeree – a completed copy of the lease mailed by the lessee – prior to actual receipt of the withdrawal, the contract is complete and the cancellation is

17 *Adams* v *Lindsell* 1 B. & Ald. 681
18 *Household Fire Insurance Co.* v *Grant* (1879) 4 Ex. D 216
19 *Henthorn* v *Frazer* (1892) 1 Ch. 27

ineffective.[20] Withdrawal of an offer by a lessor is further complicated by the fact that he will have signed the lease under seal. This aspect is discussed in more detail *infra*.

The courts have, on several occasions, pondered the status of parties to a lease signed by the lessor but not yet signed by the lessee. The results undoubtedly depend to a very great extent on the individual fact patterns; nonetheless, there are some useful guidelines to be found.

OPTION

The ordinary circumstances of a typical lease acquisition do not lend themselves to the concept of an option. It sometimes happens, however, that for one reason or another, the lessee desires to tie up the lands for a period of time without committing itself to the expenditure of a substantial bonus consideration. If the documentation properly reflects this posture, then the relationship will be treated as one of optionor and optionee. On the other hand, the negotiations may be such that they may even alter the nature of a document which on its face purports to be an option.

In *Canadian General Associates Ltd.* v *Fedor*[21] the documentation consisted of a typewritten portion with a printed form of lease attached to it. Originally the typewritten part was entitled 'Option to Lease,' but the word 'Option' was struck out because the lessor stated he wanted a deal not an option. The court paid careful attention to all of the circumstances surrounding the actual negotiations. The document was signed by the lessor after a discussion of about one and a half hours at which the president of the lessee company was present, as well as other witnesses who also testified. Despite the deletion of the reference to 'Option,' there remained language in the instrument which was consistent only with an option. For example, the operative words were: 'Do hereby offer to lease,' and there were two other clauses that were cast in terms of an option. They related to the manner in which the offer could be accepted and the period for which it remained open, together with a right of extension.

$1,900.00 cash upon completion and return of papers from Calgary, $2,000.00 cash if and when No. 3 Imperial well is declared a producer, $10,000.00 cash upon the first producing well obtained on the above lease, 8 per cent royalty on each well thereafter drilled on the NE¼ Section 19, Township 51, Range 25, W.4th and continuous drilling until such time as the property is drilled out. I,

20 Chitty, *supra* n. 1, 21, 29, and 30. Harris's Case (1872) L.R. 7 Ch. App. 587
21 [1948] 2 W.W.R. 287 (Alta.)

J.F. Anderson, to return from Calgary not later than Monday, May 12th, 1947.

The lessor contended that the document was an option only and that the limit of time fixed for payment of the $1,900.00 was May 12, 1947, when Anderson, the president of the lessee company, would return from Calgary. Since the required payment of $1,900.00 was not made by that date he argued that the option had lapsed.

The evidence as to the meeting revealed that the document was discussed clause by clause, with both parties agreeing on each clause as they proceeded. The sum of $100.00 was given to the lessor as a deposit at the time the agreement was signed, and the $1,900.00 referred to in the above clause represented the remaining balance of the initial $2,000.00 payment. It had been agreed between the parties that the lessor, who was purchasing the land under an agreement for sale, would produce a copy of it for inspection by the lessee's solicitors and that the $1,900.00 would be paid upon approval of this document. The lessor, who obviously repented of his bargain, refused to produce a copy of the agreement and the court found this refusal to be deliberate.

When it became apparent to the lessee company that the lessor would not co-operate in producing the document, it left two cheques, one for $1,900.00 and a further one in the sum of $2,000.00 payable because the Imperial well was a producer, with the lessor's agent. This was done on June 6, long after the expiration of the May 12 date referred to in the typewritten portion. Under all these conditions, the court found:

I am unable to construe the document as granting an option only to lease the oil and gas rights on this land for the consideration of $100.00. The lessee did not merely purchase the right to obtain a lease. It undertook, if my interpretation of the meaning of the words quoted is sound, to pay definite sums of money for the lease, the terms of which are set out therein. In my opinion, it was intended to be a lease operative from its date, with the initial cash payment of $2,000.00, divided into $100.00 deposit, and the balance of $1,900.00 deferred for such time as was considered sufficient for the title of the defendant Fedor to be inquired into and passed upon by the solicitor for the plaintiff at Calgary. (Wording re-arranged to correct obvious printing error in original report.)

It should be noted that both parties had signed the document. The sole issue was whether the document amounted to a mere option or a valid and binding lease. The court held it was the latter and that it was not defeated by any delay in making the required payments since this was occasioned by the deliberate act of the lessor.

OFFER

A lease signed by a lessor, but not the lessee, has been characterized by the Saskatchewan Court of Appeal as an offer under seal. The facts in *McAlester Canadian Oil Company* v *Petroleum Engineering Company Limited*[22] were quite typical. During January 1956 a landman employed by the lessee company contacted a representative of the company which owned the minerals. The lessee had its offices in the United States and its landman was not authorized to make binding commitments on its behalf. The negotiations between the agent and the representative of the lessor company led to a lease being signed by the lessor company under seal. It was dated January 11, 1956, and together with a certificate of title and a certified copy of a caveat filed on the property, was delivered to solicitors for the lessee. These documents were immediately forwarded to the head office of the lessee in the United States where it was signed by the lessee on February 2, 1956, but was retained in its possession. On February 8, 1956, the lessor's solicitors withdrew the offer to sell the mineral rights and asked for return of the documents. At this point there had been no indication from the lessee that the offer had been accepted. On the next day the completed lease was received by the lessee's solicitors in Regina, who prepared and filed a caveat against the land. On February 21 they wrote the lessor's solicitors stating that the title had been approved and they had requisitioned a cheque to cover the bonus payment. This cheque was duly tendered on February 29 but was refused by the lessor.

There are two things that should be noted in this case; (a) the landman had no power to bind his employer; (b) the fact that the lessee had executed the lease was not 'communicated' to the lessor, by mailing or otherwise, before the offer was withdrawn. The lessee contended that, since the document had been sealed, it could not be revoked. This was defeated by the Supreme Court of Canada decision in *Davidson* v *Norstrant*:[23]

I agree that a unilateral offer of an option without consideration can be revoked at any time, unless under seal as this contract was.

I am of the opinion that if the offer is made under seal and not accepted it may be withdrawn within a reasonable time and that the measure of such time might under certain circumstances be very brief indeed.

I am further of opinion that, if there is no other consideration than mutual promises, an agreement for an option without seal may be enforceable.

22 (1958) 25 w.w.r. 26 (Sask. c.a.)   23 (1921) 61 s.c.r. 493; 1 w.w.r. 993

On the question of what was a reasonable time, the court cited *Barrick* v *Clark*,[24] which held that an offer to sell farmland, not containing a definite time limit, dated November 15 had expired prior to a purported acceptance made on December 10. The Saskatchewan Court of Appeal emphasized that the value of oil and gas rights fluctuates very rapidly, 'at any rate, far more rapidly than farmlands which were offered for sale in the *Clark* case.'[25] An offer, even under seal, can be withdrawn after it has been in force for a reasonable time, before acceptance by the lessee.

The power, or lack of it, of the agent to bind the lessee can be of decisive importance. In *Sial Explorations Ltd.* v *Leask*[26] the Alberta Appellate Division indicated in the course of argument, that the signing of a lease by the lessor may be the acceptance of an offer made by the lessee. In this case there had been considerable negotiation as to the price per acre to be paid prior to the meeting which resulted in the execution of the lease by the lessor. The land agent had been expressly authorized to make a binding commitment in this regard. Under these circumstances the court was inclined to treat the lease as having been completed when signed by the lessor subject only to the fact that the lessor could not have sued upon it since it did not comply with the Statute of Frauds.

CONSIDERATION AND PAYMENT AS A CONDITION PRECEDENT

A lease may be executed and delivered subject to certain conditions which do not appear on its face but are embodied in a collateral instrument or by verbal understanding. These conditions most often refer to the mode of payment, but they may deal with other matters such as the verification of title.

In *California Standard Co.* v *McBride*[27] the lease had been executed by both parties and contemporaneously they had also signed a receipt. The lease specified a bonus consideration of $16,000.00, while the receipt acknowledged payment of $5.00 and an agreement that the balance was to be paid upon the company's solicitors being satisfied as to title. It turned out that there was a defect in the lessor's title which required some curative documentation from both the Crown and an intervening transferor. The lessee, faced with this defect, and a demand by the lessor for the balance of the bonus monies, deposited $15,995.00 with the depository bank pending correction of the title. The lessor did not cure the defect until nearly two years after the lease had been executed. In the meantime he had served notice upon

24 [1951] S.C.R. 177
26 [1971] 4 W.W.R. 654 (Alta. C.A.)
25 *Supra* n. 22, 30
27 (1963) 38 D.L.R. (2d) 606 (Alta. C.A.)

the lessee requiring it to either remove the caveat or commence proceedings. As soon as the lessee was advised by its solicitors that the lessor's title was in order, it notified the bank to release the bonus consideration, but the lessor refused to accept it. The lessor argued against the validity of the lease on the basis that the proper payment of the bonus money was a condition precedent. The receipt, however, was admitted to prove that payment within any given period of time was not meant to be a condition precedent to the lease, but had been expressly postponed until the title was examined and the lessee's solicitors were satisfied with it. Since the receipt would be fatal to the lessor's position, it was attacked on a variety of grounds, including one that its language was so vague and uncertain as to be meaningless and ineffective. It required the solicitors to be satisfied with title and, since this was a purely subjective test, they could grant or withhold their satisfaction capriciously. The court rejected this and declared that once the lessor had produced a good and valid title the lessee could have been compelled to pay the balance of the purchase price. A claim that its solicitors were not yet satisfied would not have been a valid defence for payment. This statement can have a wide application since many deals in the oil industry are made subject to title approval. Clearly, the court is prepared to substitute its judgment as to title for that of a solicitor where the latter may attempt to withhold approval on unjustifiable grounds. As the court pointed out, the lessor was not in a very good position to complain about the lessee's delay in making payment since it had been occasioned by the former's lackadaisical approach to perfecting his title.

When a lessor signs the lease it will contain a typewritten insert of the amount of the bonus consideration, followed by a printed parenthetical phrase, 'the receipt whereof is hereby acknowledged.' Only under the most unusual circumstances will the lessor have actually received payment at the time he signed and delivered the lease. At most, he might have received a token sum as a deposit or down payment. The payment of the real consideration is almost invariably postponed until both title approval and registration of the lease or a caveat. The mode of payment will be covered in a very informal manner and very seldom reduced to writing. There are primarily two situations: (a) the parties may agree that payment will be made in any event by a certain date, or (b) the payment may be postponed until title approval and registration, with no definite time limit.

The recital in the lease that payment has been received is not a bar to the admission of evidence to establish that in fact no payment has been made.[28] The courts are also disposed to treat payment of the purchase price, or

---

28 *Cushing* v *Knight* (1912) 46 S.C.R. 555; 6 D.L.R. 820; 2 W.W.R. 704 (S.C.C.)

bonus consideration, as a condition precedent which means that, unless the condition is performed, the agreement has no force and effect. If it is determined that the parties have agreed upon a definite time period within which payment is to be made, as described in (a) above, failure of a timely payment appears to be fatal. If the court construes the agreement as requiring payment by a certain date, then no enforceable agreement is created in the absence of such payment. Nor would there seem to be any requirement on the part of the lessor to formally demand payment; he is entitled to treat the agreement as having come to an end.[29]

If the lease contains the usual acknowledgment of receipt and no payment has in fact been made, the lessor, in the absence of any collateral agreement, can immediately terminate the lease on the ground that the condition precedent has not been fulfilled. The recital of receipt has the effect of making payment a condition precedent: 'The parties do not, it is true, in formal terms provide that the payment of that sum is to be a condition; but the intention that it should be so is manifested by the frame of the agreement as a whole, the stipulations of which pre-suppose that this payment has already been made and shew unmistakably that it is upon the basis of this assumed state of facts that the parties are contracting.'[30] The lessor may be required to demand payment and give the lessee an opportunity to pay before he is entitled to terminate the lease. In *Cushing* v *Knight*, which involved an agreement for the sale of land, the vendor gave the respondents four days within which to make payment. One of the Supreme Court judges notes that fact in his judgment but seems to treat it as merely adding weight to the termination of the contract, the main thrust of the case being that developed in the above passage, namely, that the contract required payment of the specified sum before it became enforceable.

The position of a lessee where there has been some agreement or understanding that payment would be postponed until title approval and registration was illustrated in *Davidson* v *Norstrant*.[31] This case, which culminated in a fragmented decision in the Supreme Court, involved an option to acquire an undivided half-interest in certain lands. The option agreement was under seal and recited a consideration of $100.00 'now paid.' In fact, the $100.00 was neither paid nor demanded. The evidence, which was purely oral, established that both parties agreed the option was not to become operative unless and until the optionee, who was the agent for the owners, had disclosed his position to them and obtained their consent to his becoming a part purchaser. This led the court to conclude that the signed option was merely tentative,

29 *Sial* v *Leask, supra* n. 26
30 *Supra* n. 28   31 *Supra* n. 23

depending for its coming into effect upon the agent obtaining the consent of his principals. The court treated the non-payment of the $100.00 as not being fatal to the agreement. The transaction was not 'closed' unless the necessary consent was obtained and, when it was obtained, there was no unreasonable delay on the optionee's part in tendering the money.

The element of demand and refusal was introduced by Idington J, who took the view that an option could not be revoked unless and until the offeror has demanded payment and been refused. None of the other members of the court dealt with this point. The *Davidson* case contains elements that do not appear in the lease situation, mainly that the $100.00 consideration was purely nominal when compared to the purchase price of the property. Under a lease, the initial bonus consideration is the entire purchase price. This feature, plus the fact that all five judges who sat on the case wrote individual judgments – including two dissents – encompassing a wide variety of points, undermines the effectiveness of the *Davidson* decision as an authority. It may, however, be held to apply where payment of the bonus consideration has been verbally agreed to be postponed pending title approval, and it does appear to reinforce the element of demand and refusal as a necessary in-gredient prior to termination.

Both the circumstances of the industry, where the courts are prepared to take judicial notice of the rapid fluctuations in value, and the wording of the lease which expressly acknowledges receipt of the bonus consideration make it virtually certain that payment of the purchase price will be treated as a condition precedent.[32]

The parol, or extrinsic, evidence rule continues to be a troubling possibility in this area. The rule deals with the admissibility of evidence and may be paraphrased: if a transaction has been put in writing, extrinsic evidence is, in general, inadmissible to *contradict, vary, add to,* or *subtract from* the

---

32 If it were to be treated otherwise and regarded merely as a condition subsequent, there is no doubt that a lessor wishing to terminate the lease would be required to give notice to the lessee allowing a period of time within which to make payment. In *Sims v Jenkins* (1951–52) 4 w.w.r. (N.s.) 352 (Alta. c.a.) the agreement involved the purchase of royalty 'points' for a stated sum, a small down payment being made at the time the agreement was entered into. The agreement did not specify any fixed date for the payment of the balance. Time was not expressed to be of the essence and the court held that there was nothing in the circumstances surrounding the transaction that would make it so. It is clear that in the view of the court there would have to be notice from the vendor making time of the essence, i.e. specifying a time within which payment must be made, before he could terminate the agreement for failure to pay. The purchaser in fact tendered the balance within two weeks following the execution of the agreement and prior to any notice of any alleged default in payment.

written terms. The rationale underlying the rule is that, when the parties have deliberately put their agreement into writing, it should be conclusively presumed between themselves that they intended the writing to form a full and final statement of their intentions.[33] Although the evidence excluded by the rule is usually of the parol or oral type, even written materials will be excluded if they are found to be extraneous to the document under review. There are several exceptions to the exclusionary rule. Parol evidence is admissible to contradict the purported receipt of money.[34] It now appears established that oral evidence may also be admissible to explain the circumstances under which payment is to be made.[35]

The practice surrounding the determination of the lessee's obligation to pay the bonus consideration under a lease is notoriously loose. The document speaks as though the payment had actually been made, which can be contradicted by extrinsic evidence and there is seldom any firm agreement on the time within which the payment must be made. The entire area of bonus payment is uncertain and confusing. Commonly employed procedures are subject to the vagaries of the parol evidence rule, reliance on evidence which is generally vague and inconclusive, the uncertainties of what the court may consider to be a reasonable time, and whether or not prior notice is required before the lessor is free to treat the lease as at an end.

TITLE

The lessor's title to the minerals is the other condition precedent commonly encountered in lease negotiations. It is normally imposed by the lessee, who makes the entire deal contingent upon title. In *California Standard Company v Chiswell*,[36] however, it was the lessor who insisted on it. The defendants were the registered owners of both surface and minerals of a certain tract of land which they had sold under an agreement for sale. The purchaser had not troubled to register a caveat to protect his position and the payments were in arrears. The defendants had begun an action for foreclosure which resulted

---

33 See Phipson on *Evidence* 11th ed. (1970) Cs. 43–46
34 Parol evidence has always been permitted to contradict a receipt and there are numerous authorities to this effect, see for example those quoted in Phipson. For our purposes it is not necessary to go beyond *Cushing* v *Knight, supra* n. 28 wherein evidence was admitted to show that the payment had not in fact been made although the agreement said 'the receipt of which is hereby acknowledged.'
35 *Davidson* v *Norstrant, supra* n. 23. See also *Long* v *Smith* (1911) 23 O.L.R. 121 where oral evidence as to a condition precedent of the contract was admitted
36 (1955) 14 W.W.R. 456 (Alta.)

in an arrangement between themselves and the purchaser under which he had made some additional payments but not enough to put them on a current basis. The defendants executed an oil and gas lease covering the lands, and at their request the lessee's agent prepared another document which was signed at the same time. This referred to the lease and postponed the payment of the bonus consideration until the successful completion of the foreclosure proceedings. It also contained a statement that the lessee recognized that the lessors were granting only such interest as they themselves had. At about the same time the purchaser granted a lease to another oil company. The cash bonus was substantial enough to pay off the entire amount remaining under the agreement for sale and it was to be held in trust until the purchaser obtained title by paying his obligations.

When the purchaser became aware of the prior lease, his solicitor made enquiries of the defendant's solicitors and was assured that he was protected in this regard because of the collateral document. The lessee under the first lease attempted to exclude this collateral agreement on both the parol evidence rule and a clause in the lease itself to the effect that the lease constituted the whole of the agreement between the parties. The court held that neither the exclusionary clause nor the parol evidence rule could operate to prevent the collateral agreement being admitted as evidence. Since it was clear that the lease was to come into effect only if and when the condition was satisfied, namely, the successful completion of the foreclosure proceedings, the exclusionary clause could not have any vitality. It was in a state of suspended animation until the agreement became effective. Similarly, extrinsic evidence which indicated that the lease was a conditional one could not be excluded under the operation of the parol evidence rule because the prohibition against contradicting a written document can apply only to one that is fully effective.

MUST BE AGREEMENT AS TO TERMS

It is not enough for the parties to properly complete all the formalities of a contract; there also needs to be a meeting of minds as to what the arrangement encompasses. Each must comprehend what has been agreed to and the agreement must be reached on a true understanding of the circumstances. If the circumstances are such as to negative this element, then the contract, although it may appear perfect and complete on its face, is void and of no force and effect, or may be treated as voidable. There are three grounds of attack mounted against a contract arising from a failure of the parties to fully appreciate and agree upon the subject matter. Quite frequently, they are all pleaded together and to some measure are interwoven.

NON EST FACTUM

This plea, which means literally that it was not done, is directed not to the contents of the document, but to the mind of the executing party. In order for this defence to succeed, the party executing the document must show that he was mistaken not merely with respect to what the document contained, but also as to the essential nature of the contract itself.[37] The only cases in which the defendant has been successful are those in which, by the fraud of a third party, the promissor has been mistaken as to the nature of the contract into which he is entering.

Although the doctrine originated for the protection of blind or illiterate persons, there now would appear to be no doubt that it also extends to those not labouring under these disabilities so long as they can discharge the onus of establishing that they were so misled or ignorant of the nature of the document that, notwithstanding the execution, it was not their deed or act in contemplation of law. It was once thought that the omission of a literate person to read a document tendered to him would be a fatal bar to the defence, but it now appears that failure to read the contents of the document is not necessarily negligence of a type that will deprive a party of the defence. If he can show that he relied upon the fraudulent misrepresentation of the other party as to the nature and character of the instrument, he still may escape liability. On the other hand, if a party reads a document before executing it, he cannot rely on the doctrine. 'A literate person who signs a document after reading it through, or hearing it fully read, must, I think, be presumed to know the nature of the document which he is signing.'[38]

Once *non est factum* has been established, the instrument is deemed to have been void *ab initio* on the basis that the deed or contract never came into existence, since the mind of the party did not follow his pen. The consequences of this is that subsequent purchasers or assignees for value are not afforded any protection, their title deriving from a document which by operation of law is deemed never to have come into existence.

The boundaries of the doctrine were outlined in two English cases, both decided in the first decade of this century. In *Howatson* v *Webb*[39] the defendant, formerly the managing clerk to a solicitor, acted as the nominee for the solicitor in a building speculation. Shortly after leaving the solicitor's employment he was requested to execute certain deeds and, on asking what they were, was informed that they were transfers of the property in question,

37 Anson's *Law of Contract* (23rd ed.) (1969) 287
38 *Prudential Trust Co. Ltd.* v *Forseth, supra* n. 9 (S.C.R.) 220
39 [1907] 1 Ch. 537

and he then signed them. One of the deeds was in fact a mortgage between the defendant as mortgagor and a third party and contained the usual covenant for payment of principal and interest. In an action by the transferee of the mortgage for payment of the principal the defendant pleaded *non est factum*. It was held that the representation was only as to the contents of a deed and that the defendant knew that the deed dealt with the property. Therefore, the plea of *non est factum* failed. In the view of the court the fact that the defendant was told the deeds related to property was sufficient.

His mind was therefore applied to the question of dealing with that property. The deeds did deal with that property. The misrepresentation was as to the contents of the deed, and not as to the character and class of the deed. He knew he was dealing with the class of deed with which in fact he was dealing, but did not ascertain its content. The deed contained a covenant to pay. Under those circumstances I cannot say that the deed is absolutely void. It purported to be a transfer of the property, and it was a transfer of the property. If the plea of *non est factum* is to succeed, the deed must be wholly, and not partly, void. If that plea is an answer in this case, I must hold it to be an answer in every case of misrepresentation. In my opinion the law does not go as far as that.

A wider concept was entertained in *Carlisle Cumberland Banking Company* v *Bragg*,[40] where the defendant pleaded *non est factum* with respect to a document which he had signed without reading, having been induced by the fraud of another to believe that it dealt with insurance. The document turned out to be continuing guarantee of the indebtedness of the fraudulent party to the plaintiff, the banking company. The deliberate act of misleading the signing party as to the nature of the document led the court to uphold the defence of *non est factum*.

The true way of ascertaining whether a deed is a man's deed is, I conceive, to see whether he attached his signature with the intention that that which preceded his signature should be taken to be his act and deed. It is not necessarily essential that he should know what the document contains: he may have been content to make it his act and deed, whatever it contained; he may have relied on the person who brought it to him, as in a case where a man's solicitor brings him a document, saying, 'this is a conveyance of your property,' or 'this is your lease,' and he does not inquire what covenants it contains, or what the rent reserved is, or what other material provisions in it are, but signs it as his act and deed, intending to execute that instrument, careless of its contents, in the sense that he is content

40 [1911] 1 K.B. 489

to be bound by them whatsoever they are. If, on the other hand, he is materially misled as to the contents of the document, then his mind does not go with his pen. In that case it is not his deed. As to what amounts to materially misleading there is of course a question. *Howatson* v. *Webb* was a case in which the erroneous or insufficient information was not enough for the purpose.[41]

The doctrine was extensively ventilated in litigation arising from certain mineral transactions that took place in Saskatchewan during the early 1950s. The pattern was substantially as follows: A land agent, acting on behalf of an undisclosed principal (Prudential Trust figured prominently as a trustee for the beneficial owner) would approach a farmer who had already leased his mineral rights. In consideration of a cash payment, usually quite insignificant, the farmer would grant an option to take a lease in the event of the expiry of the then existing lease. The usual period for the exercise of the option was 99 years. In addition, the transaction involved an assignment of one-half of the owner's interest in the mines and minerals and one-half of any royalties that might become payable under the existing lease if the land became productive.

It was the assignment of the minerals and the royalties that gave rise to the litigation, the mineral owners claiming that, while they realized they were granting an option to lease, they were not aware that they had disposed of one-half of their ownership in the minerals and royalties. The only cases in which the owners were successful in having the transaction set aside were those in which the evidence established a definite act of misrepresentation.[42] In *Prudential Trust Co. Ltd. and Canuck Freehold Royalties* v *Cugnet*[43] the court was persuaded the landowner had relied on the misrepresentation of the agent that the documents were nothing more than an option. It is noteworthy that the agent himself was not called as a witness since his whereabouts were unknown. The trial judge found that Cugnet was mistaken as to the nature and character of the assignment and that this mistake was induced

---

41 Ibid, 495
42 These transactions ultimately led to some extraordinary legislation; The Mineral Contracts Re-negotiation Act, 1959, s.s. 1959, c 102, which set up a Board to which an aggrieved mineral owner could apply. If the Board found that the contract constituted an unconscionable bargain, or that the owner was induced to enter into the contract through misrepresentation, it would attempt to re-negotiate the contract. If its efforts at re-negotiation proved unavailing, the Board could call a public hearing. If the hearing failed to produce a re-negotiation and the Board found the mineral owner entitled to relief, it would extend financial aid so he could seek relief in the courts.
43 (1956) s.c.r. 914, 5 d.l.r. (2d) 1

by the fraudulent misrepresentation of the agent. Thus, the necessary ingredient was established and the plea of *non est factum* prevailed. In the Supreme Court of Canada, Nolan J extensively reviewed the authorities on *non est factum* and preferred the approach of *Carlisle* v *Bragg*, as opposed to that of *Howatson* v *Webb*. In dealing with the latter he noted that the defendant was a solicitor and he should have realized that he was signing a mortgage and not a transfer. Furthermore, when the defendant asked what the deeds were, he was told that they were just deeds transferring the property. In fact, one deed was a mortgage, but as the court pointed out, in England a mortgage is an actual transfer of property by way of a mortgage. Thus, the court could treat the documents signed by the defendant as not being of a character 'wholly different' from that which was represented to him. In the *Cugnet* case, however, while the defendant knew he was dealing with his petroleum and natural gas rights, the representation made to him was as to the nature and character of the document, not merely as to its content. The agent led him to believe it was merely an option to grant a petroleum and natural gas lease when it was really an assignment to Prudential of an undivided one-half interest in the mineral rights. Accordingly, the mind of the defendant Cugnet did not go with his hand.

One of the plaintiffs, Canuck Freehold Royalties Limited, was a subsequent transferee for value without notice and it contended that the transaction could not be set aside as far as it was concerned. This argument was met by the fact that a transaction set aside on the ground of *non est factum* is void and not merely voidable. Hence, a plea of *bona fide* purchaser for value could not assist the plaintiff since there is no way to breathe life into a transaction that never existed.

The Alberta Trial decision in *Falcon Exploration Limited* v *Gunderson*[44] which struck down a contract for an oil and gas lease on the basis of *non est factum* is difficult to reconcile with the main stream of authority on the doctrine. Negotiations between the parties resulted in an exchange of telegrams which commenced with an offer from the plaintiff oil company as follows: 'Reyurlet May thirty first fifty six we hereby offer twelve thousand dollars consideration for a standard ten year lease offer open until midnight June fifth nineteen fifty six please confirm by wire.' In reply the defendant lessor wired on June 5: 'Retel June first 56 I accept offer of twelve thousand dollars for standard ten year petroleum and natural gas lease of Section eight Township nineteen Range 29 West of the Fourth Meridian subject to reservation to McIrvine and reduction of acreage as described in Certificate of Title 102R65 with twelve and one half per cent gross royalty reserved and annual

44 (1958) 25 w.w.r. 416 (Alta.)

rental of six hundred and forty dollars.' After this the plaintiff wrote a letter on June 7 to the defendant in which were enclosed partially completed forms for execution and which stated: 'This is our approved standard lease form and you will note that the terms are as agreed upon, namely: The sum of twelve thousand ($12,000.00) dollars, as consideration, the sum of six hundred and forty ($640.00) dollars as annual delay rental, and twelve and one-half per cent (12½%) gross royalty reserved to the lessors,' and added: 'It will be necessary for the beneficiaries of the estate to give their consent to the lease and there are several forms included for execution on their behalf.' The letter also enclosed ten per cent of the consideration although there had been no previous mention of a deposit.

The two telegrams amounted to an offer and acceptance in the clearest possible terms. Nonetheless, the oil company was unsuccessful in its attempt to have the documentation declared a binding lease. Cairns J held, as the first ground for not enforcing the agreement, that the minds of the parties had not met in such a way as to constitute a contract. He reached this result on the basis that, while the oil company was at all times thinking of its standard form of lease which by judicial definition was in fact a *profit à prendre*, the defendant, who was not familiar with the oil and gas industry, thought that he was required to give a lease. This distinction is not altogether convincing. There can be no doubt that both parties knew they were dealing with an oil and gas lease; the fact that such a document fits within the legal category of interest in land known as a *profit à prendre* would not appear to warrant the finding that the parties were not addressing their minds to the same thing. 'Lease' is a term generally used in the industry to mean that very document which constitutes a *profit à prendre* and since both telegrams specifically referred to a lease, the defendant's telegram being even more particular as it referred to a 'petroleum and natural gas lease,' there would not appear to be any misunderstanding as to what was to be granted.

SUFFICIENCY OF TERMS

The *Falcon* decision also relied upon another ground, namely, that there were not sufficient terms agreed upon to constitute an agreement for a lease. There is a close relationship between the two requirements: the minds of the parties must not only meet, they must do so with sufficient precision and amplitude to constitute an enforceable agreement.

The telegrams and the plaintiff's letter covered a good many features of the proposed arrangement, namely, the initial consideration to be paid, and that it was a 'standard ten year lease' embodying a 12½ per cent gross royalty and an annual rental of $640.00. The defendant introduced expert testimony at the trial to establish that there were many other important matters which must form part of the lease agreement, such as a pooling clause, a drilling commitment, and an off-set drilling provision. The expert also testified that the industry did not have something which would represent 'a standard petroleum and natural gas lease.'

The trial judge found 'because of these features, that there had not been sufficient essential terms agreed upon between the parties, even if there had been agreement upon some of the terms usually found in leases, to constitute a binding agreement to grant a lease.'

The law concerning sufficiency of terms has been summarized for conventional real estate leases as follows: 'To be valid, an agreement for a lease must show (1) the parties, (2) a description of the premises to be demised, (3) the commencement and (4) duration of the term, (5) the rent, if any, and (6) all the material terms of the contract not being matters incident to the relation of the landlord and tenant, including any covenants or conditions, exceptions or reservations.'[45] Despite this summary of the necessary ingredients, it is difficult to predict just when any particular court will be satisfied that documentation, which falls short of a properly executed and completed lease, should be treated as constituting a lease.

In the early Ontario case of *Acme Oil* v *Campbell*[46] there was a claim for specific performance of a document under which the mineral owner agreed to lease to Acme 'at such time as the company shall move a drilling rig into this immediate district preparatory to drilling for oil.' It was specified that the royalty would be one barrel in every ten, that the lessor would have gas to heat his house and an annual rental would be paid if the well was not completed. The agreement further provided that the lease would be null and void if a well was not started in the district within sixty days from the date on which the drilling rig was moved into the area. The agreement was found lacking in two essential conditions: the time from which the term was to commence because there was no indication as to when, if ever, the company would move a drilling rig into the general area and there was no provision as to the duration of the term. Accordingly, the court refused to grant specific performance.

Welland County v *Shurr*[47] illustrated a different approach by the Ontario judiciary when it enforced an undertaking by a mineral owner to give 'the usual oil leases.' He was required to 'execute a lease to the plaintiffs in the form in which gas and oil leases were framed in 1903,' that being the year in which the undertaking was given.

When this decision, where an undertaking to give the usual 'oil leases' was

45 Williams, *Canadian Law of Landlord and Tenant* (3rd ed.) (1957), 68
46 (1906) 8 o.w.r. 627
47 (1912) 23 o.w.r. 397, 4 o.w.n. 336, 8 d.l.r. 720

implemented, is compared with *Falcon*, which refused to uphold the arrangement embodied in the telegrams and correspondence, it must remain a matter of conjecture as to what will or will not be accepted as a binding agreement.

Kopf v *Superior Oils Ltd.*[48] does not illuminate this area to any great extent since the preliminary documentation was remarkably detailed. The company sought to implement a document which was in reality a check list of terms to be later inserted into a surface lease. The check list contained such detail that it would have been remarkable had it not been enforced:

Owner: (Mrs.) Aurelia Kopf
Wife or Husband: Widow
Company: Superior Oils Ltd.
Commencement date: When road conditions permit.
Lands: (Legal Description) LSD 8 SE ¼-Sec. 14-50-22-w.4th

Note: Plans of wellsites, roadways, etc. to be made up by Company and forwarded to owner for lands required for Company's operations. Areas used to be reduced as operations may permit. Term: For as long as petroleum and natural gas produced or until company surrenders lease. Rental per acre per year: $80.00

Owner agrees:
(a) To pay taxes;
(b) That he has good title;
(c) To accept surrender of lease when lands not required by the Company;
(d) Wife and husband each consent hereto and release each other in respect of dower, and agree to execute formal consent under Dower Act.

Company agrees:
(a) To pay taxes resulting from its operation;
(b) To pay the annual rental per acre, annually in advance;
(c) To fence wellsite and roadways;
(d) To comply with provincial regulations;
(e) To pay compensation for damage to fences, buildings or growing crops;
(f)   To bury pipe lines below plow depth;
(g) To forfeit prepaid rental on surrender of lease.

Dated April 20–1959.   Signed: (Mrs.) Aurelia Kopf (Owner)
At New Sarepta   Signed: N.A.
                       (Wife or husband of Owner)
                       Company: Superior Oils Ltd.
                       Per: A.C. Jensen

48 (1951–52) 4 w.w.R. (N.S.) 682

Note:
Lease to be drawn containing above terms, at Company's expense, and forwarded for execution.

The landowner subsequently refused to execute the formal lease as prepared by the oil company. The outline or check list by itself was held to be a valid and enforceable agreement.

MISREPRESENTATION

A completed contract or lease may be set aside if it can be established that one of the parties entered into it by reason of a fraud or misrepresentation on the part of the other. This attack differs from *non est factum* in that the misrepresentation can be as to the contents or legal effect of the document, as well as its nature. Furthermore, it is not essential that the fraud or misrepresentation go to the root of the contract itself so long as it relates to a material point and affected the mind of the party executing the document. Also, unlike the doctrine of *non est factum,* a contract vitiated by misrepresentation is not void *ab initio,* but merely voidable. Thus, it cannot be a good defence against a party who has acquired rights under the document *bona fide* and for value.

The ingredients that must be established for the defence of misrepresentation have been laid down by the Supreme Court of Canada in *Robert* v *Montreal Trust Company.*[49]

In order to maintain a plea that he was induced by false representation to make the contract sued upon, a defendant must establish (1) that the representations complained of were made; (2) that they were false in fact; (3) that the person making them either knew that they were false or made them recklessly without knowing whether they were false or true; (4) that the defendant was thereby induced to enter into the contract; and (5) that immediately on, or at least within a reasonable time after, his discovery of the fraud which had been practised upon him he elected to avoid the contract and accordingly repudiated it.

It is to be noted that the court refers to fraud and false statements made knowingly or recklessly. Mere innocent representation is not sufficient to set aside a completed contract. The party who seeks to upset a contract on the basis of misrepresentation faces an uphill struggle. The main problem is a matter of evidence, the misrepresentation must be established at the trial

49 (1917–18) 56 s.c.r. 342, 355

and the trial judge's finding in this regard is not likely to be revised. In *Bakker* v *Winkler*[50] the Supreme Court of Canada restored a finding by the trial judge that there had been a fraudulent misrepresentation and that the contract was induced by such misrepresentation. The issue revolved around a sub-lease under which the plaintiff granted rights under an existing lease. The head lease contained obligations on the part of the plaintiff to drill wells by certain specified dates. The plaintiff had failed to meet the prescribed commencement date but had managed to obtain an extension of the time. At this point the defendants entered the picture and negotiations led to the execution of a written agreement which simply provided that upon payment of certain cash considerations a sub-lease would be granted. There was also a verbal agreement which was admitted on the grounds that it showed the true consideration for the granting of the sub-lease under which the defendants agreed to drill the first well and commence operations thereon as required by the terms of the head lease. The plaintiff sued to set aside the agreement and to be freed from the obligation to grant a sub-lease to the defendant on the basis that he had been induced to enter into the agreement because of verbal assurances given him as to the financial ability of the defendants to carry out their drilling commitments. The trial judge pointed out that it was of vital importance to the plaintiff that the well should be commenced on the required date because it was on this that all his rights under the head lease depended. Apparently, the plaintiff did not extend his investigations beyond enquiring of the defendants themselves and relied on their assurances. As matters turned out, the defendants were of no substance and did not have the financial ability to drill the well. The trial judge held that the verbal assurances of the defendants as to their financial condition amounted to a fraudulent misrepresentation which had the effect of inducing the plaintiff to sign the agreement[51] and the Supreme Court re-instated this finding after it had been upset by the Appellate Division.

Misrepresentation upset an 'assignment' type of transaction in *Brown* v *Prairie Leaseholds Ltd.*[52] The facts are fully set forth in chapter 2 *ante*. It was one of those situations where the agent visited the farmhouse and ended up with both an option to take a lease on the expiration of the existing lease and an assignment of one-half of the mineral rights including royalties. In *Brown* there were two parcels of land, only one of which was subject to a prior lease. The Browns granted a lease on the other parcel and its validity was not challenged. The lessor and his wife (she for dower only) also signed

50 [1931] S.C.R. 233, (1930) 4 D.L.R. 266
51 (1929) 4 D.L.R. 107 (Alta.); 1929, 24 Alta. L.R. 258 (C.A.)
52 (1953) 9 W.W.R. (N.S.) 577, aff'd (1954) 12 W.W.R. (N.S.) 464

an assignment and transfer of a one-half interest in the mines and minerals in the other portion of land, together with an assignment of one-half of the royalty interest under the existing lease. There was a direct conflict of evidence between the testimony of the lessor and his wife and that of the agent. The trial judge accepted the evidence of the former and concluded that the parties had discussed only the granting of an option to take a lease upon the expiry of the existing lease and not an assignment of one-half of the interest in mines, minerals, and royalty. The mineral owners did not read the documents when they signed them, nor did they give more than a cursory glance at the completed documents when they were returned by the defendant. The two cheques that accompanied the completed documents were cashed by the landowner. It was not until some conversation with neighbours had alerted his suspicions that Brown realized the documents might have done more than he had bargained for. The court put aside the entire transaction noting, 'mere negligence and unwise reliance upon a stranger will not make a man a party to a contract he does not intend.'

Under the plea of misrepresentation everything turns on the findings as to the facts and credibility. In *Prudential Trust Co.* v *Forseth*[53] the trial judge believed the evidence of the agent and preferred it to that of the landowner and his wife. He held that there was no fraudulent misrepresentation and that the owners were not misled as to the real nature and character of the documents. The Court of Appeal reversed these findings but they were restored by the Supreme Court of Canada on the fundamental principle that the findings of fact by the trial judge who had the benefit of observing the witnesses in the stand should only be reversed or upset under the most exceptional circumstances.

In *Prudential Trust Co. Ltd. and Canadian Williston Minerals Ltd.* v *Olson*[54] there was a direct conflict of evidence. The mineral owner asserted the agent had led him to believe that he was granting only an option. He had not troubled to read the assignment document before signing it. The agent testified he had worked on and off for four or five months during 1951 making similar deals; that he interviewed about one hundred farmers in all and was successful in obtaining agreements in about two dozen instances. He did not remember Olson or the transaction in question but declared that he followed the same procedure in all cases. He would introduce himself, explain that he was representing Prudential and was interested in acquiring one-half of the mineral rights. If the existing lease expired or was cancelled, Prudential would have the option of leasing the mineral rights. After hearing the

---

53 [1960] s.c.r. 227, 21 d.l.r. (2d) 603 (s.c.c.); 17 d.l.r. (2d) 341 (c.a.)
54 [1960] s.c.r. 227

evidence, the trial judge stated that he did not believe Olson's story that the agent had been guilty of misrepresentation and found that when Olson signed the documents he was fully aware of their contents. He specifically stated that in the event of any conflict he preferred the evidence of the agent to that of the owner. The Court of Appeal, however, reversed the judgment on the basis that the landowner's evidence was uncontradicted because the agent stated he did not recognize Olson and did not have any recollection of the particular transaction. Martland J speaking for the Supreme Court of Canada, commented on this:

I do not think that such a conclusion must follow because of that evidence, since Fesser (the agent) went on to say that he had followed the same pattern in his dealings with Olson as that which he followed in his interviews with other persons who had executed similar documents, which pattern he described ... it seems to me that a person can properly deny fraudulent representation attributed to him on a specific occasion, even though he may not remember the exact occasion or the person who alleges that such representations were made, if he is able to say that he followed the same pattern as in other cases and describes what that pattern was. Having made such a denial of fraud, I do not think that it can properly be said that the allegations were uncontradicted. (*parenthetical words added*)

PROCEDURE FOR TAKING A LEASE

The hazards discussed in this and the preceding chapter all arise from the circumstances which lead up to and surround the execution of the lease. They are a mixture of form and substance and combine both the status and conduct of the parties. A lessee can do much to improve the chances of its lease being sustained by following proper procedures. The lessee (or agent) should:

1 Keep a full record, by memos to file, of all that transpired in each meeting or contact with the lessor.
2 Enquire into the homestead status of the lessor and the property, ensure that the statutory requirements of the particular province are strictly complied with (the most common defect occurs in the 'separate and apart' feature of the spouse's acknowledgment).
3 Inform the lessor of the exact nature of the instrument itself; in normal circumstances where the documentation is limited to an oil and gas lease, this may almost be taken for granted, but any variation such as an option or assignment of minerals must be clearly indicated.
4 Complete the lease form filling in all blanks prior to execution by the lessor.

5 Review the contents of the lease clause by clause with the lessor.
6 Affix a proper seal (the common wafer form will do) opposite the lessor's signature prior to execution.
7 Pay some portion of the bonus consideration, however nominal, at the time of execution.
8 Reach a firm understanding as to the terms on which the balance is to be paid and have them reduced to writing signed by the lessor. The time period should be sufficient to permit the proper investigation of title, curative title work, and registration of either a caveat or the lease itself. Under most circumstances a time period of 30–45 days should be sufficient (the lessor cannot take advantage of any title defect by neglecting to cure same).
9 Pay the full bonus consideration prior to the expiration of the specified time.
10 Mail or deliver a copy of the lease duly executed by the lessee to the lessor prior to the expiration of the time set for payment.

PART THREE
THE LEASE

5
What the lease grants

A standard lease as such does not exist in Canada. Indeed there is not even uniformity as to the use of the 'unless' or the 'or' form, although the former undoubtedly is more frequently encountered. An examination of the various forms of lease does indicate, however, that the great majority of them contain clauses that are virtually identical or differ only in areas of minute detail. Because of this, one may engage in a review of the individual clauses with the assurance that any observations are applicable to most Canadian leases. For convenience, the commonly used version of each clause will be referred to as the 'standard clause.'

AMERICAN AUTHORITIES

Since the Canadian lease is derived directly from the United States, it would seem reasonable to suppose that the body of case law and authority that has grown up around its American counterpart would be of particular assistance to Canadian courts. It has not worked out this way. The lower courts have indicated some willingness to consult American authorities.[1] The Supreme Court of Canada, however, has examined the terms of oil and gas leases on

---

1 The Alberta Appellate Division in *East Crest Oil Company Limited* v *Strohschein* (1951–52) 4 W.W.R. (N.S.) 553, [1952] 2 D.L.R. 432, applied the California case of *Richfield Oil Corpn.* v *Bloomfield* (1951) 229 P. (2d) 838 to hold that an 'unless' form of lease terminates automatically if drilling has not commenced, or delay rental payment not made within specified time.

at least fifteen occasions and has referred to American authorities in only one instance, and that was merely a passing bow where the court acknowledged that some American authorities took a different view of the *habendum* clause than the one it entertained. The brief discussion was followed by this statement: 'the essential task in the present case is to construe the terms of the lease which is in question.'[2]

CANADIAN JURISPRUDENTIAL APPROACH

The lack of enthusiasm for American authorities provides a useful clue to the approach of the Canadian Supreme Court to the oil and gas lease. The American cases, in addition to suffering from a considerable divergence of result arising from the differing views of individual state courts, introduce other elements such as equitable considerations, relief against forfeiture, intention of the parties, and implied covenants. The Canadian approach, on the other hand, has been to look only to the actual words of the lease and to exclude any outside influences or considerations.

This has led on occasion to interpretations so much at variance with what the draftsmen undoubtedly intended that it prompted Locke J to remark, 'I am by no means satisfied that the result accords with the intention of the parties to the instrument,'[3] and has dismayed writers and commentators.[4] Some writers have suggested that the approach may have been caused by judicial sympathy for the plight of the lessor under a document drafted by the other party and heavily weighted in favour of the lessee.[5]

The actual decisions of the court itself, however, do not reveal any particular bias for or against either party. The common theme that runs throughout all the judgments is that of strict attention to the actual wording of the particular lease itself, and a determinedly literalistic application of that language. The literalistic approach is subject to one further refinement in that if the language creates an ambiguity it should be construed against the party who prepared and tendered the document.[6] The lessee, almost invariably, will be the party who proffers the document so that if there is any ambiguity it will be resolved in favour of the lessor.

---

2 *Canada-Cities Service Petroleum Corporation* v *Kininmonth* [1964] s.c.r. 439, 447, 448
3 *Shell Oil Co.* v *Gibbard* [1961] s.c.r. 725, 732
4 Lewis and Thompson, *Canadian Oil and Gas,* § 100
5 Angus, 'Voluntary Pooling in Canadian Oil and Gas Law' (1955–61), 1 *Alta. L. Rev.* 481
6 This maxim is one of those that, regrettably, is still most frequently pronounced in Latin. In that language it takes the following formidable form: *verba chartarum fortius accipiuntur contra proferentem.*

The court has very seldom been forced to rely upon the maxim since the wording of the individual clauses has usually been found to be clear and free from ambiguity. This is so despite the fact that the court's view of the 'clear meaning' has frequently astounded those who originally prepared the document and has caused a good deal of frantic re-drafting to reverse the interpretation of the courts. Virtually every lease now contains language that has been revised in an attempt to repair the judicial ravages. As might be expected, the lease is drafted so as to adequately protect the position of the lessee.[7] A general attack was made, on one occasion, against a form of lease on the ground that it was unconscionable and should be set aside.[8] Milvain J rejected this contention on the basis that, in order to succeed, the lessor must establish the existence of a relationship between the parties which makes him subservient to that of the lessee. If this is the test and such a relationship must be established, regardless of the effect of the actual terms of the agreement, then it would appear that the lease is virtually unassailable from attack based on its being an unconscionable bargain.

Against this background let us now examine the standard clauses in their present form, together with any judicial interpretations. A number of the clauses acquired their present form as a result of drafting changes to avoid the effect placed on their predecessors. Hence they can best be understood when seen against this background. Wherever applicable, we will trace such clauses through their earlier version and judicial fates. A number of the decisions resulted in the abrupt and involuntary termination of the leases. This has become such an important feature of the Canadian law that the cases are given full and exhaustive treatment in Part Six, Involuntary Termination. Here they are discussed only in enough detail to indicate the development of the present form of certain clauses in the lease.

THE PARTIES AND LEASED LANDS

The lease commences with a description of the parties, that of the lessee being printed as part of the form while the name and description of the lessor is typed in as occasion serves. The lessor is further described as the owner of the leased substances 'within, upon or under' lands which are set forth in their

---

7 Some writers dispute this and advance the claim that many of the provisions in the lease are for the express protection of the lessor. See, for example, Burden, 'Capped Gas Well Clause, and the Gunderson Case,' 5 *Can. Bar Journal* 37. Lewis and Thompson, *supra* n. 4 § 100, however, acknowledge 'at the same time, it is stretching credulity to contend that there are many clauses inserted solely for the benefit of the lessor.'

8 *Crommie* v *California Standard Company* – reported in part, (1962) 38 w.w.r. 447 (Alta.) and in full in Lewis and Thompson, *supra* n. 4 Dig. 190

full legal description, including the Certificate of Title number, if one exists. Usually all the lands that may be owned by a lessor in a given locality are included in one lease; for example, if he has title to a full section rather than the more customary quarter section, all 640 acres will be leased. Some very important consequences flow from this practice and they may not be fully appreciated by the average lessor. Since the covenants and undertakings of the lessee relate to all the lands covered by the lease, certain operations conducted by the lessee anywhere on the lands will keep the lease in force. If one lease embraces a number of sections, even though they may not be adjacent or contiguous, they will all be lumped together under the definition of 'said lands,' with the result that the drilling of one well on the lands will satisfy the drilling requirement. Similarly, production from only a portion of the entire area serves to prolong the lease with respect to the entire leased area. It is very much to the benefit of the lessee to embody all the lands owned by a single lessor under one lease and, conversely, it is to the advantage of the lessor to enter into a separate lease for each parcel.

CONSIDERATION

The description of the lands covered by the lease is immediately followed by the bonus consideration which is typed in after the negotiated figure has been agreed upon. The dollar figure is followed by the phrase 'paid to the Lessor by the Lessee, (the receipt whereof is hereby acknowledged), and in consideration of the covenants of the Lessee hereinafter contained.' In view of the practice followed by most lessees in paying the initial bonus consideration, described in chapter 4 *ante*, the clause has several drawbacks. It recites that the full consideration has been paid, which usually is not the case until after title check and registration of the lessee's interest, and contains the phrase 'the receipt whereof is hereby acknowledged.' This can be contradicted by evidence to the effect that the payment has not been made; furthermore, the wording has the effect of making payment a condition precedent to the agreement itself. It ignores the fact that the usual practice is to agree upon some time period within which full payment must be made. There is no provision for a deposit or payment of a portion of the bonus consideration as a down payment. The courts will likely regard the effect of the express acknowledgment of receipt as making payment of the full sum a condition precedent and it is unlikely that embodiment of the 'covenants of the Lessee hereinafter contained' as part of the consideration would be very useful to counteract the necessity of immediate and full payment, or, alternatively, a collateral agreement as to when a postponed payment must be made.

The bonus consideration has tax consequences to both lessee and lessor.

The lessee may treat it as a drilling or exploration expense. Conversely, the lessor must treat the payment as income. Under the former Income Tax Act he was not required to include such a payment in income if (a) he owned the property before April 10, 1962, or (b) acquired it after that date by inheritance or bequest.[9] These exemptions are no longer available under the Income Tax Act 1972, payments of this nature now being considered income under Sec. 59(1). However, if the lessor owned the property prior to April 10, 1962, and leases it after 1971, he is entitled to the benefit of the transitional provisions under Sec. 59(3). For example, if such a lessor granted a lease in 1972, only sixty per cent of the bonus consideration would be treated as income. This amount increases by five per cent, in each of the eight years subsequent to 1972, so that if the lease were granted in 1976, eighty per cent of the bonus would be treated as income.

THE GRANT

The operative words of an oil and gas lease are those which grant or lease the substances. There is a remarkable degree of unanimity insofar as the wording is concerned:

DOTH HEREBY GRANT AND LEASE unto the Lessee all the petroleum, natural gas and related hydrocarbons (except coal and valuable stone), all other gases, and all minerals and substances (whether liquid or solid and whether hydrocarbons or not) produced in association with any of the foregoing or found in any water contained in any reservoir (all hereinafter referred to as 'the leased substances'), subject to the royalties hereinafter reserved, within, upon or under the lands hereinbefore described and all the right, title, estate and interest, if any, of the Lessor in and to the leased substances or any of them within, upon or under any lands excepted from, or roadways, lanes, or rights-of-way adjoining, the lands aforesaid, together with the exclusive right and privilege to explore, drill for, win, take, remove, store and dispose of the leased substances and for the said purposes to drill wells, lay pipelines and build and install such tanks, stations, structures and roadways as may be necessary.

The clause is an outright grant of the substances. It is not enough to merely lease the minerals as they are to be reduced into the possession of the lessee. A conventional real property lease envisages the eventual return of the premises in an unchanged condition, normal wear and tear excepted. Under

9 The Income Tax Act – R.S.C. 1952 c 148 as amended, s 83A (5c), now replaced by the Income Tax Act, 1972, S. Can. 1970–71 c 63 c 59

an oil and gas lease, however, the parties recognize that the minerals are to be exhausted prior to the termination of the lease.

The granting clause also confers upon the lessee certain exclusive rights. The words of grant and lease are probably the most unambiguous ones in the entire document. Possibly for this reason the granting portion of the clause has been free from litigation. As we have seen in chapter 3, the rights granted by the clause amount to a *profit à prendre*. A right of this nature is not necessarily exclusive, although it is hard to conceive that a right to remove minerals would not be so considered. In any event, the standard clause removes all doubt by expressly providing that the specific rights and privileges are, in fact, exclusive.

Some leases insert the exclusive feature as an integral part of the lease and grant itself: 'DOES HEREBY LEASE AND GRANT exclusively.' This would seem to be the better practice.

RULE OF CAPTURE

Despite the unrestricted language of the grant, the lessee only receives those substances that are ultimately reduced into its possession regardless of what quantities originally may have underlain the leased lands. The 'rule of capture,' succinctly phrased by Hardwicke, 'the owner of a tract of land acquires title to the oil and gas which he produces from wells thereon, though it may be proved that part of such oil and gas migrated from adjoining lands,'[10] is firmly entrenched in Canadian law. In *Borys* v *Canadian Pacific Railway and Imperial Oil Limited*,[11] the Privy Council said:

The substances are fugacious and are not stable within the container although they cannot escape from it. If any of the three substances is withdrawn from a portion of the property which does not belong to the appellant, but lies within the same container and oil or gas situated in his property thereby filters from it to the surrounding lands, admittedly he has no remedy. So, also, if any substance is withdrawn from his property, thereby causing any fugacious matter to enter his land, the surrounding owners have no remedy against him. The only safeguard is to be the first to get to work, in which case those who make the recovery become owners of the material which they withdraw from any well which is situated on their property or from which they have authority to draw.

10 'The Rule of Capture and Its Implications as Applied to Oil and Gas' (1935), 13 *Tex. L. Rev.* 391, 393
11 (1952–53) 7 W.W.R. (N.S.) 546, 550

THE SUBSTANCES THAT ARE GRANTED

The present version of the standard granting clause uses an all-embracing definition of the minerals covered by it. The wording is the result of experience and knowledge of the difficulty in defining the various substances, hydrocarbons or otherwise, which might be produced from a well. Earlier leases had definitions that were much more limited, typically: (i) petroleum and natural gas; (ii) petroleum, natural gas and all related hydrocarbons (except coal and valuable stone); (iii) oil, gas, casing head gas, casing head gasoline, and related hydrocarbons.

These narrower definitions are often found in leases negotiated during the early 1950s, many of which still continue in force by reason of production. Some substances produced from a well are not hydrocarbons, but do have a commercial value. The most significant example is sulphur, which is produced in vast quantities from 'sour' gas and now constitutes a multimillion dollar industry by itself. There are other materials, such as helium and carbon dioxide which, while not as common or important, have, or could have, a commercial value. Are they included in a grant of 'petroleum, natural gas and related hydrocarbons'? The issue is further confused by the changing physical nature of the hydrocarbon substances themselves. They may be in liquid form at reservoir pressure, but turn into a gas when brought to the surface. Are they petroleum or natural gas?

The judicial starting point for considerations of this sort must be the decision of the Privy Council in *Borys* v *Canadian Pacific Railway and Imperial Oil Limited*.[12] The issue here did not involve a lease, but rather the reservation in a transfer of land; the proper interpretation of the word 'petroleum,' however, was in question. Borys was the owner of an estate in fee simple in a section of land that had been acquired from the Canadian Pacific Railway Company through a conveyance that reserved 'all coal, petroleum, and valuable stone.' In 1949 the CPR leased to Imperial Oil Limited all petroleum under the lands together with the exclusive right to work and carry away the same.

Imperial commenced drilling pursuant to its lease, but before the well had reached the productive formation Borys obtained an interim injunction prohibiting Imperial from drilling into the formation. Simultaneously he brought an action for a declaration that he was the owner of the natural gas within the land and a permanent injunction restraining Imperial from interfering with or disposing of his natural gas.

12 Ibid

The trial court granted a declaration that Borys was, in fact, the owner of all gas whether it was free, or in solution. The Appellate Division of Alberta held that the gas in solution under reservoir conditions was part of the petroleum, that Imperial was entitled to extract all of the substances belonging to them, i.e. the petroleum, even if their action caused interference with and wastage of the gas belonging to Borys, so long as modern methods were used.

Borys appealed to the Privy Council claiming that he was the owner not only of the gas contained in the cap situated on top of the petroleum, but also any gas in solution with the petroleum. The other parties claimed that the reservation of petroleum included all gas whether it was in the cap or in solution. In dealing with this question the Judicial Committee agreed that the vernacular meaning should be applied if one could be ascertained. The court referred to a statement in *Glasgow Corpn.* v *Farie*[13] with respect to mines and minerals: ' "Mines" and "minerals" are not definite terms; they are susceptible of limitation or expansion, according to the intention with which they are used.' Similarly the court felt that the meaning of petroleum could vary according to the circumstances in which it was used. After examining all the evidence, expert and otherwise, the Privy Council concluded it was impossible to find any clear indication as to what the uninstructed mind would define as petroleum, at the time of the original grant or, indeed at any time. Receiving no help from a non-existent vernacular meaning, the court was driven to consider, purely as a matter of construction, the meaning that the word 'petroleum' bears when the substance referred to is *in situ* in a container below ground. Their Lordships agreed with the observations of the Appellate Division that the test as to what was included in petroleum was the state of affairs in the reservoir, since what had been reserved to the railway company was petroleum in the earth and not a substance when it reached the surface. The fact that a change in pressure and temperature releases gas at the surface should not affect the original ownership.

Insofar as the word 'petroleum' is concerned, therefore, we may safely say that under the circumstances of the normal lease it includes all hydrocarbons in a liquid state under reservoir conditions. While the Privy Council has informed us what substances are included in or excluded from the word 'petroleum,' the problem becomes more complicated when additional words are included, and substances other than hydrocarbons are produced. The potential ambiguity of 'petroleum, natural gas and related hydrocarbons' may be shown by asking whether or not sulphur would be included in the grant.

Over the years the courts have evolved certain rules as guides to aid in the

13 (1888) 13 App. Cas. 657, 58 L.F.P.C. 33

interpretation of documents.[14] The rules are easy to describe, even though some have been graced with Latin tags, but are not always so easy to apply.

1 If the phrase has a plain and unambiguous meaning, then that meaning must be implemented. To apply this to our example, if the word 'sulphur' occurred in the grant there would be no need for further enquiry.

2 The vernacular meaning, if there is one, will control, and it will be the meaning existing at the time the document was drafted. Since sulphur is not a hydrocarbon if it is to be found anywhere in the above phrase, it can only be in 'natural gas.' Sulphur under reservoir conditions is normally encountered as a gas known as hydrogen sulphide, so one would think it might well be included in 'natural gas.' Is there, however, a popular meaning to the words 'natural gas' which restricts them to hydrocarbon substances? Certainly some evidence could be led to establish that until ten years ago, at least, the average person when he spoke of 'natural gas' had in mind the fuel used for space heating and which consists only of hydrocarbons. Despite this, it is doubtful that a court could be persuaded that there was a popular meaning sufficiently precise to exclude all non-hydrocarbons.

3 *Expressio unius est exclusio alterius*, which may be translated to mean that the expression of one person or thing implies the exclusion of other persons or things of the same class but which are not mentioned. The rule is usually illustrated by this example: 'Suppose one man says to another: "we are looking forward to seeing you on Tuesday, bring the family with you; my wife wants to meet your mother." Does "the family" include everybody living in the other man's house or only his wife and children with the expressed addition of his mother? Is his father or his sister-in-law not invited?'[15] This principle, if held to be applicable, would favour the exclusion of sulphur, because since the words 'natural gas' are preceded by 'petroleum' and followed by 'and related hydrocarbons,' they include only hydrocarbons.

4 The document as a whole should be looked at to interpret a particular provision. This might be of assistance if, for example, the lease contained in its royalty provision a specific reference to sulphur. There might then be an implication that the parties must have intended to include sulphur in the grant.

5 The *ejusdem generis* rule to the effect that if there is a particular description of property sufficient to identify what the parties intended, accom-

14 See generally, Odgers, *The Construction of Deeds and Statutes* (5th ed. 1967)
15 Ibid, 94. Odgers warns that this maxim must be applied with great caution, as it is capable of being stretched beyond its proper limits.

panied by some general description, the latter will be confined to objects of the same class or kind as those particularly described. The rule is sometimes paraphrased; a word is known by the company it keeps. If this maxim were applied, it could lead to the exclusion of sulphur since the references to both 'petroleum' and 'related hydrocarbons' are clearly specific as to hydrocarbons, thus limiting the general phrase 'natural gas.'

In the absence of any judicial decisions the question as to whether sulphur in its gaseous form is included in the grant of 'petroleum, natural gas and related hydrocarbons' remains open. It seems abundantly clear that, if sulphur were encountered in solid or crystal form in the reservoir, then such could not be included in the grant. On balance, one must incline to the view that the words 'natural gas' are sufficiently wide to include any constituents that are found in a gaseous state. This is lent some support by American decisions, notably *Lonestar Gas Co.* v *Stine*,[16] which concerned the right of the gas owner to liquid hydrocarbons separated from the gas at the surface. Since the substances in dispute were all hydrocarbons, the issue as to natural gas being limited to hydrocarbons did not arise. The judge examined the term 'natural gas': 'The term "all natural gas" would include all the substances that come from the well as gas, and that regardless of whether such gas be wet or dry. It is undisputed in the evidence that the term "natural gas" includes numerous elements or component parts, but the very language of the conveyance is such as to include therein all those component parts which were in gaseous form when they came from the wells.'

The American courts edged somewhat closer to the problem in *Navajo Tribe of Indians* v *The United States*,[17] where the lease was a grant of 'all the oil and gas deposits.' The question was whether such a grant included helium. The plaintiff asserted that the term 'gas deposits' referred solely to gaseous hydrocarbons because of the presence of the word 'oil.' The court had this to say:

The position asserted by plaintiff appears to overlook the fact that gases existing in nature do not fall into neat, mutually exclusive categories such as 'hydrocarbon' and 'non-hydrocarbon.' The various elements are co-mingled. With respect to the Rattlesnake gas, the hydrocarbon content could not be produced separately from the other components and, even under plaintiff's view, the lessee would have the right to produce the hydrocarbon gases. Perhaps, plaintiff would impose upon the lessee an obligation to produce the gas, extract the helium, and deliver the refined helium to the lessor. Of course, it would have been possible for the parties to create such an arrangement ... However, the lease in question contains no such

16 41 s.w. (2D), 48   17 25 *Oil & Gas Reporter* 858

provision, and there is no basis for holding that such an understanding arose by implication.

We consider defendant's approach to be the proper one. Although the parties to the lease may have been thinking mainly of fuel-type gases, it is still more realistic to presume that the grant included not only hydrocarbons but the other gaseous elements as well. It follows that, whether its percentage was high or low, the helium component was part of the 'gas deposit' which passed to the lessee.

Popular dictionaries display the same lack of certainty as to whether 'natural gas' is confined to hydrocarbon substances. Webster defines natural gas as 'a mixture of gaseous hydrocarbons, chiefly methane, occurring naturally in the earth in certain places.' The Random House dictionary, while acknowledging the predominance of hydrocarbons, also admits the possibility of other substances forming part of natural gas. It defines 'natural gas' as 'Combustible gas formed naturally in the earth, as in regions yielding petroleum, consisting usually of over 80 per cent of methane together with minor amounts of ethane, propane, butane, nitrogen, and, sometimes, helium: used as a fuel and to make carbon black and acetylene.' The reference to nitrogen and helium indicates that natural gas is not necessarily confined to hydrocarbons, and the definition also emphasizes the naturally occurring feature of gas.

The natural origin aspect appears in scientific definitions which also make it clear that natural gas may contain substances other than hydrocarbons, although such may be considered to be impurities.

Natural gas is defined as any gas of natural origin as produced from or existing in oil or gas wells and consisting primarily of the light hydrocarbons methane and ethane.

Deposits of natural gas occur in rock of sedimentary origin wherein layers of rock are folded upward to form anticlines or dome-shaped structures with oil and gas being trapped under non-porous layers of rock which cover the structure, thus forming a structural trap.

Natural gas may contain undesirable impurities such as carbon dioxide, nitrogen, water vapour, hydrogen sulphide and thiols or other organic sulphur compounds.

Hydrogen sulphide is one of the more important impurities present in natural gas.

In some instances, the presence of appreciable concentrations of impurities has been turned to economic advantage. Natural gas containing high concentrations of hydrogen sulphide, such as the Olds Field gas and the Laq Field gas shown in Table 5, are processed for recovery of hydrogen sulphide, which in turn is reduced to elemental sulphur, a valuable, basic, chemical raw material. As a result of the Laq installations, France has become one of the world's major suppliers of sulphur. Numerous sulphur-recovery plants are also in operation in the U.S. and Canada. The recovery of sulphur from natural gas is an important economic factor to the sulphur industry as well as segments of the natural gas industry.

Helium is present in a few natural gases, but should be regarded as a valuable component rather than an impurity if present in concentrations sufficiently large for economical recovery (about 0.3–0.7% or higher).[18]

On the basis of the above, therefore, it seems at least probable that a Canadian court, faced with the question of whether or not substances such as hydrogen sulphide, nitrogen, helium, and carbon dioxide which form part of the natural gas in a reservoir are included in a grant of 'petroleum, natural gas and related hydrocarbons,' would hold that they were so included.[19]

The result might be otherwise under another description of the minerals which is occasionally encountered: 'oil, gas, casinghead gas, casinghead gasoline and related hydrocarbons.' The non-hydrocarbon substances, if included at all, could only be found within the word 'gas.' All the other words used in the grant relate specifically to hydrocarbons; oil, casinghead gas, casinghead gasoline, and related hydrocarbons, although it is possible that 'casinghead gas' could also include impurities and other substances in a natural state. One might speculate that in view of the number of references to hydrocarbon substances, 'gas' might be limited through association to hydrocarbons.

MINERALS UNDER THE STANDARD CLAUSE

The current description of minerals is cast in very wide terms: 'All the petroleum, natural gas and related hydrocarbons (except coal and valuable stone), all other gases, and all minerals and substances (whether liquid or solid and whether hydrocarbons or not) produced in association with any of the foregoing or found in any water contained in any reservoir.' There is a specific reference to 'all other gases,' which makes it abundantly clear that substances found in gaseous form, although not hydrocarbons, are meant to

18 Kirk and Othmar, *Encyclopaedia of Chemical Technology* (2 ed) (1966) vol. 10, 443, 441 and 449
19 The opposite view is expressed by Holland, 'Is Helium Covered by Oil and Gas Leases?' (1963), 41 *Tex. L. Rev.* 408. See also Lewis and Thompson, *supra* n. 4 § 102A where the authors suggest that the mere fact that helium is intermingled with 'natural gas' may not be enough to treat it as being included

be included. The reference to all 'minerals and substances' is wide-ranging although qualified by the words 'produced in association with any of the foregoing or found in any water contained in any reservoir.' Certainly this phraseology would be broad enough to capture substances such as hydrogen sulphide, nitrogen, carbon dioxide, and helium since those substances are produced in association with natural gas. The wording, although broad, does not include, nor is it meant to include, any solid or 'hard' minerals, since 'minerals' are limited to those produced in association with the other substances, which are only those substances normally produced from an oil or gas well in liquid or gaseous state. The reference to 'found in any water contained in any reservoir' is clearly meant to reflect the fact that formation water is very often produced with the petroleum substances and the grant makes it clear that any substances found in such formation water also belong to the lessee.[20]

INCOME TAX CONSIDERATIONS

The description of the substances used in the standard clause is tax-inspired to some extent. Section 83A (5a) of the Income Tax Act, 1952, as amended permitted the deduction as a drilling or exploration expense of the acquisition cost of an agreement or contract or arrangement for the right, licence, or privilege to explore for, drill for, or take in Canada petroleum, natural gas, or other related hydrocarbons (except coal) as long as no other right was acquired over the land *except*: 'materials and substances (whether liquid or solid and whether hydrocarbons or not) produced in association with the petroleum, natural gas or other related hydrocarbons (except coal) or found in any water contained in an oil or gas reservoir.'

Obviously there was a strong incentive to make sure that a lease was not disqualified by the inclusion of other substances. Prior to 1972 the standard

20 For an interesting and worthwhile discussion of what is included in the reservation from land transfers of 'All Mines and Minerals,' see Stewart, 'The Reservation or Exception of Mines and Minerals' (1962), 40 *Can. Bar Rev.* 329. This, of course, is a different matter from the grant under an oil and gas lease where the reference to minerals is referable back to petroleum, gas, and hydrocarbons. See also the Sand and Gravel Act R.S.A. 1970 c 328 which makes it clear that, regardless of any reservations that may have occurred in the transfer, the owner of the surface of land is deemed to be also the owner of sand and gravel obtained by stripping off the overburden, excavating from the surface, or otherwise recovered by surface operations. The Act is effective with respect to any patent, title, grant, deed, conveyance, etc. issued or made before or after the 7th day of April, 1951. Certainly sand and gravel together with other 'hard' minerals, including potash, are outside the ambit of the granting words in the average oil and gas lease.

clause may have gone too far by the inclusion of 'all other gases,' and by changing 'materials' as used in the Act to 'minerals.' In the unlikely event that a non-hydrocarbon gas, such as helium or carbon dioxide, occurred by itself and free of any association with hydrocarbons, it would have been covered by the standard clause but excluded by the language of the Income Tax Act. The taxing authorities have not questioned the clause on this point, although wording that granted 'all mines and minerals' has been disallowed. The Income Tax Act, 1972, by Sec. 66(1), 66(15)(b) and (c), has altered this situation and the specific prohibition against the acquisition of any other right has disappeared. Sec. 66(15)(c)(i) defines 'Canadian resource property' as any right, licence or privilege to explore for, drill for, or take petroleum, natural gas or related hydrocarbons in Canada, and Sec. 66(15) (c)(ii) extends this definition to any right, licence or privilege to prospect, explore, drill or mine for minerals in a mineral resource in Canada. The description of the substances granted by a lease now can be expanded without risk of disqualification for income tax purposes.

MOTHER HUBBARD CLAUSE

After describing the substances, the standard clause continues: 'and all the right, title, estate and interest, if any, of the lessor in and to the leases substances or any of them within, upon or under any lands excepted from, or roadways, lanes, or rights-of-way adjoining the lands aforesaid.' It commonly happens that a person's title will be subject to certain exceptions; portions of his land are carved out of his title because of utility easements, roadways, and similar public uses. Ownership of the minerals under any excepted portion is often a complex legal question. The provision, usually known as the Mother Hubbard clause, simply ensures that if the lessor, in fact, owns minerals under these parcels, they will be included automatically within the grant. The language imposes a definite geographical limitation on the operation of the automatic inclusion to either lands excepted from the leased lands or adjoining roadways, lanes, or rights-of-way.

EXPRESS POWERS UNDER THE GRANT

The granting clause also confers special rights that are related to the exploration for and production of the substances. Those enumerated in the standard clause are almost universal throughout Canada; they confer upon the lessee the exclusive right and privilege to 'explore, drill for, win, take, remove, store and dispose of the leased substances and for the said purposes to drill wells, lay pipelines and build and install such tanks, stations, structures and roadways as may be necessary.' These express powers fall into two classifications: those that relate to the surface of the land and those that deal with underground matters. There has been very little litigation on the scope and effect of these powers although there has been considerable academic speculation as to what rights may or may not be included.[21] There are a number of factors which complicate the question; the grant of minerals rights *per se* involves a corollary grant of the right to work the same, the frequent severance of title as between surface and minerals, the effect of legislation that greatly modifies the common law position and the precise nature of the ownership under the words of grant, i.e. is it only the minerals that are granted or is there also a grant of the surrounding space, stratum, or formation?

The wording purports to make the powers exclusive to the lessee. As has been discussed above, the grant of a *profit à prendre* is not automatically exclusive. Some of the express powers, those related to the sub-surface; to drill, win, take, remove, store and dispose, and to drill wells are undoubtedly exclusive. It is doubtful, however, if the mere use of the word 'exclusive' in such a grant would deprive an owner who is entitled to both the surface and the sub-surface of his right to make additional grants of the surface to others for the purpose of laying pipelines and building station structures or roadways thereon. Similarly, if there had been a division of the grant of the petroleum rights so that a particular oil and gas lease granted only the rights to the substances within certain horizons, it would not seem that the landowner could be prevented by the use of the word 'exclusive' from granting similar rights, including the rights to drill wells to the grantee of the petroleum substances within the other formations. The exclusive feature must be interpreted in relation to the grant itself, that is, the rights are exclusive to the lessee, but only insofar as they relate to the particular substances granted. Even this refinement is not sufficient to explain the position of the landowner who, having made a grant under an oil and gas lease that confers these exclusive rights, is still clearly entitled to grant to others the rights to use portions of his surface for such purposes as laying pipelines and building roads. The bare reference to 'exclusive' as commonly encountered is inaccurate and does not properly describe the true legal position between the parties.

While the surface rights may not be exclusive to the lessee, the wording enables the lessee to choose any portion of the lands for his purposes. In the

21 Lyndon, 'The Legal Aspects of Underground Storage of Natural Gas' (1961), 1 *Alta. L. Rev.* 543; Stewart, *supra* n. 20; McRae, *Granting Clauses in Oil and Gas Leases*, Second Annual Institute on Oil and Gas Law, 43

United States the rule is that the lessee is entitled to use such portions of the surface as may be reasonably necessary for the purposes specified in the lease.[22] Indeed, this right exists even if not definitely expressed. It arises by implication under the rule that 'when a thing is granted all the means to obtain it and all the fruits and effects of it are also granted.'[23] In fact, the express rights spelled out in the typical granting clause are all powers which American courts have, at one time or another, held that the lessee has by implication.[24]

MINERAL TITLE DOMINANT

Where, as frequently happens, there is a severance of the surface and the mineral title, those powers that relate to surface use in an oil and gas lease are clearly beyond the right of the lessor to grant, except as an incident of the mineral estate. As between the two estates, the mineral title is dominant to the surface insofar as those rights and privileges necessary to secure and produce the minerals are concerned. The mineral owner has the right of ingress and egress over the surface and the right to use the surface to carry on operations that are necessary to the mining or production of the minerals underneath the surface. The surface cannot be used by the mineral owner to mine or produce minerals that are not located under the lands; this distinction is of more significance with hard minerals than in the case of petroleum substances which are subject to migration and the rule of capture. In *Borys* the Privy Council stated: 'Inherently the reservation of a substance, which is of no advantage unless a right to work it is added, makes the reservation useless unless that right follows the grant. The true view is that such a reservation necessarily implies the existence of power to recover it and of the right of working.'[25] Their Lordships also quoted with approval the following passage from *Ramsay* v *Blair*:[26]

In the case of Hamilton (Duke) v Graham 1871 LR 2sc & DIV 166, it was clearly pointed out what the exact right of a proprietor was in respect of a property excepted from a demise; and as to which therefore all the original rights of the demising proprietor remain, together with all the incidents to that property necessary to its working and enjoyment, that which the owner has reserved to

22 *Mosley* v *Magnolia Petroleum Co.* (1941) 114 P 2d
23 *Squires* v *Lafferty* (1924) 121 SE 90: see also Brown, 'The Law of Oil and Gas Leases' (2nd ed.) sec. 3.06
24 See Brown, ibid, for an extensive review of the cases
25 *Supra* n. 11, 558
26 [1876] 1 App Cas 701 (H.L.)

himself being as much his as other parts of his land of which he has made no demise whatsoever.

RIGHT OF SURFACE OWNER TO SUPPORT

The Privy Council pointed out that so far as they were aware that general proposition had never been controverted except in the case of interference with the surface of land which had been granted to another. In such a case there is in general a right to support. The right to support, which means the mineral owner cannot conduct his operations so as to cause the surface to subside, has long been recognized as a limitation on the dominant position of the mineral title. As to what constitutes the right to support, the classic statement seems to be that in *Humphries* v *Brogden*:[27] 'The only reasonable support is that which will protect the surface from subsidence and keep it securely at its ancient and natural level.'

An example of how the right to mine minerals could cause subsidence to the surface and thus be enjoined is found in *The Trinidad Asphalt Company* v *Ambard*,[28] where the owner of the asphalt had excavated right to the border of an adjoining property so that asphalt from the adjoining property seeped over the boundary and the surface subsided. Normally, however, there can be no suggestion that the withdrawal of petroleum or natural gas will interfere with the right of support of the surface. They are usually produced from formations deep within the earth with many intervening structures between them and the surface. There is little likelihood that production of oil or gas will affect the level of the surface.

Under the common law the dominant mineral title probably would include by implication many of the rights that are spelled out in the granting clause of the oil and gas lease. It is doubtful if the express references to the powers actually enlarges the rights of either the mineral owner himself or his lessee. Insofar as the lease is concerned, the lessor by the grant of minerals also by implication grants such rights to work them as he himself possesses. Such implied rights would necessarily include the right to explore, the right to drill wells, together with the right to remove and dispose of the substances.

SURFACE FACILITIES

The American cases indicate that the mineral owner could use the surface to construct such tankage as would be reasonably necessary to store the sub-

27 12 Q.B. 739, 745
28 [1899] A.C. 594, 68 L.J.P.C. 114

stances produced from the lands. But this would not include the right to construct storage facilities for production from other lands, i.e. it would not include the right to construct a battery of tanks to store production from a number of leases. The lessee by implication may have the right to construct access roadways, and lay flowlines to conduct the production from the lease. These powers, and probably others if necessary to the proper recovery of the minerals, would be bestowed upon the lessee by operation of the common law. There is the always present hazard, under the rules of interpretation, that by specifically enumerating certain powers, the parties have excluded others that otherwise might be implied. Although one can understand the reluctance of draftsmen to rely on implied powers, the lessee might be better served if the words of grant and lease were supplemented by the phrase 'together with the right to work the same,' with no mention of any specific powers.

In Canada the common law dominance of the mineral title has been displaced or affected by legislation.[29] The legislation, which varies to some

29 The Surface Rights Act 1972 S.A.C. 91 s 12 reads:
    1 No operator has a right of entry, user or taking of the surface of any land for
    a the removal of minerals contained in or underlying the surface of such land or
      for or incidental to any mining or drilling operations, or
    b the laying of pipe lines for or in connection with any mining or drilling
      operations, or the production of minerals, or
    c the erection of tanks, stations and structures for or in connection with a mining
      or drilling operation, or the production of minerals, until the operator
      has obtained the consent of the owner of the surface of the land and of the
      occupant thereof, or has become entitled to right of entry by reason of an
      order of the Board, pursuant to this act.
    2 Notwithstanding anything contained in a grant, conveyance, lease, licence or
      other instrument, whether made before or after the coming into force of this Act,
      and pertaining to the acquisition of an interest in a mineral, an operator thereby
      does not obtain the right of entry in respect of the surface of any land
      unless the grant, conveyance, lease, licence or other instrument provides a
      specific separate sum in consideration for the right of entry of the surface
      required for his operations, but this subsection does not apply in a case
      where the operator, prior to July 1, 1952, has for any of the purposes
      referred to in subsection (1), exercised the right of entry in respect of the
      surface of land in accordance with the provisions of a grant, conveyance,
      lease, licence or other instrument.
    There is legislation in other provinces to somewhat similar effect, see Manitoba,
    Mines Act R.S.M. 1970, M160, s 20; Ontario, The Mining Act R.S.O. 1970, c 274
    s 101; Petroleum and Natural Gas Act, S.B.C. 1965, c 33 s 18. These acts require
    the written consent of the surface owner, plus compensation for damages, or some-
    times, as in Ontario, provide only for compensation. With respect to Manitoba
    and British Columbia which require the consent of the owner, or an entry order,

degree from province to province, effectively precludes the lessee from relying solely on the grant or lease of the minerals, despite any express powers
it may give, for the right to use the surface. Something more is required – the
express consent of the owner and payment of separate compensation. As is
pointed out by the authors of *Canadian Oil and Gas*,[30] the objects of the
legislation are to ensure reasonable user of the rights and to provide adequate
compensation to surface owners and occupants for disturbance of the surface. The legislation arose because ownership of minerals was severed from
ownership of land to such an extent that the landowners, usually farmers,
very often found the development of minerals to be 'of a barren and disturb-
ing nature.' Since oil and gas leases do not normally embody a separate
consideration for surface rights, it is necessary for the mineral lessee to deal
with the surface owner and attempt to obtain rights from him by agreement
or, failing that, to resort to the entry arbitration procedures. This has become
the accepted practice and the oil and gas lease is not treated as creating any
rights to the surface.

Once these rights have been obtained, the common law rules may again
come into force, although it would seem that most matters between the
parties, such as liability for damage, would be governed by surface lease or
the entry order. The Alberta Act refers to the right of entry, user or taking of
the surface in view of the purpose of the legislation, and would seem to rule
out some of the more extravagant express powers sometimes included in a
lease such as those which permit a lessee to 'house and otherwise care for
its employees.'

GEOPHYSICAL EXPLORATION

The right to explore for the leased substances is among the specific powers
enumerated in the granting clause. Apart from drilling, the most common
method of exploring for petroleum and natural gas is by seismograph. This
involves the movement of mobile equipment, and vehicles, across the land,
the drilling of shallow 'shot' holes, and the temporary laying of wires. Small
explosive charges are detonated in the 'shot' holes and the reflections from
the sub-surface formations are recorded. A right of this type would probably
be included in the specific power to 'explore,' but here again the situation

it would seem that the powers contained in the oil and gas lease would constitute
the necessary consent. For an interesting but somewhat confusing review of
'expropriation' under The Alberta Right of Entry Act see *Murphy Oil Company*
v *Dau and Dau* (1968) 66 w.w.r. 553 (Alta. D.C.), reversed (1966) 70 w.w.r.
339; aff'd by s.c.c. (1970) 73 w.w.r. 269, 12 D.L.R. (3d) 19.

30 *Supra* n. 4, § 76

has been altered by legislation. In Alberta and Saskatchewan there is a prohibition against any person conducting geophysical operations on privately owned land except with the consent of the owner.[31] The regulations also prescribe in detail the manner in which such operations are to be carried out.

SECONDARY RECOVERY

Today there is an increasing reliance on secondary recovery methods. Essentially this is the supplementing of original reservoir drive, by the injection into the reservoir of water, or gas, or a mixture of both. This increases or at least maintains the pressure within the reservoir. Secondary recovery involves several concepts which appear to be outside the scope of the normal oil and gas lease.

There is the injected material itself. Does the lessee have the right to use water which may be located under the lands for the purposes of secondary recovery? It would seem that the right to drill for and remove water which may underlie the leased lands is not one which is granted under the lease. In fact, the mineral owner may not have the power to grant such a right. Underground waters are treated in the common law as 'percolating waters.' The landowner has no right to them unless he reduces them to his possession, nor does he have a right of action against a person who does.[32] In some jurisdictions, underground water is vested in the Crown.[33]

---

31 Geophysical Regulations, Alta. Reg. 26/59 s 5; Geophysical Exploration Regulations, Sask. o.c. 933/64 s 15

32 *Acton* v *Blundell*, 12 M & W, 324, *Chasemore* v *Richards*, 29 L.J. Ex. 81

33 The Water Rights Act R.S.S (1965) c 51, s 7. The same result is achieved in Alberta by The Water Resources Act, R.S.A. 1970, c 388 s 2(2):
'2 All reference in this Act to water in any river, stream, water course, lake, creek, spring, ravine, canyon, lagoon, swamp, marsh, or other body of water, applies to water under the surface of the ground, commonly referred to as ground water, but does not apply to water obtained incidentally as a result of drilling for oil or the operation of an oil well.' In the light of other provisions in the Act, it now seems clear that the operator is free to produce water along with the oil, but if he desires to produce water by itself for re-injection into a reservoir, he must deal with the province. See also Manitoba Water Rights Act, R.S.M. 1970, c w80 s 7(1). The British Columbia Water Act, R.S.B.C. 1960 c 405 as amended by The Water Act Amendment Act, 1966, S.B.C. (1966) c 54, s 2. In the absence of such legislation it is a somewhat moot point as to whom an operator should turn to for the right to take underground minerals. Under the common law, the surface owner has the right to appropriate percolating waters to his own use, but if there are separate titles, ownership of the underground waters may have passed to the mineral owner. It is entirely possible that both the surface and mineral owner would have the right to use underground water for their own purposes. Maybe the unfortunate operator has to deal with both.

Nor would the words of grant appear to confer upon the lessee the right to take gas and re-inject it back into the reservoir for pressure maintenance, at least without payment of royalty to the lessor. Any such injection is also, of course, subject to the provisions of existing provincial legislation dealing with conservation. The implementation of a secondary recovery scheme also requires the actual physical injection of the substances into the reservoir. Normally, this is done by converting existing wells, either producing or suspended, into injector wells. This represents a substantial change in the status of the minerals owned by the lessor as they will no longer be produced. The power to inject substances into a formation underlying the lessor's lands is not, in our view, included within the ambit of the ordinary oil and gas lease.

Practically all secondary recovery schemes are conducted on lands that have been unitized, which greatly simplifies the problems that otherwise would occur under the lease. Unitization has such a profound impact on the lease that it warrants separate and detailed treatment, see *infra*, chapter 11.

UNDERGROUND STORAGE

Underground storage of natural gas, liquid petroleum, and condensate is now a recognized means of storing large volumes at a low unit cost. Various types of underground caverns, including salt domes, have been used for this purpose. One of the best receptacles for underground storage is a depleted oil or gas reservoir. The growing importance of this type of storage has focused attention on the ownership of such a right; does the lessee under an oil and gas lease acquire some ownership in the reservoir space itself, or does it remain the property of the mineral owner? Under a series of old English cases on mining it was established that the owner of a 'mine' had ownership of the 'whole containing chamber.'[34] This holding in connection with mines was consistent with the principle of 'outstroke,' which is the right to excavate so much of the surrounding rock as may be necessary to build adequate passageways for the transportation of the mineral to the surface. This right, however, was connected with the grant of 'mines,' a grant not usually found in oil and gas leases. Since the minerals granted under the oil and gas lease are not 'mined' but are withdrawn from the reservoir through a drill hole, it is not likely that the grant of such minerals would be held to also include the grant to the surrounding spaces. Nor is the right to underground storage among the enumerated specific powers.

Underground storage is most effective when located close to major markets, thus enabling pipelines to utilize unused capacity during the off-

34 *Proud* v *Bates* (1865) 34 L.J. Ch. 406. These and other cases are discussed in Stewart, *supra* n. 20

seasons to transport the gas and store it against periods of heavy demand. Not surprisingly, Ontario and British Columbia have taken the lead in legislating on the subject of gas storage. The Ontario Energy Board Act, 1964[35] specifically authorizes the storage of gas in Section 21:

AUTHORITY TO STORE

(1) The Board by order may authorize a person to inject gas into, store gas in and remove gas from a designated gas storage area, and to enter into and upon the land in the area and use the land for such purposes.

RIGHT TO COMPENSATION

(2) Subject to any agreement with respect thereto, the person authorized by an order under sub-section 1, (a) shall make to the owners of any gas or oil rights or of any right to store gas in the area fair, just and equitable compensation in respect of such gas or oil rights or such right to store gas; and (b) shall make the owner of any land in the area fair, just and equitable compensation for any damage necessarily resulting from the exercise of the authority given by such order.

RECOVERY OF COMPENSATION

(3) No action or other proceeding lies in respect of such compensation, and, failing agreement, the amount thereof shall be determined by a board of arbitration in a manner described in the regulations, and The Arbitrations Act does not apply.

The Act specifically authorizes the storage of natural gas but also provides that both the owners of the oil or gas rights or of storage rights and the owners of the surface shall be compensated in a fair, just, and equitable manner. The provisions of this Act were interpreted in *re Wellington and Imperial Oil Limited*,[36] where the applicant sought to have payments made by the lessee, who had an order to store gas under the land, classified as being royalty payments for the undepleted reserves of gas left in the ground at the time storage operations commenced rather than compensation under the Act for the storage privileges. The Ontario High Court held that it was barred by privative language in the Act itself from determining the question which lay solely within the jurisdiction of a Board of Arbitration to be appointed under the Act. In the course of judgment, however, the court noted that, while the

35 R.S.O. 1970 c 312 s 2; British Columbia has enacted a special statute on the subject, The Underground Storage Act, S.B.C. 1964, c 62, Alberta and Saskatchewan to date have confined themselves to bringing underground storage under the control of the respective Conservation Boards, but have not legislated on private rights, see The Oil and Gas Conservation Act, R.S.A. 1970 c 267, ss 37, 38; The Oil and Gas Conservation Act, R.S.S. 1965, c 360, s 51 (D(b)).

36 (1970) 8 D.L.R. (3d) 29

applicant lessor and Imperial Oil Limited as lessee had entered into both oil and gas leases and unit agreements concerning the lands, none of these documents contained a clause giving the lessee right to store gas. When interpreting the Energy Board Act, the court observed that the consideration and construction of both oil and gas leases and unit operating agreements must have been within the contemplation of the legislature when it enacted the particular provision authorizing the storage of gas. Although it was not called upon to decide that precise point, it is clear from the decision that the Energy Board Act did confer the right to store gas and that such right would override any conflicting claims that might be advanced by the mineral or surface owners.

In British Columbia, the Minister of Mines and Petroleum Resources may designate certain areas as 'storage areas' and may grant the right to explore for suitable reservoirs of structures for underground storage as well as a licence to store. The Act provided for agreement with the owner of the mineral rights or storage rights as to compensation or a determination of 'fair, just, and equitable compensation' by the Board of Arbitration. If the surface is owned in freehold, the Act appears to make the written consent of the owner and lawful occupant of the land mandatory.

It has now become common practice to include the right to use underground storage along with the right to inject substances into the formation as specific provisions in unitization agreements.

SALT WATER DISPOSAL

Large quantities of formation salt water are frequently brought to the surface in the production of oil. The disposal of these unwanted volumes of salt water becomes a serious problem in logistics. Small and very carefully controlled volumes can be stored in surface pits but the conservation legislation imposes strict limits on the amount that can be so dealt with, and the harmful effects of salt water leaking from surface pits are creating pressure to eliminate the privilege entirely. The commonest means of disposing of salt water is to inject it back into a formation, not necessarily the one from which it is produced. Frequently salt water will be trucked considerable distances to a well which has been converted to salt water disposal. There is a charge per barrel for the privilege of injecting the salt water. Clearly, such a right is not conferred under the lease and here again a mineral operator desiring to use an existing well for salt water disposal or to drill a well for that purpose must deal with the owner of the mineral rights on the basis that such ownership includes the actual cavern or reservoir in which the minerals may be located.

6
The *habendum* and interpretation clauses

This clause, together with its provisos, is the heart of the lease. It sets forth
the conditions under which the lease continues in force and thus accounts for
much of the litigation that has swirled about the document. The *habendum*
and its provisos define the primary term of the lease, the manner in which it
may be extended, and what happens when drilling results in a dry hole or
production ceases, both before and after the expiration of the primary term.
Strangely enough, it also contains a provision which describes the position of
the lessee with regard to drilling operations on the land.

Drilling has little relation to the primary or extended term of the lease,
and why it was structured into the first proviso to the *habendum* in Canadian
forms remains a mystery. True, a failure to comply with its terms may result
in a termination of the lease, but this applies as well to other provisions
which are written as separate and distinct clauses. Because of its importance
and its lack of connection with the *habendum* the drilling proviso will be
treated separately. The standard form of the *habendum* clause, complete with
its provisos, reads:

TO HAVE AND ENJOY the same for the term of Ten (10) years from the date hereof
and so long thereafter as the leased substances or any of them are produced from
the said lands or the pooled lands subject to the sooner termination of the said
term and subject also to extension of the said term all as hereinafter provided.

PROVIDED that if operations for the drilling of a well are not commenced on the said lands or the pooled lands within one (1) year from the date hereof, this Lease shall terminate and be at an end on the first anniversary date, unless the Lessee shall have paid or tendered to the Lessor on or before said anniversary date the sum of......................Dollars ($......................) (hereinafter called the 'delay rental'), which payment shall confer the privilege of deferring the commencement of drilling operations for a period of One (1) year from said anniversary date, and that, in like manner and upon like payments or tenders, the commencement of drilling operations and the termination of this Lease shall be further deferred for like periods successively;

PROVIDED FURTHER that if at any time during the said Ten (10) year term and prior to the discovery of production on the said lands or the pooled lands, the Lessee shall drill a dry well or wells thereon, or if at any time during such term and after discovery of production on the said lands or the pooled lands such production shall cease and the well or wells from which such production was taken shall be abandoned, then this Lease shall terminate at the next ensuing anniversary date hereof unless operations for the drilling of a further well on the said lands or the pooled lands shall have been commenced or unless the Lessee shall have paid or tendered the delay rental, in which latter event the immediately preceding proviso hereof governing the payment of the delay rental and the effect thereof, shall be applicable thereto;

AND FURTHER ALWAYS PROVIDED that if at the end of the said Ten (10) year term the leased substances are not being produced from the said lands or the pooled lands (whether or not the leased substances have theretofore been produced therefrom) and the Lessee is then engaged in drilling or working operations thereon, or if at any time after the expiration of the said Ten (10) year term production of the leased substances has ceased and the Lessee shall have commenced further drilling or working operations within Ninety (90) days after the cessation of said production, then this Lease shall remain in force so long as any drilling or working operations are prosecuted with no cessation of more than Ninety (90) consecutive days, and, if they result in the production of the leased substances or any of them, so long thereafter as the leased substances or any of them are produced from the said lands or the pooled lands; provided that if drilling or working operations are interrupted or suspended as the result of any cause whatsoever beyond the Lessee's reasonable control, or if any well on the said lands or the pooled lands or on any spacing unit of which the said lands or any portion thereof form a part, is shut-in, suspended or otherwise not produced as the result of a lack of or an intermittent market, or any cause whatsoever beyond the Lessee's reasonable control, the time of such interruption or suspension or non-production shall not be counted against the Lessee, anything hereinbefore contained or implied to the contrary notwithstanding.

The clause confers upon the lessee the right to hold the grant for a specified number of years. This is known as the primary term. The great majority of printed forms specify a term of ten years, although there is a growing tendency on the part of the lessor to demand a shorter primary term and it is now not uncommon to find a period of five years or less inserted in the clause. Under this provision, and if there is no default with respect to the other requirements of the lease, the lessee may continue to hold the lease for the specified number of years without either drilling or production. While the lessee must make annual payments during the primary term, it is obvious that the shorter the primary term the sooner the lessee will be required to drill, or lose the lease.

EXTENSION OF THE PRIMARY TERM

A fixed primary term by itself would not serve the particular needs of an oil and gas lease. If the term were for a fixed period of years and nothing more, the lease could terminate during the height of production, a state of affairs which would not be welcomed by the lessee. Hence the inclusion of words which continue the lease in force beyond the primary term if the leased substances are being produced. Like so many other features of the lease, this provision is a balance between the rights of the two parties. On the one hand it continues the lease in force if there is production, so that the lessee is not deprived of whatever reserves might have been discovered, while the requirement that there be production guarantees to the lessor that he will get his lands back unless the lessee has done something by the end of the primary term to explore their potential. This result is achieved by the phrase 'and so long thereafter as the leased substances or any of them are produced from the said lands or the pooled lands.' Since there is no way to predetermine the precise date on which production may cease, the length of such a term cannot be definitely established until after the event. Such uncertainty would be fatal to a conventional property lease, but not to a *profit à prendre* which may be for an uncertain term.[1]

WHAT IS PRODUCTION?

The primary term is extended if the substances 'are produced.' The intent seems clear enough, but there may be some borderline situations: will actual production, no matter how small and uneconomic, be sufficient, or is there

---

1 *Berkheiser* v *Berkheiser* [1957] S.C.R. 387

some requirement that it be of economic and commercial value? Must there be production at the very moment the primary term expires? What happens when production is interrupted or ceases altogether?

PRODUCTION IN PAYING QUANTITIES

The standard *habendum* clause requires that the substances 'are produced' in order to extend the primary term. There is no minimum quantitative limit. American courts in most of the important oil producing states interpret the word 'produced' as 'produced in paying quantities.'[2] This engrafting of a quantitative requirement works to the advantage of the lessor since it prevents the lease from being extended without any worthwhile benefit to him by way of royalties. So far this issue has not arisen in Canada in connection with the 'are produced' language. In view of the approach taken by the Supreme Court on other aspects of the lease, it must be considered highly unlikely that the words would be enlarged to include any economic or volume conditions. If an operator is prepared to physically produce a well, regardless of profit or loss, it is submitted that a Canadian court would hold that the 'are produced' test had been met.

The occasional lease form does refer to 'production in paying quantities.' The Ontario courts dealt with a variation of this wording in *Stevenson* v *Westgate*,[3] where the fixed term of the lease was for one year 'and for such longer period as oil or gas is found thereon in paying quantities.' The use of the verb 'found' rather than 'produced' deflects the precise applicability of the decision; nonetheless, the court had to concern itself with the implications of 'paying quantities.' Indeed, the trial judge appears to have treated 'found' as synonymous with 'produced.' The dispute arose from this fact pattern. The lease was dated October 13, 1938. The lessee drilled two wells and produced some oil from them, but more drilling apparently was required to fully develop the property (the wells were shallow and one must assume there were no minimum spacing restrictions at that time). The lessee entered into a development agreement with a third party, but at this time the problem posed by a prior mortgage became critical. The mortgagee would consent to the lease only if the lessor agreed to assign his royalty, which he avoided doing, and the developer refused to perform the work until the mortgagee

2 Summers, *Oil and Gas*, vol. 2, 298. Many American courts have also interpreted 'found,' 'discovered,' 'obtained,' and 'produced' as meaning the same thing, namely, 'produced in paying quantities.'
3 [1941] 2 D.L.R. 471 (Ont.); [1942] 1 D.L.R. 369 (C.A.)

had consented to the lease. As a result of this impasse, operations, including production, were suspended. At the end of the year, the lessee was ordered from the land.

The trial judge ignored any distinction between 'found' and 'produced' and referred to 'produced in paying quantities.' During the year the lessees had produced $539.00 worth of oil and they had expended over $4,000.00. Most of their expenditures, however, were of a capital nature; the operating costs were only $228.00. It was held that the true test was the relation between the oil produced and the cost of running and operating expenses. Capital expenditures, such as the cost of drilling the wells, were not to be included in the calculation.

The Court of Appeal seemed to place more emphasis on the meaning of the word 'found.' Experts had testified at the trial that the wells could be produced profitably. 'The situation that developed was this: oil had been found upon the property in marketable quantities.'[4] It is clear, however, that the court agreed with the trial judge in excluding capital costs. 'Oil had been found and it was possible to pump it in quantities that were more than sufficient for the then current charges.'[5]

So far as it goes, then, *Stevenson* v *Westgate* stands for the proposition that a Canadian court, faced with the test of 'produced in paying quantities,' would opt for revenues versus operating costs, rather than some other guideline such as whether a 'reasonably prudent operator' would continue to operate the well.

CONTINUOUS PRODUCTION DIFFICULT TO ACHIEVE

A literal interpretation of the phrase 'and so long thereafter as the leased substances are produced' would appear to require continuous and uninterrupted production. There are many circumstances under which production may be suspended or interrupted: a well may be shut down for reworking or maintenance; the permitted allowable may have been produced within a portion of the month and the well shut-in for the balance of the period; an over-production penalty may be imposed with the result that a particular well is shut down completely for a prolonged period; a road ban may make it impossible to transport production from a wellsite not connected to a pipeline. These are but a few of the circumstances, unrelated to the productive capacity of the well, which may lead to a temporary halt in production. There are many others. If a well is productive of gas, the peculiar conditions

4 Ibid, 371   5 Ibid, 372

of the market could lead to an entire field being shut-in for several months out of each year. A particular gas field may be connected to a local utility company which will produce it only during periods of great demand such as December, January, February, and March.

All of these reasons are in addition to the more ominous one where production ceases because of the physical characteristics of the well and the reservoir. If production dwindles owing to the deterioration or depletion of the reservoir, the lessee will be able to contemplate the ultimate loss of its lease with more equanimity than where the lease is terminated 'accidentally' in the full flood of its producing capacity.

Production may cease or be suspended either during the primary term or after its expiration.

CESSATION OF PRODUCTION DURING PRIMARY TERM

The second proviso to the *habendum* clause covers the situation that occurs when there is a well but no production during the primary term. In the absence of such a provision it could be argued that the result under the usual form of lease would be that the lease continues in force during the balance of the primary term without the requirement of either any further drilling or the payment of delay rentals. The *habendum* grants the lease for the specified primary term, subject to earlier termination if the lessee does not commence drilling or pay the annual fee for deferring same. In the case of a dry hole or of a well becoming unproductive, the lessee will have met the drilling commitment and thus there should be no basis for terminating the lease prior to the expiration of the primary term. Nor would the lessee be liable for any further payments of the delay rental since the undertaking to commence drilling has been met. When the primary term has elapsed the lease would terminate for want of production.

The second proviso makes this type of argument unnecessary and provides that the lessee may continue the lease in force by drilling or paying the delay rental on or before the next anniversary date. In effect, the proviso treats the drilling of a dry hole or the abandonment of a well during the primary term as if no drilling operations had in fact taken place. This is consistent with the basic concept of a lease which requires that there be drilling operations, or payment of a deferral fee, or production during each year of the primary term. The same approach is taken in the 'or' type of drilling clause which, under the same circumstances, while it does not provide for automatic termination on failure to do so, obliges the lessee to commence drilling or pay the deferral fee.

CESSATION OF PRODUCTION AFTER THE PRIMARY TERM

If production comes to an end after the primary term, the lease will terminate. In *Krysa* v *Opalinski*[6] production continued for some years beyond the primary term, but eventually was halted because the wells could no longer produce on an economic basis. The wording of the 'thereafter' portion of the *habendum* was held to result in an automatic termination. The third proviso comes into operation at this stage. *Canada Cities-Service Petroleum Corp.* v *Kininmonth*[7] demonstrates what happens when the proviso is treated as being inapplicable. In *Kininmonth* the clause was an earlier and unsuccessful version of the third proviso.

AND FURTHER ALWAYS PROVIDED that if at any time after the expiration of the said ... 10 ... year term the said substances are not being produced on the said lands and the Lessee is then engaged in drilling or working operations thereon, this Lease shall remain in force so long as such operations are prosecuted, and if they result in the production of the said substances or any of them, so long thereafter as the said substances or any of them are produced from the said lands, provided that if drilling, working or production operations are interrupted or suspended as the result of any cause whatsoever beyond the Lessee's control, other than the Lessee's lack of funds, the time of such interruption or suspension shall not be counted against the Lessee, anything hereinbefore contained or implied to the contrary notwithstanding.

The lessee delayed drilling until very close to the end of the primary term. When the ten-year period had expired the well had encountered production and was ready for a treatment which would open up the formation. This occurred during the months of March and April – the lease was dated May 11 – and the usual road bans were in force, with the result that the equipment required to treat the well could not be trucked to the lease until after the primary term had expired. The work was eventually completed and the well produced briefly in June and July before it was shut down by a Conservation Board order because the lessee did not have the proper spacing unit. This latter point is irrelevant for our purposes; we need only concern ourselves with the situation as it existed on May 10, when the well was awaiting a fracturing treatment and was not producing. It should be noted that the clause in *Kininmonth* referred to 'after the expiration of the said ten year term.' Because of this, Martland J declared that it could not apply where there was no production when the primary term expired. It could not mean

6 (1960) 32 w.w.r. 346 (Alta.)   7 [1964] s.c.r. 439, 47 w.w.r. 437

that 'even though no production has been obtained within the ten year primary term, the lessee may thereafter carry on drilling operations on the land which, if successful, will then serve to extend the lease for a further period during the continuance of such production.'[8] The proviso quoted above, referred to by the court as 'the fifth paragraph' did not apply, and 'without the fifth paragraph the lease would automatically terminate upon the cessation of production.'[9]

In its most recent interpretation of the 'thereafter' clause with its provisos, the Supreme Court displayed an uncharacteristic regard for the intention of the lessee. While the facts in *Canadian Superior Oil Ltd.* v *Cull*[10] were generally similar to the *Kininmonth* structure, the result was totally different. In the *Cull* case the *habendum* clause was for a term of ten years 'and as long thereafter as oil, gas or other mineral is produced from the said land hereunder, or as long thereafter as Lessee shall conduct drilling, mining or re-working operations thereon as hereinafter provided and during the production of oil, gas or other mineral resulting therefrom.'

The lease also contains a clause that extended the primary term if the lessee were engaged in drilling operations at the time of its expiration.

12. If Lessee shall commence to drill a well within the term of this lease or any extension thereof, Lessee shall have the right to drill such well to completion with reasonable diligence and dispatch, and if oil or gas be found in paying quantities, this lease shall continue and be in force with like effect as if such well had been completed within the term of years herein first mentioned.

Clause 7 of the lease was a combination of the standard form of the second and third provisos to the *habendum* clause.

7. If prior to the discovery of oil or gas on said lands Lessee should drill a dry hole or holes thereon, or if after the discovery of oil or gas the production thereof should cease from any cause, this lease shall continue in force during the primary term, if on or before the rental paying date next ensuing after the expiration of ninety (90) days from date of completion of dry hole or cessation of production Lessee commences drilling or re-working operation or commences or resumes the payment or tender of rentals, or after the primary term if Lessee commences

---

8 Ibid, s.c.r. 445
9 Ibid
10 [1971] 3 w.w.r. 28 (s.c.c.); (1970) 75 w.w.r. 606 (c.a.); (1970) 74 w.w.r. 324 (Alta.). I commented on the implications of this decision in Ballem, 'The Continuing Adventures of the Oil and Gas Lease' (1972), 50 *Can. Bar. Rev.* 423

additional drilling or re-working operations within sixty (60) days from date of completion of dry hole or cessation of production, and if production results therefrom then so long as such production continues.

The dispute arose on this fact pattern:

1   The primary ten-year term would have expired on December 30, 1957.
2   The well had been spudded on November 28, 1957, and drilled ahead until December 23, 1957.
3   On December 24 and 25 the well was cored and a drill stem test was run with results that led the lessee to believe the well should be completed as an oil well.
4   Drilling was resumed and continued to total depth which was reached on December 28 and a radioactive log was run on the same date.
5   Production casing was set on December 29 and a Christmas Tree (the wellhead equipment that controls production) was set on the well.
6   The drilling rig was released on December 30, 1957, and it took two days for the rig to be dismantled and moved off the site.
7   A service rig (much smaller and less expensive to operate than a drilling rig and commonly used for completion operations) was moved onto the site and rigged up on January 2, 1958.
8   On January 3 it commenced completion operations, including the recovery of dropped casing, the running of a radioactive log, and perforations into the prospective formations. Production tubing was run and on January 6 the well was acidized – a process designed to open up the formation and increase the flow.
9   On January 7 the well was swabbed, an operation where outside oil is introduced into the well to stimulate the flow of substances, and both load and formation oil began to flow and were discharged into a disposal pit. The service rig was released on the same date.
10 By January 7, 1958, the well was capable of producing oil for the first time – on this date the well had started to flow and the Christmas Tree was shut to stem the flow and the service rig released and removed from the site.
11 There was no equipment then ready on the site to pick up the production although some of the material was on the site but not hooked up. On January 8, 9, and 10 a 500-barrel tank, a separator, and miscellaneous equipment were erected and installed. After this work was completed the well was reopened on January 11, 1958, and began to flow into production. Subject to the production allowable established by the Oil and Gas Conservation Board, production in paying quantities has continued ever since.

12   The oil began to flow into the tank on January 11, and, as was pointed
out by the court, such oil was probably a mixture of outside load oil
which had been introduced during the swabbing operations and only
partially recovered during tests and some was formation oil. For accounting purposes the lessee treated all of the oil produced on January
11 and 12 as paying back the load oil from other sources and treated
production as having commenced on January 13.

The lessor argued against the continued validity of the lease primarily on
two grounds: that the lease expired at midnight December 29–30, 1957,
because the lessee was not then engaged in *drilling* the well to completion
since total depth had been obtained and clause 12 referred to the right 'to
drill such well to completion.' The trial judge, Sinclair J held that the non-
drilling operations such as perforating, acidizing, and swabbing constituted
drilling the well 'to completion' and the lease was thus extended during the
continuance of these operations. Both the Appellate Division and the Supreme Court agreed with this conclusion.

The second ground of attack was that, if the well had been drilled to
completion on January 7, 1958, at which time it was capable of producing,
it terminated automatically according to its terms on that date since it was
not produced until January 13. Although the trial judge was prepared to
include those operations necessary to place the well in a position where it
was capable of production as being included in the phrase 'drill ... to completion,' he was not prepared to extend such phrase to include the installation
of tanks and other surface facilities needed to treat and save the oil. Therefore, he agreed with the lessor's contention that the lease was extended only
until January 7, 1958, and that there being no production for a period of
several days thereafter, the lease terminated on January 7 by its own terms.[11]

Both the Appellate Division and the Supreme Court of Canada concluded
that, under the circumstances above described, the lease had never terminated. The senior courts were obviously impressed by the fact that the well
produced and marketed its full quota of oil for the month of January and the
lessee had received the royalty. The trial judge had rejected the production
allowable argument on the basis that it could not work until the well had
produced to the point where the restriction would come into play. In other
words, if the well had produced its monthly quota and had been shut in at the
time its primary term expired, Sinclair J would have relied on the previous

11 The trial judge upheld the lease on the ground of estoppel created by a subsequent
document. This point will be discussed *infra* under the heading Estoppel. Neither
the Appellate Division nor the Supreme Court found it necessary to deal with
estoppel.

production to continue the lease in force. But the Appellate Division went even further by holding that allowable production that took place *after* the end of the term but during the same month in which it expired was sufficient.

The Appellate Division also paid attention to the mechanics of completing a well; Johnson JA was troubled that there might always be a time gap which would make it impossible to effectively extend the life of the lease by the use of a clause such as the one contained in the *Cull* lease. 'Given a ready market for oil does the combined effect of these clauses require that production be taken the very moment that the well has been completed? I have said "the very moment" for it must be realized that in every case there will be a period, however short, while the well is connected to the gathering systems and the valves are being turned on, when no production is obtained.' He then answered his own question: 'It is not reasonable, I suggest, to apply so stringent an interpretation. Wells are not permitted to produce constantly. The Conservation Board sets a quota for each well ... Considering the effect to be given to paragraph 2 of the lease the question is not whether the well was flowing at the exact moment that the term of the lease expired (in this case when the well was completed) but whether oil can be taken and marketed so that the lessor and lessee will be entitled to the full benefit of the well's production.'[12]

The lessor had relied very heavily on a trio of Supreme Court of Canada decisions, in each of which the term of the lease was held not to have been extended. All three cases, *Canadian Superior Oil Ltd.* v *Murdoch*;[13] *Canadian Superior Oil of California, Ltd.* v *Kanstrup*;[14] and *Canadian Superior Oil Ltd.* v *Hambly*[15] involved gas for which there was no currently available market and the failure to make timely payment of the suspended well royalty. The Supreme Court of Canada agreed with the ground on which the Appellate Division distinguished these authorities, namely, that in all three cases there had been no present intention on the part of the lessee to place the wells on production and that since the suspended well royalty had not been made on time, the lease could not be continued beyond the primary term by reason of constructive production.

In the *Cull* situation all the courts found that the lessee had a *bona fide* intention to proceed diligently to place the well on production and that this intention was carried out with reasonable diligence and dispatch. The Supreme

12 (1970) 75 w.w.r. 610, 611
13 (1969) 70 w.w.r. 768 (s.c.c.) affirmed without written reasons the decision of the Appellate Div. (1969) 68 w.w.r. 390
14 1965 s.c.r. 92
15 (1970) 74 w.w.r. 356

Court also relied upon the provision in Clause 12 that 'if oil or gas be found in paying quantities, this lease shall continue and be in force with like effect as if such well had been completed within the term of years herein first mentioned.' Oil had been found and the court held that the language enabled the lessee to put the well into production and thereby continue the lease.

The *Cull rationale* should really be compared with that of the *Kininmonth* case rather than with those three decisions involving suspended gas wells and untimely payment of the suspended well royalty. The *Kininmonth* case dealt with an oil well which the lessee was unable to complete prior to the expiration of the primary term. In that case, however, it will be recalled that the language of the 'fifth paragraph' (the approximate counterpart of the third proviso in the standard form of lease and of clause 7 in the *Cull* lease) did not apply according to its language until after the expiration of the primary term. Accordingly, it could not be relied upon by the lessee. The *Cull* decision illustrates what might have been the result in *Kininmonth* if the 'fifth paragraph' had been worded so as to apply during as well as after the primary term. This gap which was fatal in *Kininmonth* and caused much judicial soul-searching in *Cull* is expressly covered in the opening words of the third proviso now currently in use. It must be borne in mind, however, that many of the old forms are still to be found in existing leases.

The standard version of the proviso attempts to deal with two situations: (a) that occurring at the end of the primary term with no production but where the lessee is then engaged in drilling or working operations on the lands. The proviso continues the lease in force so long as such drilling or working operations are prosecuted with no cessation of more than ninety consecutive days and, if such operations result in the production of leased substances, so long thereafter as such substances are produced. (b) Where the lease has been continued beyond its primary term and then production ceases. The lease continues in force if the lessee shall commence further drilling or working operations within ninety days after the cessation of such production and remains in force provided that such drilling or working operations are prosecuted with no cessation of more than ninety consecutive days and for the duration of any production resulting therefrom.

Both situations are also covered by a *force majeure* provision which provides that, if the drilling or working operations are interrupted or suspended as the result of any cause beyond the lessee's reasonable control, the time of such interruption or suspension or non-production shall not be counted against the lessee. There is a further application of *force majeure* in that, if the production is shut-in or suspended or not produced as a result of a lack of or an intermittent market or any cause whatsoever beyond the lessee's reasonable control, then such time shall not be counted against the lessee.

The wording of this portion is somewhat unfortunate where it refers to 'shall not be counted against the lessee.' Presumably it is meant that, where *force majeure* applies, the time intervals of ninety days shall not run, but one has to speculate that this is the desired result; it does not emerge clearly from the language.

Some versions of this proviso refrain from expressing the period during which production may cease, and rely simply on a reference to 'a reasonable time.' Certainly where the clause spells out a ninety-day period it is unlikely that the court would permit any longer periods, but it remains an open question as to what the court might interpret as constituting 'a reasonable period.' Much would depend upon the circumstances of the individual case. A well with a serious technical problem located in an isolated area might be granted a longer period of interruption than would a readily accessible well with only a minor breakdown. Factors such as weather conditions or spring break-up might also be taken into consideration.

In any event, where the lessee has spelled out in detail the manner in which an interruption in production is to be treated, one may say with assurance that the terms of such a clause represent the utmost relief that will be granted by Canadian courts.

The lessees continue to improve upon the lease form. There are other versions of the proviso which confer a broader protection upon the lessee in the event of a temporary stoppage of production. One of them incorporates the idea that, so long as the well is capable of production and compensatory royalties, equal to the delay rental, are paid in each year, the lease continues in force.

The effect of a temporary cessation of production under a lease with no equivalent of the third proviso remains a matter of conjecture insofar as Canada is concerned. American courts take the approach that a temporary cessation of production will not terminate the lease. 'The law is well settled that a temporary cessation of developments or operations under an oil and gas lease does not, as a matter of law constitute an abandonment.'[16] In *Frost* v *Gulf Oil Corp.*[17] the court held that 'the lease in question does not say that it shall be in force so long as minerals are *continuously* produced.'

This approach has enabled lessees to maintain a lease where the production has ceased for a period of months or sometimes even years. The courts apply the test of whether the cessation of production was for an 'unreason-

---

16 *Wisconsin-Texas Oil Co.* v *Clutter* 268 sw 921
17 238 Miss 775, 119 So 2d 759 (1960). For a detailed review of the American authorities on this point, see Brown, *The Law of Oil and Gas Leases* (2nd ed) 1967 Sec. 5.09.

able' period of time. The decisive factor in whether or not the elapsed time was unreasonable seems to be the efforts, or lack of them, made by the lessee to restore production. If the lessee has acted in good faith and carried out operations designed to reactivate the wells or drill new ones, the American authorities seem disposed to continue the lease in force.

It is doubtful if this approach would commend itself to Canadian courts with their strict approach to the language of the lease. In the absence of the third proviso, a Canadian court is more likely to treat the wording of the *habendum* clause as requiring virtually continuous production, with cessations of very limited duration for routine maintenance repair and re-working being the only permitted exceptions. The following passage from the Ontario Court of Appeal in *Stevenson* v *Westgate* may forecast the attitude of Canadian courts:[18]

The question whether respondents' rights under the agreement of October 13, 1938 continued beyond the expiration of one year depends upon the proper effect to be given to the words 'for as much longer period as oil or gas is found thereon in paying quantities.' While appellants are entitled to have a construction placed upon these words that will assure them of the continued operation of any well upon their land, so that they may be assured of a reasonable return so long as respondents continue to occupy, at the same time this is a business arrangement, and regard must be had to the reasonable requirements of the business. It is not the fair meaning of the agreement that without interruption respondents must produce a constant flow of oil in paying quantities, or lose their right to continue operating. Operation may be interrupted from causes not chargeable to respondents. There may be times in the course of the operations when it cannot be said that they are paying. In my opinion a more liberal interpretation must be placed upon the terms of the agreement than to say, 'if there is any such occasion, the lease terminates.'

It must be borne in mind however that the thereafter clause referred to oil or gas being 'found' rather than being 'produced.' Indeed the trial judge used this to distinguish the *Stevenson* case in *Can. Superior Oil Ltd.* v *Cull*.[19]

DRILLING

Having dealt with the primary term and its extension, we may now return to the first proviso and the lessee's position *re* drilling on the lands. The standard proviso quoted at the beginning of this chapter provides that, if the lessee has not commenced operations for the drilling of a well within the specified annual period or paid the specified delay rental, the lease will terminate. This type of provision is the one commonly found in Canada and is known as the 'unless' drilling clause. The termination of the lease on failure to commence drilling operations on time or make payment is clearly set forth: 'THIS LEASE shall terminate and be at an end on the first anniversary date, *unless* the lessee shall have paid or tendered to the lessor on or before the said anniversary date the sum of ... dollars ... which payment shall confer the privilege of deferring the commencement of drilling operations for a period one year from said anniversary date.' It has been held time after time that under the clear language of the lease itself the termination is automatic unless one of the alternatives of drilling or payment has been fully complied with. There have been many judicial pronouncements on such niceties as what constitutes the commencement of drilling operations, what amounts to proper payment and what are the precise time limits within which such operations or payments must be commenced or made. These matters are fully reviewed Part 6 dealing with INVOLUNTARY TERMINATION, chapters 13 and 14, *infra*. The historical reasons which led to the widespread use of the 'unless' type of clause in Canada are described in chapter 1, *ante*.

There is another generally accepted form of drilling commitment which does not contain the built-in hazard of the 'unless' type. Under this alternative the lessee is obligated to commence drilling operations *or* pay an annual sum of money; hence its name, the 'or' clause. For a variety of reasons the 'or' clause, although seemingly advantageous to the lessee, has not yet become prevalent in Canada. A typical 'or' clause is as follows:

PROVIDED, however:
(i) that if drilling operations are not commenced on the said lands within one year from the date hereof, the lessee shall not later than thirty (30) days after the expiration of the said one (1) year period, pay or tender to the lessor rental at the rate of $........................ per acre of the said lands, (hereinafter called 'the annual acreage rental') as the annual acreage rental for the next ensuing year of the primary term and that similarly during successive years of the primary term, if drilling operations are not commenced, the lessee shall make like payments for tenders.

The 'or' clause does not contain any words of automatic termination. The lessee is merely obliged to either commence drilling operations *or* pay a specified rental. Because there is no automatic termination, the obligation of the lessee to make the rental payment continues so long as the primary term exists, but this obligation can be terminated by the lessee through a positive act of surrender under a subsequent clause in the lease.

There are no obligations on the lessee under the 'unless' clause to either commence drilling operations or make the payment. The lessee's position has been defined repeatedly by the courts as that of a person who has an option and not an obligation, but the result of this freedom of action can often be fatal to the lease. The annual payment made to defer the commencement of drilling operations is normally referred to as a 'delay rental,' the reference to 'delay' recognizing that by such payment the commencement of drilling operations may be postponed or delayed. The courts have also pointed out on many occasions that the payment is not a rent. 'This sum was not paid as rent but was paid for the privilege of postponing the obligation to drill, ... obviously, the sum of money paid each year by the oil company to the appellants was not rent but was the purchase price of an extension of the time fixed for drilling. The payments had none of the characteristics of rent.'[20]

The amount of the delay rental, left blank in the printed form to be filled in on execution of the document, is almost invariably computed at the rate of one dollar per acre, so that if the lease covers one quarter section, 160 acres, the amount of the delay rental will be $160.00 and $640.00 for a full section. One dollar per acre was the standard rental under Alberta Crown leases and was enshrined in the former Income Tax Act, although the original provisions disappeared in 1962. Until then the deduction for a right, licence, or privilege to explore for, drill for, or take petroleum or natural gas was limited to an annual payment not exceeding one dollar per acre. Because of this, the figure of one dollar per acre became universally accepted as the annual delay rental. That monetary limitation was partially removed by a new Sec. 83A (5) in 1962 and was confined to rights acquired prior to April 11, 1962. Annual payments, without limitation as to amount, for the preservation of a lease were then specifically included in deductible 'drilling and exploration expenses' by Sec. 83A (5a) and this has been continued by Sec. 66(1), (15)(b) and (d) of the Income Tax Act, 1972.

It should be borne in mind that the ability to deduct annual delay rentals under the former Income Tax Act was limited to payments made with respect to a lease that qualified under Sec. 83A (5a) and that if a lease went beyond the limits specified by such Section, i.e. by granting 'all mines and minerals,' the annual payment could not be deducted. Under the operation of the Income Tax Act, 1972 annual payments made to maintain a lease that was disqualified under the old Act are now deductible.[21]

Although the reason for limiting the annual delay rental to one dollar per

20 *Duncan* v *Joslin* (1965) 51 w.w.r. 346, 348, Porter JA
21 Under the Income Tax Application Rules ss 29, 34, expenses incurred up to the end of 1971 will continue to be deductible for the 1972 and subsequent taxation years on the same basis as under the Income Tax Act 1952.

acre per year has disappeared, the figure remains popular and accepted and, in truth, the lessee has little reason to disturb the pattern.

Until modified in 1962 by Sec. 83A (5c) of the former Income Tax Act, the general rule was that delay rental payments in the hands of the lessor were not considered as income to him but rather were treated as capital receipts. The annual payments were nothing more than additional consideration for parting with the control of and right to use an asset that had income bearing possibilities; *Sparrow* v *Minister of National Revenue*.[22] This has been reversed by Sec. 83 (5c), however, so that delay rentals were considered income unless the lessor owned his mineral rights prior to April 10, 1962, or acquired them subsequently by inheritance or bequest. Thus, if a lessor purchased mineral rights after that date and then leased them, all delay rental payments made to him would be taxable income. The provisions that exempted annual payments from inclusion in taxable income where the property was owned prior to April 10, 1962, or acquired by inheritance or bequest, have disappeared under the Income Tax Act, 1972. Sec. 59(1) makes such payments taxable income in the hands of the lessor, although the present wording of the section is troublesome. It refers to the amount 'receivable' for the disposition of a resource property. It is at least questionable if a delay rental under an 'unless' type of lease could be regarded as 'receivable,' since the payment is purely optional on the part of the Lessee. There is little doubt that such payments are meant to be taxable and one may expect an amendment to the language of Sec. 59(1) if a delay rental is held not to be an amount 'receivable.'

INTERPRETATION

Under the usual sequence of clauses in the lease form, the *habendum* is followed by a clause which defines the precise meaning of certain words and phrases that occur throughout the lease. The standard form of interpretation clause defines 'commercial production,' 'spacing unit,' 'pooled lands,' and 'said lands.' With the exception of the last named, these phrases relate to subsequently occurring clauses in the lease and will be dealt with in conjunction with them. The phrase 'said lands' is defined as the lands described in the opening part of the lease, 'or such portion or portions thereof as shall not have been surrendered.'

22 (1957) 11 D.T.C. 453 (Income Tax Appeal Board)

7
Royalties, suspended well payments, and taxes

THE ROYALTY CONCEPT

The royalty is the means by which the mineral owner shares in production of the substances from his land. Both the concept and the word 'royalty' originated in England, where it designated the share in production reserved by the Crown in grants of mines and quarries.[1]

The royalty clause accomplishes its purpose by providing that a certain portion, normally expressed as a percentage, of the production shall be deliverable or payable to the lessor. The percentage is usually specified as 12½ per cent which is a one-eighth share. This figure is so common that in most lease forms the percentage is actually printed in the document itself. Apart from its prevalence over many years and the natural reluctance of the lessee to increase it, there is no magic in the one-eighth share, and one now encounters leases which contain different and usually higher percentages. A royalty of 15 per cent is often asked for and obtained by lessors with respect to natural gas. The amount of the royalty share is a matter of negotiation between two parties to the lease, but there is no doubt that the tradition of one-eighth as the usual royalty share weighs heavily against any increase.

TYPES OF CLAUSES

There is probably more variation in the royalty provision among the individual lease forms than in any other clause of the Canadian oil and gas lease.

1 Brown, *Royalty Clauses In Oil And Gas Leases*, Sixteenth Annual Institute on Oil and Gas Law and Taxation, 139

In general there are three types of clauses: (a) those under which the lessor *reserves* a share of the production; (b) those which embody the concept of *delivery* to the lessor of a share of the production; and (c) those under which the lessee agrees to *pay* to the lessor a percentage of the value of the substances. The type of clause under which the lessor reserves a share as under (a) is the most common type, and is the one expressed in the standard clause.

ROYALTIES

The Lessor does hereby reserve unto himself a gross royalty of Twelve and one-half per cent (12½%) of the leased substances produced and marketed from the said lands. Any sale by the Lessee of any crude oil, crude naphtha, or gas produced from the said lands shall include the royalty share thereof reserved to the Lessor, and the Lessee shall account to the Lessor for his said royalty share in accordance wtih the following provisions namely:

The Lessee shall remit to the Lessor, on or before the 20th day of each month, (a) an amount equal to the current market value on the said lands of Twelve and one-half per cent (12½%) of the crude oil and crude naphtha produced, saved and marketed from the said lands during the preceding month, and (b) an amount equal to the current market value on the said lands of Twelve and one-half per cent (12½%) of all gas produced and marketed from the said lands during said preceding month.

Notwithstanding anything to the contrary herein contained or implied, the Lessee shall be entitled to use such part of the production of the leased substances from the said lands as may be required and used by the Lessee in its operations hereunder, and the Lessor shall not be entitled to any royalty with respect to said leased substances.

Those clauses under (b) which contemplate delivery are usually worded to make either delivery or payment optional to the lessee.

As royalty, the Lessee covenants and agrees:
(a) To deliver to the credit of the Lessor, in the pipe line to which the Lessee may connect its wells, the equal one-eighth part of all oil produced and saved by the Lessee from the said lands, or from time to time, at the option of the Lessee, to pay the Lessor the current market value of such one-eighth part of such oil at the wells as of the day it is run to the pipe line or storage tanks, the Lessor's interest, in either case, to bear one-eighth of the cost of treating oil to render it marketable pipe line oil.

A modern form of the covenant to pay type under (c) would be as follows:

ROYALTY

The Lessee shall pay to the Lessor a royalty in an amount equal to the current market value at the well as and when produced of Twelve and one-half per cent (12½%) of all leased substances produced, saved and sold from the said lands. Notwithstanding anything to the contrary in this lease contained or implied, the Lessor shall not be entitled to any royalty with respect to any of the leased substances produced from the said lands, or pooled lands or unitized lands, as may be required and used with respect to operations hereunder, or unavoidably lost.

This type of clause where the obligation is only to pay would appear not to create an interest in land, but only a contractual right.[2] The lessor's position under other aspects of the lease, however, does create an interest in land. It is astonishing that there has been so little litigation in Canada over the royalty clause when one considers its importance. Once the lands have been placed on production, the whole lease is virtually reduced to this one provision.

RIGHT OF LESSOR TO TAKE ROYALTY SHARE IN KIND

The standard clause reserves the royalty share to the mineral owner. Does he have the right to demand that his share of the leased substances be actually delivered to him or must he be content with the proceeds from the sale of such royalty share? Under most circumstances, this point will have little practical application, for the average lessor will not have the inclination, or the means, to dispose of his share of production and is only too happy to have that particular chore assumed by the lessee. This is borne out by the declaration, nearly always found in the royalty clause, that any sale by the lessee shall include the royalty share thereof reserved to the lessor. Consequently there can be no doubt that the lessee is under a duty to share any available market with the lessor,[3] although in the standard form this obliga-

---

2 *St. Lawrence Petroleum Limited et al* v *Bailey Selburn Oil & Gas Ltd.* (No. 2) [1963] S.C.R. 482, 41 D.L.R. (2d) 316, 45 W.W.R. 26 (S.C.C.); *Saskatchewan Minerals* v *Keyes* [1972] 23 D.L.R. (3d) 573, [1972] 2 W.W.R. 108 (S.C.C.). Both cases dealt with agreements rather than leases, but make it clear that if the right is only to receive money payments, it will not be considered as creating an interest in land.

3 In the absence of such a provision, is the lessee under any duty to market the lessor's royalty share? In the United States the lessee may be under an implied duty to do so, *Wolfe* v *Prairie Oil & Gas Co.*, 83 F 2d 434. In view of the strict construction placed on the terms of the lease by Canadian courts and their

tion is limited to 'crude oil, crude naphtha or gas.' Presumably the lessee is not obligated to market any leased substances which do not fall within such classes.[4] However, if the lessor insists on delivery of the substances themselves, can he succeed? It is entirely conceivable that if a lessor were itself an oil company with a ready market, and if the volumes were sufficiently large, it might seek to enforce such a right.

The lease is silent on the mechanics of any such delivery. It does not, for example, provide that if the lessor is to take his share in kind the lessee must provide surface storage and other facilities. This type of provision would normally be included if the lease contemplated such delivery; understandings of this nature are frequently encountered in operating agreements and over-riding royalty agreements where both parties are oil companies. While their absence may indicate that the parties did not expect the lessor to take his share in kind, express reservation by the lessor of his share surely preserves whatever title he might have had to that portion of the substances. Such rights would necessarily include the right to take them into his own possession and dispose of them. The requirement that imposes upon the lessee a duty to share any market does not seem to derogate from this right of the lessor; there is no provision that requires the lessor to use the lessee as his exclusive marketing agent. Under the standard type of clause therefore a lessor, if he were so inclined, might insist successfully upon delivery to him of his royalty share, although he would be faced with the necessity of either installing his own storage and transportation facilities or entering into some agreement with the lessee to share the existing ones. It is doubtful if a similar right would accrue to the lessor under types (b) and (c) above. Certainly, under (b) the option on the part of the lessee to pay the lessor for his share rather than deliver it to the pipeline vests the lessee with the power to dispose of the lessor's share. Even if that option were not included in the (b) form (and sometimes it does not appear) it could be argued that the lessor has appointed the lessee as his agent to deliver the oil produced and that such a power must by implication be exclusive to the lessee.

On the other hand, the (c) type of clause which requires the lessee to pay the lessor his share as royalty would appear to exclude any right of the lessor to insist upon actual delivery of the substances, his entitlement being to a share of the proceeds of sale and nothing more.

reluctance to imply any terms into such a detailed document, the lessor would be well advised to ensure that his lease expressly imposes such an obligation.

4 This could give rise to some interesting questions: is the lessee obliged to market sulphur, frequently a glut on the market? See the discussion as to the substances covered by the grant, chapter 5, *ante*.

SUBSTANCES SUBJECT TO THE ROYALTY

The standard royalty clause makes it clear that the royalty applies to all the substances granted by the lease. There is an all-inclusive reference to 'the leased substances' which, by definition, includes all the minerals covered by the grant. If, as sometimes happens, different substances attract a different royalty rate or there are variations in the permitted deductions, the clause may be subdivided to provide separately for each substance. This can lead to some question as to whether an individual substance not specifically mentioned is included. Usually, however, the question is put to rest by an omnibus provision which embraces 'all other minerals' or 'all other leased substances.'

Certain of the substances are excluded from the imposition of a royalty. These, however, do not relate to the nature or quality of the substances but rather to their use. The lessee is not required to pay royalty on substances that are used for the purposes of producing operations on the lease. The theory is that the lessor, having the benefit of production, should share in the cost and expense thereof. One way is to exclude substances used for such purposes from the computation of royalty. Additionally, a certain amount of loss on the surface after production is inevitable and unavoidable because of evaporation, spillage, and other circumstances often referred to as 'shrinkage.' Accidents, under which substantial quantities of production are lost prior to sale, occur from time to time and the lessee seeks to ensure that the mineral owner will bear his share of such loss.

These objectives frequently are accomplished by specific provisions, but the same purpose may be served by a description of the substances. The ultimate disposition of the materials becomes the criterion by which the applicability of the royalty is determined. The leased substances are qualified as being 'produced and saved,' 'produced, saved and sold,' 'produced and marketed,' and other words designed to carve out from the royalty those minerals which, although produced, are not sold by the lessee. Under the usual language, the production must actually be sold or marketed by the lessee before it becomes subject to the royalty. Good conservation practices, which are rigidly enforced by the regulatory bodies, also may require the return of gas to the reservoir when it is produced in association with oil. This recycling may be due to the necessity of maintaining reservoir pressure or the absence of an existing market for gas. An operation of this type, where a substance is produced and then returned to the reservoir, does not produce any direct monetary return to the lessee. There are also circumstances under which non-commercial or economic volumes of gas are produced in association with oil and these small quantities are permitted to be flared and burnt.

All these exclusions from the impact of royalty appear to be equitable. There are, however, circumstances under which substances, although not sold or marketed in the true sense, may be used in such a way as to confer a substantial benefit to the lessee. For example, gas produced from a lease may be used in a gas injection secondary reserve scheme in a reservoir where the lessor has no interest, although the lessee may have a substantial interest. The substances may be used by the lessee as a fuel for a processing plant which it may operate and which processes substances other than those produced from the lease. For internal accounting reasons, the lessee may not charge for the substances so used as fuel, and therefore such substances are not considered as having been sold or marketed.

The right of the lessee to use the substances free from royalty to the extent necessary to produce the substances from the leased lands is normally covered by an express proviso in the royalty clause. Under such a proviso the lessee is granted the use of the leased substances for its operations 'hereunder.' The reference to operations under the lease would encompass the exploration and drilling for and the removal, storage, and disposal of the substances. There seems to be, although it is nowhere spelled out, an intention that such royalty-free substances are to be used on the lease itself and that any attempt by the lessee to use them off the premises would not qualify as being in relation to 'operations hereunder.' Presumably the lessee could use the substances, without payment of royalty, as fuel in a drilling rig on the lands, or to thaw the ground for the laying of flowlines to carry production from the lands (probably only to the extent that such flowlines were located within the lands covered by the lease), or to fuel machinery and equipment for the same purposes and to operate treaters and dehydrators located on the lands and not used to treat or process substances from other lands. The qualifications that the substances must be 'produced and marketed' or 'produced and sold' before royalty attaches seems to go further and to exclude substances other than those used in 'operations hereunder.' To be consistent and to protect the lessor's royalty in circumstances where the lessee obtains a benefit other than proceeds from the sale of the substances, it is suggested that the phrase 'produced and marketed' be enlarged to read: 'produced and marketed from the said lands or used off the said lands.'

VALUE FOR COMPUTING ROYALTY

If the lessee, having marketed the royalty share, is to pay the lessor, there must be some yardstick for determining the value of such share. The lessor would not be sufficiently protected by simply taking his share of whatever the lessee received, since the lessee might be selling to itself or an associated company and hence might be satisfied with a depressed price. Thus, the standard reference to 'the current market value.' This qualification is designed to ensure that the lessor will receive the going price for his royalty share. In most instances, and particularly in the case of oil, this value is relatively easy to ascertain. It is common practice for purchasing companies to post a specified price per barrel for certain types of crude oil in each field. Such price would automatically become the current market value.

There may, however, be a complicating factor when the royalty substance is natural gas. Unlike oil, which is usually sold on a short term basis under contracts terminable on thirty-days notice, natural gas is sold under long-term agreements which will last the life of the field – twenty or more years. This type of arrangement is made necessary because of the heavy capital requirements for gas pipelines and the need to assure supplies to constantly growing markets. Gas does not have the portable qualities of oil and it requires large diameter pipeline systems for its economic transportation. The usual long-term gas contract will contain price escalation clauses and may also contain price renegotiation provisions which, if present at all, will occur only at lengthy intervals. The wellhead price for gas is constantly increasing as the demand grows, and new contracts will contain more favourable prices than earlier versions. Gas from the same area or field may be subject to both old and new contracts. What then of the situation where a lessor's royalty share is under an early gas contract, but other volumes of gas in the same immediate area have the benefit of a substantially improved price? Could it not be argued that the new price prevalent in the area represents 'the current market value' and that the lessee must account to the lessor on the basis of the best possible price? Such an interpretation would create a very severe financial hardship on the lessee who receives the lower price, but it is one which could easily be held to be the plain meaning of the words. The only countervailing argument is one based on the fact that the current market value is to be determined 'on the said lands,' and, since the gas is already committed under the earlier contract and cannot be sold under any other arrangement, the price actually obtained represents the current market value 'on the said lands.' Such a construction, however, appears somewhat forced, and a court might very well prefer the plain meaning of the phrase 'the current market value' as meaning the best existing price paid in the area at any given point of time. The specific inclusion of the word 'current' is difficult to reconcile with any other interpretation.[5]

5 This problem is discussed in Rae, 'Royalty Clauses In Oil and Gas Leases' (1965), 4 *Alta. L. Rev.* 323, 327, 328, and by E.H. Brown, 'Royalty Provisions of Oil and Gas Leases,' *The Landman*, September 1964, 6.

SULPHUR

The price or value of most of the leased substances is relatively stable. The price of oil is regulated by competition from domestic, American, and foreign sources; gas is normally subject to long-term arrangements with specified prices. Sulphur, however, is the exception, and its world price, and consequently the price received by the Canadian producer, has been subject to abrupt fluctuations between $6 and $50 a long ton. This has led to the inclusion, in some leases, of a fixed dollar royalty amount regardless of the actual price received by the producer. 'To pay to the Lessor One Dollar ($1.00) per long ton (2,240 pounds) on all sulphur mined and marketed by the Lessee from sulphur deposits within or upon the said lands.'

This practice originated when the sulphur market was severely depressed and guaranteed to the lessor a certain fixed amount. While there is no consistent pattern in sulphur prices, past experience would indicate that the fixing of a dollar royalty on sulphur will be more to the advantage of the lessee than the lessor in the long run. This is particularly true since leases, if productive, will continue in force for many years.

POINT WHERE VALUE DETERMINED

The point or place at which the royalty value is determined is an essential provision. The value of the leased substances, whether oil or gas, will vary in accordance with the point at which it is measured, increasing in value as it leaves the well and approaches the end consumer. Gas which has been treated and processed is obviously more valuable at the plant outlet where it is delivered to the pipeline than in its raw state at the well; similarly oil refined into its various components is worth more as gasoline in service station tanks than as crude oil back at the lease. When it comes to determining the value of the lessor's royalty, the leases are virtually unanimous in providing that such value shall be determined 'at the well' or 'on the said lands,' or even more specifically 'at the mouth of the well.'

The intention of the reference to 'the well' or 'the said lands' is to establish those points as the basis for measuring the value and to permit the lessee to deduct all costs subsequently incurred. The lessor's share is not subject to any of the costs of producing the substances and bringing them to the surface but is burdened with its share of the costs beyond that point. This approach works remarkably well in the case of crude oil, since it coincides with the manner in which that substance is customarily sold. For the most part, crude is sold either at a pipeline connection at the wellhead or from storage tanks on or in the vicinity of the well site. The general practice in computing royalty is to ignore any surface storage costs and to pay royalty computed on the actual selling price of the crude. This results in a more generous treatment of the lessor than would appear to be required by the clause itself.

The reference to 'on the said lands' could, under a given set of circumstances, lead to some results not contemplated by the lessee, particularly where gas is involved. (If the precise wording were to be followed, there could be a significant difference between a reference to 'at the well' or 'on the said lands.') If, for example, a reference to 'at the well' were to be strictly construed, the lessee would be entitled to deduct all costs beyond the wellhead, including separating and dehydrating facilities on the lease and storage either on the lease or at a central battery. An oil and gas lease sometimes covers very substantial areas of land since lessees prefer to include as much of the lessor's lands as possible under one lease. If plant facilities for the processing of gas were constructed within the area of the said lands, the wording suggests that the value for the purposes of computing the royalty would be at the outlet of such plant and that the lessee would not be able to deduct the costs of transportation and processing to such point. The reference to the well as the determination point would seem to be much more precise and accurate, rather than a general reference to 'on the said lands.'

Both references, however satisfactory they may be for crude oil, leave many questions unanswered when dealing with gas and other products. If the gas is sweet and of a merchantable quality, it may be picked up by the pipeline company through a wellhead connection and the determination of its value at the well is reasonably straightforward. Gas, however, often contains impurities and other constituents which must be removed. This is particularly true of the gas from deeper high-volume reservoirs which now produce the greater part of natural gas in western Canada. Gas of this type must be transported to a processing plant where it is cleaned, treated, and processed. The resulting dry residue gas and by-products are sold at the plant outlet. There is no such thing as a wellhead price and, in order to determine the 'value' at the well, it is necessary to deduct from the price obtained at the outlet of the plant the cost and expenses of transporting it to that point and of rendering it merchantable.

The lease does not contain any guidelines for determining the amount of such deductions, and many questions remain unanswered. Is the lessee entitled to include a rate of return on the investment in the gathering pipelines and processing plant? on what basis should the capital structure be apportioned as between equity and indebtedness? are income taxes to be taken into account? and what is the proper period of amortization of the investment? In practice, the average freehold lessor simply accepts the calculations and formulae used by the lessee and its accounting department. When the Crown or an experienced oil operator is the lessor, these matters are negotiated in great detail.

In Alberta at least, the issues may be resolved by an order of the Public Utilities Board. The Gas Utilities Act[6] provides:

Determining prices. 9(1) When gas produced from any land is to be gathered, treated or processed by the producer of the gas, the Board may, for the purposes of determining or establishing the value of the gas or any of its components as at the time and place of production from the well or on the location of the well, fix and determine,
  (a) the just or fair and reasonable costs, charges or deductions, or
  (b) the method, formula or basis to be applied, adopted or followed for ascertaining the just or fair and reasonable costs, charges or deductions,
to be made or to be deducted by the producer for or incidental to the gathering, treating or processing of the gas or any of its components.
(2) An order made pursuant to subsection (1),
  (a) applies and extends to such lands or areas as may be designated therein,
  (b) applies to and is effective and binding upon the producer and all parties to or for whom he is or may be liable to pay or account for the gas or any portion thereof or interest therein, except only in so far as the order is inconsistent with any express contractual obligation of the producer that fixes or establishes
  (i) specific costs, charges or deductions, or
  (ii) the specific method, formula or basis for ascertaining the costs, charges or deductions, that are to be made or deducted by the producer for or incidental to the gathering, treating or processing of the gas, and
  (c) may be for a fixed or determined period or periods, or be made subject to future review by the Board, as provided in the order, and the order shall not be otherwise changed or varied by the Board except and only insofar as the change or variation is consented to by all of the parties affected thereby.

Subsection (2)(b) makes such an order binding upon the producer and all parties to or for whom he may be liable to pay or account for the gas, except only if the order is inconsistent with any express contractual obligation that fixes or establishes specific costs, charges, or deductions or a specific method, formula, or basis for ascertaining such costs, charges, or deductions. The royalty clause in the lease does not contain any specific charges; therefore, an order made by the Public Utilities Board would be

6 R.S.A. 1970, c 158

binding on the lessor. The main purpose of the Gas Utilities Act is to regulate gas utilities and, upon application of an interested party or municipality or upon its own motion, to fix the price or prices of gas.

The power given to the Board under Section 9 is an incident of this jurisdiction and has been held in Alberta to be a power that can be exercised by the Board, even though such exercise involved the Board placing its own interpretation on contracts. The power given to the Board under Section 9 of the Gas Utilities Act was once contained in the Public Utilities Act in a section that is essentially the same as the current form.[7] The right of the Public Utilities Board to make such a determination was challenged in *Rabson Oil Co. Ltd. v Shell Exploration Alberta Ltd.*[8]

Shell and Rabson had entered into agreements, not leases, under which Rabson reserved an overriding royalty share and the agreements specifically provided that, if Shell had to process any natural gas, it had the right to deduct from the royalty payments a pro rata share of the reasonable costs of processing the same. The lands in question were in the Jumping Pound field. Rabson objected to the deductions as made by Shell, and Shell applied to the Public Utilities Board for an order fixing and determining the deductions and charges that could be made. Rabson then issued a statement of claim in the ordinary courts, seeking a declaration that the costs charged by Shell were not reasonable under the terms of the agreement. Shell then moved to strike out the statement of claim on the grounds that an application was before the Public Utilities Board to determine the very points in issue.

The trial judge held that, if the Board had jurisdiction to determine such questions, it was not an exclusive jurisdiction and did not override the traditional jurisdiction of the courts to interpret contracts. This decision was appealed and reversed by the Appellate Division on the ground that the Board could be given the right to place its own interpretation on contracts as necessarily incidental to its proper decision.

The Board then issued an order stating that, in principle, certain deductions could be made. These items are summarized as follows: (1) the wellhead value can be determined by working back from the sale price; (2) the lessee is entitled to receive a return on invested capital; (3) income taxes

---

7 R.S.A. 1955, c 267 s 72 (8) (9)
8 This case, decided in 1953, is unreported, but the trial decision of Egbert J is reported in Lewis & Thompson Dig. 68A. The decision of the Appeal Court is also unreported, but is quoted in the judgment of Milvain J in *Calgary & Edmonton Corporation Ltd. v British American Oil Co. Ltd.* (1963) 40 D.L.R. (2d) 964, 970. It reversed the decision of Egbert J and held that the Province had the right to appoint a Board with the power to interpret contracts 'as necessarily incidental to its proper decision.'

were proper items to be allowed and included in the cost of operations; (4) intangible costs (interest charges, etc.) incurred prior to and during construction of the plant should be allowed as part of the cost of the plant; (5) working capital should be allowed as part of the cost of the plant; (6) depreciation should be allowed as an operating charge.

Subsequently, the Board issued an order setting out the specific costs, charges, and deductions which could be charged by Shell and which charges were based on actual operating experience. The second order also favoured a capitalization of 50 per cent debt and 50 per cent equity. These orders established what has now become known as 'The Jumping Pound Formula' and is accepted by the Crown. It would be applied by the Public Utilities Board in the event of an application made pursuant to Section 9.

It was clear from the *Rabson* case that, while the Board could have jurisdiction to interpret the contracts when such were incidental to their decision, such jurisdiction was not necessarily exclusive to the Board. Since the *Rabson* decision, the Board has displayed reluctance to interpret private contracts. In *Calgary and Edmonton Corp. Ltd.* v *British American Oil Co. Ltd.*[9] there was a dispute between the lessor and the lessee concerning a royalty provision which involved not only the items to be deducted but also the rate of royalty applicable to the various types of substances. British American, as lessee, made an application to the Public Utilities Board and the c & e Corp. commenced an action in the ordinary courts. The Board held that, if it did have jurisdiction to interpret contracts, such jurisdiction was not exclusive and that the court also had jurisdiction to determine the matter. Under those circumstances the Board suggested that the proper course would be to have the parties apply to stay either the proceedings before the Board or the action before the courts. An application was made to have the court action stayed. The trial judge refused to stay the action on the ground that what the Board was being asked to do was not merely to determine what were reasonable costs of processing, but also to settle a dispute between contracting parties as to the proper construction to be placed upon their agreements. The proper forum for such a dispute was a court of law. On appeal, the trial decision was upheld, but on the grounds that the court had not been denuded of its jurisdiction, there being no express language in the Gas Utilities Act taking away the jurisdiction of the court. Because of this, the Board was not 'the only competent tribunal.' Furthermore, the Board had plainly indicated that it would not deal with the issues between the parties unless the action was stayed or the contract construed by the court.

9 *Supra* n. 8

This was the end of the litigation as the parties negotiated a settlement of their dispute.

It is unlikely, therefore, that an Alberta lessee could expect the active co-operation of the Public Utilities Board in resolving any dispute with the lessor. Nonetheless, there has been a sufficient background of Board awards and judicial interpretation to establish the factors that a lessee is entitled to deduct to determine the value of the substances 'on the said lands.' The Jumping Pound formula may be said to constitute the standard for such deductions insofar as Alberta freehold leases are concerned and would be of persuasive weight in other jurisdictions.

Individual variations in the royalty clauses also sometimes lead to results totally unexpected by the lessee. For example, the clause of the (b) type requires the lessee to deliver the royalty share to the credit of the lessor in the pipeline to which the lessee connects its wells. If the wells are not connected to a pipeline and the lessee must truck the oil some distance to a terminus of the pipeline, it is doubtful if the cost of such transportation could be deduced, as the obligation is to deliver it into the pipeline.

DIFFERENT ROYALTY RATES APPLICABLE TO
LEASED SUBSTANCES

Royalty clauses sometimes specify a different royalty rate for individual classes of the leased substances. For example, the royalty on oil might be the customary 12½ per cent, while the royalty rate on gas may be set at 15 per cent. It then becomes essential to classify each substance as it is produced from the well. Some of these classifications are not too easy to make. Is casinghead gas, which is produced in association with crude oil, to be considered as oil or natural gas? By a sudden decrease in the pressure, gas may produce hydrocarbon liquids at the surface or at a surface separator. Are such substances to be considered as oil or natural gas for the purposes of royalty?

The only judicial guide presently available in Canada is the *Borys* v *Canadian Pacific Railways*.[10] The Privy Council determined what substances were included in 'petroleum' by its composition in its container within the ground. If this reasoning were to be applied, the royalty on gas produced in association with oil and separated from it at the surface would be subject to the oil royalty. Similarly, liquids that are produced in association with gas

10 [1953] A.C. 217, 7 W.W.R. (N.S.) 546, [1953] 2 D.L.R. 65 (P.C.). This case is
discussed extensively in chapter 5, *ante*

but are separated from it at the surface would fall under the gas portion of the clause.

ROYALTY PAYABLE WHEN LESSOR OWNS LESS THAN ENTIRE ESTATE

The royalty clause reserves to the lessor or requires the lessee to pay the lessor a share of the leased substances produced and marketed 'from the said lands.' The wording appears to be remarkably straightforward and free from ambiguity. What is the situation where the lessor turns out to own something less than the entire mineral interest? For example, his interest may be determined to have been only an undivided 25 per cent rather than the whole. This situation is now provided for in the oil and gas lease by a separate clause on the following lines: 'LESSER INTEREST: If the Lessor's interest in the substance be less than the entire and undivided fee simple estate therein, then the royalties herein provided shall be paid to the Lessor only in the proportion which his interest bears to the whole and undivided fee.'

The Supreme Court of Canada has indicated that, even without such a clause, the lessee cannot be compelled to pay royalty upon oil which does not belong to the lessor. This statement, which is clearly *obiter dicta*, was made by Martland J in *Imperial Oil Limited* v *Placid Oil Co.*[11] In this case, the problem concerned the royalty payable under lands affected by the Saskatchewan Road Allowances Crown Oil Act, 1959, which provided that in every producing oil reservoir 1.88 per cent of the recoverable oil shall be deemed to be under road allowances and the property of the Crown. Imperial, as the original lessee, took the position that it was required, despite the existence of the Act, to pay the freehold lessor his royalty on the basis of 100 per cent of the substances produced from the lands. The particular lease contained the lesser interest clause in the same form as set forth above. Imperial was not content to rely on the protection of this clause, possibly on the ground that it might not apply to the situation created by the Saskatchewan Act. The Supreme Court held that the effect of the Road Allowance Act was to make the specified percentage of 1.88 the property of the Crown. The court considered the effect of this upon the lease in the following passage: 'Insofar as the lease is concerned, the obligation to pay royalty is upon the leased substances owned by the lessor and leased and granted by him to the lessee. The lessee cannot be compelled to pay royalty upon oil which

11 [1963] S.C.R. 333, 43 W.W.R. 437

does not belong to the lessor and this conclusion, which, I think, must follow, even apart from the provisions of clause 4 of the lease, is reinforced by the terms of that clause.'[12]

The interesting portion of this passage is the statement that the lessee's obligation is to pay royalty only upon the substances *owned* by the lessor *even apart from the lesser interest clause.* Since the lease did contain such a clause, the observation is no more than *dicta,* but it is, nonetheless, remarkable. It seems to impart the concept of ownership into the royalty clause. The actual words used in the clause do not contain any reference to ownership, but only to production from the said lands. The view that the royalty is applicable only to the leased substances 'owned' by the lessor seems to vary the express terms of a contract between the parties, particularly in view of the rule of capture. If the parties see fit to impose a royalty on all the substances produced from the said lands, then that result should not necessarily be altered by the subsequent discovery that the lessor may own something less than 100 per cent. If such a result were to be achieved, surely the proper method would be in an action for rectification on the ground of mistake. In most cases, the point may be academic because of the almost universal existence of the lesser interest clause. There may, however, be circumstances which lie outside the ambit of its language or where it is absent from the lease, and then the *obiter dicta* of Martland J would become very material.

NO AUTOMATIC TERMINATION FOR FAILURE TO PAY ROYALTY

The royalty clause does not contain words of automatic termination. The obligation of the lessee is to remit to the lessor on or before the 20th day of each month an amount equal to the royalty share of the substances produced and sold in the previous month. Since the lessee is obligated to make the payments by the specified date, failure to do so falls within the default clause discussed in more detail *infra.* In brief, if the lessee fails to remit royalty payments as required, the lessor may give a default notice and, unless the lessee commences to remedy such default within a period of ninety days from receipt of such notice, the lease will then terminate.

In the absence of a default notice and the expiration of the period of grace without remedial action by the lessee, the failure of the lessee to pay the royalty would not terminate the lease. The *habendum* clause maintains the

12 Ibid, S.C.R., 339

lease in force for the primary term and so long thereafter as the leased substances are produced. So long as the substances are being produced, the lease is continued regardless of whether or not the royalty payments are made.

ENTITLEMENT TO ROYALTIES AS BETWEEN LIFE INTEREST AND REMAINDER MAN

Royalty proceeds, while they may partake of the nature of a rent, also have the quality of being a share in a substance which is removed from the land and not replaced by the processes of nature. Is royalty income, or is it capital, is it the proceeds from an estate, or part of the *corpus* of the estate? This enquiry becomes very material when, as frequently occurs, a testator leaves a life interest in his estate to his widow with the remainder to his children. If a lease forms part of that estate, to whom does the royalty belong – the wife as the owner of the life interest, or the children as owners of the remainder?

The English law has long drawn a distinction between produce which would be restored and replenished by nature, such as fruits and crops, on the one hand, and minerals which form part of the soil, on the other. According to this principle, the holder of the life estates was entitled to the replenishable proceeds from the estate, but had no interest in the mineral rights. This was subject to a limitation where mines or quarries had been opened and worked prior to the death of the testator. Under such circumstances, the owner of the life interest was entitled to continue to work the open mines and to receive the benefit therefrom.

In Canada the judicial disposition has been to treat royalty as belonging to the owner of the life estate. The English cases which held that, with the exception of open mines, the royalty interest was to be retained for the owner of the remainder have been distinguished on the grounds that the intention of the testator must be controlling. Canadian courts look to the intention of the testator or the creator of the trust and generally conclude that payments of royalty would have been considered by him to be income and therefore intended to benefit the owner of the life estate.[13] In *Re Moffat Estate*[14] it was held that the owner of the life interest was entitled to have the receipts from the royalties invested in trustee security and to have the income from such

13 *Re Murray* [1961] o.w.n. 189; *Hayduck* v *Waterton* (1968), 64 w.w.r. 641, where the Supreme Court of Canada held that the term 'liferent,' as used by the parties would include all the fruits of the land, including oil royalties
14 (1955), 16 w.w.r. 314 (Sask.)

investments paid to her and on her death the accumulated funds to be paid to the owner of the remainder. This seems to be an unnecessary refinement and one that probably would not be followed by a court seeking the intent of the testator or settlor as to what would be included or excluded from the concept of income.

APPORTIONMENT

Somewhat similar is the problem of who is entitled to the royalty when the land covered by a lease has been subsequently conveyed by the lessor to separate owners and production occurs on one parcel but not on the other. Is the owner of the parcel on which there is production entitled to the royalty exclusively or must he share it with the owner of the other parcel?

The one Canadian decision on this point had a fact pattern which contained all the ingredients for the principle of apportionment. In *Re Dawson and Bell*[15] the lessor had granted a lease covering portions of two lots. During the primary term two gas wells were brought into production on one lot, but there was no drilling on the other. The lease, of course, was continued beyond the primary term by the presence of production. The lessor then died and by agreement among his heirs-at-law the land was divided into two portions, one comprising the area on which the two wells were located. The question was whether the owner of the non-productive lot was entitled to any share of the royalty. The Ontario Court of Appeal applied English mining law to hold that the royalty 'is the compensation which the occupier pays the landlord for that species of occupation which the contract between them allows.'[16]

Once royalty had been equated to rent, the court applied long established principles of English law to hold the right to receive the proportionate part of the rent passed under the grant of land. The owners of the freehold were entitled to have it apportioned, in the event of a subsequent sub-division of the freehold, notwithstanding that all of the oil or gas may be produced from only one portion. The division of the freehold did not have the effect of severing the *profit à prendre*.

The application of the English rule of apportionment really settled the matter although the Court of Appeal also looked to the existing American authorities. As quite often happens, the court found that there were two conflicting lines of authorities, depending on whether the particular state

15 [1946] 1 D.L.R. 327 (S.C.C.)
16 *Reg.* v *Westbrook* (1847) 10 Q.B. 178, 204–5; 116 E.R. 69

took the view that a lease vested in the lessee an estate in the land only, or absolute title to the oil and gas in place.[17]

The *Dawson and Bell* case is not binding on any courts outside of the province of Ontario, so it is not yet possible to determine how widespread will be the Canadian acceptance of the doctrine of apportionment. It has an appeal to equitable considerations and it has the support of English mining law. Some forms of leases finesse the problem by including, usually in the assignment clause, an express provision for apportionment of royalties. Such a clause was considered by the Alberta Trial Division in *Prudential Trust Company Limited* v *National Trust Company Limited*.[18] The lease contained this provision: 'If the leased premises are now or shall hereafter be owned in severalty or in separate tracts, the premises, nevertheless, shall be developed and operated as one lease, and all royalties accruing hereunder shall be treated as an entirety and shall be divided among and paid to such separate owners in the proportion that the acreage owned by each such separate owner bears to the entire lease acreage.'

The lessor entered into two agreements, subsequent to executing the lease, in which he disposed of portions of his royalty to two different owners. The Trial Division applied the provision of the entirety clause and apportioned the royalty among the two assignees. Because of the existence of this clause, McDermid J expressly refrained from deciding whether the rule of apportionment as applied in *Re Dawson and Bell* was in force in the province of Alberta.

ROYALTY AS RENT

Just as the lease itself falls somewhat uneasily between an outright grant and a mere lease, it is difficult to conceive of royalty as being rent in the true sense. Nonetheless, this appears to be the legal category in which royalty finds itself. A long line of English decisions has refused to concede that,

---

17 Rae *supra* n. 5 points out that in applying the Texas cases, the Ontario Court of Appeal may have overlooked the fact that the Supreme Court of Texas subsequently reversed one of the decisions, overruled another, and distinguished the third of the three cases cited. Nonetheless, the apportionment theory seems to be firmly established in the States of California, Mississippi, and Pennsylvania, although the non-apportionment theory according to Rae is followed in the States of Arkansas, Colorado, Illinois, Texas, Kansas, Kentucky, Louisiana, Nebraska, New Mexico, Ohio, Oklahoma, and West Virginia. As McRuer JA pointed out, the American decisions are only useful insofar as they may expound the law consistently with the principles of English law.

18 (1965) 50 w.w.r. 29 (Alta.)

because royalty is paid not in respect of replenishable produce of the land but for a portion of the land itself, this makes it something more than rent. As far back as 1847, an English court was confronted with this argument over royalty paid under a lease for the purpose of mining fire brick clay. The argument was met as follows:

We come, then, to the bare objection that the royalty is paid, not for the renewing produce of the land, but for several portions of the land itself, mixed up with foreign matter: The expense of this, however, must of course have been cast off before the royalty itself was fixed. That was a sum which, after all such expenses paid, the occupier could afford to render to the landlord. When the case is thus laid bare, there is no distinction between it and that of the lessee of coal mines, of clay pits, of slate quarries: In our lease the occupation is only valuable by the removal of portions of the soil: And whether the occupation is paid for in money or kind, is fixed beforehand by the contract, or measured afterwards by the actual produce, it is equally in substance a rent: [19]

In an earlier case[20] the same court held that, where an agreement required the payment of a yearly sum based on a rate per yard for all the material removed from the land and an additional sum for each one thousand bricks made, the owner of the land was entitled to distrain for rent.

The practical effect of equating royalty under an oil and gas lease to rent is somewhat difficult to gauge, although it does lead to apportionment and may confer upon a mineral lessor the common law right of distraining for arrears of royalty against the well and equipment of his lessee.

CONSTRUCTIVE PRODUCTION

Once the primary term has expired, the effect of the 'thereafter' language of the *habendum* clause is to automatically terminate the lease unless there is production. There are circumstances under which the lessee having discovered oil or gas would be forced to stand by and wait helplessly for the lease to expire because of a lack of market. This situation most frequently occurs with gas, since marketing can be a very lengthy and uncertain procedure. A lessee with a gas discovery may know full well that the primary term of the lease will expire long before it can be placed on production. This

19 *Reg.* v *Westbrook, supra* n. 16, 204–5
20 *Daniel* v *Gracie* (1844) 6 Q.B. 145, 115 E.R. 56; generally, see also Davies, 'The Legal Characterization of Overriding Royalty Interests in Oil and Gas' (1972), 10 *Alta. Law. Rev.* 232

led to the development of a clause which creates constructive production under the lease. In its simplest form (often still encountered in existing Canadian oil and gas leases) the clause was limited to gas and to a failure to produce the gas because of no market. A typical clause of this type reads: 'Where all wells on the said lands producing, or capable of producing, gas only are shut in, suspended, capped or otherwise not being produced as the result of a lack of or an intermittent market, lessee may pay as royalty the sum of $100.00 per well per year, and if such payment is made it will be considered that gas is being produced from the said land.'

A clause of this type designed to meet a specific situation is quite restrictive in its application and has many deficiencies insofar as the lessee is concerned. Because of its reference to 'gas only,' it clearly does not apply to an oil well, and there may be considerable question as to whether it would apply to a well which produces distillate, condensate, or sulphur along with the gas. This particular point has never been decided in Canada although it was argued both before the Trial and Appellate Divisions of Alberta in *Canadian Superior Oil Ltd.* v *Hambly*.[21] Here the well, in addition to encountering gas, also discovered volumes of heavy oil in deeper horizons. It was argued that, because of the oil, although it might not have been economically expedient to produce it at that time, the well could not be considered as one producing 'gas only.' This point was not dealt with by the courts as the lease was struck down on other grounds.

The application of this early type of capped gas well royalty clause is confined to circumstances where the gas is shut-in and not being produced as a result of a lack of or an intermittent market. Only these special circumstances where a market does not presently exist can activate the clause. It is easy to visualize many other circumstances where production may be suspended or shut-in, such as the necessity of reconditioning the well, temporarily impassable road conditions, conservation orders, and many others. Under the above type of clause the lessee would be powerless to prevent the lapsing of the lease if the primary term had expired.

There is also a problem as to when the capped gas well royalty may be relied upon to preserve the lease. Many of the early forms of lease simply provide that, if production ceases during the primary term, the lease shall terminate at the next ensuing anniversary date unless drilling operations have been commenced or unless the delay rental has been paid. Under such language it would seem conclusive that, if a well were shut-in or suspended, this would amount to the cessation of production and only the payment of a

---

21 (1969) 67 w.w.r. 525, [1969] 3 d.l.r. (3d) 10 (c.a.); 65 w.w.r. 461 (Alta.).
The issue was not raised before the Supreme Court of Canada, (1970) 74 w.w.r. 356.

delay rental or further drilling operations could continue the lease in force. Under these circumstances, the prudent lessee would be well advised to pay both the capped gas well royalty and the delay rental payment. This confusion does not arise when a well is suspended after the expiration of the primary term, but then the time of payment of the royalty becomes of critical importance.

There are three factual situations wherein the shut-in royalty provision may operate to maintain a lease in force beyond the primary term:

1   Where there is a completed well on the lands but no production and the primary term expires. Here the payment must be made prior to the expiration of the primary term as the lease will terminate automatically upon the expiration of the primary term unless there is production, actual or constructive, to operate the 'thereafter' provision.[22]

2   Where at the expiration of the primary term there is no producing well but the lessee is drilling on the land and such well is completed as a potential producer. In this case it is necessary that the lease, as most do, contain a provision that extends the primary term for so long as the drilling operations continue. The result in this situation is the same as in 1 above, with the exception that the primary term is treated as having been extended by the operation of the clause that permits the lessee to continue the drilling operations. The individual wording of such clauses will be closely scrutinized – i.e., does the lessee have the right to complete the well? or will the wording of the particular clause in his lease protect him for a certain period beyond the actual completion? Regardless of the period by which the primary term may be extended, it is clear that any capped royalty payment must be made prior to the expiration of such extended term.[23]

Once again the lessee is faced with a critical time factor. First of all, it must be determined that the well qualifies under the terms of the clause, i.e., it must be capable of production of the particular substances mentioned, whether gas or others; then, that the payment is made prior to the expiration of the extended term. It is no easy matter to predict at what point of time a court will hold the extension to have ended.

3   Where the primary term has been extended by actual production but then production ceases or is suspended. In the early type of clause quoted above, which is limited to gas wells being suspended as the result of a lack of or an intermittent market, there would be considerable difficulty in qualifying the suspension. Assuming, however, that the suspension was

22 *Can. Superior Oil of Calif. Ltd.* v *Kanstrup and Scurry-Rainbow Oil Ltd.* [1965] s.c.r. 92, 49 w.w.r. 257, 47 d.l.r. (2d) 1 (s.c.c.)
23 *Canadian Superior Oil Ltd.* v *Hambly, supra* n. 21

caused by a market interruption, or by another cause under the broader forms now in use, it would seem that the payment should be made immediately upon cessation of production as the 'thereafter' provision only applies where there is actual or constructive production. This would hold true, in the absence of any other provision, for even the briefest of suspensions. Most modern lease forms attempt to overcome this by changes in the wording of the suspended well clause itself and by other provisions, notably in the proviso to the *habendum* which deals with cessation of production after the expiration of the primary term.

The standard shut-in well clause is an attempt to overcome the shortcomings that became evident in the early type of clause discussed above.

SHUT-IN WELLS

If all wells on the said lands or the pooled lands are shut-in, suspended or otherwise not produced during any year ending on an anniversary date as the result of a lack of or an intermittent market, or any cause whatsoever beyond the Lessee's reasonable control, the Lessee shall pay to the Lessor at the expiration of each said year a sum equal to the delay rental hereinbefore set forth, and each such well shall be deemed to be a producing well hereunder.

This type of clause does several things: it removes the restriction that the well must be a producing or potential gas well and embraces all types of wells, while the reference to a lack of or an intermittent market remains the failure to produce can also qualify if it is induced by 'any cause whatsoever beyond the Lessee's reasonable control'; and it seeks to give the lessee considerably more latitude as to the time within which the payment should be made by providing that the payment is to be made at the expiration of each year in which the wells remain off production.

As we have seen, the standard form of the third proviso to the *habendum* also deals with the suspension of production after the expiration of the primary term: 'If any well on the said lands ... is shut-in, suspended or otherwise not produced as the result of a lack of or an intermittent market, or any cause whatsoever beyond the Lessee's reasonable control, the time of such interruption or suspension or non-production shall not be counted against the Lessee.' The wording is somewhat unclear, as it is difficult to gauge what is meant by 'shall not be counted against the lessee,' but it would appear that, if the failure to produce is due to market conditions or any other cause beyond the lessee's control (the identical reasons as set forth in the shut-in royalty provision), then such time shall not be included in computing the ninety-day periods within which the lessee must commence other drilling operations. The effect seems to be that the cessation of production due to reasons beyond the control of the lessee gives an indefinite and permanent extension of the lease, regardless of whether or not the shut-in well payment is actually made. If the two provisions are meant to co-exist, a cross-reference to the payment of the shut-in royalty should be included in the third proviso of the *habendum*.

The operation of the current form of shut-in well payments affords a great deal of protection to the lessee and obviates those critical decisions as to the precise time within which payments must be made. Now it is sufficient that they be made at the expiration of each year. Under the requisite conditions, a lease could be maintained in force for an indefinite period of years without any actual production. Canadian lease forms do not contain any obligation on the part of the lessee to develop a market for the leased substances, and it is at least questionable if Canadian courts would imply any such term. The operation of the shut-in well clause is such that it might justify the inclusion of a marketing-type covenant or the imposition of a time limit beyond which non-production payments cannot maintain the lease.

RESPONSIBILITY FOR TAXES

Most leases attempt to allocate the responsibility for taxes that may be levied against the ownership of the minerals and the operations conducted on the lands. Generally, the lessor is made responsible for the taxes arising out of his interest (the royalty share) in production obtained from the lands and his ownership of mineral rights. He is also charged with the responsibility for payment of such taxes as may be levied against the surface of the lands if he owns same.

The lessee is charged with responsibility for the taxes levied in respect of its operations on the said lands and interest in production.

From the point of view of the lessor, the most significant tax is the provincial tax imposed on his ownership of the actual mineral rights. Because he is the registered owner, the government collects the tax from the lessor, but the lessee normally will undertake to reimburse the lessor for seven-eighths of all such taxes. While the lessor specifically agrees to pay and discharge the taxes levied against his interest, his continued failure to do so may result in a situation where his mineral interest may eventually be taken from him.[24] The prudent lessee will incorporate in the terms of the lease a provision that will enable it to take action under such circumstances.[25]

24 See, for example, The Mineral Taxation Act R.S.A. 1970, c 236. Although not required to do so, the provincial government departments notify any person having registered or caveated an interest in the minerals, of the existence of tax arrears.
25 The standard clause that does this is discussed in Chapter 9, *infra*, under the heading *Encumbrances*.

Responsibility for taxes is allocated by these two standard clauses which are self-explanatory:

TAXES PAYABLE BY THE LESSOR

The Lessor shall promptly satisfy all taxes, rates and assessments that may be assessed or levied, directly or indirectly, against the Lessor by reason of the Lessor's interest in production obtained from the said lands, or the Lessor's ownership of mineral rights in the said lands, and shall further pay all taxes, rates and assessments that may be assessed or levied against the surface of the said lands during the continuance of the term hereby granted or any extension thereof if and so long as the said surface of the said lands is or continues to be owned by the Lessor.

TAXES PAYABLE BY THE LESSEE

The Lessee shall pay all taxes, rates and assessments that may be assessed or levied in respect of the undertaking and operations of the Lessee on, in, over or under the said lands, and shall further pay all taxes, rates and assessments that may be assessed or levied directly or indirectly against the Lessee by reason of the Lessee's interest in production from the said lands. The Lessee shall on the written request of the Lessor, accompanied by such tax receipts, statements or tax notices as the Lessee may require, reimburse the Lessor for seven-eighths (7/8ths) of any taxes assessed or imposed on the Lessor during the currency of this Lease by reason of the Lessor being the registered owner of the leased substances or being entitled to become such owner.

8
Drainage – offset drilling and pooling

The ambulatory nature of oil and gas raises both the hazard of drainage and economic advantage of producing them through a minimum number of wells.

PROTECTION AGAINST DRAINAGE

Loss of production through drainage can be counteracted by drilling a well on the leased lands and placing it on production. This is the purpose of the offset drilling clause – to impose upon the lessee an obligation to drill if certain conditions are met. Here again, the clause has been refined and improved over the years to the lessee's advantage so that there is a marked difference between the forms in vogue ten or fifteen years ago and those of the present day. The best way to understand the current version of the clause is to trace its development from the earlier forms (many of which are still to be found in existing leases) and to consider the reasons that led to its amendment.

This clause is typical of the early versions:

In the event of commercial production being obtained from any well drilled on any spacing unit laterally adjoining the said lands and not owned by the lessor, then unless a well has been or is being drilled on the spacing unit of the said lands laterally adjoining the said spacing unit on which production is being so obtained and to the horizon in the formation from which production is being so obtained, the lessee shall, within six (6) months from the date of said well being placed on production, commence or cause to be commenced within the six (6) month period aforesaid operations for the drilling of an offset well on the spacing unit of the said lands laterally adjoining the said spacing unit on which production is being so obtained, and thereafter drill the same to the horizon in the formation from which production is being obtained from the said adjoining spacing unit; PROVIDED that, if such well drilled on lands laterally adjoining the said lands is productive primarily or only of natural gas, the lessee shall not be obligated to drill an offset well unless and until an adequate and commercially profitable market for natural gas which might be produced from the offset well can be previously arranged and provided.

The clause is designed to protect the interest of the mineral lessor and at the same time to avoid placing the lessee in an uneconomic position with regard to the drilling of a well. It does not impose an absolute drilling obligation but is conditional upon the fulfilment of certain prerequisites, namely:

(a) The well which creates the obligation must have encountered 'commercial production.' This is one of the terms defined in the interpretation clause and means such output from a well as, considering the cost of drilling and production operations and the price and quality of the leased substances, would commercially and economically warrant the drilling of a like well in the vicinity thereof after a production test of thirty days. This requirement ensures that the creating well must have encountered production in economic volumes which were maintained for at least a thirty-day period.

(b) The creating well must have been located on a spacing unit laterally adjoining the leased lands. This condition is apparently based on the theory that no significant drainage will occur over greater distances. 'Spacing unit' is another defined term and means the area allocated to the well for the purpose of drilling for or producing the leased substances under the existing conservation and production laws. The provincial conservation laws now permit a very substantial variation in the size of a spacing unit; it may range from a quarter section to several sections depending on the type of substance and reservoir conditions. The requirement that the spacing unit must be 'laterally adjoining' is virtually universal. A diagonal offset which occurs when the producing spacing unit corners on the leased lands will not activate the clause.

Alberta has enacted legislation[1] which provides that, where a well is drilled and produces oil or gas from a drilling spacing unit which laterally adjoins a drilling spacing unit subject to an oil and gas lease which contains an offset drilling provision, then the well that creates the obligation shall be deemed, regardless of its actual location on the drilling spacing unit, to give rise to the offset obligation. This legislative provision is meant to take care

1 The Oil and Gas Conservation Act, R.S.A. 1970 c 267, s 130

of the situation that may arise where a 'drilling spacing unit' under the Act consists of several sections of land comprising several leases. In such a case, the producing well could be located on one lease with another lease, comprising part of the drilling spacing unit, intervening between the well and yet another lease with an offset clause.

(c) The creating well must be on land not owned by the lessor. This requirement is justified on the theory there would be no actual monetary loss to the lessor if the creating well were situated on his lands, even if not included within the subject lease, as all the petroleum substances drained from the leased lands would be recovered to his possession through the other well. A lessor, if he were so inclined, could circumvent this limitation by simply transferring the rights to a relative or other 'friendly assignee.'

The standard clause contains a modification of this limitation under which the offset will accrue with respect to land owned by the lessor unless the land is also leased by the lessee. This variation, although the logic behind it is not readily apparent, can only be beneficial to the lessor since it widens the applicability of the obligation.

TERMINATION ON FAILURE TO DRILL OFFSET WELL

Unlike the drilling commitment, failure to comply with an offset drilling obligation does not lead to automatic termination of the lease. It may ultimately result in termination if the lessor sets in motion certain procedures. Most leases contain a provision under which the lessor may give the lessee written notice of a default, and, if the lessee shall fail to commence to remedy such default within a ninety-day period, the lease will terminate. Since the offset clause creates an obligation on the lessee and not a mere option, failure to drill constitutes a default. Therefore, if the lessor gives notice and the required period of time elapses without remedial action, the lease will terminate.

DAMAGES FOR FAILURE TO DRILL AN OFFSET WELL

The question of termination or non-termination may not be of too much importance to the parties. Presumably the lessee will refuse to drill under conditions where it has reason to believe that the reserves are of little commercial value. For example, the creating well after producing satisfactorily for the thirty-day period may start to produce excessive volumes of water, cease production altogether, or a neighbouring dry hole or other discouraging geological information may have dampened enthusiasm for the prospect. Under such circumstances the lessee would be quite happy to forget about the lease, while its mere surrender would confer a doubtful benefit upon the lessor. The question then becomes whether the lessor can collect damages against the lessee, and, if so, in what amounts.

TERMINATION OF LEASE DOES NOT EXTINGUISH LIABILITY FOR DAMAGES

Although failure to drill under an offset obligation may terminate the lease and forfeit the lessee's interest therein, this by itself does not remove the already accrued liability to drill.[2]

QUANTUM OF DAMAGES

At first glance, the proper measure of damages would appear to be the cost of drilling the well. Such damages would place the lessor in the same position as though the obligation had been performed. If he wished he could take the proceeds, amounting to the cost of drilling the well, and have the well drilled on his own. Until recently, however, the cost of drilling the well had been totally discarded as a proper measure of damages. A recent decision of the Canadian Supreme Court may have reopened the door to the utilization of the drilling cost in determining damages.

The principal difficulty with the cost concept of damages in an offset situation is the likelihood that there will be convincing geological evidence which discredits the prospects of success if the well were to be drilled. The underlying principle in computing damages is expressed in *Wertheim* v *Chicoutimi Pulp Company*:[3] 'And it is the general intention of the law that, in giving damages for breach of contract, the party complaining should, so far as it can be done by money, be placed in the same position as he would have been in if the contract had been performed.'

For a period of twenty years, following the decision of the Canadian Supreme Court in *Cotter* v *General Petroleums Limited* and *Superior Oils, Limited*,[4] the lower courts have felt that they could not apply the cost of drilling as a measure of damages. The trial judge in the *Cotter* case had, in fact, awarded damages based on the cost of drilling,[5] but this was repudiated by the Supreme Court. The *Cotter* case involved an obligation that arose not

2 *Prudential Trust Co. Ltd. and Wagner* v *Wagner Oils Limited* (1954) 11 W.W.R. (N.S.) 371
3 [1911] A.C. 301, 80 L.J. P.C. 91
4 [1951] S.C.R. 154; [1950] 4 D.L.R. 609 (S.C.C.)
5 [1949] 1 W.W.R. 193

from a lease but rather an option under which the defendant could earn an interest by commencing the drilling of a well within a specified time. The agreement also contained a covenant to exercise the option. This curious legal situation troubled the courts, but the Supreme Court treated it as either a binding covenant to drill, or at least an undertaking which gave rise to liability. The defendant was not to receive a sub-lease until the option had been exercised. This fact enabled the Supreme Court to treat the document as one under which consideration had not passed and was the ground on which it distinguished two earlier mining cases where the cost of performing the work had been used as the measure of damages.

Under the oil and gas lease, however, the consideration will have passed to the lessee since it obtains its rights under the lease immediately and those rights are substantial, involving as they do the right to explore, drill, take and remove the substances from the lands. Cartwright J (as he then was) reviewed the circumstances and held, 'I do not think that the cost of drilling is the proper measure of damages.'[6]

The *Cotter* case has been treated as eliminating the cost of doing the work as the measure of damages. The same trial judge who had used the cost of drilling as the measure of damages in *Cotter* was once again faced with the problem a few years later. In *Prudential Trust Company Limited and Wagner v Wagner Oils Limited*[7] the obligation arose under a lease, although not under the offset clause. The lease form in question was quite unusual in that it contained an absolute commitment to drill. The defendant refused to drill and the geological evidence at the trial was most discouraging on the prospects of success for any well. The trial judge, McLaurin J, stated:

If it were not for the Cotter decision, I would be disposed to fix the damages at some substantial amount, probably the cost of drilling a well. I still see nothing unfair in visiting a defaulting party with damages in this amount. The whole foundation of legitimate promotional efforts in the exploitation of oil is based on the assumption that the parties will not renege on such deals. However, the Cotter case has established that such damages must not be awarded, but it does hold that nominal damages are recoverable even though no nominal damages were fixed in that case.

As to damages, I assume that I would be loyally following the Supreme Court of Canada by fixing some relatively inconsequential amount. I accordingly fix damages at $500.00.[8]

---

6 *Supra* n. 4, s.c.r. 175
7 *Supra* n. 2   8 Ibid, 374

Both the *Cotter* and *Wagner* decisions were applied in *Albrecht* v *Imperial Oil Limited*,[9] which involved the breach of an offset drilling clause in a petroleum and natural gas lease. The creating well produced satisfactorily during the thirty-day period but, shortly thereafter, water began to intrude into the formation and led to the abandonment of the well within seven months after it had been placed on production. The plaintiff claimed damages for drainage of petroleum substances during the productive period of the creating well. In the light of evidence given by geological experts, the trial judge found that royalty payments which the plaintiff might have received from any production drained from his land would not exceed the trifling sum of $11.50. The main contention, however, arose over the claim for damages for breach of contract. Evidence at the trial indicated that the cost of drilling a well would amount to $40,000.00, with an additional $4,000.00 for production equipment. The court accepted geological evidence to the effect that a well on the plaintiff's land would be non-productive. Riley J rejected out of hand the cost of drilling the well as a basis for determining the damages, citing the *Cotter* and *Wagner* precedents.

American authorities, to the effect that the measure of damages for failure to drill an offset well is the amount of royalty the lessor would have received had the well been drilled, were quoted with approval. The geological evidence had, in the view of the court, affirmatively disproved that the plaintiff would have received any royalty whatsoever had the well been drilled on his land.

The plaintiff was not totally deprived of damages, however. The court correctly held that the *Cotter* case did not necessarily restrict the plaintiff to nominal damages. Once again the difficulty lay in establishing damages as a matter of evidence. The plaintiff had led evidence to the effect that, prior to the first well going to water, there had been offers of substantial cash considerations plus commitments to drill immediately; that the plaintiff had gone to the defendants and offered to purchase the lease back for the sum of $10,000.00; that they had been offered $3,000.00 for each one point of royalty – an offer they did not accept; and that, had the defendants spudded in the well on the plaintiff's land, each one point of the plaintiff's royalty would have increased in value to $6,000.00. The court felt that at the material time the plaintiff possessed a valuable asset. Riley J pointed out that the plaintiff had apparently refused the offer of $3,000.00 a point and that there was some doubt as to whether concrete offers in the amount of $6,000.00 per point would have been made if the well had been spudded, or accepted by the plaintiff, if made. Indeed, the spudding in of the offset well

9 (1957) 21 w.w.r. 560

would seem to affect only the possible increase in value of the points from $3,000.00 to $6,000.00. Nonetheless, the plaintiff was deprived of an opportunity to sell the whole or a portion of the points at an attractive price. Without attempting any detailed mathematical analysis, the court awarded damages in the sum of $6,000.00 for a loss of the opportunity to sell, plus $11.50 for the drainage claim.[10]

This case is interesting as an example of how a court, while inhibited by geological evidence that downgrades the property, nonetheless may conclude that the lessor is entitled to something more than purely nominal damages. While it was not cited in the *Albrecht* decision, an earlier Ontario case had developed a similar approach. In *Carson* v *Willitts*[11] the Ontario Court of Appeal declined to base damages on the cost of drilling, but was prepared to grant the lessor damages on the basis of a loss of a sporting or gambling chance that valuable oil or gas would be found if the drilling was performed.

Although the *Cotter* case has afforded much comfort to delinquent lessees over the years, its scope appears to have been severely restricted by *Sunshine Exploration Limited* v *Dolly Varden Mines Ltd. (NPL)*.[12] The dispute arose from a mining situation: the defendant had undertaken to carry out certain operations such as de-watering an existing mine, a substantial amount of diamond drilling to determine the extent of ore bodies, and other exploratory work. In return, the defendant received an assignment of an interest in the mining property, plus certain releases concerning alleged prior acts of default and extension of earning periods. The defendant did not carry out the work which it had agreed to do, and this failure admittedly terminated the agreement. It was also conceded that the defendant Sunshine was in breach of its

---

10 This decision and its predecessors are analysed in Ballem, 'Damages for Breach of Drilling Commitment' (1957), 35 *Can. Bar Rev.* 971; Bjornson, Boyd, Bredin, Brown, and MacWilliam, 'Problems in Development of Leased Lands' (1965), 4 *Alta. L. Rev.* 302, 306; see also Sychuk, 'Damages for Breach of an Express Drilling Covenant' (1970), 8 *Alta. L. Rev.* 250.

11 (1930) 65 D.L.R. 456; see also *Kranz* v *McCutcheon* (1920) 18 O.W.N. 395; 19 O.W.N. 161 (C.A.)
   In *Medalta Potteries Limited* v *Medicine Hat* [1931] 1 W.W.R. 217, purely nominal damages of $5 were awarded in a case which had some aspects of the failure to drill situation, but the plaintiff was required to have incurred expenditures as a condition to receiving a benefit under the breached contract. This feature makes it clearly distinguishable from the oil and gas lease where the lessor is not required to do anything other than receive the benefit of having the well drilled on his property.

12 (1970) 8 D.L.R. (3d) 441. The effect of this decision is discussed in Ballem, 'Some Second Thoughts on Damages for Breach of a Drilling Commitment' (1970), 48 *Can. Bar Rev.* 698.

obligations to carry out the work, and the sole issue was reduced to the quantum of damages. The defendant relied heavily on *Cotter* in support of its contention that only nominal damages should be awarded. The court refused to apply the *Cotter* decision and distinguished it on the ground that it was based upon the fact that no consideration had passed. In the *Sunshine* case there was valuable consideration because of the assignment of the interest and other items mentioned above.

This distinction of the *Cotter* case renders it virtually inapplicable to the normal offset drilling requirement in the oil and gas lease. It cannot be argued that a defendant lessee has not received consideration under the lease since, upon its execution, it grants substantial rights with respect to the mineral and the lessee immediately receives the benefit of those rights: to enter upon the lands, to drill, to explore, and to produce any substances. The consideration has passed in full and, moreover, the obligation under the offset clause is absolute once the conditions have been met.

The *Sunshine* decision held that the proper measure of damages was in fact the cost of performing the work that the defendant had obligated itself to do. The work which was described in the agreement would have been of advantage to the properties and the defendant undertook to perform that work, obviously because it considered the results would be of value. The plaintiff had given up a half interest in the property because, if the results of the work were favourable, it would obtain further development of the property, and in any event would be the recipient of useful information concerning the property. Both parties considered that the work would be worth the expense and Martland J pointed out that it would be of advantage to both. He rejected the test that seems to have been used in the oil and gas cases, namely that a comparison be made between the value of the mining property with and without the work being done, because the result of the work would be unknown. To a somewhat lesser extent this observation would be also true with respect to the drilling of an offset well, although geological evidence may be more persuasive in convincing a court that an offset well would likely be of little value to either party.

If *Cotter* has been sidelined by the Sunshine *ratio*, the question of damages for breach of the offset clause can only be described as open. The *Wagner* and *Albrecht* decisions cannot be of much help since they were influenced so heavily by *Cotter*. We seem to be left with the two Supreme Court mining decisions: *Cunningham* v *Insinger*[13] and *Sunshine* v *Dolly Varden*. Both these decisions used the cost of performing the work as the proper measure

13 [1924] S.C.R. 8

of damages, apparently because at the time of entering into the obligation both parties were of the view that the work was necessary in exploring and developing the property. This test can be applied in oil and gas situations. When the parties entered into a lease containing an offset obligation, presumably both of them were of the opinion that the drilling of an offset well under the stipulated conditions would be beneficial to the property, not only to protect it against drainage, but to explore its potential when the success of nearby drilling would justify it. Even if the offset well turned out to be non-productive, it would nonetheless yield useful, if negative, information concerning the lessor's property. If, however, the disappointing performance of the creating well and other drilling in the locality made it almost certain that the offset well would be non-commercial, it could be argued that at the time the obligation accrued, six months after the first well went on production, the parties could not have felt that the drilling of the offset well would be of substantial value to the property. Against this, there is always the argument that it is impossible to completely eliminate the prospect of a property being productive without the actual drilling of a well. A court would not be disposed, however, to award the very substantial damages that would be achieved by utilizing the cost of drilling if the geological evidence was overwhelming against any prospect of success. Under these conditions the court might be tempted to adopt the principle of awarding the lessor something for the loss of a gambling or sporting chance. If, however, there is an element of doubt in the geological evidence, a court might very well apply the cost of drilling as the proper principle.

While the type of clause described at the beginning of this chapter is still encountered in western Canada, the most common current form provides the lessee with a means of side-stepping the issue of damages. This is achieved by a version of the offset clause which, upon the prerequisites being fulfilled, confers upon the lessee an option either to drill the offset well or surrender the lands. While the mere termination of the lease would not affect the lessee's liability for an already accrued obligation to drill, the existence of an option to either drill or surrender does have the effect, inasmuch as, by the act of surrendering, the lessee will have done all that is required to do under the lease. Surrender satisfies the obligation created by the clause.

There are refinements of this procedure, one of which limits the lands which the lessee is obliged to surrender to the actual spacing unit on which the offset well would have been located, that is, the spacing unit laterally adjoining the one on which the creating well is located. The standard form also provides for the situation where production may, in fact, be obtained from the lands covered by the lease, but where the creating well obtains production from a formation other than that which is being produced under the lease. Under such circumstances the lessee, if it does not wish to drill, is required to surrender only those portions of the land other than the formation from which production is being obtained.

The standard clause now reads:

OFFSET WELLS

In the event of commercial production being obtained from any well drilled on any spacing unit laterally adjoining the said lands and not owned by the Lessor, or, if owned by the Lessor, not under lease to the Lessee, then unless a well has been or is being drilled on the spacing unit of the said lands laterally adjoining the said spacing unit on which production is being so obtained and to the horizon in the formation from which production is being so obtained, the Lessee shall, within six (6) months from the date of said well being placed on regular production, either:

(a) Commence or cause to be commenced within the six (6) month period aforesaid operations for the drilling of an offset well on the spacing unit of the said lands laterally adjoining the said spacing unit on which production is being so obtained, and thereafter drill the same to the horizon in the formation from which production is being obtained from the said adjoining spacing unit; or

(b) Surrender all or any portion of the said lands pursuant to the provisions of paragraph 14 hereof, provided that the lands surrendered shall include that portion of the said lands comprised in the said spacing unit laterally adjoining the said spacing unit on which production is being so obtained; or

(c) Where production is being obtained from the said lands from a formation other than the formation from which commercial production is being obtained on the spacing unit laterally adjoining the said lands, surrender all formations which lie within the said lands except that formation within the said lands from which the Lessee is obtaining production.

PROVIDED that, if such well drilled on lands laterally adjoining the said lands is productive primarily or only of natural gas, the Lessee shall not be obligated either to drill an offset well or to surrender said spacing unit unless and until an adequate and commercially profitable market for natural gas which might be produced from the offset well can be previously arranged and provided.

In view of the likelihood that future courts may award substantial damages for failure to drill an offset well, the alternative of surrendering is obviously very beneficial to the lessee. There appears to be merit in the approach exemplified in the current standard form since the lessee would not be anxious to surrender its interest unless it was satisfied by the geological evidence that there was very little prospect of success.

POOLING

Both oil and gas wells can drain the substances from a certain area within the reservoir. The drainage area will vary with the substances in question – gas being much more fugacious than oil – and the reservoir characteristics. Because of this, it would be economic folly to drill wells in a pattern denser than that required to effectively drain the reservoir. Conservation legislation and regulations uniformly provide for a limit on the density of the drilling patterns for both drilling and production purposes. In Alberta, for example, the normal drilling spacing unit for an oil well is a quarter section of one hundred and sixty acres, while the normal drilling spacing unit for a gas well is one section of six hundred and forty acres. This reflects the greater ability of gas to move through the reservoir. The legislation also provides for expansion or contraction of the normal spacing unit in response to reservoir conditions.

The conservation legislation also provides, generally, that before an operator can obtain a drilling licence he must prove that he has the appropriate rights with respect to the entire spacing unit. A similar situation exists when an operator applies for a licence to produce. This can create problems for the lessee, particularly in the case of a gas well. The quarter section, 160 acres, farm or ranch, is the most commonly encountered type of freehold mineral title in the west. Because of this, the great majority of petroleum and natural gas leases cover a quarter section; normally this will be sufficient for oil drilling purposes, but inadequate in gas areas. The standard pooling clause is designed to cover this situation.

POOLING

The Lessee is hereby given the right and power at any time and from time to time to pool or combine the said lands, or any portion thereof, or any zone or formation underlying the said lands or any portion thereof, with any other lands or any zone or formation underlying the same, but so that the lands so pooled and combined (herein referred to as a 'unit') shall not exceed One (1) spacing unit as hereinbefore defined. In the event of such pooling or combining, the Lessor shall, in lieu of the royalties elsewhere herein specified, receive on production of the leased substances from the said unit, only such portion of the royalties stipulated herein as the surface area of the said lands placed in the unit bears to the total surface area of lands in such unit. Drilling operations on, or production of the leased substances from, or the presence of a shut-in or suspended well on, any land included in such unit shall have the same effect in continuing this Lease in force and effect as to all the said lands, as if such operations or production were upon or from the said lands, or some portion thereof, or as if said shut-in or suspended well were located on the said lands, or some portion thereof.

The pooling clause empowers the lessee to combine the lands with the adjoining lands but only to the extent of one 'spacing unit' which is defined in the interpretation section as the area allocated to a well for the purpose of either drilling or producing under the existing conservation laws. Therefore, if a lease covers a quarter section in a gas area, the lessee can enter into pooling arrangements with the holders of the leases covering the remaining three-quarter sections and obtain a licence to drill a well.

The clause also makes the necessary adjustment to royalty, by providing that the royalties shall be apportioned on the basis of the ratio the surface area covered by the leases bears to the entire surface area comprised within the unit. If, for example, there were four leases, each comprising one hundred and sixty acres, each owner would be entitled to a royalty based on one-quarter of the production of a gas well regardless of where such well might be located within the spacing unit.

For the purpose of continuing the lease in force, it is essential to equate operations on the pooled lands to operations on the lands covered by the lease. That is the purpose of the final sentence in the clause which provides that drilling operations, production, or the presence of a shut-in or suspended well on any land included in the unit shall have the same effect insofar as the lease is concerned as if the same had taken place upon the said lands. This is a necessary step in preserving the lease and its importance was vividly dramatized by *Shell Oil Company* v *Gunderson*,[14] which is discussed in detail in Part 6 dealing with Involuntary Termination, *infra*. In the *Gunderson* case, the lease covering the particular quarter section on which the well was not located did not make any reference to shut-in or suspended wells, but referred only to drilling operations on, or production of leased substances from, any land included in the unit. The existence of a capped gas well on another quarter section within the unit and the tender of a capped gas well royalty to the lessor were held by the Supreme Court of Canada not to be sufficient to extend the primary term. Since the pooling clause contained no reference to suspended or shut-in wells, there was no basis for extending the definition of 'said lands' within the lease, and thus it was only the presence of a suspended or shut-in well on the actual lands covered by the lease, plus the appropriate payment of a capped gas well royalty, that would have preserved the lease.

The omission of suspended wells was a common feature of virtually every

14 [1960] s.c.r. 424

lease entered into through to at least 1961. Similarly, the early form contained additional language, not now included in the standard form, which also created difficulties for the lessee. The original form contained these words: 'when such pooling or combining is necessary in order to conform with any regulations or orders of the government of the province of ——— ——— or any other authoritative body, which are now or may hereafter be in force in relation thereto.'[15] It sounds innocuous enough, but its effect was to make pooling virtually impossible to achieve. In *Shell Oil Company* v *Gibbard*[16] the Supreme Court of Canada held that the effect of such wording was that pooling could only be accomplished when necessary to conform with the regulations. In the view of the court this condition could only be met when there was an affirmative and specific requirement that the lands be pooled. There is, of course, no such requirement in the conservation rules.[17]

The conservation regulations, however, do provide that, before a well can be placed on production, the operator must have the right to produce from the entire spacing unit. This requirement that it may be necessary to include the leased lands with other lands in order to obtain the approval of the Conservation Board to a spacing unit and to obtain a production permit was not judged by the Supreme Court to amount to the type of regulation or order that would activate the pooling clause.

If the pooling clause spells out the reason for pooling, this may be sufficient even if there is no affirmative regulation or order requiring such pooling. In *Canadian Superior Oil of California Ltd.* v *Kanstrup*[18] the lease originally did not contain a pooling clause. During the term of the lease, however, the lessee wrote the lessor requesting the addition of a pooling clause. The letter

---

15 See discussion in Mullane and Walker, 'The Pooling Clause and the Effects of Unitization on the Oil and Gas Lease' (1966), 44 *Can. Bar Rev.* 523.

16 [1961] S.C.R. 725, (1961–62) 36 W.W.R. 529

17 This is subject to an exception in that legislation provides for compulsory pooling under certain circumstances where the parties cannot agree. The sections of the acts that provide for such compulsory pooling also stipulate that operations, or production, or the presence of a shut-in well within the unit shall have the same effect as if they were carried on or located on the lands covered by the lease. For Alberta, see the Oil and Gas Conservation Act, *supra* n. 1, ss 82–86. The question as to whether a lease with an unenforceable pooling clause can be pooled on a compulsory basis remains open. s 82 (2) (c) requires the applicant to state that an agreement to pool cannot be made on reasonable terms. Can this statement be made when the lease contains a pooling clause, albeit a defective one? The point was not in issue in the *Gibbard* decision. See also, The Mines Act R.S.M. 1970, c M160 ss 68–73; Oil and Gas Conservation Act R.S.S. 1965, c 360 ss 30–33.

18 [1965] S.C.R. 92, 49 W.W.R. 257, 47 D.L.R. (2d) 1 (S.C.C.)

contained the new clause which was identical in all respects with the one in the Gibbard lease. After reciting the clause, the letter from the lessee went on to explain why it was required. It was pointed out that the area within which the leased lands were located was a gas area and that the spacing unit was 640 acres. The lessee wrote that it desired to pool the quarter section covered by the lease with the remainder of the lands in the section for the purpose of forming a spacing unit to drill a well. The lessor signed a copy of the letter, acknowledging and agreeing to the amendment of the lease. The Supreme Court of Canada said that under these circumstances it was prepared to hold that the lessee intended the clause to be construed as providing for pooling to enable it to establish a 640-acre spacing unit and to obtain a licence from the Conservation Board to drill a well. Since the lessee had stated the purpose for which it wished to pool the lands, the pooling clause was thereby effective even in the absence of any affirmative order or regulation. It should be noted, however, that the circumstances in the *Kanstrup* case on this point are unique and not likely to be repeated. The special conditions arising from the fact that the lessee stated the purpose of the pooling clause makes it clearly distinguishable under most circumstances and does not derogate from the original interpretation of such a pooling clause as expressed in *Gibbard*.

For all practical purposes then, the pooling clause contained in virtually every lease entered into until the early sixties is totally ineffective. The current standard form has overcome these two drawbacks by, in one case omitting the reference to orders and regulations and conferring an unfettered power to pool, and on the other by including a specific reference to the presence of a suspended or shut-in well. Incredibly enough, oil companies are still executing lease forms with the old type of pooling clause.

UNPOOLING

Once the leased lands are pooled with others to form a spacing unit, can they be subsequently unpooled by the unilateral act of the lessee? Most leases are silent on this point, but there are circumstances where this ability, or lack of it, could be significant. One form used by a major company includes the express power to dissolve a unit where no operations are being conducted within the unit. If a quarter section on which there is no well is pooled with lands on which a well is located, that well is treated for all intents and purposes as though it were on the leased lands. The well subsequently might be included in a unit with the lessor refusing to execute the unit agreement. Under these conditions the lessor would be entitled to claim royalties on the actual production from the well, which is likely to be substantially greater than the share of production allocated to the leased lands under the unitization formula.

It would seem that, if the lands were pooled by an affirmative act of the lessee, the only way in which they could be unpooled would be by mutual agreement between the lessor and the lessee. The ability to unpool under these circumstances would be valuable to the lessee as by so doing it could put pressure upon the lessor to agree to unitize or forego any royalties.

POOLING BY ZONE OR FORMATION

The pooling clause grants to the lessee the right to pool the lands not only in their entirety but also with respect to any zone or formation. This fragmentation of pooling enables the lessee to retain control over the nonproductive formations which may be unexplored and potential. Even if the pooling is limited to a particular formation, the effect of the last sentence in the pooling clause would appear to hold the balance of the lease and the unpooled formations in force without any further action on the part of the lessee. So long as the lessee either produces from the spacing unit well or pays the shut-in royalty, the lease will remain in force.[19]

AGENCY

Implementation of a pooling clause may create the possibility of a principal–agent relationship between lessor and lessee.[20] If so, the lessee will owe to the lessor that very high duty, amounting to a trust, that an agent must render to his principal. These responsibilities and how they may apply to an oil and gas lease are discussed in chapter 11 dealing with Unitization. If the act of pooling does in fact create the relationship, the lessee would be in a much better position to discharge an agent's duties than would be the case under unitization, since pooling involves a much smaller area of land, fewer parties and less possibility of a conflict in interest.

19 This is not necessarily so in some American jurisdictions, where the effect of pooling by formation has been construed as dividing the leased premises into unitized or non-unitized areas. Under these circumstances the lessee has been required to pay delay rentals to maintain the lease in force even with production from the unitized acreage. *Fremaux* v *Buie* 212 So 2d 148
20 'Problems in Development of Leased Lands,' *supra* n. 10, 302

9

Administrative and procedural provisions

The pooling clause marks the end of what might be called the substantive portion of the lease in that it deals with the actual grant of the minerals and what may be done with them. The remaining clauses, for the most part, constitute the machinery for administering the lessor–lessee relationship.

OPERATIONS

Oil and gas are inflammable, explosive, and volatile. In a word, they are dangerous substances. Under the lease the lessee is given the entire management and control over the operations connected with these substances.

The relationship between lessor and lessee is such as to create a duty on the lessee to protect the lessor against damage. The lessor retains a vested interest in the minerals; he is entitled to a royalty and, if the minerals are lost or dissipated through the negligence of the lessee, the lessor has suffered damages. There are three areas in which the negligent conduct of the lessee may cause damage to the lessor: (a) wasting of the reserves; (b) if the mineral owner is also the surface owner, his property may be damaged by escape of the substances or by the surface operations of the lessee; (c) the lessor may suffer personal injury as a result of an accident at the well.

What is the standard of care required of the lessee? The common law is deliberately unspecific in this field, saying only that the standard of conduct is that of the reasonable man.[1] In each case the court must take the objective test and apply it to the facts before it. The element of foreseeability plays an

1 Salmond, *On Torts* (15th ed.), 281

important role. For example, would a reasonable man foresee the possibility of damage or injury in a particular situation? The magnitude and nature of the risk also are factors. For operations under an oil and gas lease, the standard of care of the reasonable man would be that employed by a reasonable and prudent oil operator. The fact that oil and gas are highly dangerous substances would necessarily impose a greater degree of care. Gas in the distribution system of a utility company has been classified by the Privy Council as a 'dangerous thing' imposing strict liability upon the utility company.[2]

The standard clause in effect imports the common law duty of care: 'OPERATIONS: The Lessee shall conduct all its operations on the said lands in a diligent, careful and workmanlike manner and in compliance with the provisions of law applicable to such operations, and where such provisions of law conflict or are at variance with the provisions of this Lease, such provisions of law shall prevail.'

The reference to 'diligent, careful and workmanlike manner' obviously demands an objective standard by which it can be determined whether the operations were in fact 'careful and workmanlike.' The first question that the court must address itself to is whether the operations of the lessee complied with those methods and precautions that would be utilized by other operators within the oil industry. This, of course, requires expert testimony, but in most instances should be reasonably easy to establish since, over the years, the industry has built up a vast body of experience and operational techniques.

While the practice and custom of the industry will be of great importance in determining the liability of an operator and whether in fact the lessee was negligent, the matter does not necessarily end there. The lessee may be able to establish that its operations conformed in all respects with those used by the industry under identical conditions, but the court might still hold that the practice of the indusry was not the standard of care that should have been employed by a reasonable and prudent operator, bearing in mind the dangerous nature of the substances.

STRICT LIABILITY

The dangerous nature of the leased substances raises the possibility that the operator-lessee may be faced with absolute liability for any damage regardless of negligence. If there is to be absolute liability, it will be found in that area of law generally known as the Rule in *Rylands* v *Fletcher*,[3] which has

2 *Northwestern Utilities, Limited* v *London Guarantee and Accident Company, Limited* [1936] A.C. 108   3 [1868] L.R. 3 H.L. 330, 37 L.J.E. 161

been paraphrased by Salmond as follows: 'The occupier of land who brings and keeps upon it anything likely to do damage if it escapes is bound at his peril to prevent its escape, and is liable for all the direct consequences of its escape, even if he has been guilty of no negligence.'[4]

This rule has been extensively applied, distinguished, discussed, and refined by the courts in the intervening years.[5] It would seem, however, that the operations of a lessee in drilling or producing fulfil most, if not all, of the requirements for the application of the modern version of the rule. Certainly, the substances are dangerous; there may be some difficulty over the requirement of accumulating the substances, or bringing them upon the land, but there is the undoubted fact that by producing the well the lessee may cause substances to migrate onto the land from adjoining properties. Where secondary recovery with the injection of water or other substances is used to drive the petroleum substances towards the well bore, then the element of accumulation would seem to be clearly established. Moreover, subsequent cases seem to substitute the aspect of escape for accumulation.[6] The element of escape would certainly be present under situations where damage is caused to lessor's person or property, surface or underground. One of the refinements of the rule draws a distinction between natural and non-natural user of land and holds that the use must be non-natural before the liability is absolute. It has been argued that 'an ordinary, reasonable and proper operation to produce oil and gas should not be considered a non-natural user of the land.'[7] This is similar to a refinement to the effect that the rule does not apply to the land itself or to things which are the product of natural forces operating in geological time, such as outcrops of rock. However, while a person may not be liable for *allowing* the escape of such things naturally on his land, he is responsible for *causing* their escape.[8] It is clear from the nature of the operation itself that the lessee actively causes the escape of dangerous substances. Thus there remains a strong likelihood that the lessee who causes the escape of petroleum substances from their underground location is under a strict liability for any resulting damage.

If the parties are in a voluntary relationship with each other, such as that of lessor and lessee, they can reduce the measure of care or skill which one of them might otherwise be forced to attain.[9] The importation of a standard

4 *Supra* n. 1, 401
5 Ibid, 407–30
6 *Read* v *Lyons* [1947] A.C. 156
7 Lewis & Thompson, *Canadian Oil and Gas*, § 164E
8 *Whalley* v *Lancs. & Yorks. Ry.* [1884] 13 Q.B.D. 131. See also discussion in Salmond, *supra* n. 1, 417
9 Fleming, *The Law of Torts* (3rd ed.), 115

of care stated to be 'in a diligent, careful and workmanlike manner' may have the effect of excluding the absolute liability that might otherwise be imposed under *Rylands and Fletcher,* particularly in view of a subsequent clause in the lease which excludes any implied covenant or liability.

In the case of substances such as oil and gas, however, the distinction between absolute liability and that imposed under a standard of care concept, may be of little practical significance. 'Liability for inherently dangerous chattels is strict in all but name, since the standard of care is so stringent as to amount "practically to a guarantee of safety." '[10]

SURFACE DAMAGE

The concept of strict liability, or compensation regardless of negligence, is embodied in the standard clause on surface damage. 'COMPENSATION: The Lessee shall pay and be responsible for actual damages caused by its operations to the surface of, and growing crops and improvements on, the said lands.' The undertaking to reimburse the lessor for actual damages caused by operations under the lease is independent of any element of liability. It is of consequence only when the mineral lessor is also the owner of the surface. To some extent it may be a duplication of the documentation under which the surface rights are obtained. As mentioned in the discussion of the granting clause, surface rights in western Canada at least are not acquired under an oil and gas lease, but under a separate document known as a surface lease or, in the event of a failure to agree, by expropriation under the applicable provincial acts. The surface lease most commonly encountered in Canada contains a clause virtually identical with the one quoted above. If the rights are obtained by expropriation, the tribunal is empowered to award compensation for damage to the surface of land.[11]

INDEMNIFICATION

The lessor, as registered owner of the lands, has a direct connection with them and likely would be joined as a defendant by any third party suffering

10 Ibid, 306, *Adelaide Chemical Co.* v *Carlyle* [1940] 64 C.L.R. 514, 522
11 The Surface Rights Act 1972, S.A. c 91 s 12; The Mines Act R.S.M. 1970,
   c M160 s 20; The Surface Rights Acquisition Act s.s. 1968, c 73
      An oil and gas operator may be liable to a landowner in the absence of either
   an oil and gas lease or a surface lease on the grounds of nuisance, trespass, or
   negligence. In *Philips* v *California Standard Company* (1960) 31 W.W.R. 331, an
   operator was held liable for damages to a water well occasioned by seismograph

damages as a result of operations carried out under the lease. The lessor is indemnified against this event by the standard clause:

INDEMNIFICATION
The Lessee shall indemnify the Lessor against all actions, suits, claims and demands by any person or persons whomsoever in respect of any loss, injury, damage or obligation to compensate arising out of or connected with the work carried on by the Lessee on the said lands or in respect of any breach of any of the terms and conditions of this Lease insofar as the same relates to and affects the said lands.

The wording of this clause is wide and generalized. It would appear to protect the lessor against all third party liability arising from the lessee's work under the lease and by the use of the word 'loss' indemnifies the lessor not only against the amount of the claim asserted by an injured third party, but presumably against any out-of-pocket expenses, such as legal costs.

INFORMATION AND RECORDS

The information to which the lessor is entitled under the lease is sparse indeed. Under the standard clause the lessee is obliged only to: 'RECORDS OF PRODUCTION: The Lessee shall make available to the Lessor during normal business hours at the Lessee's address hereinafter mentioned the Lessee's records relative to the quantity of leased substances produced from the said lands.' Since the lessor's royalty share is computed on production, actual or allocated, the right to inspect the lessee's production records would seem to be the least that he is entitled to do. It is noted that the above clause merely refers to 'the lessee's records relative to the quantity of leased substances.' Presumably the lessor has to take the lessee's records as he finds them. It would be preferable to expand this clause by imposing upon the lessee an

work along the road allowance bordering the plaintiff's lands. This action was founded in nuisance and not trespass since the latter required a physical entry on the plaintiff's lands. In *McWilliams* v *Carlton Royalties Limited* [1938] 2 w.w.R. 351, the operator was held liable to the landowner for damages occasioned by drilling mud escaping from a sump where it had been collected during the drilling of an oil well. In *Kopf* v *Superior Oils Limited* (1951–52) 4 w.w.R. (N.S.) 682, the document in question was headed 'Instructions for Surface Lease' and signed by the parties. It was held to constitute the requisites for a valid lease and thus could be specifically enforced. It did not, however, contain a covenant to pay damages for destruction of the surface. The court was not prepared to imply such a covenant, but awarded damages on the basis of a tort, rather than by contract.

obligation to keep full and adequate accounts of all production from the said lands and to make those records available.

This is the only reference in the entire lease to information, records, or data to which the lessor may be entitled. The lease is silent on any information relating to drilling operations on the lands. It sometimes happens that an aura of secrecy shrouds these operations as the lessee will not want to disclose any information that would impair its ability to acquire a good land position in the area. But 'tight-hole' conditions are the exception rather than the rule and could be adequately provided for by express exceptions. Most drilling information is a matter of public record and there is no reason why the lessee should not provide the lessor with a condensed, general version of it. A mineral owner has more than a passing interest in whether a well is a potential producer or a dry hole.

ENCUMBRANCES

Since the lessor is the registered owner of the lands, he can by an express act or by omission create charges, liens, and defaults that encumber the interest in the land and could eventually lead to the extinction of his title and the defeat of the lessee's interest.[12] Obviously, the lessee cannot stand idly by while its title may be defeated by the act or omission of the lessor. The lessee's right to take action under such circumstances is contained in this standard clause:

DISCHARGE OF ENCUMBRANCES
The Lessee may at the Lessee's option pay or discharge the whole or any portion of any tax, charge, mortgage, lien or encumbrance of any kind or nature whatsoever incurred or created by the Lessor and/or the Lessor's predecessors or successors in title or interest which may now or hereafter exist on or against or in any way affect the said lands or the leased substances, in which event the Lessee shall be subrogated to the rights of the holder or holders thereof and may in addition thereto at the Lessee's option, reimburse itself by applying on the amount so paid by the Lessee the rentals, royalties, or other sums accruing to the Lessor under the terms of this Lease, and any rentals, royalties or such other sums so applied shall, for all purposes of this Lease, be deemed to have been paid to and received by the Lessor.

12 For example, The Mineral Taxation Act R.S.A. (1970), c 235, which provides for the cancellation of a lessor's certificate of title after the expiration of the required number of years following default in payment of taxes and vests title to the minerals in the Crown free and clear of encumbrances.

Even in the absence of the above clause, the lessee would have the right to redeem, at least with respect to a mortgage: 'Any person entitled to an estate carved out of the mortgagor's estate is entitled to redeem, subject, of course, to any paramount equities which affect the estate.'[13] The lessee under a mineral lease, being the owner of a *profit à prendre*, has an interest sufficient to exercise the right of redemption.[14] In Saskatchewan, a mineral lessee who has redeemed a mortgage has the right by statute to have the mortgage assigned, rather than discharged.[15]

The clause enlarges this right of redemption to include any tax, charge, mortgage, lien, or any kind of encumbrance. It also subrogates the lessee to the rights of the holder or holders thereof and allows the lessee to reimburse itself from rentals, royalties, or other sums accruing to the lessor. This right of reimbursement would appear to be inconsistent with, in the case of a mortgage, the statutory right to require a transfer of the mortgage. If the lessee demanded and obtained such a transfer, that would appear to extinguish any right of reimbursement from proceeds due under the lease.

The right of reimbursement also extends to rentals due under the lease. Presumably the reference is to the 'delay rental' defined in the first proviso to the *habendum* clause. Since the term 'delay rental' is expressly defined as meaning a payment which might not be considered a rental, the reference should be amended to expressly include the term 'delay rental as defined.' In view of the extreme strictness which the courts have used in determining whether or not a delay rental has been properly paid and the disastrous consequences of any failure to do so, a prudent lessee would be well advised to continue making delay rental payments and not seek reimbursement from those payments, even though the clause expressly provides that the rentals shall be deemed to have been paid to and received by the lessor.

SURRENDER

The lessee has a unilateral right to surrender.

SURRENDER

Notwithstanding anything herein contained, the Lessee may at any time or from time to time determine or surrender this Lease and the term hereby granted as to the whole or any part or parts of the leased substances and/or the said lands, upon giving the Lessor written notice to that effect, WHEREUPON this Lease and

---

13 *Tarn* v *Turner* (1888) 57 L.J. c 452, 58 L.T. 558, aff'd (1888) 39 Ch. D. 456
14 *Gallagher* v *Gallagher* (1962–63) 40 W.W.R. 35 (Sask. C.A.)
15 The Land Titles Act R.S.S. (1965), c 115, s 136(2)

the said term shall terminate as to the whole or any part or parts thereof so surrendered and the rental, royalty or otherwise, shall be extinguished or correspondingly reduced as the case may be, but the Lessee shall not be entitled to a refund of any such rent theretofore paid.

The right to surrender is much more vital in an 'or' type of lease than in the more typical 'unless' form. If the lessee under an 'or' type did not have the right to surrender, then it would remain liable for each yearly rental during the primary term, regardless of whether or not it had any real desire to maintain the lease in force. With the right of surrender, the lessee can avoid a constantly accruing liability for yearly rentals, provided it is prepared to give up its interest in the lease.

The right of surrender granted to the lessee by the standard clause can be fragmented both as to area and zone. If the lessee desires, it may surrender any portion of the said lands or the leased substances. The right to surrender a portion of the acreage covered by the lease clearly emerges from 'or any part or parts of ... the said lands,' while the reference to 'leased substances' is meaningful only if it refers to geological zones or formations. If there is a partial surrender on an area basis, there is provision for a corresponding reduction of the rental, but this result would not seem to follow in the case of a surrender by zone. In the latter case there is no mechanism for determining the proper apportionment of rental as among the surrendered and retained zones.

The standard clause also contains a confusing reference to royalty: 'the rental, royalty or otherwise.' Royalty, *per se*, cannot be reduced by a partial surrender as it depends on the actual quantity of production from the lands and nothing else. One could guess that the reference is meant for a suspended well payment which would in fact be reduced as it tracks the delay rental payment, and would be reduced automatically.

The lessee cannot escape liability for already accrued obligations by the act of surrender. By the express wording of the clause, the lessor is not required to refund any rent that may have been advanced. Here again the word 'rent' seems to be a misnomer and the reference should be to a delay rental.

REMOVAL OF CAVEATS AND REGISTERED DOCUMENTS

The lessee will protect its interest under the lease by registration in the appropriate land titles office. Usually the registration takes the form of a caveat, but occasionally the lease itself will be registered. As a matter of mechanics, the lease provides that upon its termination any such caveat or registered document will be withdrawn or discharged from the lessor's title:

'REMOVAL OF CAVEAT: In the event of the Lessee having registered in the Land Titles Office for the area in which the said lands are situated this Lease or any caveat or other document in respect thereof, the Lessee shall withdraw or discharge the document so registered within a reasonable time after termination of this Lease.' A mineral owner should ensure that any registration is discharged. Otherwise the title would indicate that the lands are subject to an existing lease and so discourage any new attempts at leasing.

REMOVAL OF EQUIPMENT

Once the lease has been terminated, ordinarily the lessee has no further status with respect to the said lands and any further entry would amount to trespass. However, some machinery, equipment, and other materials used for drilling, production, or other operations may still be on the lands at the time of termination. The lease makes an attempt to confer the right to enter and remove such equipment for a period of time after termination: 'REMOVAL OF EQUIPMENT: The Lessee shall at all times during the currency of this Lease and for a period of Six (6) months from the termination thereof, have the right to remove all or any of its machinery, equipment, structures, pipe lines, casing and materials from off the said lands.' Similar provisions are to be found in most surface leases. Insofar as surface installations are concerned, it would appear that the right of removal is more appropriately granted under the surface lease.

Notwithstanding the express right in both the oil and gas and surface lease, it is doubtful if the lessee would have the right to remove underground equipment where such removal would impair the ability of a well to produce. This situation is most often encountered where the lease has been terminated against the desire of the lessee. Usually the lease that is terminated under such circumstances will cover a productive property. The removal of equipment would undoubtedly constitute a violation of the existing conservation laws in each province and amount to a waste or a potential waste of the resources of the province. Hence, a former lessee could be prevented from pulling out well casing and, possibly, production tubing.

There is an interesting question as to the duty, if any, of a lessor to reimburse the former lessee for the cost of such equipment or the cost of drilling the well. The Saskatchewan Court of Appeal, in an approach which was subsequently endorsed by the Supreme Court of Canada,[16] allowed recovery to a lessee where there had been production for some years from a lease

16 *Sohio Petroleum Co.* v *Weyburn Security Co. Ltd.* (1970) 74 W.W.R. 626 (S.C.C.); 69 W.W.R. 680, 7 D.L.R. (3d) 277 (C.A.); see also discussion in chapter 15, *infra*

which had, unknown to the parties, expired on its own terms prior to being placed on production. The court found it 'just and equitable' to fix the point of time beyond which the former lessee must account for all production as the date on which the action was commenced. The court noted that by the cut-off date the revenue which the lessee had received from the sale of production exceeded the amount it had expended.

By analogy it could be argued that, if a lease were terminated before the former lessee had recovered its expenditures from production, the owner might be required to reimburse the former lessee for any outstanding balance with respect to the equipment or drilling cost. This result may not be so easily achieved when the court must require the owner to actually lay out cash to the former lessee as when it is merely a matter of accounting for production already taken and sold.

PROCEDURE IN THE EVENT OF DEFAULT

The lease contains machinery for dealing with defaults by the lessee in the performance of any obligation thereunder. Such default does not result in automatic termination since the lessee is granted a time within which to remedy such default. The standard clause provides a grace period of ninety days.

In the case of the breach or non-performance on the part of the Lessee of any covenant, proviso, condition, restriction or stipulation herein contained which ought to be observed or performed by the Lessee and which has not been waived by the Lessor, the Lessor shall, before bringing any action with respect thereto or declaring any forfeiture, give to the Lessee written notice setting forth the particulars of and requiring it to remedy such default, and in the event that the Lessee shall fail to commence to remedy such default within a period of Ninety (90) days from receipt of such notice, and thereafter diligently proceed to remedy the same, then except as hereinafter provided, this Lease shall thereupon terminate and it shall be lawful for the Lessor into or upon the said lands (or any part thereof in the name of the whole) to re-enter and the same to have again, repossess and enjoy; PROVIDED that this Lease shall not terminate nor be subject to forfeiture or cancellation if there is located on the said lands a well capable of producing the leased substances or any of them, and in that event the Lessor's remedy for any default hereunder shall be for damages only.

The first thing to be noted about the clause is that it relates only to covenants, provisos, conditions, restrictions, or stipulations. In the early cases involving termination for failure to pay delay rental on time, this clause was relied upon by the lessee as requiring both notice of default and time to remedy it. The courts rejected this approach and held that, since under the 'unless' type of lease the lessee was not obligated to pay the delay rental, it could not be treated as coming within the scope of 'covenant, proviso, condition, restriction or stipulation.'[17]

Although it never seems to have been argued before the courts, it is possible that this clause could be held to apply to the shut-in well royalty which, once the conditions are met, appears to require the lessee to pay to the lessor a sum equal to the delay rental. The operative words of the shut-in well clause are: 'The lessee shall pay to the lessor ... a sum equal to the delay rental hereinbefore set forth.' If the use of the word 'shall' is construed as making it mandatory for the lessee to make the payment, then it would seem to be an obligation that would fit under the default clause. The counter-argument runs that the structure of the lease is such that the lessee is not obligated to pay shut-in royalty, since by failing so to do the lease would terminate, and in essence the lessee's decision to pay or not to pay becomes an option. The wording of the shut-in well clause, on the surface at least, seems to impose upon the lessee an absolute obligation to pay the royalty. It is true that the obligation can be extinguished by an act of surrender, but without that it appears to be an unrestricted obligation to pay. This would meet the test laid down in *Chipp* v *Hunt*[18] that it was an obligation which the lessee is legally required to perform.

If we assume that a lessee is in breach of a clear-cut obligation under the lease, such as to pay royalty on actual production or to drill an offset well, the lessor must follow a set procedure to enforce whatever rights he may have. He must first give written notice to the lessee specifying the particulars of the default and requiring the lessee to remedy same. The lessee then has 90 days from the receipt of the notice to commence to cure the default. It is important to note that the lessee is not required to complete any remedial action within the 90-day period, but only to *commence* such action, and thereafter to diligently proceed with the corrective measures. If the lessee does not commence to remedy the default within the 90-day period, the lease will terminate unless a well capable of production is located on the said lands. In such event the lessor's remedy is limited to damages and the lease will not be terminated.

The default clause plays a legitimate role in the structure of the lease. It prevents termination for a purely technical or nominal breach and yet gives

---

17 *East Crest Oil Company Limited* v *Strohschein* (1951–52) 4 w.w.r. (n.s.) 553
18 (1955) 16 w.w.r. 209 (Alta.)

the lessor a weapon he can use to enforce compliance with the terms of the lease.

WARRANTY OF TITLE AND COVENANT OF QUIET ENJOYMENT

The heading in the standard clause refers only to 'quiet enjoyment.' This can be misleading since the actual clause includes a warranty of title as well.

QUIET ENJOYMENT

The Lessor covenants and warrants that he has good title to the leased substances and the said lands as hereinbefore set forth, has good right and full power to grant and demise the same and the rights and privileges in manner aforesaid, and that the Lessee, upon observing and performing the covenants and conditions on the Lessee's part herein contained, shall and may peaceably possess and enjoy the same and the rights and privileges hereby granted during the said term and any extension thereof without any interruption or disturbance from or by the Lessor or any other person whomsoever.

The language of the clause imposes an absolute liability for title failure upon the lessor. If title failed, the lessee could sue him and be awarded damages which, under proper circumstances, would be of staggering proportions. It is unlikely the average lessor realizes that by signing a lease he has undertaken such a potentially enormous liability. There are no recorded instances where a lessee has attempted to invoke such a right against a lessor, but there is no doubt that such a claim could be advanced. The warranty of title on the part of the lessor seems inconsistent with the practice followed in the industry, whereby the lessee normally investigates any freehold mineral title with great care. If the bonus consideration under a lease is for a relatively insignificant amount, the lessee usually relies upon the current certificate of title. Before undertaking the expense of drilling a well, however, or paying a substantial bonus consideration, the lessee should, and usually does, conduct an historic search of the lessor's title. A prudent lessor should insist on the deletion of the warranty of title.

The balance of the clause amounts to an unqualified covenant for quiet enjoyment. The language goes beyond the type of covenant usually encountered in conventional landlord–tenant relationships since it is unqualified and applies not only to interruption or disturbance by the lessor or anyone claiming under him, but also from any person whomsoever. Since the covenant for quiet enjoyment was imported from the law of landlord and tenant, one would expect it to have the same scope under the oil and gas lease. The acts of interference must be physical[19] and a breach of the covenant may be restrained by an injunction.[20] The effect of the covenant is very similar to the legal principle that a person shall not derogate from his own grant. A typical example of a breach of the covenant would occur if the lessor erected a fence around the wellsite and attempted to prevent the lessee from gaining access to the well. The split between surface rights and grants of mineral rights may create some confusion in this area, and the lessee should have the covenant in both the oil and gas lease and the surface lease.

The inclusion of 'or any other person whomsoever' broadens the application of the covenant and makes the lessor responsible for disturbance of the lessee's quiet enjoyment even by strangers. This appears to be an unjustifiable extension of his responsibility, and it is suggested that the lessor should not be liable for interference except by himself and those claiming through him.

Under a conventional lease of land, a covenant for quiet enjoyment would be implied if there were no express provisions. Although an oil and gas lease is not a lease in the proper sense of the word, it is likely that such a covenant would be implied in the absence of an express provision, subject always to the effect of the entire agreement clause discussed *infra*. The covenant exists only during the term of the lease and is ended upon its termination. The sometimes energetic actions by lessors to establish that a lease has lapsed are not in any way violations of the covenant for quiet enjoyment, but are merely attempts to define the legal status of the lease.

FURTHER ASSURANCE

COVENANT FOR FURTHER ASSURANCE

The Lessor and the Lessee hereby agree that they will each do and perform all such acts and things and execute all such deeds, documents and writings and give all such assurance as may be necessary to give effect to this Lease and all covenants herein contained.

The intent of the foregoing standard clause is clear, but there is a question as to its scope. It is obviously designed as a curative measure and is one of the fundamental covenants that are now implied by statute under the English property law.[21] Presumably it would assist the lessee in cases such as these: If the land were mis-described, the lessor could be required to execute a

---

19 *Browne* v *Flower* [1911] 1 Ch. D. 219.
20 *Allport* v *Securities Corporation* (1895) 64 L.J. Ch. D. 491
21 Megarry and Wade, *The Law of Real Property*, 559

document remedying such defect. Where the seal has been omitted, the lessor may be compelled to affix one. The counter-argument to this is that, if, for example, the seal were not affixed, the document would not be an effective grant. Therefore, the covenant never came into existence. More likely, however, the covenant would be enforced between the two parties. The covenant will not assist the lessee where the act of further assurance is to be done by someone other than the lessor. For example, if the homestead or dower affidavit has been improperly taken, the covenant could not be used to force the lessor's spouse to remedy the defect.

ASSIGNMENT

Both parties have a virtually unrestricted right to assign their interest in the lease.

ASSIGNMENT

The parties hereto may each or either of them delegate, assign, sub-let or convey to any other person or persons, corporation or corporations, all or any of the property, powers, rights and interests obtained by or conferred upon them respectively hereunder and may enter into all agreements, contracts and writings and do all necessary acts and things to give effect to the provisions of this clause; PROVIDED that no assignment of royalties or other moneys payable hereunder shall be binding upon the Lessee, notwithstanding any actual or constructive notice or knowledge thereof, unless and except the same be for the entire interest of the Lessor in all of the said sums remaining to be paid or to accrue hereunder, nor then until Thirty (30) days after the Lessee has been actually furnished at its address hereinafter set forth with evidence satisfactory to the Lessee of such assignment of the entire interest of the Lessor in all the sums aforesaid, including, if effected by voluntary act, the original or a certified copy of the instrument effecting such assignment; PROVIDED FURTHER that in the event that the Lessee shall assign this Lease as to any part or parts of the said lands, then the delay rental shall be apportioned amongst the several leaseholders rateably according to the surface area of each, and should the Assignee or Assignees of any such part or parts fail to pay the proportionate part of the delay rental payable by him or them, such failure to pay shall not operate to terminate or affect this Lease insofar as it relates to and comprises the part or parts of the said lands in respect of which the Lessee or its Assignees shall make due payment of rental.

The first portion of the clause sets forth the untrammelled rights of either party to assign without the necessity of consent from the other. The provisos, however, reflect the lessee's preoccupation with making the payments required to keep the lease in force. As has been demonstrated repeatedly, proper payment of the delay rental is critical to the continued existence of the lease. An assignment of the lessor's interest in the lease can create situations where the lessee may inadvertently pay the rental to the wrong person. The outstanding example of this difficulty is to be found in *Langlois* v *Canadian Superior Oil of California Ltd.*,[22] where the lease was dated October 12, 1948, and there was an assignment during one of the years of the primary term, namely, on June 14, 1954. Notice of this assignment was received by the lessee on September 14 of that year and on the same day the lessee sent a change of depository agreement to be executed and returned by the new assignees. This agreement signed by the assignees was returned to Canadian Superior with a letter dated September 30, 1954, and on October 5, 1954, the lessee returned a copy of the depository agreement duly executed by it. In the meantime, on October 1, 1954, the lessee sent its cheque payable to the depository bank for the credit of the former lessor. The amount of the cheque was duly credited to his account, so the new assignees did not receive any payment. This failure to make proper payment was held to terminate the lease by virtue of its own terms.

The first proviso to the assignment clause is designed to avoid this unhappy result. It attempts to do this by providing that no assignment of royalties or other monies 'shall be binding upon the lessee' regardless of any notice that the lessee may have unless it is for the entire interest of the lessor in all of the sums to be paid. In addition, it does not become binding until a period of 30 days after the lessee has been furnished with evidence of the assignment. Such evidence, moreover, must be satisfactory to the lessee.

The first requirement that the assignment be of the entire amount of the monies payable obviously is meant to protect the lessee against the hazards of fragmented payments. Reading this condition in the light of the opening portion of the assignment clause, it would appear that, while the lessor may assign a portion of the interest covered by the lease, the assignment of any monies payable thereunder can be only of the entire amount if it is to bind the lessee.

The second condition of the proviso allows the lessee a period of time to get its records in order.

It is relatively easy to determine the purpose that the first proviso is meant to achieve, but the imprecision of the language is troublesome. The proviso states that, unless and until the conditions are met, no assignment 'shall be binding upon the lessee.' What is the situation where the 30-day period has not expired but the lessee, being fully aware of the assignment and of the

22 (1957) 23 w.w.r. 401 12 d.l.r. (2d) 53

identity of the new assignee, makes payment to him rather than to the original lessor? Can that be considered a good payment? Can the lessee, in effect, elect to be bound by the assignment despite the language of the proviso? It would appear that, if the date for the payment of a delay rental occurs during the 30-day period, the lessee in order to be secure must pay the assignor. There is also considerable elasticity in the 30-day period; it starts when the lessee 'has been actually furnished' with evidence satisfactory to it of the assignment. Presumably the use of the word 'furnish' means that the lessee must be in receipt of the evidence before the 30-day period starts to run. There is also a note of uncertainty inasmuch as the evidence 'must be satisfactory to the lessee.' The further reference to the original or certified copy of the instrument creating such assignment is an indication that this would be evidence satisfactory to the lessee. Would something less than that be evidence satisfactory to the lessee? Would an uncertified copy of the instrument be satisfactory evidence? Presumably it would, but under the wording of the clause one could not be certain. Although the test is expressed to be a subjective one in that the evidence must be satisfactory to the lessee, a court would probably be prepared to substitute an objective standard and hold that under certain circumstances the evidence should have been satisfactory to the lessee.[23]

The whole thrust of the proviso is to avoid the hazards of a faulty payment when an assignment is made near the anniversary date. The draftsman attempts to achieve this objective through the broad brush approach of making the assignment not 'binding' until the requirements have been met. Inasmuch as the parties to a contract can make law for themselves so long as they do not infringe on legal prohibitions or public policy,[24] a court might interpret this language to accomplish the desired result. In view of the strictness which the courts have employed in interpreting an oil and gas lease, one cannot be too sanguine that the words would be so interpreted. Surely it would be preferable to provide that any payment made to the lessor during the 30-day period would be deemed conclusively to be proper payments within the meaning of the lease.

The second proviso is the other side of the coin and likewise is directed

23 See *California Standard Company* v *McBride* (1963) 38 D.L.R. (2d) 606, where the Alberta Appellate Division held that a receipt which postponed payment until 'the Company's solicitors being satisfied that my title to the mines and minerals covered by the said Lease is valid and that the said Lease is a valid and subsisting agreement and that they form a first charge against the title to the said mines and minerals' did not make the instrument void for uncertainty. The document required payment when the Lessor produced, as the court found, a good title.

24 *Anson's Law of Contract* (23rd ed.) (1969), 1

towards payment of the delay rental. It deals with assignments by the lessee of a portion of the lands and in such event apportions the delay rental among the several leaseholders according to their respective shares of the surface area. For example, if the lease covered a full section and a quarter section was assigned to a third party, then the original lessee and the assignee would be responsible for the payment of delay rentals in the ratio of three to one.

It should be noted that the only allocation is one based on surface acreage. There is no mention of assignment by zone or formation. Under such an assignment the original lessee must continue to make payments directly to the lessor and seek reimbursement from the assignee. The assigning lessee's position is further protected by providing that, if the assignees of any part or parts of the lands fail to pay their proportionate part of the delay rental, this does not operate to terminate or affect the lease insofar as it relates to those portions where proper payment was made. The objective is clear, but one must be sceptical as to whether a partial payment can maintain a lease partially in force. The drilling proviso to the *habendum* clause is explicit as to the precise sum of money that must be paid and what happens if it is not. The payment of the delay rental is an option which the courts traditionally interpret with great strictness. This approach, together with the demonstrated reluctance to treat the grant and term clauses as being modified or amended by subsequent provisions,[25] makes it at least questionable if a partial payment could be effective. The lessee should rely on it only as a last resort under conditions where it is too late to make a full and timely payment.

MANNER OF PAYMENT

The lessor becomes entitled to a payment of money for a variety of reasons under the lease. The reasons include: the delay rental, royalties on production, a suspended well, reimbursement of taxes, and sometimes compensation for damages caused by operations. The delay rental payment is by far the most critical since it is the only one which may involve an automatic termination of the lease. The drilling proviso to the *habendum* requires that the lessee, in order to defer drilling operations, 'shall have paid or tendered to the lessor.' The use of this language by itself would seem to require the lessee to seek out the lessor personally and to pay him, or make tender, in cash.[26] Virtually every form of lease relieves the lessee from this onerous burden by

25 *Shell Oil Company* v *Gunderson* [1960] S.C.R. 424, 23 D.L.R. (2d) 81 (S.C.C.); see also *Canadian Superior Oil Ltd.* v *Kanstrup* [1965] S.C.R. 92, 49 W.W.R. 257, 47 D.L.R. (2d) 1, (S.C.C.), where the court refused to treat the *habendum* as modified by the *force majeure* clause
26 *Shockey* v *Molnar* [1948] 2 W.W.R. 1087; *Bishop* v *Gray* [1944] 3 D.L.R. 541; affirmed [1944] 4 D.L.R. 743 (Ont. C.A.)

a special provision relating to the manner in which payment may be made. One feature of the Manner of Payment clause has been subjected to judicial scrutiny. The early form – which is still frequently used today – envisaged payments either being *mailed* or *delivered* to the lessor without going into detail as to the effect of mailing.

MANNER OF PAYMENT
All payments to the Lessor provided for in this Lease shall, at the Lessee's option, be paid or tendered either to the Lessor or to the depository named in or pursuant to this clause, and all such payments or tenders may be made by cheque or draft of the Lessee either mailed or delivered to the Lessor or to said depository, which cheque or draft shall be payable in Canadian funds at par in the bank on which it is drawn. The Lessor does hereby appoint .... as the depository for the receipt of all moneys payable under this Lease, and the Lessor agrees that said depository and its successors shall be and continue as his agents for the receipt of any and all sums payable hereunder regardless of changes of owner-ship (whether by assignment, succession or otherwise) of the said lands or of the leased substances or of the rentals or royalties to accrue hereunder. The Lessor may at any time designate a new depository by giving written notice to the Lessee specifying the name and address of such new depository; PROVIDED that only a bank or trust company in Canada may be designated as depository, that only one depository shall be designated at any one time as aforesaid, and that the Lessee shall not be required to recognize any change of depository until the expiration of forty-five (45) days from the receipt by the Lessee of the notice in writing aforesaid. If any depository designated by the Lessor shall at any time resign or fail or refuse to act as depository and a successor depository shall not be designated as aforesaid within ten (10) days thereafter, or if any moneys payable hereunder become payable to more than one person and the persons to whom said moneys are payable shall have failed to designate one depository hereunder, then the Lessee may at its option designate a bank or trust company in Canada as depository hereunder, which depository shall be entitled to charge its usual fees, and said bank or trust company shall be the depository to all intents and purposes as if originally designated herein by the Lessor.

The clause affords the lessee considerable scope in making payment. It can now be made either directly to the lessor or to a depository and it can be either mailed or delivered.

TIME OF PAYMENT

The precise meaning of the phrase 'either mailed or delivered' after years of doubt has now been determined by the Supreme Court of Canada. The unresolved question was whether the phrase equates the act of mailing with delivery or must there be an actual receipt of the payment by the lessor or the depository prior to the expiration of the time period? The issue was first put in question by the Alberta Appellate Division which, in *Canadian Fina Oil Ltd.* v *Paschke*,[27] stated that, while the phrase conferred the privilege of making payment by mail, the payment nonetheless must *arrive* within the stipulated time.

After an interval of nearly fourteen years, this statement was categorized by the Alberta Appellate Division as *obiter dicta* and was not followed. In *Texas Gulf Sulphur Company* v *Ballem*[28] the court held that the mailing of a cheque prior to the expiration of the time period was equivalent to making payment directly to the lessor or to the depository and, so long as the mailing was done by the required date, the lease would be continued in force. This approach was subsequently affirmed by the Supreme Court.[29] The same conclusion was reached in *Paramount Petroleum and Mineral Corporation Limited et al* v *Imperial Oil Limited*,[30] where the Saskatchewan Trial Division held the words to mean that mailing by itself constituted compliance with the payment requirements of the lease.[31]

The doubt that for so many years clouded the effect of mailing led to the insertion of a specific provision. It is the only change in the current standard form; otherwise the clause is identical with the one quoted at the beginning of this section. The amendment provides: 'A cheque or draft in payment of delay rentals which is mailed by deposit in one of Her Majesty's Mail Boxes or Post Offices at least Forty-eight (48) hours prior to each anniversary date shall be deemed to have been received by the addressee in sufficient time to confer the privilege of deferring the commencement of drilling operations for a period of one (1) year from each such anniversary date.' This rather complex provision cures the uncertainty that existed after the *Paschke dicta*, but has been rendered unnecessary by the *Texas Gulf* v *Ballem* decision.

It should be noted that the amendment refers only to delay rentals and not to any other payments. The delay rental is the only deadly one that extinguishes the lease if it is not made on time.

27 (1957) 21 w.w.r. 260; 7 d.l.r. (2d) 473 (c.a.); 19 w.w.r. 184 (Alta.)
28 (1970) 72 w.w.r. 273 (c.a.); (1969) 70 w.w.r. 373 (Alta.)
29 *Ballem* v *Texas Gulf Sulphur Co.* [1971] 1 w.w.r. 560
30 (1970) 73 w.w.r. 417
31 American authorities hold that 'proper mailing' prior to the expiration of the critical period is sufficient. Summers, *Oil and Gas* vol. 2, s 344, 433. 'An oil and gas lease may provide for the payment of delay rentals by the mailing of a cheque, draft or other form of remittance to the Lessor. In such a situation the postal service is made the Lessor's agent to deliver the remittance, and proper mailing, although it is never delivered, constitutes payment.'

Since *Texas Gulf* v *Ballem*, the standard clause would be improved by deleting the addition and restoring the old form. The new wording not only creates the unnecessary requirement that the payment be mailed at least 48 hours before the anniversary date, it also creates a potential conflict with the preceding language 'either mailed or delivered,' which permits the mailing to be done effectively up to the critical date.

SUFFICIENCY OF PAYMENT

Payment may be in the form of cheque or draft of the lessee and such cheque or draft must be payable in Canadian funds at par in the bank on which it is drawn. Since the courts regard deferment of the drilling commitment by payment of a delay rental to be in the nature of an option, it is imperative that the payment be for not less than the precise amount required. For example, if the bank deducted even a small handling charge, this would probably jeopardize the payment. An overpayment would be valid but any shortfall would make the payment ineffective.[32]

The issue of the sufficiency of a payment was raised but not effectively dealt with in *Paramount Petroleum and Mineral Corporation and Bison Petroleum & Minerals Limited* v *Imperial Oil Limited*.[33] In this case the lessors were residents of the United States, and the lessee deducted and withheld the non-resident withholding tax from a payment of the delay rentals. In the result the sum of money received by the lessor was fifteen per cent less than the amount of delay rental specified in the lease.

Unfortunately, from the point of view of clarifying the law, the real attack on the lease was what the plaintiffs conceived to be a late payment of the delay rental. The issue as to the sufficiency of the payment was not mentioned in the pleadings and was raised for the first time in written argument following the trial. The Saskatchewan trial judge treated the contention as being merely 'an afterthought on the part of the plaintiffs,' and declined to give effect to it as the defendant had not had the opportunity to meet it with appropriate evidence. The court did not, however, decide on the merits of the argument itself.

---

32 See, generally, discussion on Tender, Di Castri, *Canadian Law of Vendor and Purchaser* (1968), para. 469–75; *Mus* v *Matlashewski* [1944] 3 w.w.r. 358 (Man.) – the insignificance of the deficiency is immaterial; *Carlson* v *Jorgenson Logging Company Limited* (1952) 6 w.w.r. (N.S.) 298 (B.C.); proper payment a condition precedent to option. Brown, *The Law of Oil and Gas Leases* (2 ed.) sec. 7.07, 7.08, examines the American authorities and concludes that, where the failure to make payment of the proper amount is due to the fault of the lessee, 'there is a strong probability that the lease will be held to have terminated.'

33 *Supra* n. 30

It would seem arguable that, since the lessee is required by Section 212 (1)(d) of the Income Tax Act, 1972, to make such a withholding, it should not be penalized for complying with the law of the land. Nonetheless, until the matter has been finally resolved by the court of last resort, a lessee would be well advised to make payment in such amount that a non-resident lessor receives not less than the full amount specified in the lease. This, of course, constitutes an overpayment, but the uncertainty of the other course makes it a sensible precaution for the lessee.

DEPOSITORY

The initial depository is appointed by filling in the blank within the clause and a new one may be designated by written notice to the lessee. The clause limits the ranks of a depository to a bank or a trust company in Canada. It also provides that there shall also be only one depository and that any change in the depository shall not be recognized by the lessee until 45 days after receipt by it of notice. This is another reflection of the lessee's anxiety regarding the critical payment of delay rentals. It is an attempt to avoid any confusion and possible error that might occur if a depository were changed near the due date. The lessee is not compelled to wait out the 45 days before acting on the change of depository; the change may be recognized prior to the expiration of the 45-day period. Although there is no specific prohibition against the lessor cancelling the appointment of a depository without appointing a replacement, it is doubtful if he has this power. The clause provides that the depository and its successors 'shall be and continue as his agents,' and this is followed by the right to designate a new depository. The clause clearly envisages the existence of a depository at all times.

DEPOSITORY AS AGENT

The depository is expressly made the agent of the lessor for the receipt of any and all sums payable under the lease. The agency, however, is confined to the receipt of sums. 'It was the duty of the bank merely to receive and deposit, nothing more.'[34] For practical purposes, the net effect of this provision seems to be that the lessee could not be held responsible for any delay by the depository in crediting the amounts paid to the lessor's account. For example, if the lessee elected to deliver a payment to the depository on the last day, then such payment would be effective, even if the depository did not actually

34 *Texas Gulf Sulphur* v *Ballem* (1969) 70 w.w.r. 373, Riley J, 389; *Rostad* v *Andreassen* (1952–53) 7 w.w.r. (N.S.) 709

credit the sums so paid to the lessor until a subsequent date. The question does not arise when the payment is mailed, as that act by itself constitutes payment.

LESSEE'S RIGHT TO APPOINT DEPOSITORY

The lessee may take action if a depository refuses to act or where, under certain circumstances, the lessor fails to appoint a depository. If a depository resigns or refuses to act and the lessor does not designate a successor within ten days, then the lessee may name a bank or trust company. The same situation applies if monies become payable to more than one person and such persons do not designate one depository. The clause as written, however, does not grant the lessee the right to appoint a depository where there is only one lessor, or person entitled to payment, the appointment of the depository has been revoked and the lessor fails to appoint a successor. Possibly the answer is, as mentioned before, that the lessor does not have the right to revoke the appointment of a depository, but only to designate a new one. The point remains troublesome under the present language.

NOTICES

The following clause sets up the procedure for giving notices between the parties. 'NOTICES: All notices to be given hereunder may be given by registered letter addressed to the Lessee at .... and to the Lessor at .... or such other address as the Lessor and the Lessee may respectively from time to time appoint in writing, and any such notice shall be deemed to be given to and received by the addressee Seven (7) days after the mailing thereof, postage prepaid.' It requires registered mail, specifies the official address of both parties, and provides for a constructive receipt, since such notice shall be deemed to be given to and received by the addressee seven days after the mailing thereof, with the proper postage. The device of 'deeming,' also used in the Manner of Payment clause, has certain drawbacks. There remains the question where a notice is actually received prior to the expiration of the seven-day period – a very likely possibility – as to which date controls, actual or deemed receipt? The point is more than academic since some time periods, such as the grace period for default, commence only from receipt of notice. Furthermore, the 'deemed' concept may have the weakness that it can be offset by absolute evidence of no receipt.

The clause refers only to 'notices' and makes no mention of payments. Inasmuch as there is a specific clause dealing with payments, it may be sufficiently clear that there are two separate time periods, one for notices and one for payments. However, since both may be mailed, a cross-reference excluding any conflict seems desirable as a matter of draftsmanship.

ENTIRE AGREEMENT

The authors of the lease made an attempt to confine the parties to the four corners of the document itself. 'ENTIRE AGREEMENT: The terms of this Lease express and constitute the entire agreement between the parties, and no implied covenant or liability of any kind is created or shall arise by reason of these presents or anything herein contained.' Despite this brave assertion, the lease falls short of constituting 'the entire agreement' between the lessor and lessee. There are a number of collateral matters which form part of the relationship between the parties and cannot be excluded by a clause such as this. The sanctity of contract theory holds that the parties to a contract may make whatever arrangement they see fit as between themselves so long as it does not offend the law itself.[35]

It has long been recognized, however, that an exclusionary clause cannot operate unless the contract itself has actual vitality. For example, this clause would not apply if the lease were executed on the condition that it was not to be effective until a certain event had occurred and that condition had not been fulfilled. In *California Standard Co.* v *Chiswell*[36] a petroleum and natural gas lease including such a clause was executed by both parties. Immediately after such execution the parties signed another agreement which recited that the bonus consideration under the lease was to be made upon the successful completion of foreclosure proceedings now pending under an agreement for sale. The lessors were in fact the vendors under an agreement for sale which was then in default. An action for foreclosure was launched against the purchaser, but this action was settled. The entire agreement clause was held to be ineffective to exclude the collateral agreement between the parties which made the lease conditional upon the successful completion of foreclosure proceedings. The court quoted *Molson's Bank* v *Cranston*:[37]

There is a plain answer to this contention. It is that the clause relied on is not binding on any one unless and until the document itself becomes operative. The rule against contradicting a written document applies, of course, only to an agree-

---

35 Fridman, 'Freedom of Contract' (1967), 2 *Ottawa L. Rev.* 1, for some limitations on this theory see Fridman, 'The Effect of Exclusion Clauses' (1968–69), 7 *Alta. L. Rev.* 281.
36 (1955) 14 W.W.R. 456, 5 D.L.R. (2d) 119 (Alta.)
37 (1919) 44 O.L.R. 58, 63 (C.A.)

ment which has actual vitality, and not to one which is in a state of suspended animation, ineffective and undelivered. No such rule of evidence can be set up until the legal relation of the parties has been established; and if the condition relied on is unfulfilled, the whole agreement fails.

Consequently the clause could not exclude a collateral agreement which constitutes a condition precedent to the very existence of the lease itself.

CONSERVATION AND OTHER APPLICABLE LEGISLATION

Nor can this clause exclude the effect of conservation legislation. Indeed, such legislation expressly overrides the provisions of any lease, in the event of a conflict.[38] In view of the express application and overriding effect of conservation legislation on the relationship between the parties to an oil and gas lease, the statement that the lease itself constitutes the entire agreement between the parties has been categorized as misleading.[39] It would be more accurate if the lease contained an express acknowledgment that it could be subject to, and its terms varied by, applicable legislation. As now written, it could mislead a lessor who could not be expected to be alive to the scope and application of conservation legislation and regulations.

IMPLIED COVENANTS

Regardless of its limitations in the areas of conditions precedent and legislation, the entire agreement clause would be effective against implied covenants. In general terms, the doctrine of implied covenants holds that, if a lease is silent on the points, the court will imply covenants on the part of the lessee to explore, develop, and operate with diligence.

38 See, for example, Oil and Gas Conservation Act, R.S.A. 1970, c 267 s 4, which provides that the Act applies to every well in Alberta and to any product obtained or obtainable therefrom, notwithstanding any terms to the contrary in any lease or grant from the Crown or from any other person; s 21(2) which provides that any terms or conditions to a contract or other arrangement that conflict with the Act, the regulations, an order of the Board, an order of the Public Utilities Board or an order of the Gas Utilities Board, are unenforceable and do not give rise to any cause of action by any party against any other party to the contract. There are also other provisions, notably those dealing with pooling, ss 82–86, which may materially vary the express terms of the lease.
39 Dea, 'A Look at the Lease from the Lessor's Point of View' (1965), 4 *Alta. L. Rev.* 208. The author describes circumstances under which the misunderstanding on the part of the lessor as to the application of conservation legislation to his arrangement with the lessee could lead to a severe deterioration in the lessor–lessee relationship.

The doctrine has flourished in American jurisprudence but is virtually still-born in Canada. There is a polite controversy among American authorities as to the classification of the obligations that will be imposed by the courts upon the lessee. Merrill[40] contends that there are four classifications of implied covenants, while others favour only three, and there are others who discern five. The point is academic. What matters is not the number and type of classifications, but rather the total impact of the implied covenants upon the relationship between lessor and lessee. Brown[41] in one of the more succinct summaries lists the covenants as follows:

1 The implied covenant to drill an exploratory well.
2 The implied covenant to conduct additional development after paying production is obtained.
3 The implied covenant for diligent and proper operation of wells.
4 The implied covenant to market or utilize the products.
5 The implied covenant to protect the leased substances against drainage by wells drilled on adjoining lands.

Implied covenants are well known to the common law, which applies the test whether such a term would have been included in the contract if the parties had addressed their minds to the point, or alternatively was the particular point so obvious it did not need to be expressed. 'A term can only be implied if it is necessary in the business sense to give efficacy to the contract, i.e., if it is such a term that it can confidently be said that if at the time the contract was being negotiated someone had said to the parties: "what will happen in such a case?" they would both have replied: "of course so and so will happen, we did not trouble to say that; it is too clear." '[42]

The basis that American courts have used for implying covenants into oil and gas leases is somewhat different and considerably wider. The relationship of the parties, that the lessor has turned over the operation and development of the lands to the lessee, and the object of the lease itself provide the reason for implying covenants that impose obligations upon the lessee.[43] The

---

40 Merrill, *Covenants Implied in Oil and Gas Lease* (2nd ed.)
41 Brown, *supra* n. 32, Sec. 16.02. See also, Summers, *Oil and Gas* 365; Thornton, Oil and Gas, vol. 1, 268; Merrill, *Lease Clauses Affecting Implied Covenants*, Second Annual Institute, 141. The doctrine of implied covenants may be one of the few remaining areas where American authority might be considered as relevant by Canadian courts.
42 *Reigate* v *Union Manufacturing Co.* [1918] 1 K.B. 592, 605
43 Some judicial bases for implied covenants are listed in Merrill, *supra* n. 40, 21. They all emphasize the mutuality of the relationship between lessor and lessee.

American approach to implied covenants was developed through the years when the oil and gas lease was still in a formative stage and very often was totally silent on many of the lessee's obligations. At the same time conservation legislation was also either non-existent or in a very rudimentary stage. This general background has been summarized as follows:

1 It must be recognized that at the outset the United States courts were faced with interpreting a type of lease very different from those commonly used today. These old forms of lease were most often granted for a long term, had no delay or other rental provision and covered very large tracts of land.
2 At the time when this implied covenant began to emerge, there were no well spacing and other conservation laws and practices such as we know them today.
3 The form of oil and gas lease in use in early days contained no express covenants on the part of the lessee with respect to exploration and development on the leased lands.
4 In the absence of express provisions for exploration and development, the courts were faced with the problem of determining what the intention of the parties to the lease was in this respect, spelling out what duties such intention imposed, how those duties must be carried out, and the penalties incurred in default of carrying out such duties.[44]

If one examines the five implied covenants, it immediately becomes apparent that at least three of them are covered either by the express terms of the Canadian oil and gas lease or by conservation legislation. Since an unwritten term will be implied into a contract only in the absence of an express covenant setting out the agreement of the parties on the same point,[45] the only areas in which Canadian courts might be tempted to imply covenants would be those two not expressly covered.

The three areas which are dealt with either by the terms of the lease or by applicable legislation are: the covenant to drill an exploratory well – the lease covers the drilling requirements in the first proviso to the *habendum*; the diligent and proper operation of wells is gone into in great detail by the conservation statutes and regulations; the covenant to protect the leased premises against drainage is the subject matter of the offset drilling clause

44 Boyd, 'Problems in Development of Leased Lands' (1965), 4 *Alta. L. Rev.* 302, 312
45 This point of view was neatly expressed in an early American decision *Mills* v *Hartz* (1908) 77 Kan 218, 94 P 142: 'Where a lease provides how and when search for oil and gas shall be made, there is no room for implications.'

found in virtually every form of lease. In some of these matters, notably that of offset drilling obligations which are confined normally to laterally adjoining spacing units not owned by the lessor, the express obligations may be substantially less severe than a court would be prepared to impose. Nonetheless the express covenants will exclude the implication of any other obligations on the same point.

The covenant to conduct additional development after production has been obtained is one which is almost never found in express terms in a Canadian oil and gas lease, nor can it be said to be covered by any legislation. While it is true that conservation measures will impose limits upon the density of wells and describe spacing units for drilling, there is nothing to affirmatively require a lessee or operator to drill additional wells. The question could be both relevant and important where one lease covers a large area of land. Even the existence of one well on production would maintain the lease in force indefinitely, although the balance of the lands remain undrilled and undeveloped. In most instances, however, the lease will cover only a quarter section, which is the customary minimum spacing unit for an oil well, or an entire section of land, which is the minimum spacing unit for a gas well. This feature of land ownership in western Canada may lessen the likelihood that a court will be called upon to imply such a term. The best protection that a large landholder can give to himself as lessor is to grant separate leases for each quarter section.

Similarly, neither the customary lease nor the applicable legislation will impose any obligation upon the lessee to market the products. The diligent development of a market is of the utmost importance to the lessor since it is only through the sale of the substances that he can enjoy the benefits of his royalty interest. The lessor has a *bona fide* interest in seeing that any substances discovered under his lands are marketed as rapidly and under as favourable terms as can be obtained. The initiative of finding a market lies entirely with the lessee and normally the lessee will be just as interested in obtaining a market as quickly as possible. There may be circumstances, however, where this mutuality of purpose does not apply.

The fact that a lease may be maintained for an indefinite number of years beyond its primary term by payment of a suspended well royalty underlines the importance that prompt marketing has for the lessor. He may find himself in a position where he is helpless to challenge a lease which has been proved to overlie substantial reserves and from which he derives no income other than the insignificant sum of the suspended well payment.

The particular nature of gas sale contracts could lead to situations whereby a lessor suffers economic hardship through his lessee's deliberate failure to market. Gas sale contracts entered into between producers and the major gas transmission companies allocate volumes based on reserves within a designated area. Thus, the total reserves allocated to a producer's holdings in an area determine the volume that he can deliver to the pipe line system. Actual deliveries, however, may take place from only a portion of the lands within the area since the entire contract volume may be produced from a relatively few wells. The unhappy lessor finds himself in a position where his reserves help the lessee establish favourable contract volumes but are not sold, with the result that he obtains no royalty.

There is another factual situation which bears upon the obligation to market. A lessee may have a number of leases in an area, all of which are capable of producing gas but may be subject to different economic burdens. The production from some may, for example, be subject to an overriding royalty, while others may be free of such charge. The lessee will be tempted to minimize production from those lands with the extra burden and maximize it from those which are free of the additional cost. The under-produced lessor would be anxious to find some means of forcing the lessee to take production ratably.

All of this leads to the suggestion that the obligation to market is the one major area in which Canadian courts might be prepared to imply a covenant. The factors involved in marketing the products will vary substantially from case to case and necessarily any such covenant would be cast in the broadest terms. The lessee would be under a duty to make diligent efforts to market production within a reasonable time and to obtain the most favourable price under the prevailing circumstances, possibly also to prorate any existing market. Using both common sense and American authorities as guides, a covenant of this type could be discharged by proof on the part of the lessee that he had made diligent efforts without success, or that the circumstances were such that any such efforts would be foredoomed to failure at that particular time.

The issue of marketing is of such importance to the lessor that he would be well advised to insist upon an express covenant imposing some duty on the lessee to use due diligence in obtaining a market for any production encountered in the demised premises.

Canadian courts have flirted with implied terms on only two occasions and the results may best be described as inconclusive. An early Ontario case, *Docker* v *London-Elgin Oil Co.*,[46] involved a contention on the part of the lessor, where the form of lease did not impose a definite obligation to commence operations, that the real purpose of the lease was for the operation of the lands for mining purposes and that the lessee was under a duty to com-

46 (1908) 11 o.w.r. 762

mence operations. The court refused to make this conclusion and confined itself to interpreting the actual terms of the lease. The fact that the lease contained a statement of its purpose 'for the purpose of enabling the lessee and his assigns ... to sink or drill oil ... subject only to the payment of the rental hereinbefore reserved' did not create any duty on the lessee to operate but merely gave him a right to do so.

In *Reynolds* v *Ackerman*[47] the lease did not follow the customary form and was described by the court as 'an informal document.' It did not contain any express covenant with respect to drilling, but simply provided for an initial period of three years and gave the lessee a right to renew it for further terms from year to year by paying in advance the sum of $1.00 per acre per year. The trial judge found the lease in question to be unenforceable and voidable for failure to comply with the Dower Act and also void for uncertainty by reason of the indefinite renewal provision. He then undertook to answer this question: 'Whether in a true and proper construction of the whole instrument ... there is an implied covenant to be read from the document on the part of the lessee, the plaintiff, to drill for gas or oil or at least to drill a shallow test well as was mentioned in the evidence.'[48] Because the lease in question was silent on the matter of drilling, McBride J stated:

If I were required to make a finding on the question now under discussion, I should find that there was an implied covenant.

What I have already said, however, to my mind sufficiently disposes of this action without the necessity of relying on an implied covenant to drill, a breach of which would terminate the lease, but, if I should be wrong as to all the other matters which I have already discussed, I would then hold that there is an implied covenant on the part of this lessee to drill. While the recital in the lease may perhaps be a limitation of its use in that it demises and leases the land to the lessee for the sole and only purpose of mining and operating for water, oil and gas, nevertheless, on the true construction of the instrument as a whole, it is clear that neither party contemplated this land of the defendant could be held for an indefinite number of years simply by paying and renewing for the comparatively insignificant rental provided in the lease.

Reference to the point in question will be found in Summers (a treatise on oil and gas) 1927 ed., vol. 3, at p. 288, and while there is no express covenant, nevertheless, the express purpose of the whole instrument would quite obviously and definitely be defeated if the lessee could take refuge in the clause in question and do nothing at all in the way of drilling. I find no excuse or explanation in

47 (1960) 32 w.w.r. 289   48 Ibid, 297

any regulations, or the fact that maybe a minimum acreage of 40 acres is required, to resolve in favour of the plaintiff the implied covenant in question which otherwise appears on the face of the instrument.[49]

The foregoing stands no higher than *obiter dicta* by a trial judge. The reception that would be accorded by Canadian courts to implied covenants to develop the lands following production, to market the products, or share a market (the only areas that seem open) remains unresolved.

If the lease contains an 'entire agreement' clause in the standard form, the lessor will have an uphill struggle to convince the court that such covenants should be implied. The language 'no implied covenant or liability of any kind is created or shall arise by reason of these presents' is clearly directed at excluding any implied covenants. In the United States such clauses, although they may be strictly construed, are generally recognized as being effective in limiting or excluding the implied covenants.[50] In Canada, bearing in mind the clear intent of the language and the literalistic approach of the Supreme Court, a clause of this type might well be successful in negativing any implied covenants.

With this examination of the entire agreement clause and implied covenants, we complete a résumé of the freehold lease form commonly and currently used in Canada. There are other forms, however, which contain additional terms and variations of those found in the 'standard' lease. In the next chapter, we shall explore the more significant of these.

49 Ibid, 298   50 Merrill, *supra* n. 40, 432, 433

10
Variations on the standard clauses and additional provisions

Some oil companies, possibly because of past experience, have worked out their own versions of the standard clauses. This is particularly true with respect to the scope of the objects and powers granted under the lease. For example, the form of lease used by one of the major companies contains this phrase after the reference to the leased substances: '... and the exclusive right to use any well on the said lands for the injection of gas, air, water or any other fluids, whether obtained from the said lands or elsewhere, into the sub-surface strata and the right to perform any operation necessary, incidental to or associated with any of the aforesaid operations of the lessee.' The phrase establishes that the lessee has the right to inject foreign substances into the sub-surface strata, thus removing any doubt that the lease grants the power to implement secondary recovery procedures. It also seems designed to permit the use of a well for such non-producing activities as disposal of salt water. It stops short, however, of granting the express right to use the strata for storage of petroleum substances, and, bearing in mind the overall purpose of the lease, namely to explore for and produce oil and gas, it is doubtful if the language would be interpreted as including such a right.

Some versions attempt to expand the surface rights by including the right to construct 'power stations, treating and processing plants, dwellings for its employees and other structures and lines of communication.' These powers go far beyond those conveyed under the standard form. For example, a lessor would be surprised and chagrined to find that, by granting the mineral lease, he had also granted the right to use the surface for the construction of a processing plant. These powers appear to be a direct importation from

American forms. In view of the dichotomy between surface and sub-surface rights that prevails in western Canada and which leads to the invariable practice of acquiring surface rights under a separate document, they would appear to be of little practical application.

DRAINAGE AND THE OFFSET WELL

The lease used by Shell Canada Limited adds a refinement to the offset drilling obligation with this proviso: 'PROVIDED that the Lessee shall not be obligated to drill an offset well if such well drilled on lands adjoining the said lands is not draining the said lands.'

This is in addition to the other requirements that must be met under the usual clause before the offset obligation arises. In a way it reflects the spirit of the offset clause since the requirement was inserted to prevent a lessor suffering drainage. In practice, however, it seems to introduce an unworkable element in that the lessor is faced with the burden of proving that his lands are being drained. In view of the partiality with which expert evidence is often tainted, this could prove to be an almost insuperable task. The normal offset clause is based on the assumption that drainage will, in fact, occur from a laterally adjoining spacing unit. This rule, while arbitrary, is purely objective and not subject to the uncertainties and possible expense involved in the test of drainage.

DEFAULT CLAUSE

The Shell lease form also contains a refinement of the default provision.

(a) In the event the Lessor considers that the Lessee has not complied with any obligations hereunder, the Lessor shall notify the Lessee in writing, setting out specifically in what respects the Lessor claims the Lessee has breached this Lease. The Lessee shall then have ninety (90) days after receipt of such notice within which to remedy or commence to remedy all or any part of the breaches alleged by the Lessor. The giving of such notice shall be precedent to the bringing of any action by the Lessor on the said Lease for any cause, and no such action shall be brought until the lapse of ninety (90) days after the giving of such notice to the Lessee. Neither the service of the said notice nor the doing of any acts by the Lessee intended to meet all or any of the alleged breaches shall be deemed an admission or assumption that the Lessee has failed to perform its obligations hereunder.

(b) Forfeiture shall be the only remedy of the Lessor for failure of the Lessee to comply with any of its obligations hereunder except such as relate to the delivery of royalty or the payment of money for which specific provision is made in this Lease. In respect of any breach relating to the delivery of royalty or the payment of such money the accrual of which the Lessee in good faith disputes, the Lessor shall have no right of declaring forfeiture until the existence of such breach has been finally judicially determined and the Lessee has not within thirty (30) days of such final judicial determination complied therewith, in which latter event the Lessor may by notice to the Lessee declare the absolute forfeiture of this Lease and of all the Lessee's rights hereunder except as to the right to remove the Lessee's property.

(c) In the event of forfeiture of this Lease for any cause, other than the Lessee's failure to deliver royalty or make any payment of money for which specific provision is made in this Lease, this Lease shall nonetheless remain in force as to each well in or upon which operations are then being conducted, together with forty (40) acres around each such well, or such larger acreage as may then be assigned to each such well as a drilling unit or for allocation of production allowable by or under any law or governmental order, as to which the Lessee is not then in default under any provision of this Lease. Such acreage shall be designated by the Lessee and be as near as practicable in a square form centred at the well, or in such form as may be necessary to comply with any governmental order.

The effect of sub-clause (a) is generally the same as that under the standard clause, except that the wording makes it abundantly clear that any action taken by the lessee shall not be construed as an admission on its part that there has been any breach of the obligations.

Sub-clause (b) expressly confines the lessor's remedies to forfeiture, with the exception of the royalty or money to be paid under the lease. If the claim is for royalty or money and if it is disputed by the lessee, the lessor's right to forfeiture is postponed until the existence of such breach to pay royalty or money has been finally judicially determined (which means the Supreme Court of Canada has ruled on the matter or the appeal periods have expired). The lessee then has a further period of thirty days after such judicial determination to comply with the requirement of royalty or money, and, if the lessee does so, this removes the lessor's right of forfeiture. The intent seems to be that the exercise of the right of forfeiture by the lessor would not eliminate his right to collect the money owed to him.

Apart from royalty and money claims, the sub-clause deprives the lessor of any remedy other than forfeiture. Thus, if the lessee were in breach of the offset drilling obligation, the lessor could not claim monetary damages for such breach. Forfeiture itself may prove to be largely illusory by reason of the operation of sub-clause (c). This provision is similar in effect to the much shorter version in the standard clause and protects any productive, or potentially productive, acreage from forfeiture.

OBLIGATION TO MARKET

The same lease form contains a provision under which the lessee assumes some obligation to market the substances. The obligation arises only when the lease is being continued in force beyond the primary term by a shut-in well payment.

PROVIDED, however, that if, at the expiration of the primary term or at any time or times thereafter, there is any well on the said lands, or on lands with which the said lands or any portion thereof have been pooled, capable of producing the leased substances or any of them, and all such wells are shut in, this Lease shall, nevertheless, continue in force as though operations were being conducted on the said lands, for so long as the said wells are shut in. If no royalties are otherwise payable hereunder during a lease year within which such shut-in period or periods occur and during such lease year no operations are conducted on the said lands, then, at the end of such lease year the Lessee shall pay to the Lessor as royalty an amount equal to the annual acreage rental hereinabove specified. The Lessee covenants and agrees to use reasonable diligence to produce and either utilize or market the leased substances capable of being produced from the said wells, but in the exercise of such diligence the Lessee shall not be obligated to install or furnish facilities other than well facilities and ordinary lease facilities of flow lines, separator and lease tank.

The provision is notable in that it specifically recognizes an obligation on the part of the lessee to do something about marketing when the lease is beyond the primary term. The obligation is to 'use reasonable diligence,' which undoubtedly would be the test applied by the courts if an obligation to market were ever to be implied. The lessee's obligation to invest in plant and equipment as a result of its undertaking to market is clearly limited to conventional well-site facilities.

The limitation of the obligation to the circumstances where the term is prolonged by a shut-in well makes it much more restrictive than the covenant to market implied by the American courts. The implied covenants come into operation within a reasonable period after discovery of the substances. Certainly the wider obligation would be preferable from the lessor's point of view, as he will be anxious to obtain royalty revenue at the earliest possible moment. The lessee's failure to market becomes particularly galling to the lessor, however, when the primary term has expired and the lease is being maintained by a small annual payment. The Shell clause is a recognition of this feature.

DE-POOLING

At least one form of lease wrestles with the problem of dismantling a pool once the pooling power under the lease has been exercised. The language is as follows: 'The Lessee may dissolve any unit established hereunder by giving to the Lessor written notice thereof if at that time no operations are being conducted in the unit for unitized leased substances. Subject to the provisions of this clause, a unit once established hereunder shall remain in force so long as any lease subject thereto shall remain in force.' Although the reference is to 'unit,' earlier references in the pooling clause established that a unit in this context means nothing more than that area allocated to one well for the purposes of production of the leased substances. This is the classic limitation on the pooling power and makes it clear that 'unitization' in the sense discussed in chapter 11, *infra*, is not involved. The power to de-pool can be used only when there are no operations underway. It could not, for example, be invoked if the well on the spacing unit were in actual production or were being re-worked, drilled or deepened. The language of this restriction is directed to physical operations and would not seem to apply to a constructive 'deeming' of operations pursuant to the suspended well clause.

It goes without saying that the provision could have no application to a compulsory pool formed by board order under conservation legislation.

GAS WELL ROYALTY – ONTARIO FORM

The form of lease most frequently encountered in the Province of Ontario has unusual features with respect to the payment of royalty for gas wells.

GAS WELLS

There is hereby excepted and reserved unto the Lessor a royalty in respect of each gas well completed on the said lands and which is capable of producing gas in paying quantities, computed as follows:

WHEN A WELL IS CAPABLE OF PRODUCING AN AMOUNT EQUAL TO OR IN EXCESS OF	BUT LESS THAN	AMOUNT
10 cubic feet per day	500,000 cubic feet per day	$100
500,000 cubic feet per day	1,000,000 cubic feet per day	$150
1,000,000 cubic feet per day	2,500,000 cubic feet per day	$250
2,500,000 cubic feet per day	5,000,000 cubic feet per day	$350
5,000,000 cubic feet per day		$500

The aforesaid royalty shall be computed in advance each year from the time each such gas well shall have been completed. The first payment for each gas well shall be based on its open flow measurement at the time of completion, and said payment for the period between the time of completion and the 30th day of September next ensuing shall be calculated at the rates above set forth and shall be paid as soon as may be practicable. Subsequent payments for each such well shall be paid in advance on or before the 25th day of October in each year and shall be based on the last open flow measurement of such well taken by the Lessee. While the said royalty is so paid it shall be deemed that each such well is a producing well hereunder and that the leased substances are being produced from the said lands.

The clause contemplates the payment of a royalty from the time the gas well has been completed. Therefore, royalty does not depend upon production and sale of the substances. The amount of the payment is based upon the capability of the well to produce and increases with potential daily volume. The annual amounts could only be considered nominal if they were a true royalty for gas actually being sold in the stated volumes. There is also the familiar provision that payment of the royalty amounts to production of the substances for the purposes of the lease.

The operation of this royalty clause can be understood only against the background that the lessee, prior to commencing production of a gas reservoir or pool, will enter into another agreement known as the Unit Operation Agreement which, *inter alia*, replaces the gas royalty payable under the lease with a royalty of two cents per m.c.f. for all gas produced, saved and marketed. Seen in this light, the gas royalty under the lease becomes the equivalent of a suspended gas well payment which, instead of being at a flat rate as in western forms, is adjusted in accordance with the potential of the well. It should be noted, however, that the small royalties specified under the clause in the lease represent the only gas well royalties due to the lessor unless and until he enters into a Unit Operation Agreement.

ADDITIONAL CLAUSES

Some leases touch upon matters not dealt with by the express terms of the standard clauses.

Use of gas by lessor
Astonishingly, many leases still grant the lessor the right to use gas for domestic purposes. The clause usually takes this form:

If as a result of drilling operations of the lessee on the said lands natural gas is produced which is not needed for the operations hereunder, which is surplus to any amounts which the lessee may have committed to deliver under contract, and which is safe and suitable for domestic use as produced, the lessee shall supply on the demand of and at the sole risk of the lessor, free of charge, and not subject to the accounting of royalty by the lessee, such surplus natural gas to the lessor for domestic use only in his principal dwelling only on the said lands, and all necessary installations for the supply of the said gas shall be made by the lessee at the sole risk and expense of the lessor.

The conditions under which the lessor can call upon the lessee for a supply of free gas are very specific. The drilling which produces the natural gas must take place on the leased lands; the gas must be surplus to the operations carried on under the lease (which means gas over and above that required for fuel and other operating purposes); and it must be surplus to any amounts which the lessee may have committed to deliver under contract – i.e., the well or wells must be capable of delivering volumes of gas in excess of that sold by the lessee under contract; the gas by itself must be safe and suitable for domestic use as produced, which means that it does not require special processing. If all these conditions are met, then the lessee is required to supply natural gas for domestic use only in the lessor's principal dwelling, which must be located on the said lands. The lessee will make the necessary installations but at the sole risk and expense of the lessor.

Although this clause, or variations thereof, is found in many past and present leases, the right of the lessor has been invoked very occasionally. There are a number of reasons for this. First, gas is a volatile explosive substance not designed to be handled by amateurs or by makeshift arrangements. Very often it will contain poisonous impurities such as hydrogen sulphide and carbon dioxide, which make it unsuitable for any use until it has been processed. In many instances it arrives at the surface under pressures impossibly high for domestic purposes.

The clause is very specific that, while the lessee may install the equipment necessary for the supply of the gas, it is at the sole risk and expense of the lessor.[1] Furthermore, the use to which the lessor may put the gas is severely restricted. He can use it only for domestic purposes in his principal dwelling. There is no Canadian authority on the scope of this description, although there has been much litigation on the point in the United States. Brown lists

1 The very concept of this clause would seem to offend against the spirit if not the letter of legislation such as the Alberta Gas Utilities Act, R.S.A. (1970) c 158, for the safe construction and operation of gas distributing systems.

the various interpretations that have been placed on this and similar phrases by American courts.[2] For example, the reference to a 'dwelling house' which is not dissimilar to 'principal dwelling' has been held to include 'the cluster of buildings in which a man with his family resides and extends to such out-buildings as are within the curtilage.'[3] Thus a Canadian court might be invited to include a garage and any outbuildings that contain, for example, boilers and other heating apparatus for the home. The only Canadian authority to date involved the interpretation of a clause, found in a memorandum of agreement, not a lease, whereunder the defendant obligated itself to supply gas 'for domestic and farm purposes.'[4] The defendant had neglected to determine how much gas the plaintiff was using for these purposes before entering into the undertaking. It turned out that the plaintiff's consumption was remarkable since, in addition to the household requirements, she had gone into the business of hog raising on a substantial scale and, for that purpose, cooked large quantities of hog food in a gas-heated steam boiler located in one of the farm buildings adjoining the house. The court held that, since the plaintiff's farm operations were of this nature at the time the agreement was entered into, the defendant had obligated itself to supply natural gas for all the farming operations including the steam boiler. Practically every clause to be found in present-day leases circumvents this difficulty and limits the use of gas to domestic purposes in the principal dwelling on the said lands.

It is suggested that this clause is not appropriate to modern conditions and its use should be discontinued. It is a very limited benefit to the lessor since both the purpose for which free gas may be demanded and the conditions under which the demand may be made are limited. Nonetheless, it can be the subject of irritation between lessor and lessee and is an open invitation to install facilities that are hazardous and unsupervised. It may have had some utility in the past when domestic fuel was both difficult and costly to obtain in remote areas. Today, however, with widespread gas distribution systems and the extensive use of propane as a farm fuel, even this justification has largely disappeared.

Force majeure
The phrase *force majeure* means a superior, irresistible force. In the context of contractual relations, it refers to intervening changes in circumstances

2 *The Law of Oil and Gas Leases* (2nd ed.) Secs. 10.10, 10.11
3 *United Carbon Co.* v *Conn*, 351 sw (2d) 189
4 *Smith* v *Inland Gas & Oil Company Limited and Wainwright Gas Company Limited* (1955) 14 w.w.r. 558 (Alta.)

which render it impossible for a party to perform his obligations. Virtually every lease form contains some reference to *force majeure*; the standard lease refers to it only in the context of an interruption or suspension of drilling, working operations, or production of the leased substances after the expiration of the primary term. The third proviso to the *habendum* clause provides that, if such interruptions or suspensions are the result of a cause beyond the lessee's reasonable control, then 'the time of such interruption or suspension or non-production shall not be counted against the lessee.' Many leases contain more extensive application of *force majeure* in a separate clause.

Force majeure
The performance of any of the obligations of the Lessee hereunder shall, notwithstanding anything contained in this Lease to the contrary, be suspended while and so long as the Lessee is prevented from complying with such obligations in part or in whole, by strikes, lockouts, acts of God, severe weather conditions and/or action of the elements, accidents, laws, rules and regulations of any governmental bodies or agencies, zoning or land use ordinances of any governmental agency, acts or requests of any governmental officer or agent purporting to act under authority, delays in transportation, inability to obtain necessary materials in the open market, inadequate facilities for the transportation of materials or for the disposition of production, or other matters beyond the reasonable control of the Lessee whether similar to the matters herein specifically enumerated or not, or while legal action contesting the Lessor's title to said lands or the Lessee's right in said lands by virtue hereof shall be pending final adjudication in a court assuming jurisdiction thereof. Time consumed in cleaning, repairing, deepening, or improving any producing well or its necessary appurtenances shall not be deemed or construed as an interruption or discontinuance of the Lessee's operations under this Lease. The Lessee need not perform any requirement hereunder, the performance of which would violate any reasonable conservation and/or curtailment program or plan of orderly development to which the Lessee may voluntarily or by order of any governmental agency subscribe or observe.

There are several points to note in the foregoing clause. It refers only to the lessee's obligations. Admittedly the lessor's positive obligations – apart from the grant itself – are modest, being confined to paying taxes and executing such further documents as may be necessary to give effect to the lease. The obligation of the lessee is merely suspended; the lease is not terminated. There is a lengthy catalogue of specific events of *force majeure*, including many references to the acts of governmental agencies. The list is not exhaustive; there is an omnibus reference to 'other matters beyond the reasonable control of the Lessee.' The insertion of 'reasonable' is an attempt to extend the application of the clause. There are matters which obviously could be remedied if cost were no object, but where no reasonable or prudent operator would incur the extra cost. In addition, the clause contains some features particular to petroleum situations. If the lessee cleans, repairs, or performs work on a well, such time shall not be deemed an interruption under the lease. This concept appears out of place in a *force majeure* clause; it is designed mainly to ensure that an interruption of production for any of the listed reasons will not terminate the lease. It is akin to the third proviso of the *habendum* in the standard lease and, as a matter of arrangement, seems more appropriate to those provisions that deal with the term of the lease and its continuance.

There is also a specific reference to conservation programs and development plans, whether voluntary or compulsory. The Lessee is excused from performing any requirement of the lease if the performance would violate such programs or plans. The precise scope of this qualification is hard to determine; certainly it attempts to go further than the usual concept that observance of the applicable legislation cannot be a breach of contract. Here the clause also includes programs voluntarily initiated.

The unique importance of litigation over the lease is recognized by the inclusion of legal action over the lessor's title or the status of the lease as an act of *force majeure*. While the existence of litigation suspends performance of obligations by the lessee, it does not expressly extend the term of the lease should the primary term expire before the litigation has been resolved.

Ironically, the clause is totally ineffective in those areas where the risk of losing the lease is highest. Most of the circumstances which give rise to an involuntary termination of the lease have been characterized by the courts as options on the part of the lessee and not obligations. Hence, the *force majeure* clause is ineffective to prevent the termination of a lease by reason of the lessee's failure to drill, pay delay rental or produce. Martland J referring to an argument based upon a *force majeure* provision said:

The answer to this argument is that, while the clause postpones obligations, in certain events, it does not purport to modify the provisions of the *habendum* clause. That clause imposes no obligation upon the appellant to produce oil, gas or other mineral from the Northwest Quarter. It only provided that the primary term could be extended if oil, gas or other mineral was produced. If none of these substances were produced within the primary term, the lease terminated at the expiration of that term.[5]

---

5 *Canadian Superior Oil of California Ltd.* v *Kanstrup* [1965] s.c.r. 92, 105; 49 w.w.r. 257, 47 d.l.r. (2d) 1 (s.c.c.)

While the clause cannot protect the lessee against the major hazards to be found in a lease, it does have a definite area of operation. If a lessor has given a default notice regarding an undoubted obligation, such as an offset well, the clause can prevent the period of grace from expiring – and with it the lease – if the delay in remedying the default is occasioned by an act of *force majeure*.

The courts can be expected to construe the language strictly and to be cautious in holding that a particular set of facts represents a cause beyond the lessee's reasonable control. The decision of the Alberta Appellate Division in *Canada-Cities Service Petroleum Corporation v Kininmonth*[6] is a good illustration of this approach. The *force majeure* language was contained in that proviso to the *habendum* clause dealing with interruption or suspension of drilling, working, or production of operations. For purposes of discussion, the court treated the proviso as though it applied to the facts of the case. The well had been commenced towards the end of the primary term in the spring of the year when the break-up of winter conditions annually required municipal authorities to impose bans on the travel of heavy equipment over certain secondary roads. In order to test and complete the well the lessee required heavy fracturing equipment which could not be moved over the roads during the prohibited period. Before the road ban was lifted, the primary term expired. The court was of the opinion that the imposition of the road ban was not a cause beyond the lessee's control. There were several grounds cited for this view: that the particular road ban in question was invalid as it did not comply with the enabling legislation (although it is hard to see just why a lessee should be required to make a determination as to whether municipal resolution had been validly enacted); that the lessee might have applied for and obtained a permit to move the equipment over the municipal roads; that the annual imposition of road bans is of such a common occurrence that the lessee could and should have anticipated it and stockpiled the necessary equipment on the well site.

All this indicates that the lessee must discharge a very heavy onus before *force majeure* comes into play. In *Kininmonth* the proviso referred to 'beyond the lessee's control.' Query whether 'lessee's reasonable control' reduces the onus.

Compliance with laws

'Laws, rules and regulations' are included among the events listed in the *force majeure* clause. Occasionally a lease will go into greater detail.

---

6 (1963) 44 w.w.r. (c.a.) 392; the Supreme Court of Canada did not deal with this precise point since they held that the clause in which the *force majeure* language was embodied did not apply to the facts of the case as it was confined to production ceasing after the expiration of the primary term; [1964] s.c.r. 439

Compliance with any now or hereafter existing act, bill or statute purporting to be enacted by Parliament of the Dominion of Canada, or Legislature of the Province of ...., or any other law-making body, or with orders, judgments, decrees, rules, regulations made or promulgated by Parliament of the Dominion of Canada or Legislature of the Province of ...., or any other law-making body, boards, commissions or committees purporting to be made under authority of any such act, bill or statute, shall not constitute a violation of any of the terms of this lease or be considered a breach of any clause, obligation, covenant, undertaking, condition or stipulation contained herein, nor shall it be or constitute a cause for the termination, forfeiture, revision or re-vesting of any estate or interest herein and hereby created and set out, nor shall any such compliance confer any right of entry or become the basis of any action for damages or suit for the forfeiture or cancellation hereof; and while any such purport to be in force and effect they shall, when complied with by the Lessee or its assigns, to the extent of such compliance, operate as modifications of the terms and conditions of this Lease where inconsistent therewith.

Basically, clauses of this type reflect what would appear to be the situation in any event; the parties to a contract remain subject to the applicable legislation and regulations regardless of what may or may not be contained in the contract itself.

Like the *force majeure* provision, the clause will afford only scant protection against termination of the lessee's estate. Canadian courts can be expected to follow the traditional approach that the lease will be terminated by a choice or option of the lessee, and not a failure to fulfil an obligation or the exigencies of a law or regulation. The foregoing clause attempts to deal directly with the question of forfeiture and termination in the following phrase: 'Nor shall it be or constitute a cause for the termination, forfeiture, revision or revesting of any estate or interest herein.' One can safely predict that a Canadian court would pay little attention to this provision on the basis that it was not the compliance with any 'act, bill or statute' that caused the termination, but rather the choice or election of the lessee not to do that which would have been required to keep the lease in force, i.e. commence drilling, make timely payment, or put a well on production.

In any event, it would appear that only a positive, affirmative requirement by statute, regulation, or order would engage the protection of the clause. In *Shell Oil* v *Gibbard*[7] the fact that the Conservation Board required that a section of land be pooled to form a spacing unit before it would grant a permit to produce gas was held not sufficient to meet the test 'necessary in order to conform with any regulations or orders of the Government of the

7 [1961] S.C.R. 725, 36 W.W.R. 529, 30 D.L.R. (2d) 386 (S.C.C.)

Province of Alberta or any other authoritative body.' The Supreme Court made it plain that only an affirmative stipulation that the lands must be pooled would meet the test.

Non-forfeiture
Occasionally a lessee, possibly driven beyond endurance by the judicial hazards to the lease, will insert this type of clause.

This lease shall not be forfeited or cancelled for failure to perform in whole or in part any of its covenants, conditions or stipulations until it shall have first been finally judicially determined that such failure exists, and after such final determination, the Lessee is given a reasonable time therefrom to comply with any such covenants, conditions or stipulations.

The purpose of the clause is abundantly clear. It is to afford the lessee complete protection against involuntary termination of the lease, regardless of circumstances. While such a clause has never been interpreted by Canadian courts, it is unlikely to be of much benefit to a lessee. It would be dismissed on the familiar basis that termination of the lease does not constitute a forfeiture and that those requirements which cause the lease to terminate prematurely are not 'covenants, conditions or stipulations' but are options or elections on the part of the lessee.

Perpetual renewal
A lease currently in widespread use by at least one company in western Canada contains the following provision:

Always provided that on the expiration of the primary term hereof, if the leased substances or any of them are not then being produced from the said lands, the Lessee shall have and is hereby granted the sole and exclusive option to renew the within Lease for a further primary term of Ten (10) years to commence as of the date of termination of the within Lease, subject to the same terms, covenants and conditions as are herein contained including this covenant for renewal. This option shall be open for acceptance for a period of Thirty (30) days immediately following the expiration of the primary term hereof, and may be exercised by notice in writing to the Lessor given in the manner herein specified, accompanied by the Lessee's cheque for the same amount as the cash consideration for this Lease.

The unrestricted right to renew, which is tucked away as a proviso to the surrender clause, is an ingenious attempt by the lessee to avoid termination at the end of the primary term, even in the absence of any production, actual or constructive. The right can be exercised even if there has been no drilling whatsoever on the lands during the entire primary term. In fact, this is the most likely circumstance under which the right to renew would be exercised, as it is unlikely that a lessee would desire to renew a lease over lands which had been disproved by a dry hole. The lessee has 30 days after the end of the primary term to exercise the right of renewal and the bonus consideration is the same as the original payment given as consideration for the lease. Inasmuch as cash considerations for wildcat acreage have generally increased through the years, such a payment usually means a very poor bargain from the lessor's point of view. This provision has never been tested in the courts, but it has been acted upon in practice on numerous occasions.

The proviso specifically includes the covenant for renewal in the terms of the renewed lease. (If this were not done, the right to renew would not extend beyond the first renewed term.) The inclusion of the specific covenant for renewal makes it clear that the lessee has a perpetual right of renewal and that the lease can be renewed for an indefinite number of ten-year periods. This aspect makes the proviso subject to attack on the grounds that it offends the rule against perpetuities. This principle was evolved by the common law to limit the practice of rendering property perpetually or indefinitely inalienable.[8] Although it has numerous ramifications and exceptions, it can be summarized that no interest is good unless it must vest (if it vests at all) not more than twenty-one years after some life in being at the creation of the interest. Thus it is common to protect against the operation of the rule by inserting a provision that the right of any party to acquire any interest from any other party 'shall cease, terminate and be at an end not later than the expiration of 21 years after the death of the last surviving lawful descendent now living of His Late Majesty King George VI.'

An indefinite option to *grant* a lease would be struck down as offending against the rule. In *United Fuel Supplies Co.* v *Volcanic Oil & Gas Co.*[9] the instrument which was executed under seal granted 'the first right or option of leasing the last-mentioned lands for oil or gas purposes.' That option was held to create a remote interest in the land and to be invalid under the rule.

When it comes to options to renew an existing lease, rather than to grant one, however, it appears that the rule does not apply. This result has been described as anomalous: 'It might have been supposed that an attempt to provide for the perpetual renewal of the lease would have brought the matter within the rule against perpetuity. For some reason which has never been definitely laid down or satisfactorily explained, a covenant for the perpetual

---

8 *Halsbury's Laws of England* (3rd ed.) vol. 23, 628; *Lewis* v *Stephenson* (1898), 67 L.J.Q.B. 296; *Wilson* v *Kerner* [1912] 3 D.L.R. 11. The applicability of this principle in Canada has been reaffirmed by the Supreme Court of Canada in *Harris* v *Minister of National Revenue* [1966] S.C.R. 489.
9 [1911] 3 O.W.N. 93, 20 O.W.R. 78

renewal of the lease does not come within the rule.'[10] The usual explanation for holding that perpetual covenants to renew a lease do not offend the rule is that the covenant is one which runs with the land.[11] In any event the cases clearly establish that a covenant for perpetual renewal of the lease will be enforced.[12]

These cases, however, dealt with conventional property leases. The oil and gas lease has been categorized by the Supreme Court of Canada as a *profit à prendre*.[13] The rule against perpetuities applies to *profits à prendre* as well as to leases.[14] Since the nature of an oil and gas lease differs so radically from an ordinary lease of real estate, a perpetual covenant to renew would appear to offend the rule. There is no reason to suppose that a court would extend the anomalous exception that protects a lease to cover a *profit à prendre*. Nonetheless, the lessor should be alert to make sure his lease does not confer this right on the lessee.

If the renewal clause were struck down, it would be treated as severable and the original lease would stand. However, any attempt by the lessee to renew the lease would be ineffective.

USE OF WATER

Underground water
A number of leases, even although water is not included in the description of the substances under the granting clause, provide in the royalty clause that the lessee may have the use of water free of royalty. 'Notwithstanding anything to the contrary herein contained or implied the Lessee, in its operations hereunder, shall have the use, free from royalty, of water, other than water from the Lessor's water wells or from the Lessor's artificial surface reservoirs, and of gas produced from the said lands.'

---

10 *O'Brien's Conveyancing Law & Forms* (9th ed.) (1955) vol. 2, 1425, 1426
11 Anger and Honsberger, *Canadian Law of Real Property*, 412, 413. In those provinces which have enacted legislation dealing with perpetuities, options to renew a lease are specifically excepted from the rule. See The Perpetuities Act, R.S.O. 1970, c 343
12 See, for example, *Llanelly Railway & Dock Co.* v *London & North Western R. Co.* [1875] L.R. 7 H.L. 550; *Baynham* v *Guy's Hospital* (1796) 3 Ves. 295, 30 E.R. 1019; *Hare* v *Burges* (1857) 4 K. & J. 45, 70 E.R. 19; *London & South Western R. Co.* v *Gomm* (1882) 20 Ch. D. 562; *Swinburn* v *Milburn* (1884) 9 App. Cas. 844; *Clinch* v *Pernette* (1895) 24 S.C.R. 385; *Alexander* v *Herman* [1912] 2 D.L.R. 239, 3 O.W.N. 755, 21 O.W.R. 461; *Gibson Holdings Limited* v *Principal Investments Limited* [1964] S.C.R. 424 (S.C.C.)
13 *Berkheiser* v *Berkheiser* [1957] S.C.R. 387, 7 D.L.R. (2d) 721 (S.C.C.)
14 *Edwards* v *Edwards* [1909] A.C. 275; *Thomas* v *Thomas* [1902] L.T. 58 (C.A.)

The right to use water, somewhat misleadingly placed in the royalty clause, can be very significant in view of the enormous volumes that may be required for water injection schemes. The power to use water is limited to operations under the lease, and expressly excepts water wells and surface reservoirs used by the lessor. This exception makes it clear that the lessee does not have the right to utilize the lessor's domestic water supply and that the provision is obviously designed with deeper water rights in mind. The restriction to 'operations hereunder' prohibits the lessee from transporting water for injection in a water-flood scheme being conducted on other lands. One may speculate that the true intent was only to enable the lessee to use water free of royalty for routine operations such as boilers, mud pits, and engine coolants, similar to the manner in which gas may be used for fuel. There appears, however, to be nothing to prevent the lessee from utilizing huge volumes of underground water for secondary recovery so long as the injection is performed on lands covered by the lease and the lands are within a water-flood project.

Surface water

Frequently the wording of a royalty clause demonstrates that water and its possible use came as an afterthought to the draftsman as he dealt with the use of the leased substances for operational purposes. 'The Lessee shall have free use of oil and gas from the said lands, and, where the Lessor is the owner of the surface, of water therefrom, except water from the Lessor's wells, dugouts or tanks, for all operations hereunder and the royalties on the said substances or any of them shall be based on the net quantity after deducting any portion thereof so used for the Lessee's operations.' This language clearly limits the lessee's right to use water to that which may be deemed to be attached to the surface rights and would not include the right to use underground water for purposes such as injection.

Disposal of salt water

In a seemingly endless quest to extend the rights granted under a lease, the right to use a well for the disposal of salt water is sometimes included.

DISPOSAL OF SALT WATER

The Lessor hereby grants to the Lessee the right to drill, maintain and operate on the said lands, wells for the disposal of salt water produced from the said lands, or other lands, subject to obtaining the consent of the Energy Resources Conservation Board of the Province of Alberta; and for such purposes the Lessee shall have the right to use and occupy all or any part of the surface of the said lands subject to the terms and conditions herein elsewhere provided.

Formation water is often produced with the leased substances. Disposing of it can be an embarrassment, particularly since conservation authorities are becoming ever more concerned about the surface damage that can be done by a saline solution. The obvious answer is to re-inject the salt water underground, and an operator who produces water along with each barrel of oil is willing to pay for the privilege. Under the proper conditions it becomes economical to convert a depleted well to water disposal or even to drill one for that express purpose. Nevertheless, such a utilization of the underground characteristics seems removed from the purposes contemplated by a mineral owner and oil operator when they enter into a lease.

INJECTED SUBSTANCES

The practice of injecting foreign substances into a formation in order to maintain pressure and reservoir drive could, under some circumstances, give rise to royalty problems since these substances are produced from the well. If the injected substances are water, as is quite commonly the case, the problem does not arise. Frequently, valuable hydrocarbons such as gas and propane are used. Sometimes a lease will attempt to deal with the situation.

AND FURTHER PROVIDED that no royalty shall be payable in respect to any substance whether similar to or dissimilar to leased substances not initially obtained from reservoirs or strata underlying the said lands which is injected into the reservoir or strata underlying the said lands and is subsequently produced therefrom and sold, regardless of whether the same is produced in conjunction with the leased substances or otherwise.

One must applaud the intention of such a provision. The problems of identification, however, are formidable. How does one divide gas and liquid hydrocarbons appearing at the well head between *in situ* and injected hydrocarbons? Engineering techniques would cast some light, but any such division could be challenged in the courts. The problem transcends any one lease, but disappears under unit operation.

COST OF TREATING LEASED SUBSTANCES

Some lease forms are not content to rely upon the computation of royalty as the value of the substances 'at the well' or 'on the said lands,' but go into detail as to the deductions that may be made.

PROVIDED THAT the Lessor shall bear his proportion of any expense of treating oil, gas, and liquid hydrocarbons to render same merchantable, or of absorption or other process by which products are recovered from gas, or of treating, boosting or transporting of gas or residue gas in connection with the disposal thereof. And Lessor shall bear its proportion of any expense of treating, processing, refining and manufacturing from other minerals produced, mined and marketed to render such minerals merchantable.

LESSOR TO DEFEND TITLE

One lease form, notable for the unusual burdens it imposes upon the lessor, contains in addition to a warranty of title a commitment by the lessor to defend the title to the leased substances in the said lands, or at the lessee's option to permit the lessee so to defend.

And the Lessor agrees to defend the title to the leased substances in the said lands, or at the Lessee's option to permit the Lessee so to defend and the Lessee to that end may and is hereby authorized to bring or defend to the Lessor's name and at the Lessor's sole cost and expense, any action necessary or incidental to the defense of such title. In the event of default of payment by the Lessor, the Lessee shall have the right to pay the expenses and costs of any such action, and may at its option deduct any amount so paid by it from rentals and royalties payable to the Lessor herein.

The provision places an unjustified burden on the lessor who may not be particularly anxious to defend his title to the minerals granted, but, nonetheless, could be made responsible for all the costs and expenses of so defending. The lessee's right to collect such costs and expenses appears to be limited to a right of reimbursement from rentals and royalties. The entire concept seems inconsistent with the normal lessor–lessee relationship.

WELL INFORMATION

One sophisticated and substantial lessor, the Canadian Pacific Railway Company, which has extensive mineral holdings and an operating oil company, has developed its own lease form. As might be expected, the lease contains much more in the way of protection to the interests of the lessor than is normally found in oil and gas leases. In particular, the form imposes very detailed requirements on the lessee with respect to furnishing information on any drilling performed on the lands. The lease contains in effect the same requirements as to information, data, testing, and access as oil companies normally require of each other in joint venture projects.

(a) Prior to commencing the drilling of each well on the said lands, the Lessee shall furnish to the Lessor a copy of application for well licence and of the plan of survey of the proposed wellsite and access roadway.

(b) During the drilling of each well on the said lands, the Lessee shall:

(i) furnish the Lessor with written advice of the date of spudding thereof;

(ii) furnish the Lessor with daily drilling reports;

(iii) take formation samples at such intervals and at such depths as the Lessor may prescribe and furnish the Lessor with a complete set of samples, washed and in suitable containers;

(iv) furnish the Lessor with chip samples at 2 foot intervals and at lithologic changes throughout the length of all cores taken;

(v) furnish the Lessor with immediate advice of any porous zones or showings of the leased substances;

(vi) test, to the extent required by good oilfield practice, any porous zones or showings of the leased substances encountered or indicated by any survey;

(vii) take representative mud samples and drillstem test fluid samples in order to obtain accurate resistivity readings of mud filtrate and formation water and furnish the Lessor with all information relative thereto;

(viii) furnish the Lessor with two copies of the drillstem test and service report on each drillstem test run, including copies of pressure charts;

(ix) permit representatives of the Lessor to have access to the wellsite including derrick floor at all reasonable times to inspect and observe and make records relating to the operations of the Lessee.

(c) During the drilling of each well on the said lands and upon each such well reaching total depth, the Lessee shall run mechanical log surveys necessary to provide the optimum evaluation possible of all horizons penetrated. Such surveys shall include, but shall not be restricted to, a satisfactory resistivity log over the full length of the hole and a satisfactory porosity log over the full length of the hole. The Lessee shall furnish the Lessor with two copies of the final prints of each log run, not later than fifteen (15) days from the running thereof.

(d) Within thirty (30) days of the date of completion of each well drilled on the said lands, the Lessee shall furnish the Lessor with:

(i) two copies of any directional, temperature, caliper or other well survey (exclusive of a velocity survey) or oil, gas, water or other analyses made;

(ii) a complete summary of the drilling and completion of such well;

(iii) written notice of the commencement of production of any of the leased substances;

(iv) all production information and such other data as the Lessor may reasonably require.

(e) Within thirty (30) days from the date of running production casing in each well drilled on the said lands, the Lessee shall:

(i) if production composed predominantly of leased substances, other than natural gas is encountered, subject such well to a production test of a duration not exceeding any maximum period for such test which may be laid down by any conservation authority. The Lessee shall furnish the Lessor with daily written advice of the oil, gas and water content of oil produced during such production test.

(ii) if production composed predominantly of natural gas is encountered, subject such well to a back pressure test; provided, however, that, if a market for natural gas does not exist, such back pressure test may be postponed until a market is available or until such time as the Lessor requests such test. The Lessee shall furnish the Lessor with written advice of the data derived from such back pressure test and the calculations and conclusions based thereon.

(f) With respect to each well drilled on the said lands, the Lessee shall furnish the Lessor with a copy of all reports required to be filed with any government body, such copies to be furnished to the Lessor at the time reports are filed with such government body.

(g) Except for information which is available to the public from any governmental authority, the Lessor, if requested by the Lessee, shall treat as confidential during the term of this Lease all or any part of the information contained in any reports of the Lessee furnished, given or delivered to the Lessor pursuant to this clause, provided, however, that this sub-clause (g) shall not prevent the Lessor from divulging any information to a subsidiary of the Lessor.

INSPECTIONS BY LESSOR OF LESSEE'S OPERATIONS

The Lessee shall permit authorized representatives of the Lessor, at all reasonable times during the term of this Lease, quietly to enter upon the said lands and into all buildings erected thereon and to survey, examine and inspect the state and condition of the same and of any wells, provided that in so doing no unnecessary interference is caused to the operations of the Lessee; and the Lessee shall in every reasonable way aid such representative in making such entry, survey, examination and inspection.

The advantage of such stipulations to a lessor with widespread mineral rights and operations is obvious. The average lessor has no need for such detailed information, but he does have a legitimate interest in knowing that a well or wells have been drilled on his lands and the results obtained.

There would seem to be no compelling reason why the lease should not obligate the lessee to advise the lessor of the fact that a well will be commenced on the land on or about a certain date and to advise the lessor in general terms of the status of such a well, i.e. abandoned, completed for production, or suspended to await a market or pipeline connection. The interest of the lessee could be protected by specifying that such abandonment or completion information need not be provided until the expiration of the period when it would become generally available by law, provided that the lessee took whatever steps are required to clothe the well with confidential status.

RIGHT TO TAKE ROYALTY SHARE IN KIND

The average lessor is in no position to deal with the oil and gas as physical substances and is only too happy to have the responsibility for disposing of his royalty share assumed by the lessee. Some lessors, however, large-scale oil operators in their own right, may wish to dispose of the royalty share directly. The Canadian Pacific form contains the following provision:

The Lessor shall have the option exercisable at any time and from time to time, on thirty (30) days' written notice to the Lessee, to take in kind, in lieu of the royalty payable under sub-clause (a) of this clause 4 in respect of crude oil and liquid hydrocarbons, ... Per cent (................%) of all crude oil and all liquid hydrocarbons produced and saved from the demised estate, and on like notice may at any time and from time to time revoke its exercise of such option; if the Lessor so exercises such option, the Lessee shall at the Lessee's cost remove basic sediment and water from the Lessor's said share in accordance with usual oil field practice so that such share will meet pipe line, refinery or other market specifications in that respect and the Lessee shall provide at the Lessee's cost storage facilities for at least ten (10) days' accumulation of such share and shall deliver the same to the Lessor or the Lessor's nominee at the outlets of such storage facilities in accordance with the usual pipe line and shipping practices and free and clear of all charges, liens and encumbrances.

Under this provision the lessor has the option on 30 days' notice to take its share of crude oil and liquid hydrocarbons in kind. The 30-day notice period coincides with the usual practice under which crude oil is sold through purchase contracts which have a 30-day termination clause. This permits the lessee to cancel any existing contract under which it is selling the lessor's share and thus place itself in a position to make delivery to the lessor. If the lessor has exercised its option, the lessee is required at the lessee's cost to remove certain impurities and water from the liquids as required to meet pipeline specifications. This involves a basic form of treating and separating on the well site and requires vessels and equipment that the lessee would need for treating its own share. The lessee is also required to provide at its cost tankage sufficient to store at least ten days' royalty share.

The situation with gas is different in that it is normally sold under long-term contracts that extend for upwards to twenty-five years. Obviously, such arrangements do not lend themselves to the periodic exercise by a lessor of his option to take the royalty share of natural gas in kind. This is overcome by granting to the lessor the right to 'opt out' of the contract prior to the lessee entering into it. If the lessor does not elect to take his share in kind, then he is bound by the terms of the contract. This is achieved by the following provision:

Within ninety (90) days, but not less than thirty (30) days, before the Lessee produces for the Lessee's use, or makes a contract for the sale or other disposition of any natural gas from the demised estate, the Lessee shall give to the Lessor written notice of the Lessee's intention so to do together with full particulars of such contract, if any, and the Lessor shall have the option, exercisable by notice in writing mailed or delivered to the Lessee within thirty (30) days after receipt of such written notice, to take in kind, in lieu of the royalty payable under sub-clause (a) of this clause 4 in respect of natural gas .... Per cent (............%) of all natural gas produced and saved from the demised estate; if the Lessor so exercises such option the Lessee shall at the Lessee's cost deliver the Lessor's said share at such point in a pipe line or gathering system used in respect of such natural gas as the Lessor may determine.

As discussed in chapter 7, the standard royalty provision empowers the lessor to demand his royalty share in kind, although it does not spell out the right in express terms. If he did so, however, the burden and cost of treating the substances or storing them would fall upon the lessor.

In view of these uncertainties and other complications that could arise if a lessor attempted to exercise his right to take in kind with respect to natural gas that had been sold on long-term contracts, it would seem preferable to either make specific provisions for these matters, as is done in the proviso set forth above, or to negate the right to take in kind entirely. There has been some reluctance to expressly negate this on the assumption that the ultimate right to take the substances in kind may be a factor in qualifying a royalty interest for the depletion allowance under the Income Tax Act. In view of the approach taken by the Tax Appeal Board in *Harrington & Bibler Ltd.* v *M.N.R.*,[15] where a royalty was defined as 'a payment, measured by production, for the temporary or complete cession of some right or interest in

15 (1967) 21 D.T.C. 1

property,' the right to take in kind is not an essential ingredient of a royalty.[16]

There are, of course, clauses other than the foregoing that are found from time to time in leases. Their number is limited only by the imagination and ingenuity of the draftsmen. But those discussed above are both the most important and most commonly encountered. The one exception is that clause which grants the lessee the power to unitize the lands. The act of unitization so profoundly alters the relationship between lessor and lessee that it deserves special treatment and is discussed in detail in chapter 11, *infra*.

16 Under the Income Tax Act, 1972, and Regulations, the automatic depletion will cease at the end of 1976 and thereafter will be related to eligible expenditures which basically are exploration and development costs.

PART FOUR

UNIT AGREEMENT AND TOP LEASE

11
Unitization

WHAT IS A UNIT?

Hydrocarbon substances are accumulated in underground traps of various types. These traps prevent the further migration or dissipation of the substances and may be referred to as 'reservoirs,' 'pools,' or 'fields.' Regardless of what they are called, each accumulation will have a finite geographical area, which may be just a few sections of land, or many square miles in extent. Each field is a homogeneous whole with the substances free to move within it. From an operational point of view it makes good engineering and economic sense to operate a field as an entity without regard to any artificial distinctions created by the ownership sub-divisions. Since the average freehold lease will comprise a quarter section of land or, at best, a full section, a field will include many different ownerships and individual leases within its boundaries.

If the parties enter upon an arrangement under which a field or pool is to be operated as a common unit without regard to the boundaries imposed by lease ownership, then the field will be described as having been 'unitized.' There has been in the past a good deal of interchange of the terms 'pooling' and 'unitizing' and one still encounters documents where the two terms appear to be used interchangeably. It now, however, seems to be recognized that the term 'pooling' refers to a combining of interest to form an area not in excess of a drilling or producing spacing unit as prescribed by the applicable regulations or orders. In practice this means that pooling for oil normally will not extend over more than one quarter section or a full section in the case of gas. 'Unitization,' on the other hand, has now come to bear the meaning of the common operation of a reservoir or field without geographical limitation.

Any arrangement that ignores lease boundaries must create fundamental changes in the relationship between a mineral lessor and lessee. Wherever possible, unitization is achieved by agreement among the various parties within the field, although some provinces have provision for compulsory unitization.

UNIT AGREEMENT

A brief analysis of a unit agreement will illustrate the changes that unitization imposes upon the lessor–lessee relationship. Both working and royalty interests enter into a unit agreement. Execution is by counterpart and all parties become bound by the one agreement. In addition, the working interests will enter into a unit operating agreement among themselves, but this document is confined to the manner in which the joint working interests will be operated and does not affect the royalty or mineral owner. In the western provinces the unit agreement will follow closely the form approved by Petroleum and Natural Gas Committee at the 25th Mines Ministers Conference and known as The Model Oil and Gas Unit Agreement. Although some operators have their own version of certain of the clauses contained in the model agreement, it serves as the starting point for all unit negotiations and most units become subject to it, sometimes with a few minor modifications.

UNITIZED ZONE

It is not the entire leased substances that are unitized; normally unitization embraces only the productive horizon or zone. Thus, the unit agreement will define 'unitized zone' as being a specific formation within the unit area. Similarly, the substances that are unitized will be only those in the unitized zone.

EFFECT OF UNITIZATION

The model agreement provides that, upon the interests of each royalty and working interest owner being unitized, then the unitized zone shall be treated as though it had been included in a single lease executed by the royalty owners as lessors to the working interest owners as lessees and as if the lease had been subject to the unit agreement. This is the fundamental effect of unitization and thereafter individual lease boundaries may be disregarded for all operational purposes.

PRODUCTION OF SUBSTANCES

Each lease subject to the unit agreement is continued in force by operations on or production from the unit, regardless of whether such operations or production take place on the leased lands. This is achieved by a clause, rather similar in effect to the pooling provision under a lease, which states that operations conducted with respect to the unitized zone or production of the unitized substances shall be deemed conclusively to be operations upon or production from all of the unitized zone in each tract, and shall continue in force and effect each lease as if such operations had been conducted on and a well was producing from each tract. Unit production maintains the entire lease in force; there is no differentiation between the unitized zone and other formations.

UNIT TRACTS

Each individual lease comprised within the unit is treated as a separate tract. The unit agreement assigns a participation factor to each tract which is that tract's share of ownership in production from the unit and its corresponding share of expenses incurred by the unit.

The agreement provides that the unitized substances when produced shall be allocated to each tract in accordance with its tract participation and the amount so allocated is deemed conclusively to have been produced from the tract. This is so, regardless of whether or not there was any production from the tract or whether the amount so allocated was greater or lesser than the amount actually produced from a tract.

DISTRIBUTION WITHIN TRACTS AND CALCULATION OF ROYALTY

The working interest owner (the lessee) is responsible for the distribution of each tract's allocated production to whatever other parties may be entitled to an interest in the tract. The production of unitized substances allocated to each tract becomes the basis on which royalty is payable under the lease and the royalty owner (the lessor) of each tract agrees to accept payment of royalty so calculated in satisfaction of the royalty payable under the lease.

The model agreement also provides for an allowance, in calculating royalty on everything except crude oil, for the costs and expenses of processing, gathering, and compressing. The allowance is to include a reasonable return on investment. This provision is a more detailed statement of the royalty provision in the lease which normally refers to value 'at the well' or 'on the said lands.' To arrive at the value at the well of residue gas, it is necessary to deduct from the price paid at the outlet of a plant all the costs incurred in transporting it from the wellhead, processing it at the plant, and compression, if necessary to meet pipeline requirements.

OPERATIONS

The agreement authorizes the working interest owners to develop and operate the unitized zone without regard to the provisions or the boundaries of the individual leases. The working interest owners are also given the specific right to inject substances into the unitized zone and to convert any wells into injection wells. This power permits the institution of secondary recovery schemes, and, if it is not an extension of the powers granted under the normal lease, at least makes the right an express one instead of possibly being implied as necessary or incidental in order to 'win, take, remove the leased substances from the said lands.'

STORAGE

The later forms of the model agreement include a specific provision granting the right to inject unitized substances for storage. This is clearly an extension of the grant contained in the customary lease. The storage is confined to unitized substances and does not confer the right to use the unitized formation for storage of substances produced outside the unit. The clause also delays the payment of royalty for any injected substances until they are recovered from storage and sold.

USE OR LOSS

The agreement authorizes the working interest owners to use whatever of the unitized substances, other than crude oil, are necessary for the operation and development of the unitized zone. They are specifically given the right to inject the substances into the unitized zone, i.e. for purposes of secondary recovery drives. No royalty is payable with respect to any substances so used or injected.

NO TRANSFER OF TITLE

Although the unitization plan authorizes the common operation of the field, the agreement is not to be construed as a transfer or exchange of any interest in the leases or in the unitized substances before production. In other words, each party retains title to its own interest, and execution of the unit agreement does not operate as an automatic cross-transfer of title.

AMENDS THE LEASE

The unit agreement substantially changes the terms of any lease. A clause in the agreement provides that each lease is amended to the extent necessary to make it conform to the agreement.

LEASE RATIFIED

By executing the unit agreement a lessor, unless a court action has been commenced or is pending, ratifies and confirms the lease and agrees that no default exists with respect thereto and that the lease is in effect. The intent of this provision is clear. The lessee is taking advantage of the opportunity to fortify the status of the lease. This is a purely gratuitous act not necessary for the purposes of unitization, and its presence in a unit agreement is hard to justify. Since the lease itself requires execution under seal and the unit agreement purports to amend and ratify the lease, the agreement should also be under seal.

UNIT OPERATION IN ONTARIO

Productive pools within Ontario tend to be of very limited areal extent. The reservoirs are small, sharply defined pinnacle reefs. The small amount of acreage comprised within a pool, plus the reluctance of an operator to drill until one hundred per cent of the land has been leased, results in one lessee owning all the rights within a reservoir. This situation in turn has given rise to the Unit Operation Agreement.

The only signatories to an agreement of this type are the lessee and the individual lessor. All the lands comprising the unit area are described in a schedule attached to the agreement, and another schedule lists the leases held by the lessee in the unit area. The list is further broken down into the acreage within each lease that is included in the 'participating section' of the unit area, and that which is included in the 'non-participating' section. The distinction between 'participating' and 'non-participating' depends on whether the land is within or outside the limits of the reservoir. Although the documentation stops short of establishing one overall agreement, it clearly envisages a common operation of the unit area. The lessee is to endeavour to have similar agreements executed by all other lessors in the unit area and 'this Agreement together with any such other agreements entered into and executed shall be interpreted and treated as a common agreement by the lessors and the Lessee for the purpose of developing and obtaining production of the leased substances from those portions of the unit area.' Insofar as the lease is concerned, the unit operation agreement has many of the effects of the conventional multi-party unitization agreement. The royalty is allocated on an acreage basis (if non-participating acreage is retained, the lessor receives an annual payment of a stated sum per acre); payment of the royalty is deemed to be production from the lease; the lessee is given complete discretion in operating the unit area; and is given the right to carry out secondary recovery procedures, to inject substances and exercise similar powers.

The lease is deemed to be amended to the extent necessary to carry out the agreement, and is expressly ratified and confirmed.

The arrangement contemplated by the unit operation agreement works only when there is just one working interest owner. If it became necessary to enter into a multi-party unitization arrangement in Ontario, it is likely that the model agreement, or a variation thereof, would be utilized.

ADVANTAGES OF UNITIZATION TO LESSOR

The principal advantage that a lessor obtains from unitization is that of security. Instead of relying on the continued production from one well on his lands for royalty revenue, he shares in a number of wells, effectively spreading the risk. Unitization also lends itself to the implementation of secondary recovery measures which are designed to improve the economics of the operation and to increase the ultimate recovery of the substances.

Operating economies made possible by unitization should filter back to the lessor in the form of reduced deductions from his royalty. Only those savings which relate to above ground operations are of any benefit to the lessor since his royalty is not subject to deductions for drilling or lifting costs. There is no doubt that unit operation facilitates economies in gathering and processing costs, mainly through the construction of one large central plant, instead of several smaller ones and the avoidance of duplication in gathering flowlines.

ADVANTAGES OF UNITIZATION TO THE LESSEE

The real beneficiary of unitization is the working interest owner, the lessee. In the first place, the lessee's economic stake is much greater, usually in the ratio of seven to one. The lessee obtains the same benefits as the lessor by allocation of reserves and production over a number of wells and properties with its greater assurance of continued revenues. The benefits of enhanced recovery accrue to the working interest owner as well as the lessor, multiplied by a greater interest in the minerals.

It is in the area of cost saving, however, that the lessee reaps the greatest benefits. The unique feature of unitization, in contrast to all other types of joint venture associations, is that under unitization it is not necessary to drill and produce wells in order to preserve individual leases. Wells can be located and operated to achieve optimum production and recovery with the least number; thus one very substantial area of savings is in the diminished number of wells required. The reduction in drilling and well operating costs accrues solely to the lessee.

There is a secondary economic advantage to the lessee which is not available to the lessor. The unit facilities, gathering flowlines, processing plants, and compressor facilities are financed so as to yield a satisfactory rate of return on the invested capital. Although the primary reason for the construction of the facilities is to process the substances and make them marketable, the fact remains that investment in such facilities is an attractive proposition with a built-in profit factor.

Unitization also confers upon the lessee an almost unassailable title to the minerals covered by the leases. Once a lease is included in a unit by the lessor executing the unit agreement, any and all operations anywhere within the unit have the effect of continuing the lease in force. It is not surprising that unitization has grown increasingly popular with each passing year. It has become almost the rule with respect to gas fields, and is normally completed before production commences. The trend to unitize oil fields is steadily growing.

It is impossible to say anything against the principle of unitization. It undoubtedly achieves better operating procedures, enhances recovery, and implements good conservation practices, all at a reduced cost. It is not surprising, therefore, to find that unitization is encouraged by public conservation bodies. In the purely private area of contract between the lessor and lessee, different factors may come into play. Under current industry practice the lessor is expected to execute a unit agreement without any additional consideration, the benefits described above evidently being regarded as sufficient incentive.

SHOULD A LESSOR ENTER INTO A UNIT AGREEMENT?

The lessor plays no part in the negotiations that lead to unitization. The chances are that the first knowledge he will have of unitization will be when he receives in the mail a twenty-page Unit Agreement with attached Exhibits. These Exhibits usually consist of a list of the tracts with their allocated tract factors; a map outlining the unit area; and a copy of the electric logs in certain wells that define the unitized zone. If the agreement is mailed to the lessor, it is usually accompanied by a letter which points out the benefits of unitization, and is followed by a visit from a representative of the lessee company. Sometimes the first contact with the lessor will be made by the company representative who will review the agreement with the lessor.

In either event the lessor is confronted with a decision: should he accede to unitization, or be a hold-out? Apart from a vague awareness that unitization is 'a good thing,' the average lessor will have little idea of the consequences flowing from it. Nor will the unit agreement do much to enlighten him since an understanding of its impact upon the lease demands a specialized knowledge far beyond that possessed by the average mineral owner. There are two situations in which a lessor may find himself when requested to unitize: (a) there is a well on the leased lands or on lands pooled with them; (b) there is no well on the leased or pooled lands.

WELL ON THE LANDS

If the lessor refuses to execute the unit agreement and there is a well capable of producing on his lands, these are the most important consequences:
1 The lessee must produce from the well or lose the lease. The suspended well royalty provision will not come to the assistance of the lessee under these circumstances since failure to produce would not be considered as resulting from a cause beyond its control. Unitization presupposes an existing or near-term market, and the fact that other wells in the immediate area are producing would render the suspended well clause ineffective. A lessee faced with a reluctant lessor can place the lands on production in two ways: (a) the well can be tied into the unit system and the production therefrom processed, if required, through unit facilities on an agreed charge basis; or (b) the lessee can 'indemnify' the lands into the unit. The model unit agreement contains a provision that permits a working interest owner whose lessor will not become a party to the unit agreement, to nonetheless include the lands by indemnifying the other working interest owners against loss or damages resulting from any claims or demands by the lessor.
2 Royalty must be paid to the lessor on the basis of actual production from the well. This result arises from the wording of the lease that requires a royalty to be paid on the basis of those substances produced and mar-

keted from the lands.[1] There would be no problem to the lessee where the well remains outside the unit since the lessee will be receiving its price on all the substances actually produced. It becomes much more significant, however, where the lands have been included in the unit. Since one of the main benefits of unitization is production through a minimum number of wells, it is likely that the well in question will be producing from an area several times the production spacing unit that would have been allocated to it under conservation regulations. Hence, it may be producing at several times the rate that would prevail in the absence of unitization. Only a portion of the actual production will be allocated to the lessee in accordance with the tract participation of the lands. The lessee, however, will be forced under the express terms of the lease to pay a royalty on the full amount produced through the well.

3   If the reserves are exhausted under the lands and production ceases, the lessor has no claim for royalty on production from other wells in the unit.

4   The existence of a non-unitized lease can complicate secondary recovery procedures. For example, consider the implementation of a water flood in an oilfield. Under such a scheme, water is injected into the formation through wells located in a certain predetermined pattern and position. As the water flood advances, it drives before it the crude oil so that some lands on the periphery of the drive are soon flooded out, while the quantity of crude under lands in the target area is increased enormously. If the non-unitized lease were located on the outskirts of the field, the lessor would soon find his lands underlain with nothing but water, while if he were fortunate enough to be located near the target area his reserves would be greatly enhanced. Under unitization this result is of no consequence since all share in accordance with their tract participation.

If the lessor's reserves are enhanced by secondary recovery measures, it would appear that he could take the benefit of this without any legal recourse against him. Under the law of capture the oil under the non-unitized land belongs to the owner when reduced into his possession, regardless of the fact that it had been driven from its original location by an artificial reservoir drive.

The rule of capture is modified to some extent at least by the effect of

1   One American court has rebelled at this result. In *Dobson v Arkansas Oil & Gas Commission* 235 sw (2d) 33, the court refused to allow the lessor to 'share the fruits of unitization while being relieved of its burdens' and held that royalty should be payable on the rate at which the well was producing prior to unitization and not at the enhanced volumes resulting from unitization. It is doubtful if a Canadian court would stray from the plain meaning of the lease.

conservation legislation and regulations. Those operators who have invested in an enhanced recovery scheme are entitled to have their allowable production increased by the application of an adjustment factor.[2] If a lease was not included in a unit and remained a 'window' as a result of the lessor's failure to execute the agreement, the other wells within the unit would enjoy this additional allowable, while the non-unitized well would not. If the lessee, however, 'indemnified' the lease into the unit, then the lessor would be entitled to royalty on actual production which would be increased by the application of the recovery factor modifier.

What of the position of the lessor who does not unitize and whose lands are quickly flooded out by the operation of the unit? At common law he would seem to have an action for restraint or injunction against the implementation of such a scheme if he could demonstrate that the result would be to destroy his property. The Alberta legislature has intervened and if a scheme for the enhanced recovery in any field or pool has been approved by the appropriate board, the performance of any act required to be done under the approved scheme cannot be prevented or restrained by an injunction, judgment, or order of any court.[3] It is to be noted that the legislation does not take away the lessor's right to claim damages but it effectively takes away his right to restrain the implementation of a scheme.

NO WELL ON THE LANDS

If there is no well on the leased or pooled lands and the lessor refuses to join in a voluntary unitization, the position seems to be
1   There would be no royalty payable as there is no production, either actual or constructive.
2   The lease will expire at the end of the primary term, since there would be no production to activate the 'thereafter' feature. The lessee can avoid this result, but only at the cost of drilling a well and placing it on actual production. This would be done at the lessee's sole cost and risk as the well would confer no benefit to the unit.
3   If the lease were beyond the primary term at the time the unit became effective and had been maintained in force by a suspended well payment, it would terminate, either immediately or at the end of the payment

2 See, for example, Alberta Oil and Gas Conservation Regulations,
   Alta Reg. 183/69 s 914
3 Oil and Gas Conservation Act R.S.A. 1970 c 267, s 39. Such prohibition is not
   necessary in other provinces where unitization can be made compulsory.

period, depending on the wording of the clause, as the *raison d'être* of the suspended well clause would have disappeared.

4 The lessor might be able to activate the offset drilling clause if a unit well on a laterally adjoining spacing unit were to be placed on production.

5 A non-unitized lessor might be able to obstruct the implementation of secondary recovery procedures that would flood out his property.[4]

COMPULSORY UNITIZATION

The advantages of unitization are so substantial that three of the four provinces where freehold mineral rights are of importance have decreed that it may be imposed compulsorily. The Ontario Energy Board Act[5] authorizes the board to require and regulate the joining of various interests within a field or pool for the purpose of drilling or operating wells. Saskatchewan provides that, upon the application of any interested party or the Minister of Mineral Resources, the Oil and Gas Conservation Board may hold a hearing and order that a field or pool is to be operated as a unit.[6] The Saskatchewan Act further provides that, if a unit is formed, then any production allocated to a tract shall be deemed to have been actually produced from that tract and that all operations within the unit area are deemed to have been carried on within each tract. In 1966 the Saskatchewan legislation was amended to recognize a voluntary unitization as well as compulsory unitization imposed by the Board and the voluntary form has been more commonly followed since that date. In Manitoba the Board upon its own motion or upon its application of a working interest owner may make an order for compulsory unitization, but only if the royalty owners having seventy-five per cent of the royalty interests in the oil and gas produced from the unit area have agreed to the plan of unit operation.[7] There is the usual statutory protection of the lessee's interest in that production or operations within the unit area are deemed to take place on each tract.

Alberta, undoubtedly in deference to the 'freedom to contract' has been much more circumspect in its approach to compulsory unitization. The Oil

4 Subject to the legislative restriction discussed in n. 3. Once again the American courts have gone further than the Canadian courts are likely to follow. *Tidewater Associated Oil Co.* v *Stott* 159 F (2d) 174 denied a lessor damages for drainage when the lessor had refused to join in a gas recycling plan for the recovery of condensates, with the dry gas being reinjected for lack of a market.

5 R.S.O. 1970 c 312 s 24

6 The Oil and Gas Conservation Act R.S.S. 1965 c 360, as amended by s.s. 1966 c 66

7 The Mines Act R.S.M. 1970, c M160 ss 76–7

and Gas Conservation Act[8] contains a fully articulated part which sets forth the manner in which a field or pool can be unitized with provisions that would continue a lease in force by virtue of unit production or operations, regardless of the location within the unit. While the machinery of compulsory unitization has been fully spelled out in the Alberta legislation, it has not yet been proclaimed in force. Until that part of the Act is brought into force, unitization can be achieved in Alberta only by agreement.

The British Columbia Petroleum and Natural Gas Act of 1965[9] contains passing references to unitization but, as is the case with most of that province's legislation, they seem to be directed solely to Crown mineral rights.

UNITIZATION CLAUSE

The desirability of unitization has led more and more lessees to include in their printed form of lease a clause that purports to give them the right to unitize the land. This power is usually mixed in with the clause that grants the right to pool the lands to form a spacing unit. A common form reads as follows:

10 POOLING
The Lessee is hereby given the right and power at any time and from time to time
(a) to pool or combine the said lands or any portion thereof, or any zone or formation underlying the said lands or any portion thereof, with any other lands or any zones or formations underlying the same, but so that the area of the lands resulting therefrom (herein referred to as a 'unit') shall not exceed one (1) spacing unit as hereinbefore defined, and
(b) to unitize the leased substances, or any of them, produced from the said lands or any portion thereof, or any zone or formation underlying the said lands or any portion thereof (whether or not the same has been pooled or combined, as aforesaid) with like substances produced from any other lands, or any zone or formations underlying such other lands, and for that purpose to enter into such agreements with respect to the said lands and the leased substances as the Lessee may deem advisable.
In the event of such pooling or combining, the amount to be paid in respect of the royalty hereinbefore reserved shall be paid on the production of leased substances from the resulting unit, only in the proportion that the surface area of the said lands in the unit bears to the surface area of all of the lands included therein. Drilling operations on, or production of any of the leased substances from, or the

8 *Supra* n. 3 ss 87–95   9 S.B.C. 1965 c 33 notably ss 113 (u) and 118

presence of a shut-in or suspended well on, any land included in such unit or the happening of any other event which occurs on or in connection with such land shall continue this Lease in force and effect to the same extent as would have been the case had such drilling operations, production of leased substances, the presence of a shut-in or suspended well, or other event occurred on or in connection with the said lands; and any well on any land included in such unit, whenever the same may have been drilled, whether producing, or shut-in or suspended, shall be deemed for all purposes to be a producing well drilled on the said lands under the provisions of this Lease.

In the event of any unitization as provided for in paragraph (b) of this Clause, the provisions of Clause 9 hereof shall no longer be applicable in respect of leased substances affected thereby, and the amount to be paid by way of royalty in respect of such substances shall be paid only in respect of such quantity thereof as have been allocated to the said lands under the terms of the agreements affecting such unitization.

The indiscriminate references to pooling and unitization in the same clause create confusion and ambiguity, but so far as unitization is concerned, the clause attempts to (a) give the lessee the right to unitize the leased substances, (b) allow the lessee to enter into whatever agreements with respect to such unitization it feels advisable, (c) ensure that drilling or other operations, or production or the existence of a suspended well on any land included in such unit will continue the lease in force as though it had all taken place on the leased lands, (d) provide that the royalty shall not be computed on actual production from the said lands, but on production allocated to the lands under the unit agreement.

The status of such clauses in Canadian law remains shrouded in doubt.[10] The issue as to whether a lessee, acting under the authority purportedly conferred by the clause could effectively commit its lessor's property to a unit agreement has never been before Canadian courts. As a matter of practice, lessees prefer not to rely upon such a clause even when present in their lease form, but rather to obtain the voluntary execution of a unit agreement. If the lessor remains adamant in his refusal to unitize, the lessee may be tempted to rely upon the clause, at least to the extent of supporting a decision to indemnify the lease into the unit. So used, the clause becomes a shield rather than a sword. Sooner or later, however, the lessee must face the final test.

10 In the United States this type of clause appears to be enforceable if the lessor was made fully aware of it and its consequences at the time of execution of the lease and if the lessee carried out such unitization in good faith. See, *Phillips Petroleum Company* v *Peterson et al*, 218 F (2nd) 926

Can unitization under the clause effectively preserve the lease? Can production allocated to the lease as a result of unitization without the actual execution of the unit agreement by the lessor amount to actual production from the lands covered by the lease?

The enforceability of a power such as that conveyed in the unitization clause immediately confronts two legal hurdles: (1) the rule against perpetuities, and (2) the question of whether it is void for uncertainty.

RULE AGAINST PERPETUITIES

Allocation of production lies at the very heart of unitization. It is this feature that validates the entire concept of operating a field or pool regardless of individual lease boundaries. In a sense, the allocation of production can be said to involve property rights. The lessor, and the lessee, agree to accept a theoretical production rather than the actual barrels of oil or thousands of cubic feet of gas produced from the lands. The unitization clause is not defined as to the time within which it must be exercised; it lasts as long as the lease. The ultimate term of the lease depends upon reserves, reservoir characteristics, and the rate of production, and could result in a period extending beyond that permitted by the rule.[11]

However, the allocation of production for the purposes of determining the computation of royalty probably falls short of that degree of vesting or title transfer required for operation of the rule. Moreover, every unit agreement specifically negatives any transfer of an interest in the leases: 'EFFECT OF UNITIZATION ON TITLES   Nothing herein shall be construed as a transfer or exchange of any interest in the Leases, Tracts or Unitized Zone or in the Unitized Substances before production thereof.' It is probable, therefore, that the clause would survive an attack made against it on the basis of the rule against perpetuities.

VOID FOR UNCERTAINTY

There are many fundamental elements of a unitization agreement that are totally unknown at the time the lease is executed. The general terms of the model unit agreement are certainly ascertainable, but no one will know the extent of the unit area, the unitized zone or the unitized substances, or the formula for the determination of tract factors. The unitization clause attempts to overcome these obstacles by delegating to the lessee complete discretion and authority to enter into such agreements 'as the lessee may deem advisable.'

11 The operation of the rule against perpetuities is outlined in chap 10, *ante*

This is truly an unfettered power to commit another party. It would appear, however, that, if the intention to delegate can be clearly demonstrated by the language, there is no legal reason why such power cannot be exercised by the lessee. The closest analogy is a Supreme Court of Canada decision involving not a lease, but a combining of interest between two permit holders. In *Calvan Consolidated Oil & Gas Company Limited* v *Manning*,[12] the two parties agreed to exchange a certain percentage of their interests in petroleum and natural gas permits. The agreement was embodied in a letter agreement which provided that the parties would exchange twenty per cent of each permit and that one of the parties, namely Calvan, would have the right to 'dispose of, or deal with Permit 120 on behalf of us both in such manner as you see fit. If the Permit is sold, then you will account to me and my partners for 20 per cent of the proceeds of the sale. If the Permit is not sold, then the 20 per cent interest is a working interest, which will be reduced proportionately as Calvan's interest is reduced, should a farmout be negotiated.'

Calvan proceeded to enter into negotiations which resulted in the execution of an agreement with Imperial Oil Limited. Manning was not consulted during these negotiations, and subsequently he attacked a number of the terms of the farmout agreement on the basis that they represented a breach of trust on the part of Calvan. That company then brought an action for a declaratory order that there never had been a contract between itself and Manning. The Supreme Court of Canada carefully confined itself to the question as to whether or not there was an existing contract between Calvan and Manning and avoided any consideration as to whether the performance of such a contract by Calvan had been adequate.

The court found the letter agreement was not void for uncertainty. The parties understood what was meant by a 'farmout' agreement, the percentage interest which the third party would earn in the property was to come proportionately from both signatories and Calvan had full power of decision, subject only to its duty to preserve Manning's interest as a working interest, to account to him for his proper share of the proceeds of the transaction, and to observe its duty to him as a co-owner. In the words of the court, 'There is no uncertainty here. There could, of course, have been an endless variation in the type of "farmout" agreement that might have been negotiated by Calvan but this was entirely a matter for Calvan's determination subject to the limitations that I have mentioned.'

This situation, where one party in effect abdicates its rights of negotiation to another for the purposes of farming out the lands, is closely parallel to that under the unitization clause. Here the lessor delegates his right to unitize

12 [1959] s.c.r. 253, 17 d.l.r. (2d) 1 (s.c.c.)

and to determine the basis of unitization to the lessee. The lessee becomes the agent of the lessor and has the power to bind him to a unitization agreement. Like any agent, however, the lessee may find itself confronted with a very high standard of duty and care.

DUTY OF CARE

The relationship between principal and agent has been defined as follows: 'Agency is the relationship that exists between two persons when one called the *agent*, is considered in law to represent the other, called the *principal*, in such a way as to be able to affect the principal's legal position in respect of strangers to the relationship by the making of contracts or the disposition of property.'[13]

A lessee working under a unitization clause with other interest owners in a field would appear to occupy this position vis-à-vis the lessor. As always in the law, responsibility walks hand in hand with authority. The lessee agent may find himself affixed with a duty of care to the lessor that, under the normal circumstances of unitization, is almost impossible to discharge. The unitization clause is silent on the duties owed by the lessee; indeed, it stops short of creating an agency relationship in express terms. Nonetheless, the agency relationship under the common law is one of trust. Fridman groups these duties owed by an agent under the general principle that 'the agent must not let his own personal interest conflict with the obligations he owes to his principal.' This generalization in turn is divided into a number of compartments which define the agent's responsibility. The ones which seem particularly appropriate to unitization are: (a) That the agent must perform the undertaking with due care and skill. This particular responsibility will be onerous on a lessee with exclusive knowledge of the data and information relating to reserves, deliverability, and character of the leased substances, and with professional experience in the industry. (b) If the agent is in a position where his own interest may affect the performance of his duty to the principal, he is required to make a full disclosure of all the material circumstances, so that the principal can choose whether to consent to the agent acting on his behalf.

The duty of disclosure, in the event of a possible conflict, is of peculiar significance to unitizaton. Almost invariably, the lessee will have interests in other tracts to be included in the unit, while the lessor will be interested only in one particular portion of the lands. The individual tract participation is worked out by representatives of the working interests prior to unitization in accordance with a formula that is tied in to reserves and deliverability. The

13 *Fridman's Law of Agency* (2 ed.) (1960) 8

formula will incorporate such factors as areal extent, estimated pay thickness, porosity, permeability, and other geological and engineering factors. Within the limits of these parameters, however, there remains considerable room for negotiation in the assignment of individual tract participations. If a lessee has interests in several tracts, it may be willing to make concessions with respect to one in the expectation of receiving more favourable treatment for others.

This atmosphere of 'give and take' in the allocation of tract factors places the agent in a position where its interest may affect the performance of its agency. Under these circumstances the agent is placed under a duty to make full disclosure of the material circumstances, and the principal after receiving such disclosure may elect whether to consent to his agent continuing to act.[14] If the fact that the lessee held interest in other tracts is construed as being such a special interest as would affect the principal–agency relationship, and in the light of the decided cases, it seems likely that such would be the result, the power contained in the unitization clause could be withdrawn or revoked at the very moment that it is to be utilized. If the agent fails to make proper disclosure, the lessor on subsequently learning of the conflicting interest of his lessee may set aside the act of the agent and claim from the agent any profit received from the transaction.[15]

The impact of such an upset, several years after the event, upon a unit achieved in part through the unitization clause may well be imagined. That these hazards of principal and agent are real in the world of oil and gas is evidenced by *Manning* v *Calvan Consolidated Oil & Gas Company Limited and Imperial Oil Limited* (No. 2).[16] Manning, having been assured by the Supreme Court of Canada in the earlier case[17] that the letter agreement between himself and Calvan was binding, set out to prove that Calvan was in breach of trust because of the deal it negotiated with Imperial Oil Limited. Calvan acting under the power granted by the letter agreement to deal 'as you see fit' with the property did not consult Manning at any stage of its negotiations with Imperial. The results of the negotiations could be summarized as follows: The arrangement involved three Permits, two of which were owned outright by Calvan and one of which was Permit 120, in which Manning was entitled to an undivided 20 per cent interest pursuant to the letter agreement. The evidence indicated that in so far as Imperial was concerned the entire transaction was 'a parcel deal' for all three Permits. In general, the agreements required Imperial to pay in cash to Calvan the sums

---

14 Ibid, 125, 126; *Bowstead on Agency* (12 ed.) (1959) 93–7
15 *McPherson* v *Watt* (1877) 3 App. Cas. 254
16 Unreported but digested in Lewis & Thompson, *Canadian Oil and Gas*, vol. 1, Dig. 183
17 *Supra* n. 12

already spent on the Permits and thereby to acquire a 50 per cent working interest in each of the Permits, with a further condition that upon completion of drilling a well Imperial's working interest in the Permits would increase to 75 per cent. With respect to Permit 120, $80,000.00 was paid, representing the expenditure that had been made. Calvan accounted to Manning for 20 per cent of this sum. Imperial initially took exception to the costs which were claimed to be $150,000.00 for one of the Permits which was wholly owned by Calvan. Despite this original objection, Imperial when it concluded a concurrent deal on all three Permits paid Calvan the entire cash consideration. There were individual agreements relating to all three Permits, but they were described as being identical in form. The performance of exploratory work created, under existing legislation and regulations, certain work credits which, broadly speaking, replaced the requirement to pay rental fees. Within limits, excess work credits earned on one permit could be allocated to others. The Permit 120 agreement provided that excess credits could be applied to the other two permits which were solely owned by Calvan. As a result of drilling carried out by Imperial on Permit 120, excess work credits were transferred in the amount of $71,000.00 to Permit 118 and $140,000.00 to Permit 119.

Manning claimed a breach of trust on the part of Calvan in the negotiations leading to the treatment of the excess credits. This allegation was upheld by the trial judge who observed 'that it is well settled that a trustee must deal with property of a *cestui que trust* as he would prudently deal with his own; he must not make a profit or gain an advantage over the *cestui que trust* by the use of his office as trustee.' He further quoted from *Regal and Hastings Ltd.* v *Gulliver*:[18] 'The general rule of equity is that no one who has duties of a fiduciary nature to perform, is allowed to enter into engagements in which he has or can have a personal interest conflicting with the interests of those he is bound to protect.'

The trial judge viewed the transaction as one in which Calvan used joint property to secure a special advantage for itself. There was evidence that the excess work credit could not have been used by Manning as he did not have other permits that qualified or that there were still excess credits available to him if he were able to use them. This was not considered relevant by the court which seized upon the point that these rights had been bargained away for other considerations which accrued solely to the benefit of Calvan. Damages were assessed at the not inconsequential sum of $40,000.00.

If the unitization clause is to be effective, the most likely legal approach is that of a principal–agent relationship. Thus the unitization clause which creates this relationship by implication, if not expressly, is subject to a very

18 [1942] 1 All E.R. 378, 381

serious limitation in that the likelihood of a conflict of interest requires disclosure with a right of revocation (or subsequent repudiation in the event of non-disclosure) and also makes the lessee vulnerable to attack on the ground that it has failed to carry out the high degree of skill and care required of an agent.

CAN LESSEE BIND LESSOR TO PROVISIONS THAT ADVERSELY AFFECT LESSOR'S POSITION?

The unitization clause empowers the lessee to enter into such unitization agreements as it 'may deem advisable.' The model unitization agreement contains several provisions which expressly affect and modify the relationship between lessor and lessee, including those that: (a) ratify and confirm the lease, (b) permit storage of the substances in underground formations, and (c) spell out and probably enlarge the deductions that may be made by the lessee in computing royalty.

If the lessor has not executed the unitization agreement and the lessee is relying on the unitization clause, can the lessee place the lessor in a position where he is bound by provisions of this type? The ratification provision is designed to work a type of estoppel against any attack by the lessor on the validity of the lease. If the lessor has not signed the agreement, it is hard to see how any estoppel by deed could be claimed against him. Similarly it seems doubtful that the powers granted under the lease, or the right to deduct charges, could be enlarged as against the lessor where he has not himself signed the agreement.

UNITIZED ZONES

Unit agreements are confined to specific formations and the substances contained therein. Nonetheless the effect of the unit agreement and any operations thereon or production therefrom is to continue the entire lease in force. Under existing practice, oil and gas leases normally convey all the lessor's interests and are not confined to any particular formation. Hydrocarbons may occur in formations other than those unitized. Thus a lessor called upon to execute a unit agreement might be well advised to insist upon an amendment that restricts the continuing effect of the unit agreement upon his lease to the unitized formation or formations.

INGREDIENTS OF UNITIZATION CLAUSE

The inclusion of a unitization clause in the lease can be very tempting to the lessee. Unitization has many benefits and a reluctant lessor, in Alberta (also in British Columbia, if freehold rights become important) and to a lesser extent in Manitoba, can prove to be very troublesome. The mere existence of a unitization clause can be a powerful tool to persuade a lessor to execute the unit agreement. The present form seems to be deficient in several respects. If, as seems probable, the principal–agency route is the one most likely of success, then the clause should make the relationship express. It is suggested that the unitization clause would be both more enforceable and more manageable if it contained these elements:

(a) a specific reference to the model form of unit agreement which the lessor would acknowledge having read;

(b) an express appointment of the lessee as the lessor's agent to negotiate the tract participation to be allocated to the leased land;

(c) an express acknowledgment by the lessor that he is aware of the fact that the lessee may have interests in other lands to be comprised within any future unit and an express waiver of any disclosure;

(d) the appointment of the lessee as the attorney of the lessor to enter into a unit agreement identical with the model form;

(e) express agreement that in the event the said lands are unitized all operations with respect to, or production of unitized substances from, the unitized zone shall be deemed to be operations on or production of the leased substances from the said lands;

(f) inasmuch as most of the advantages resulting from unitization flow to the lessee, it might not be inappropriate to include a provision for some additional consideration to the lessor in the event the lands are unitized. An additional cash payment of $1.00 per acre, for example, has much to recommend it both from the point of view of equity and because the powers granted under the clause might appear more acceptable to a court if supported by a separate consideration.

A clause drawn on the above lines might enable a lessee to effectively unitize the lease. Nonetheless, unitization achieved in this manner has so many drawbacks when compared to voluntary unitization that it should be regarded only as a last resort. It has all the hazards of the agency relationship, the possibility of a successful repudiation by the lessor, and it is doubtful if it could effectively amend the lease.

12
Top lease

The judicial hazards that threaten the existence of oil and gas leases have given rise to a curious document known as a 'top lease.' The agreement is entered into when there is an existing lease on the property, and reflects the hope or expectation that the current lease will expire or be terminated while the mineral rights under the property still retain some value. The Supreme Court of Canada has defined a top lease succinctly if not too helpfully: 'A top lease is one which takes effect upon the termination of a prior existing lease.'[1] However expressed, the top lease makes the lessor's reversionary interest subject to the top lessee's right to take a lease.

The top lease arrangement may follow any one of a number of forms. The ones most commonly encountered are: (a) a conditional lease, (b) a right of first refusal, (c) an option to take a lease.

CONDITIONAL LEASE

Under this method the lease form is identical with the conventional lease, with the exception that it contains the following proviso:

PROVIDED that this Lease and Grant shall not become effective until the Petroleum and Natural Gas Lease dated the .... day of ...., A.D. 19........ made between .... as Lessor, and .... as Lessee, hereinafter called 'the current lease', affecting the said lands, shall have termin-

---

1 *Meyers* v *Freeholders Company Limited and Canada Permanent Trust Company* [1960] S.C.R. 761, 766

ated, expired or ceased to have any force and effect. Upon the current Lease having terminated, expired or having ceased to be of any force and effect, the Lease and Grant herein created shall become effective and the term shall be deemed to commence as of such date, hereinafter called the 'effective date'. The current Lease shall be deemed to have terminated, expired, or ceased to be of any force and effect upon that date determined as follows:

(a) If any court proceedings are commenced with respect to the current Lease, when the Court having final jurisdiction in the matter shall have determined that the current Lease has so terminated, expired or ceased to be of any force and effect;

(b) When the current Lease terminates, expires, or ceases to exist by any other happening or by operation of law, PROVIDED that if the current Lease shall not have terminated, expired, or ceased to be of any force and effect, within twenty-one (21) years after the death of the last surviving direct descendant, now living, of Queen Elizabeth II of the United Kingdom, the Lease and Grant herein created shall terminate and be at an end.

Within thirty (30) days after the collective date has been determined as aforesaid, the Lessee shall pay the Lessor the sum of .... ($................) provided that in the event a bona fide dispute exists as to the date on which this Lease and Grant commences, the Lessee's obligation hereunder shall be postponed until the resolution of such dispute.

RIGHT OF FIRST REFUSAL

A typical clause of this type reads:

DOTH HEREBY grant unto the Grantee the sole and exclusive preferential and prior right to acquire from the Grantor any interest of the Grantor in the petroleum substances or any of them within, upon or under the said lands from time to time and at any time during the currency hereof, such rights being granted upon and subject to the following terms and conditions: 1. If at any time during and throughout a period of four (4) years commencing as of the date hereof, the Grantor shall receive or make a bona fide offer acceptable to both him and his offeror and/or his offeree as the case may be, to sell, transfer, lease, license or otherwise in any manner howsoever dispose of any interest in and to the petroleum substances or any of them within, upon or under the said lands or any part or parts thereof, or to renew or extend the term of any estate or interest in the said petroleum substances, whether now or hereafter created, the Grantor shall forthwith advise the Grantee by notice in writing, as hereinafter prescribed, (hereinafter called the 'Grantor's Notice') of all of the terms of such offer, whereupon the Grantee, or its nominee, shall have the first preferential and prior right for a period of thirty (30) consecutive days, (hereinafter called 'the period of first refusal') commencing and including the first day following receipt by the Grantee of such notice, to acquire from the Grantor the interest so intended to be disposed of by the Grantor, as aforesaid, upon and for a consideration Ten (10%) Percent greater than that disclosed in such offer but otherwise on the same terms and conditions as are contained in the said offer.

OPTION

The top lease concept is probably best suited to the option. A top lease may be created by an option which becomes effective only when the current lease has terminated.

The Optionor, being the beneficial owner of the petroleum, natural gas and all related hydrocarbons within, upon or under ... (160 acres) ... in consideration of the sum of .... Dollars paid to the Optionor by the Optionee (the receipt whereof is hereby acknowledged) the Optionor DOTH HEREBY GRANT to the Optionee the sole and exclusive option, irrevocable for a period of five (5) years from the date hereof, to acquire a Petroleum and Natural Gas Lease in the form hereinafter set forth, of all the petroleum, natural gas and related hydrocarbons, except coal (hereinafter referred to as 'the leased substances') within, upon or under the lands hereinbefore described, and insofar as the Optionor owns or controls the same all the right, title, estate and interest of the Optionor in and to the leased substances or any of them within, upon or under any lands excepted from, or roadways, lanes or rights-of-way adjoining the lands aforesaid, together with the exclusive right and privilege to explore, drill for, win, take, remove, store and dispose of the leased substances and for the said purposes to drill wells, lay pipe lines and build and install such tanks, stations, structures and roadways as may be necessary.

The option hereby granted shall be open for acceptance at any time within a period of five (5) years from the date hereof, or on or before, but not after, a date thirty (30) days from the date of receipt of notice by the Optionee from the Optionor pursuant to the provisions of Paragraph 19 hereof of the termination, cancellation or expiration of the existing Petroleum and Natural Gas Lease affecting the said lands.

The option may be exercised by the Optionee delivering to the Optionor, or mailing postage prepaid and addressed to the Optionor at the address specified in Paragraph 23 hereof, written notice of its intention to exercise this option accompanied by payment of such amount of lawful money of Canada as shall be necessary to increase the amount paid as consideration for this option to the sum of .... Dollars per acre, which amount shall represent the consideration for the granting of this option and the petroleum and natural gas lease herein-after set out. The term of the said Petroleum and Natural Gas Lease shall be deemed to commence as of the date of the exercising of the said option (which date is hereinafter referred to as 'the effective date').

A simpler form of option ignores any lease that may be existing:

... the Optionor, being the owner of the Petroleum and Natural gas rights in and under the lands herein described, DOES HEREBY GIVE AND GRANT to the optionee the sole and exclusive Option, irrevocable within the time herein limited for acceptance, to lease all the petroleum, natural gas and related hydrocarbons, all other gases, and all other substances (whether fluid or solid and whether similar or dissimilar and whether hydrocarbons or not) produced in association with any of the foregoing or found in any water contained in an oil or gas reservoir, excluding, however, coal and valuable stone, in and under all or any part of the following lands, including the interest of the Optionor in such substances within, upon or under any lands excepted therefrom or roadways, lanes or rights-of-way thereto adjoining.

From the top lessee's point of view, the option route seems infinitely preferable. The conditional lease suffers from the defect that it is binding upon the lessee when the existing lease comes to an end. Once that happens, the lessee becomes obligated to pay the stipulated bonus and to assume the obligations of the lease. From the lessor's viewpoint, the fact that the lessee becomes obligated to at least pay the bonus consideration upon termination of the existing lease may be very desirable.

The first refusal technique suffers from the deficiency that it requires the positive act of some party other than the grantee to activate the right. Before the grantee's right to acquire comes into force, there must be a *bona fide* offer involving a third party.

INTEREST IN LAND

The right to acquire a lease as expressed in the top lease arrangement has been characterized as an equitable contingent interest in land.[2] The fact that

2 *Pan American Petroleum Corporation* v *Potapchuk and Scurry-Rainbow Oils Limited* (1964), 46 w.w.r. 237 (Alta), aff'd (1965) 51 w.w.r. 700 (CA) aff'd (1965) 51 w.w.r. 767 (S.C.C.). This decision applied *Frobisher Ltd.* v *Canadian Pipelines & Petroleums Ltd.* [1960] S.C.R. 126; commented on by La Forest, 'Real Property – Options Rights of Pre-Emption – Accrual Interest in Lands – Personal Contractual Obligation – Rule Against Perpetuities' (1960) 38 *Can. Bar Rev.* 595

it is an interest in land makes a top lease registrable by caveat or otherwise under the various provincial registry systems. Since the top lease effectively ties-up the reversionary interest of the lessor and authorizes the top lessee to call for a conveyance of a *profit à prendre*, it is difficult to see how it could be treated as anything but an interest in land.

RULE AGAINST PERPETUITIES

A top lease, by its very nature, postpones the actual vesting of an interest to some future time, which automatically calls into question the rule against perpetuities. The scope and effect of this principle are discussed in some detail in chapter 10, *ante*, although it may be useful to summarize once again the rule: 'No interest is good unless it must vest, if at all, not later than 21 years after some life in being at the creation of the interest.'[3] The examples of the various approaches to a top lease set forth at the beginning of this chapter are careful to avoid the application of the rule by embodying a time limit after which the right to acquire a lease will expire. The fixing of a definite time limit, regardless of whether or not the original lease has expired or terminated, will effectively counteract the rule so long as the period within which the vesting must occur does not exceed the perpetuity period. Since the only reason for imposing a time limit is to avoid the rule, one may safely assume that the time period will never offend against the rule.

Some of the earlier forms of top lease did not take precautions against the rule; even in these circumstances there is an indication that Canadian courts might be prepared to enforce the option as a personal covenant against the optionor.

PERSONAL COVENANT

If the optionor remains in possession of the mineral rights, the optionee can enforce specific performance of a covenant to grant a lease, even if the arrangement offends the rule against perpetuities. The optionor remains personally liable on the covenant and must perform it so long as it is within his power so to do. If the optionor disposes of the property to a third party, however, the optionee will be able to obtain only damages for breach of contract and cannot insist upon specific performance.

The issue was lightly touched upon by the Canadian Supreme Court in *Prudential Trust Company Limited and Canadian Williston Minerals Limited*

3 Morris and Leach, *The Rule Against Perpetuities* (2nd ed.) (1962), 1

v *Forseth*[4] and in a manner which made it clear that Martland's J comments were *obiter dicta*. After disposing of various attacks upon documentation which transferred an undivided half interest in the minerals and granted an option to take a lease upon expiration of the existing one, the learned judge dealt with the argument that the option to lease was void because it offended the rule against perpetuities. The option could be exercised within ninety days of the termination of the current lease. The original lease could, of course, extend well beyond the perpetuity period. The court noted that because there were no less than eight producing oil wells on the property, the issue was really academic since the original lease would be continued indefinitely by production.

We are being asked, therefore, to determine questions of law which are unlikely to arise and which, if they arise at all, can only arise in the remote future.

It is sufficient to say that at this stage I would not be prepared to hold that the option is void. The law regarding the subject of contracts relating to rights in the future has been well summarized in Halsbury's Laws of England, 2nd ed., vol. 25, at p. 109, as follows:

'A contract relating to a right of or equitable interest in property *in futuro* may be intended to create a limitation of land only, in which case, if the limitation is to take effect beyond the perpetuity period, the contract is wholly void and unenforceable; or the contract may, upon its true construction, be a personal contract only, in which case the rule does not apply to it; or it may, upon its true construction, be, as regards the original covenantor, both a personal contract and a contract attempting to create a remote limitation, in which case the limitation will be bad for perpetuity, but the personal contract will be enforceable, if the case otherwise admits, against the promisor by specific performance or by damages, or against his personal representatives in damages only. In all cases it is a question of construction whether the contract is intended to create a limitation of property only, or a personal obligation only, or both.'

I am not prepared to say that the assignment did not constitute a personal contract by Forseth, especially when it is borne in mind that the agreement contemplates a future petroleum and natural gas lease to be granted, not by Forseth only, but by both Forseth and Prudential as co-owners. The real effect of his covenant was to give assent to a leasing of his share of the petroleum and natural gas rights along with the share of his co-owner Prudential.[5]

---

4 [1960] s.c.r. 210, the same reasoning was also applied by the Supreme Court of Canada in *Prudential Trust Company Limited and Canadian Williston Minerals v Olson* [1960] s.c.r. 227   5 Ibid, 225, 226

Thus it would appear that even an indefinite top lease can be enforced as a personal covenant against the lessor so long as he remains the owner of the minerals.

AMENDING A LEASE SUBJECT TO A TOP LEASE

Not only does a top lease overhang the current lease like a Damoclean sword, it also represents an ever-present obstacle to any attempts by the lessee to improve its status under the lease. The inhibiting effect of a top lease was strikingly illustrated in the *Potapchuk* case[6] where the trial judge, Cairns J, analysed the impact of a top lease with great care. His judgment was followed by the two higher courts.

The *Potapchuk* fact pattern is a good example of how a top lease works. The lands were subject to a lease dated January 16, 1951, with a primary term of ten years plus the usual 'thereafter' provision.

On May 16, 1956 (during the primary term of the original lease) the mineral owner granted to one Minnie Potapchuk an option, irrevocable for five years, to lease the minerals. The form of option was identical with the first one set forth in the beginning of this chapter under the heading *Option*. Potapchuk was in fact an employee of Canadian Pipelines & Petroleums Limited and she assigned her interests to that company. A caveat was filed in the appropriate land registry office on June 1, 1956. The Canadian Pipeline company on May 9, 1957, assigned its rights under the option agreement to the Defendant Scurry-Rainbow which registered a caveat on July 18, 1957.

The original lease suffered from a defective pooling clause which, like the one that had been interpreted in *Shell Oil Co.* v *Gunderson*,[7] did not provide that the existence of a non-producing gas well on some part of the spacing unit, other than lands covered by the lease, could have, with the appropriate payment, the same effect in extending the primary term as though the well were on the said lands. Pan American, the lessee by assignment from Shell Oil Co. of the current lease, realized its perilous position as a result of the *Gunderson* decision and was successful in obtaining from the lessor a letter dated May 20, 1960 (during the last year of the primary term) in which he consented to the pooling of his lands with the other three-quarters to form a

---

6 *Supra* no. 2. The *Potapchuk* decision and its effect on amending the lease was extensively canvassed by Curran, 'Effect of Amendments to Petroleum and Natural Gas Leases' (1965–6), 4 *Alta. L. Rev.* 267

7 [1960] S.C.R. 424, 23 D.L.R. (2d) 81 (S.C.C.)

spacing unit and agreed that, if production of natural gas was encountered and such production was not sold because of lack of market, he would accept as royalty the annual acreage rental and it would be deemed that, while such payments were made, production was being taken from the lands and that the payment would be treated as royalty. This, of course, materially improved the lessee's position under the lease since it could continue it in force by payment of a capped gas well royalty.

Armed with this amendment, the lessee drilled a well in August 1960 on lands other than the leased lands but within the section that had been pooled. This well was capped as a shut-in gas well.

The primary term of the original lease expired on January 16, 1961. On May 1, 1961 (within the five-year option period), Scurry exercised the option and paid the option price. Scurry also, on May 23, 1961, registered a caveat in support of its lease. The mineral owner returned the bonus consideration to Scurry with a letter in which he stated he was not entitled to it because of the arrangements that had been made with respect to pooling and shut-in royalty payments with Pan American.

The case boiled down to a single issue: if the amendment as to pooling and capped well payments were effective, then the original lease would continue in force. In order to succeed on its option, the plaintiff had to strike down the amendment that had been made during the primary term of the lease. The trial judge found that by registering its caveat in 1956 the claim of the plaintiff Scurry was protected as from that date from anyone else taking an interest, or bettering or increasing any interest already held in derogation of the claim of the caveator. He quoted and applied a passage by Anglin J from *Alexander* v *McKillop and Benjafield*:[8]

But whatever its effect as notice (and I incline to the view that it must be deemed notice to every person who claims to have acquired, subsequently to its being lodged, any interest in the lands, or to have increased or bettered any such interest already held), inasmuch as it is the only means provided for the protection of unregistered interests and it was obviously intended by the legislature thus to afford adequate and sufficient protection for them, I am of the opinion that a caveat when properly lodged prevents the acquisition or the bettering or increasing of any interest in the land, legal or equitable, adverse to or in derogation of the claim of the caveator – at all events, as it exists at the time when the caveat is lodged.

The *Potapchuk* decision stands for the proposition that, once a lessor has

8 (1912) 45 s.c.r. 551, 582, 583; 1 w.w.r. 871, 881

granted a top lease and the top lessee records its interest on the registry system, the lessor and the original lessee are prohibited from doing anything that would lead to the acquisition or the bettering or increasing of any interest in the land which would be adverse to or in derogation of the claim of the top lessee.

While Cairns J did not go into specifics as to what would be an 'acquisition or the bettering or increasing of any interest in the land, legal or equitable, adverse to or in derogation of the claim of the caveator – ,' it is implicit in his judgment that anything which would have the effect of extending the term of the lease or increasing the chances of it being extended would be so considered.[9]

In fact, virtually every change or amendment that the original lessee would want to make in the lease would be directed to the improvement of or protection of the interest which it originally obtained in the lease, and thus automatically be adverse to or in derogation of the interest under the top lease. The ramifications of the *Potapchuk* approach are far reaching indeed.

PRIORITY OF REGISTRATION

The *ratio* of the *McKillop* decision makes it clear that registration is all important. It is the rights which exist at the time that the caveat is registered that cannot be 'bettered or increased.' Under the Torrens System which is in effect throughout most of the oil and gas areas in Canada, the usual procedure is to register the interest claimed under a lease by a caveat. The instrument of caveat normally would include a summary of the rights claimed under the instrument. In view of the approach taken by the Supreme Court of Canada in *Ruptash and Lumsden* v *Zawick*[10] where the rights were limited to those expressed in the caveat, regardless of what was conferred by the document itself, it would seem that the better practice would be to attach a copy of the lease to the caveat. In this way, the lessee could at least depend upon the full rights granted under the lease document being protected. Otherwise, a too brief summary of the rights in the caveat might open up an even broader field for a caveated top lease to invade and proscribe.

9 Curran *supra* n. 6, argues that the amendment in the *Potapchuk* case merely changed the mode of performance of certain covenants in the existing lease and gave the lessee the right to pool lands, pay royalties, and drill a well on a different basis than that provided in the existing lease. While that may be so, the fact that such changes also had the effect of permitting an extension of the primary term of the lease, where otherwise it would have terminated, obviously was regarded by the court as being 'adverse to or in derogation of the claim of the caveator.'

10 [1956] S.C.R. 347

WHAT IS AN AMENDMENT TO A LEASE?

The net cast by the *McKillop* case is a wide one. It includes anything that affects the interest protected by an intervening caveat. In *Potapchuk* a letter agreement which changed the pooling provision in the original lease was prohibited because it would have one of the proscribed effects on the caveated top lessee's position. If a broadening of the pooling clause is not to be allowed, the fundamental changes that are worked in a lease by a unit agreement certainly must be an even more serious derogation from the claim of the top lease. It will be recalled from the discussion in chapter 11 that the voluntary execution by a lessor of the unit agreement makes the then existing lease virtually impregnable. It would be hard to conceive of anything more 'adverse to or in derogation of the claim' of the top lessee. The limitation of the ability to enter into subsequent unit agreements must be considered as one of the most serious probable effects of an intervening top lease upon the original lease.

EFFECT OF CLAUSES IN THE LEASE

The caveat in support of the original lease, where the lease is attached to it, will protect whatever rights are therein described. What if the lease contains an express clause to the effect that amendments may be made by agreement, or giving the right to unitize? It is questionable if either of these devices could assist the original lessee. In the first place the right to amend is implicit in any agreement and the express provision for amendment by agreement would not appear to enlarge any of the rights that may be protected by the caveat. The type of unitization contemplated by a unitization clause in the lease is not the voluntary type that is created by the execution of the unit agreement by the lessor. So the fact that a caveated lease contains a compulsory unitization clause would not appear to enable a lessor to execute a voluntary unit agreement with his original lessee against the interest of a caveated top lessee.

TOP TOP LEASE

The frustration felt by the original lessee who had been top leased, together with a natural desire to strike back, led to the brief emergence of a grotesque document which might be best described as a top top lease. Under this arrangement, the original lessee obtained from the lessor an undertaking that the new lease would become 'effective' on the later of the date of termination of the existing lease, or the expiration of the top lease.

One might speculate that the original lessee sought to obtain through this device a form of protection which would allow the lessee to finance and otherwise support an attack upon the top lease. So long as the lessee successfully tied up the mineral rights upon the top lease being terminated, it would be feasible to launch an attack on the validity of the top lease along the lines of the *Forseth* and *Cugnet* cases and other decisions discussed in detail in chapter 4, *ante*. Without some hold on the reversionary interest it would not confer much benefit on a lessee to have a top lease set aside on some grounds such as misrepresentation, mistake, or *non est factum*. To do so would only free the lessor to deal independently with the minerals, if the current lease had also been invalidated, or to himself attack the current lease.

Secondly, the registration of the rights acquired under a top lease by caveat or otherwise would, in accordance with the *Potapchuk ratio*, effectively freeze the top lessee's ability to improve or alter its position.

The obstacles and restrictions that would surround a lessor's freedom of movement where his lands are subject to a lease, a top lease, and a top top lease are mind-boggling. Fortunately, the latter document never came into widespread use.

INGREDIENTS OF A TOP LEASE

The top lease device is utilized under a number of different conditions. Primarily it is predicated upon the extinguishment of the existing lease at some point in time, but there are many degrees of the urgency with which the existing lease is to be attacked. The top lessee may know of a fatal flaw in a particular lease and so enter into an arrangement whereby the lease will be challenged forthwith and, if the attack is successful, the top lessee will have the option, or may be bound, to acquire a new lease. Under such circumstances both the option fee and the bonus consideration for the lease are likely to be very substantial. On the other hand an operator might seek a large number of top leases within a given area and thereafter challenge the validity of one or more of the current leases in the form of a test case, or may be content simply to have the option to take a new lease without seeking to set aside any existing leases.

Obviously there are many individual terms and conditions that might be negotiated between the parties. Generally, however, it may be stated that a top lease should at least:

1   Have the lease form attached to it, or incorporated as a part of the document.
2   The lease form should be filled out in all details, i.e., the bonus consideration, delay rental, primary term, royalty rate and all other items should be stipulated. A definite time limit, calculated to avoid the rule against

perpetuities, and beyond which the option will expire, should be imposed.
3 The right of the top lessee should take the form of an option. (Under certain circumstances a top lessee might feel justified in committing to take a lease upon the expiration of the current one, but normally the option route is preferred.)
4 Contain an undertaking by the optionor that he will not waive any default under, or consent or agree to any modification of, or grant any renewal or extension of the term of the existing lease. This undertaking should be carefully worded so that it, in turn, cannot be said to be adverse to or in derogation of the claim of the original lessee. Some top lease forms go much further and make the lessor the ally of the top lessee in defeating the current lease. In view of the strictures of *Potapchuk* against derogating from rights protected by registration, such provisions could be held invalid. It is suggested that a top lease should not exceed the obligations listed at the beginning of this paragraph.

Above all, the top lease must be registered in order to freeze the lessor–lessee documentation.

PART FIVE

INVOLUNTARY TERMINATION

13
Commencement of drilling operations

A suitable, if irreverent, subtitle for this Part would be 'The Lessor's Guide to Lease-Breaking.' Unquestionably, the oil and gas lease, hastily imported from the United States and superimposed on Canadian jurisprudence, has led a very hazardous existence. Many a lease has come to an untimely and unexpected end.[1]

It is the cases in this area that oil company lawyers have in mind when they complain of the attitude taken by the courts. The list of commentators who have criticized the approach of the Supreme Court is long; this passage from an article by Currie epitomizes their concern:

The decisions of the Courts have continued to ignore or reject the argument by lessees that petroleum leases should be viewed as a business arrangement between the parties and be interpreted in a more liberal fashion. In some instances, for example, lessees have lost their leases due to late performance by a mere three or four days. The Courts refuse to recognize the extreme variables which affect the scheduling of wells, the drilling days lost due to equipment failures, the delays in obtaining equipment and many other postponements caused by circumstances over which the lessee has little or no control. The Courts continue to insist that the lessee is the victim of its own procrastination by not drilling in ample time to complete its well within the primary term. Although in certain instances there is a great deal of merit to this criticism this attitude generally fails to take into consideration the justifiable reasons for 'sitting on' leases. The exploration phase of the petroleum industry is a waiting game. Good business judgment in such a

---

1 See Ballem, 'The Perilous Life of an Oil and Gas Lease' (1966) 44 *Can. Bar Rev.* 523

high-risk business requires the lessee to wait on plays to develop in the vicinity; to drill only the most prospective structures in the early stages of exploration; and to acquire lands under lease in adjacent areas before commencing drilling. It is argued that the petroleum industry should construct leases which take into consideration these emergencies, but this is just what the industry has attempted to do in its evolution of the present petroleum and natural gas lease. As long as the Courts continue to construe leases so literally as to ignore the basic purpose of the lease it is doubtful that a lease will ever be drafted successfully to protect the interests and rights of the lessee.[2]

It is impossible not to feel some sympathy with this lament; the results of the cases often have been the exact opposite of what might reasonably have been expected by the lessee. Nonetheless the following observations seem justified:

(a) The lease has been created by the very people who bewail its results.
(b) A lease is more than a 'business arrangement,' it is a *grant* of a very substantial interest in land.
(c) The approach suggested by Currie and others would confer a very substantial benefit to the lessee; as between the parties the lessee now enjoys the advantage of drafting the document and also has the benefit of expert advice and counsel, not always available to the lessor.
(d) The importation of a substantial compliance rule would introduce an element of uncertainty which the strict interpretation now employed by the courts has largely avoided.
(e) Mineral rights can fluctuate violently and abruptly in value. Time is of the essence and the mineral owner should know his precise right to deal with his mineral ownership at all times. If the courts were to import considerations of 'the basic purpose of the lease' and vary their decisions accordingly, there would be many occasions during which a lessor could not know whether he was free to deal with his minerals or not.

There are a number of areas in which the lease has proved to be vulnerable:[3]

(1) Commencement of drilling within the stipulated time,
(2) Payment of delay rental,

2 Currie, 'Recent Cases and Developments in Oil and Gas Law' (1971) 9 *Alta. L. Rev.* 452, 462, 463
3 Where a third party takes an option or top lease, attacks the validity of the underlying lease and settles the action for a monetary sum, such money is taxable income in his hands; *Pawnee Petroleums Limited et al.* v *M.N.R.* (1972) 72 D.T.C. 1273 (Tax Rev. Bd.)

(3) Operations at the end of the primary term,
(4) Pooling,
(5) Payment of suspended well royalty,
(6) Interruption or cessation of production.

COMMENCE DRILLING

It will be recalled that the most common type of lease provides for automatic termination if the drilling deadline is not met.[4] 'PROVIDED that if operations for the drilling of a well are not commenced on the said lands within one year from the date hereof, this lease shall terminate and be at an end ...'

The question as to whether drilling operations have been *commenced* within the required time becomes critical in a number of situations. The lessee may have elected in any year of the primary term to drill rather than pay delay rental. The primary term may be about to expire so that drilling can no longer be postponed. The lease itself may impose a definite time limit, without the option of deferment.

Even under the typical lease which does contain the right to defer, the time limit will expire eventually and if the lease is to continue, drilling must be carried out prior to the end of the primary term. In a sense, the last year of the primary term is shorter than the preceding years insofar as drilling is concerned. During any of the initial years all that is required is that the lessee shall have commenced drilling before the end of the year. In the last year, however, by virtue of the way in which the *habendum* clause is worded, mere commencement of drilling will not suffice since the lease is continued only if the leased substances are produced, either actually or constructively, from the said lands. It has become customary to ameliorate the effect of this by a further proviso that permits a lessee, where a well has been commenced prior to the end of the last year, to continue such drilling operations with a resultant extension of the lease if production occurs.

WHAT CONSTITUTES COMMENCEMENT OF DRILLING OPERATIONS?

The critical question is always whether what has been done on the lands prior to the critical date amounts to the commencement of drilling operations. In the instances that have come before the courts to date the leases or agreements contained several different expressions of the drilling requirement: i.e., 'if operations for the drilling of a well are not commenced'; 'a well has

---

4 Subject, of course, to the right to defer drilling by payment of a delay rental

not been commenced'; and 'commence drilling operations' are the ones most commonly encountered. Regardless of the individual variations in the wording, the courts uniformly have treated such phrases as though they read 'commenced the drilling of a well.'

To date there have been nine cases in Canada involving this question; two of them reached the Supreme Court of Canada but neither of these involved commencement of drilling as a fundamental issue.

The pattern began to emerge as early as 1909 in *Lang* v *Provincial Natural Gas and Fuel Co.*[5] where the lease provided 'that if within six months from the date a well has not been commenced on said premises this lease shall be null and void.' At the end of the six-month period the lessee had done the following things: placed a stake on the land at the spot where the well was to be drilled; erected a derrick; and moved on to the land an engine, belt-house, drive pipe, and casing.

The trial judge noted that in oil contracts, time is of the essence of the bargain and also that a strict rather than a lax reading of the agreement would be appropriate. He reviewed English and American building cases which held that 'to commence work' meant to 'break the ground' and that excavation for the foundation represents 'the commencement of the building' within the meaning of the law. He concluded that the phrase 'to commence work' as used in these building cases did not include mere preparations for the execution of the work. With these precedents as a guide, the court held that some breaking of the ground was essential to meet the test of commencement of a well. That element being absent, the lease was terminated.

In *Wulff* v *Lundy*[6] the operative language was found in a sub-lease. The land was held under a petroleum and natural gas lease granted by the Crown in the right of the Province of Alberta and the original lessees entered into a sub-lease which contained the following clause: 'The Lessees agree to commence operations on the said lease with a view to the drilling of a well on the lands on or before June 15th, 1937, and will continue said operations until said well is completed, it being understood that the continuing shall be in accordance with the established practice of the field and having regard to unavoidable delays or other causes.' A company was incorporated on March 31, 1937, to carry out the drilling venture, but for want of capital it was never in a position to allot shares or to commence operations.

On May 31, 1937, the parties entered into another agreement which recited that, owing to the difficulty of financing the well drilling operations, an extension of the drilling obligation was granted to November 1, 1937, 'and that in case at the said November 1st conditions are such that there would be

5 (1909) 17 o.l.r. 262 (Ont.)
6 [1940] 1 w.w.r. 444

difficulty and it would not be advisable to consider financing or the conditions in general are not real good the parties of the first part will on application by the parties of the second part give consideration to a further extension.' There was another agreement dated November 12, 1937, which granted a further extension of commencing operations to May 1, 1938, and provided 'in case the requirement of commencing operations are not complied with by ... May 1st, 1938, that the said agreement ... be thereupon null and void.' By May 1, 1938, all that had happened was that the company had been incorporated and that a geological survey had been made. Both of these events had occurred prior to the first extension that had been granted on May 31, 1937.

The sub-lessees argued that the reference in the agreements to 'operations' did not necessarily mean 'drilling operations' and that they could include such things as incorporation of a company, surveys, and attempts to raise capital. The Alberta Appellate Division agreed with a statement in *Thornton's Law of Oil and Gas* that there was no reasonable distinction to be made between commencing 'operations' or commencing 'drilling operations' under an oil and gas lease which provided for the commencement of work within a specified time.

Dealing with the acts which the defendants contended amounted to 'operations,' the court held that the incorporation of a company and the carrying out of a geological survey could not meet the test. This conclusion was fortified by the fact that both of these events took place prior to the first extension agreement of May 31, 1937, and, if these acts by themselves had constituted 'operations' within the meaning of the original sub-lease, there would have been no necessity for any extension.

OPERATOR'S GOOD FAITH

A trio of cases has elevated the operator's true intent and *bona fides* to an all-important factor. In *Wetter v New Pecalta Oils Company Limited*[7] the lease was dated April 8, 1947, for a primary term of twenty-one years, but provided:

the Lessees shall commence drilling operations not later than one year from the date hereof (if not commenced by that date the lease to be null and void unless the lessees pay $1.00 per acre rental in advance, and if so paid the date for beginning drilling to be extended another year) and this same procedure shall be

7 (1951) 2 W.W.R. (N.S.) 290, [1951] 3 D.L.R. 533 (Alta. C.A.)

observed from year to year but not beyond December 31st, 1950. This lease shall be null and void if no well has been commenced to be drilled on the said demised premises by that date.

The rental was duly paid up to that point in time where drilling operations had to be commenced if the lease were to be preserved, namely December 31, 1950.

The lease also contained a requirement that the lessees pay to the lessor $200.00 per annum per well for surface rights at the time that drilling operations were begun. On December 28, 1950, the lessees paid this surface rental. On December 30 and 31, 1950, a bulldozer was operated on the land and a drilling site was surveyed. During the first week in January 1951 (after the critical date) a service drilling rig was moved onto the premises and it drilled to a depth of 300 feet, after which it was removed. It is significant that a service rig has only a limited capacity and could not have reached the depth of any prospective horizon.

The trial judge found there had been no default under the lease, but this finding was reversed on appeal. It is clear from the judgment of the Appellate Division that the court might have been prepared to concede that the bulldozer work could have qualified as being preliminary to drilling if the actual drilling had been properly and continuously prosecuted. The court pointed out, however, that the actual drilling took place in January 1951 (after the cut-off date) and lasted only a week before the rig was removed. This persuaded the court that the work done was merely a pretence to continue the lease.

O'Connor CJA adopted the language of *Summers on Oil and Gas*:

The general rule seems to be that actual drilling is unnecessary, but that the location of wells, hauling lumber on the premises, erection of derricks, providing a water supply, moving machinery on the premises and similar acts preliminary to the beginning of drilling, when performed with the *bona fide* intention to proceed thereafter with diligence toward the completion of the well, constitute a commencement or beginning of a well or drilling operations within the meaning of this clause of the lease.[8]

The same court, seventeen days later, handed down its decision in *Oil City Petroleums (Leduc) Limited* v *American Leduc Petroleums Limited*.[9] The instrument was not a lease but an agreement which set forth the manner in

8 *Summers on Oil and Gas*, 362
9 (1951) 2 W.W.R. (N.S.) 371, [1951] 3 D.L.R. 835 (Alta. C.A.)

which the lands were to be drilled and developed. In particular it specified that if the first well produced in commercial quantities, a second well was to be commenced on the adjoining legal sub-division by a date fixed by reference to the production date of the first well. The agreement continued 'that in the event that the operator fails to comply with such terms or to continue such leases in effect or fails to drill within the time set out or limited thereafter (providing the owners shall not be in default hereunder) they shall be liable to the owners for such default, or at the option of the owners, the owners may notify the trustees in writing and this agreement shall forthwith cease and determine in all its terms except as to those legal sub-divisions upon which commercial wells have been drilled ...' The time limit expired on October 18, 1950, and a notice of termination was given by the owners on October 27, 1950.

By the critical date of October 18, 1950, the operator had prepared the surface, drilled a 30-inch hole to a depth of 300 feet, cased it for a short distance, and placed a water tank on the drill site. It was admitted that the operator had not entered into any drilling contract. Although it does not appear from the written judgment, the rig which had drilled the 300-foot hole had been removed from the well site; this fact would tell heavily against the intention of the operator to proceed.

The Appellate Division examined these activities and concluded that, while they might 'be regarded as a preparation to drill,' by themselves they did not satisfy the test of 'commencement of drilling.'

This view was endorsed on appeal to the Supreme Court of Canada which contented itself by observing: 'I think that the small amount of drilling relied upon by the appellant company as an answer to the allegation of default against it in this respect is not to be taken seriously as a compliance with its obligations.'[10]

There is one case in which the court decided in favour of a lessee who had done something less than breaking ground with a rig capable of drilling to the projected depth. *Risvold and Mallory* v *Scott and Granville Oils Limited*[11] was decided in 1938 and involved a resolute course of action that a modern-day lessee, more aware of the hazards, would be reluctant to follow. In the *Risvold* case, the covenant was contained in an assignment of a lease and the lessee undertook 'that he shall and will commence the erection of a derrick, will install proper and adequate drilling equipment and machinery as soon as

10 [1951] 3 D.L.R. 577, 578 (S.C.C.)
11 [1938] 1 W.W.R. 682 (Alta.) The test as to 'commence drilling' discussed in this decision was expressly approved by the Saskatchewan Trial Division in *Kendall* v *Smith and Northern Royalties Limited* [1937] 2 W.W.R. 609.

possible, and shall and will commence actional drilling operations on the said lands, but not later than the 31st day of December, 1936 A.D.'

The presence of the word 'actional' is unusual, but had no influence on the decision as the trial judge determined that the word did not add anything material to the words which followed, namely 'drilling operations,' so that the phrase became the conventional 'commence drilling operations.'

The wording of the first covenant of the lessee to 'commence the erection of a derrick and will install proper and adequate drilling equipment and machinery as soon as possible' was very broad and indefinite and for all practical purposes was discarded by the court, so that the entire issue turned on whether or not the lessee had complied with the covenant to commence drilling operations by the specified date.

On December 31, 1936, the following work had been done: a surface lease had been obtained, a cellar – a large hole about 10 feet by 12 feet and from 12 to 15 feet deep – had been dug and cribbed and completed with a runway, contracts had been let for the erection of a derrick, a drilling contract had been awarded, and certain other contracts for the use of the required equipment had been entered into. By that time the lessors had become alive to the potential of the land and were following the progress of operations very closely. On February 11, 1937, they purported to cancel the lease and warned the lessees that they would continue operations at their peril. The basis of the cancellation was the failure of the defendants to commence drilling operations by the required date. There was a further exchange of correspondence asserting and denying the breach, culminating on March 9, 1937, in the commencement of the action for a declaration that the lease had been terminated. Among the relief claimed by the lessors was an interim injunction; this remedy was not pursued, although the defendant company continued its drilling operations.

Despite the perils of the situation, the lessees pressed on with commendable determination. As the court pointed out, the work was continued without intermission during the very severe winter weather in January and February 1937 and despite the fact that a storm of unprecedented severity blew down the defendants' derrick. The well was completed in September 1937 (long after the commencement of the action) and became a substantial producer.

Since this was one of the earlier decisions, there was little in the way of Canadian precedents to guide the court and it relied upon and quoted extensively from that well-known American authority, *Summers on Oil and Gas*, notably the passage quoted above, which emphasized the good faith of the operator.

Evidence had been given at the trial by a number of witnesses as to what they understood by the meaning of the term 'commence drilling operations' as used in the oil fields. Their understanding of the phrase, as might be expected, conflicted. It was analysed by the trial judge in this passage, and the uncertainty that it reveals is still relevant today:

Evidence was given at the trial by various witnesses as to the meaning of the term 'commencing drilling operations', as used in the oil fields with which they were familiar. Their evidence is conflicting but I think for the most part these witnesses are not close observers of expressions used. Mr. Adams says that neither erecting a derrick nor installing drilling machinery is part of a drilling operation. Mr. Muir says that neither drilling a cellar nor erecting a derrick is part of a drilling operation, although he said that if he were asked to estimate the cost of drilling a well he would include everything. Mr. Snyder, on the contrary, says that all these are part of drilling operations. Mr. Davies, who is a petroleum engineer and geologist of long experience and therefore as an educated man more likely to weigh carefully expressions which he hears in the practice of his profession, says that in his opinion on the facts of the case the defendant company had commenced drilling operations before December 31, 1936.[12]

The decision of the court really turned on the question of *bona fides* as stressed by Summers. In the *Risvold* case there could be no doubt as to the good faith of the defendants. This had been proved by the fact that once having commenced operations they pursued them to completion despite adverse conditions and repeated warnings and threats from the plaintiffs as to the uncertainty of their position.

The obligation to 'commence drilling operations' is expressed in broad and non-specific terms. For this reason the obligation is one which can be stretched to include almost any activity if the court so inclined. It would appear that a Canadian court might find that there had been no default if (a) at least *something* had been done on the lands by the critical date and (b) the good faith of the lessee could be established. The manner in which the *bona fides* appear to be established is by the diligent prosecution of the drilling of a well to its completion. This is an expensive operation and it would take a very courageous and determined lessee to continue drilling a well in the face of knowledge that its title might be open to challenge. The diligent completion of a well would be a very effective defence by a lessee whose title was attacked after the fact. But a lessee whose status was questioned before being too

12 Ibid, 687, 688

deeply committed to the well might well conclude that it would be foolhardy to proceed until the question had been resolved.

RELIEF FROM FORFEITURE

The courts have an equitable jurisdiction to grant relief from forfeiture where the rigid exercise of the legal right would produce a hardship if adequate compensation to the injured party can be made by some means other than forfeiture of the estate.[13]

There is an obvious application of this equitable remedy to oil and gas leases. A lessee may argue, and many have done so, that the termination of the lease for tardiness in commencing the drilling of a well or in payment of a delay rental is forfeiture of the type against which the courts should relieve. The point has been considered in numerous cases, dealing with failure to commence drilling on time or a late payment of delay rental. As discussed in chapter 14, the argument appears to have been completely rejected in the delay rental situation, but it still may retain some vitality when it comes to the commencement of drilling operations.

In the *Risvold* case there was *obiter dicta* that the court would relieve against the forfeiture. This observation is clearly in the category of *dicta* since Ewing J found that the defendants were not in breach of the drilling obligation. He went on to note that the defendant had proceeded in good faith and that the performance of a contract was not open to criticism. He coupled this with the fact that the plaintiff, with full knowledge that the work was proceeding, did not attempt to restrain the work by injunction. The circumstances of the *Risvold* case were extraordinary and not likely to be duplicated since the defendant company actually drilled the well to completion.

The Alberta Appellate Division conceded in the *Wulff* decision that the claim for relief from forfeiture gave 'much difficulty.' It pointed out, however, that the breach of an agreement to drill a well was no light matter and approved a statement from *Thornton's Law of Oil and Gas* that 'neglect to sink the well cannot be compensated in damages.' Accordingly, the court refused to apply the equitable remedy.

In *Wetter*, the trial judge after holding that there had been no default, went on to state that he would have been prepared to relieve against forfeiture on condition that 'a drilling permit was applied for forthwith; that within thirty

13 See Anger and Honsberger, *Law of Real Property*, 955; *Snyder v Harper* [1922]
   2 w.w.r. 417

days a rig be moved on the premises, that actual rigging be commenced and drilling operations be diligently prosecuted.'[14] On appeal, however, relief against forfeiture was not given because the work relied upon as commencement of drilling was not, in the view of the court, performed with the *bona fide* intention to proceed with diligence.

Relief from forfeiture received its most thorough review, insofar as commencement of drilling was concerned, in the *Oil City* case, where the Alberta Appellate Division emphasized the nature of the oil business with its pressures of time. The drilling obligation was considered to be an essential term of the contract and to deny relief to a party in breach of it could not be said to transgress any principle of equity. The court also noted that the evidence indicated a lack of financial ability on the part of the plaintiffs to carry out their obligation and that no proposal had been placed before the trial judge under which they could be granted a reasonable period of time within which to commence drilling. This portion of the Appellate Division's judgment is significant as it indicates at least a disposition, under proper circumstances, to grant an extension of time within which drilling operations could commence.

On appeal, the Supreme Court of Canada expressly left the question open: 'With respect to the contention that the appellants should be relieved from the consequences of their default, I see no grounds, assuming but without deciding there is jurisdiction to do so, upon which relief should be granted.'[15]

It must be noted, however, that the documentation in the *Oil City* case involved an agreement rather than a lease. The granting of an extra period of time within which to commence drilling would seem to be totally excluded by the precise wording of the 'unless' clause. Nonetheless, when dealing with the commencement of drilling, the courts have been reluctant to totally reject – as they have in the case of delay rental payments – relief against forfeiture. There is a distinction between the two situations; payment of the delay rental is a definite act, it is either done or not done, whereas the commencement of drilling is a more indefinite concept and allows the courts a greater scope as to whether what has been done constitutes drilling operations. As will be seen, the courts have discarded the remedy with respect to delay rentals as they regard the payment of delay rentals as a mere option. The same may be true of drilling, but the latitude to construe almost any form of activity as amounting to the commencement of drilling lays the groundwork for the application of relief from forfeiture, if the facts of the case so incline the court.

14 *Supra* n. 7, 291   15 [1952] 3 D.L.R. 577, 580 (S.C.C.)

NOTICE OF DEFAULT

Most leases, including the standard lease, contain a clause that requires the lessor to give the lessee notice of a default and grants a period of grace to remedy it, before the lease can be terminated. The operation of this type of clause was discussed in chapter 9, *ante*. The courts have refused to hold that a notice of default must be given before a lease could be terminated as a result of failure to commence drilling.[16] The ground for so refusing has been that the commencement of drilling by the required time is considered all essential by the parties. Put another way, it is clear from the language of the 'unless' clause that the lease will terminate automatically if drilling operations have not been commenced. There is no default on the part of the lessee in failing to commence since there is no absolute obligation to do so; the only consequence is that the lease will terminate.

NO PROVISION FOR TERMINATION

Occasionally, one suspects more by accident than design, the document in question will impose an obligation to drill, but does not expressly provide for termination in the event the deadline is not met. In what appears to be the first Canadian case on drilling obligations, *Docker* v *London-Elgin Oil Co.*,[17] the drilling clause did not contain words of automatic termination: 'will commence operations upon the said premises on or before the 1st day of November, 1902, or will pay to the lessor or his assigns the sum of $6.00 per month from the date hereof until operations are commenced on the said premises: provided that the said term hereby granted shall cease and determine if the lessee and his assigns shall wholly cease for the space of six months continuously to operate under this lease.'

The lessee did not commence operations on or before the first day of November 1902, but did pay to the lessor, who accepted the same, the monthly rent computed from the date of the lease down to November 1, 1902. After November 1, 1902, the lessee paid further sums up to at least January 1905 and paid into court additional sums to take care of arrears that may have accumulated prior to the trial.

The lease was upheld on the basis that the lessee had an option to do one of two things, either to make a commencement of operations or to pay the required rent. In effect, the lease was of the 'or' type and did not terminate automatically for failure to carry out operations. The contract was silent as

16 *Wetter* v *New Pecalta Oil Company Limited, supra* n. 7
17 (1907) 10 o.w.r. 1056 (Ont.); aff'd (1908) 11 o.w.r. 726 (c.a.)

to any obligation to commence operations and merely provided that the lessee must pay the monthly sum of $6.00 until there be such a commencement of operations.

In *Wulff* v *Lundy* one agreement which expressly declared that it would be null and void if operations were not commenced by the specified date was held to have been terminated by such failure. There was another agreement in the same case which covered different parcels of land and contained a drilling obligation, but did not provide expressly for termination in the event of a breach of such obligation. The Appellate Division held that the only remedy for breach of the second agreement would be for damages and that, since there were no provisions for re-entry or for determination or forfeiture in case of default, the agreement should not be terminated.

Sometimes the parties, rather than use one of the more or less standard forms, will draft their own version of an oil and gas lease. The results are often bizarre. In *Reynolds* v *Ackerman*[18] the lease was set forth in two pages of typewriting and included this clause:

The lessee shall pay to the lessor for the said period of three (3) years of this lease the sum of Two Hundred ($200.00) Dollars upon the execution of this lease, (receipt whereof is hereby acknowledged). This lease shall be subject to renewal for a further term from year to year by the lessee paying to the lessor in advance, the sum of One ($1.00) Dollar per acre per year, provided that all the covenants of the lessee therein contained, shall have been fully done and performed.

The lease was completely silent on the question of drilling – there was no provision terminating the lease in the event of the lessee's failure to drill. The renewal provision was without limitation and would seem to permit the lessee to renew the term from year to year by paying rental in the sum of $1.00 per acre per year. This indeed was the precise effect which counsel for the lessee contended should be given to the provision. The trial judge, however, quoted the Supreme Court of Canada's decision in *Can. Department Stores Ltd.* v *Gourlay and Billing*:[19] 'It has long been established that a covenant in a lease, which provides for a renewal of the term, in order to be valid must designate with reasonable certainty the date of the commencement and the duration of the term to be granted.' Finding no limitation in the renewal clause, McBride J held it to be void for uncertainty; a lessee cannot overcome the necessity to commence drilling operations by simply neglecting to insert

18 (1960) 32 w.w.r. 289 (Although not reported until 1960, the actual decision was delivered in 1953.)
19 [1933] s.c.r. 329, 331

a time limit in the lease. In view of the precise language contained in the usual 'unless' lease, the last three cases mainly have a curiosity value.

INTERVENING LEGISLATION

The remaining case in this area illustrates what would seem to be a self-evident proposition, that a drilling obligation will not be enforced, nor the lease terminated, if to do so would contravene applicable regulation. In *Mercury Oils Limited* v *Vulcan-Brown Petroleums*[20] the lessee was required to drill one well within a stipulated time limit and a second one within twelve months thereafter. If the lessee failed to drill the second well, it was to have been deemed to have abandoned the property. The lessee timely drilled the first well but, before it could begin the second one, new regulations were passed by the Province of Alberta which prohibited the drilling of the second well because it would have been too close to the first one. The lease contained a clause that all operations were to be carried on in strict compliance with the statutes and regulations. The Canadian Supreme Court held that the lessee's failure to drill, when prohibited by regulation, could not be construed as a default which would terminate the lease.

CONCLUSIONS

The cases to date make it clear that each one will be decided on its own particular facts. There are few guide-posts and an almost total absence of authority at the Supreme Court of Canada level. Nonetheless the following generalizations seem to be justified:

1 An actual breaking of the ground on or before the critical date by a drilling rig capable of drilling to a prospective depth is the best means of satisfying the test.
2 An actual breaking of the ground or 'spudding' may not be required where some operations at least have been carried on at the drillsite prior to the deadline and the well is thereafter diligently prosecuted. The hazards of this approach to the lessee are obvious.
3 The courts seem willing to apply equitable considerations in this area; witness their emphasis on *bona fides* and their reluctance to totally reject relief from forfeiture.
4 There must be at least some physical activity on the wellsite even if it falls short of an actual spudding.

20 [1943] S.C.R. 37, 1 D.L.R. 369 (S.C.C.)

5 Governmental regulations which prohibit the drilling of a well may be a defence available to the lessee but may be limited to those cases where there has not been a total failure of consideration, i.e., where there is already a producing well on the property.

6 An oil and gas document, such as a lease, which ignores any drilling obligation and provides for perpetual renewal without limitation most likely would be held void for uncertainty of term.

14
Deferring the commitment to drill

The second half of the 'unless' drilling clause allows the lessee to avoid termination of the lease by payment of an annual sum in lieu of drilling.

... unless the Lessee shall have paid or tendered to the Lessor on or before said anniversary date the sum of .... ($................) Dollars (hereinafter called the 'delay rental') which payment shall confer the privilege of deferring the commencement of drilling operations for a period of One (1) Year from said anniversary date, and that, in like manner and upon like payments or tenders, the commencement of drilling operations and the termination of this lease shall be further deferred for like periods successively;

The right to defer drilling is, of course, limited to the primary term. In every year of the primary term but the last one the lessee is entitled to keep the lease in force without drilling by payment of the delay rental.

AUTOMATIC TERMINATION

The cornerstone decision on delay rentals is *East Crest Oil Company Limited* v *Strohschein*[1] which effectively demonstrated the lethal nature of the 'unless' clause. The facts were clear and agreed to by both parties.
1   The lease was dated September 13, 1948, with a primary term of six years.

1 (1951–52) 4 w.w.r. (N.S.) 70 (Alta.); (1951–52) 4 w.w.r. (N.S.) 553, [1952] 2 D.L.R. 432 (C.A.)

2 It contained an 'unless' clause to the same effect as the one quoted at the beginning of this chapter.
3 There were no drilling operations on the lands at any material time.
4 The lessee paid the annual delay rental in accordance with the terms of the lease on September 13, 1949.
5 Delay rental was not paid to the lessor or the depository on September 13, 1950.
6 On October 13, 1950, the lessor's solicitor wrote to the oil company advising that the delay rental had not been paid when due and claiming that the lease was at an end.
7 On the following day the oil company replied that the failure to pay the rental was due simply to an oversight. The oil company also referred to the default provision of the lease and forwarded a certified cheque for the sum of $160.00 (the amount of the delay rental) plus exchange.

The Appellate Division adopted the colourful expression of the California court in *Richfield Oil Corpn.* v *Bloomfield*[2] that from its own nature the document 'carries within its own phraseology an automatic termination which clicks.' That click has been heard in many Canadian courtrooms in the intervening years.

THE TIME PERIOD

The fatal results that flow from failure to make a proper payment of delay rental have created situations where the courts are called upon to make the most detailed analysis as to what constitutes a sufficient and timely payment. In *Canadian Fina Oil Limited* v *Paschke*[3] the validity of the lease depended upon the interpretation of the word 'from,' and a time interval of one day. The lease was dated October 12, 1953, and contained the following clause: 'Provided that if operations for a drilling of a well are not commenced on the said lands within one year from the date hereof, this lease shall thereupon terminate and be at an end unless the Lessee shall have paid or tendered to the Lessor the sum of three hundred and twenty ($320.00) dollars as rental which payment shall confer the privilege of deferring a commencement of drilling operations for a period of one (1) year ...'

The difficulty arose with the payment for the year 1955. On October 12 the lessee deposited in a post office at Calgary a registered postpaid letter addressed to the depository which was the Bank of Nova Scotia at Stettler.

2 (1951) 229 P (2nd) 838
3 (1956) 19 W.W.R. 184 (Alta.); (1957) 21 W.W.R. (N.S.) 260, 7 D.L.R. (2d) 473 (C.A.)

This letter contained a cheque in payment of the delay rental and was received by the depository bank on October 13 at 3:00 PM. The cheque was immediately returned by the lessor who maintained that the payment was late and therefore the lease had expired.

In concluding that the grant had commenced on the day of the date of the lease, namely October 12, and had therefore ended on October 11, Porter JA strikingly emphasized the importance of time in the oil and gas industry:

Upon argument, counsel for the appellant was critical of the reference that the learned trial judge made to the fact that time is of the essence in the oil production business, taking the position that while that might be the particular knowledge of the trial judge, because of his experience at the bar, it could not be regarded as general knowledge, of which judicial notice could be taken. Perhaps it would be useful for the guidance of those who are not familiar with the background of the development of this country, to know that the oil and gas business has been carried on with a good deal of vitality in this province for more than 50 years, from Milk River to Peace River, and from the eastern boundary of the province to the eastern slope of the Rocky Mountains. In the course of that time the people of this province have seen hopes and values dashed when a few strokes of the bit found salt water where oil had been hoped for, whereas in the other fields they have seen what was in common parlance called 'cow pasture' turned overnight from areas of hope alone, to reservoirs containing thousands of barrels per acre. It is implicit in the search for oil, and indeed in its production and marketing, that events affecting these activities can occur with great suddenness unpredictably. In consequence there are heavy shifts of value and necessary new, almost instant, reappraisals of ventures to be undertaken. These facts are common knowledge in this province.

Bearing in mind these characteristics of the business, it is my view that the appellant would have been shocked if it had been told that it could not move on to the property on October 12, 1953, that indeed, having signed the lease, its presence on the land would have made it a trespasser until the next day. This practical view is emphasized by the fact that the law does not know fractions of the day. That being so, it follows that this document was to all intents and purposes signed on the first instant of October 12.[4]

Because of the minute and often unexpected variations in wording among the various forms of lease, the existing decisions must be applied with great care. The clause in the *Paschke* case referred only to 'within one year from

4 Ibid, 21 w.w.r. 263

the date hereof' and the Appellate Division was of the view that the period of time commenced on the date the lease was signed and accordingly terminated on the day previous, one year later. The standard 'unless' proviso contains the same reference but states that the lease shall terminate on 'the first anniversary date' and the time within which the payment must be made is also related to the anniversary date. Does the insertion of anniversary date grant the lessee one extra day? Would the lessee, in the *Paschke* situation, have the right to make payment on October 12 if the clause had been identical with that in the standard lease?

The Manner of Payment clause found in the standard lease also has a bearing on the time of payment. This clause was fully discussed in chapter 9, *ante*, and permits payment or tender to be either 'mailed or delivered.' After some initial doubt, it has now been determined that the act of mailing itself is sufficient if done prior to the expiration of the time limit.[5]

RELIEF AGAINST FORFEITURE

The argument that the termination of a lease for a late payment of delay rental is the sort of 'forfeiture' that a court should relieve against was advanced in *East Crest Oil* v *Strohschein*.[6] The Appellate Division pointed out a fatal flaw to the argument: 'that on the true construction of the lease now under consideration the question of relief from forfeiture does not, at the stage to which the document has become operative, arise. There is no forfeiture to relieve against. There cannot be default in neglecting to do something one is not bound to do.'[7] The Manitoba Court of Appeal expressly adopted this view in *Langlois* v *Canadian Superior Oil of California Limited*.[8]

NOTICE OF DEFAULT

The same kiss of death was administered to the argument based upon that clause which requires a notice of default and a period of grace before termination. As they did in the drilling cases, tardy lessees contended that the default clause compelled a lessor to give notice of default in delay rental payments and to permit the lessees to remedy same, before a lease could be terminated.

In the *East Crest* case, Ford JA said:

5 *Ballem* v *Texas Gulf Sulphur Co.* [1971] 1 W.W.R. 560 (S.C.C.)
6 (1951–52) 4 W.W.R. (N.S.) 553 (Alta. C.A.)
7 Ibid, 558
8 (1957–58) 23 W.W.R. 401, 12 D.L.R. (2d) 53 (Man. C.A.)

As to the argument based upon the lack of notice under clause 18 (the default clause), quoted above, I am of the opinion, apart from what I have already said, that this clause has no application to the failure to pay delay rental. This clause, in my view, has its full force in respect to defaults arising under the second part of the lease. It can have no application to the first part which provides for the commencement and extension or continuation of the lease. The use of the word 'ought' shows clearly that clause 18 refers to those provisions which bind the lessee and have no application to the failure to do something he may or may not do as he pleases. The clause deals with 'default' and, as I have said, there is no default in not doing something one is not obliged to do. Authority for this interpretation is to be found in the decision of this Division in the *Wetter* case, *supra*, and is supported by the reasoning in the *Richfield* case, *supra*.[9] (*words in parentheses added*)

As it did with the relief from forfeiture argument, the Manitoba Court of Appeal subsequently adopted this rejection of the default clause.[10]

The logic seems irrefutable; the lessee in an 'unless' lease suffers from a lack of obligations.

In *Chipp* v *Hunt*[11] the default clause, unlike any of the other cases, contained a specific reference to 'rental': 'In case of default in payment of the rental or royalty payable hereunder, or in case of breach or non-performance on the part of the lessee of any of its covenants herein contained, Lessor may give Lessee Thirty (30) days written notice in case of default in such payment ...' The lease also contained a typical unless clause which does not create an obligation, but confers an option, upon the lessee. Nevertheless the lessee in *Chipp* v *Hunt* must have been considerably encouraged by the specific reference to 'rental' in the default clause.

The Alberta Trial Division followed the *East Crest ratio*, noting that 'default' in the *New Century Dictionary* was defined in part: '... failure to meet financial obligations; in law failure to perform an act or obligation legally required ...' This definition led the court to conclude: 'It seems to me that, before clause 10, *supra*, could have any application, the plaintiff would have to be in default under the lease of an obligation that he is legally required to perform. I do not think that he could be in default in the payment of rental, until he had first obligated himself to pay such rental. So it is my view that clause 10 does not take the case out of the law as laid down in the *East Crest* case, *supra*.'

The court was also prepared, if required, to reject that portion of the default clause which dealt with rentals, on the ground that it was repugnant to

9 *Supra* n. 6, 559
10 *Supra* n. 8   11 (1955) 16 w.w.r. 209 (Alta.)

the earlier provision dealing with the payment of delay rentals. The principle of repugnancy was described by the Privy Council in *Forbes* v *Git*:[12] 'The principle of law to be applied may be stated in few words. If in a deed an earlier clause is followed by a later clause which destroys altogether the obligation created by the earlier clause, the later clause is to be rejected as repugnant and the earlier clause prevails.' If the default clause imposed an obligation on the lessor to give notice of non-payment of the rental before the lease could be terminated, then in the view of the court, this clause could not be reconciled with the earlier unless clause which imposed no obligation and must be rejected.

WAIVER

Under the circumstances of the typical late delay rental payment, it is not surprising that the proceeds are sometimes retained by the lessor. Normally the payments are directed to a depository bank which will simply credit them to the lessor's account without inquiry, or the lessor may be unaware that the payment is late or of the significance of such tardiness.

In *Rostad* v *Andreassen*[13] the lease required payment by November 29, 1951, but the lessee did not send the cheque until December 11. It was addressed to the depository bank which routinely credited the amount to the lessor on December 13. Thus it was not until December 20 that the lessor received notice from the bank that this had been done. He immediately made arrangements to have the payment returned to the lessee. The lessee contended that the acceptance of the cheque by the bank and its act of crediting the proceeds to the lessor amounted to a waiver.[14] The Alberta Trial Court refused to treat this as a waiver and noted that the bank had no authority to receive rents except in accordance with the lease and its actions could not bind the plaintiff lessor.

In the *Langlois* case,[15] after a defective payment in one year had gone unchallenged, the lessee made a payment to the proper lessor which was credited by the depository bank to his account. In the next following year a similar payment was also made by the lessee to the depository bank and it was credited to the lessor's account and retained for several months before being returned. In the meantime, the lessor had discovered that the delay rental

12 (1922) 1 w.w.r. 250, 1 A.C. 256 (P.C.)
13 (1952–53) 7 w.w.r. (N.S.) 709 (Alta.), aff'd without written reasons, (1953) 8 w.w.r. (N.S.) 717 (C.A.)
14 Waiver is really a branch of *estoppel*. This equitable doctrine was extensively developed in those cases dealing with termination after the primary term. Because of its importance, estoppel is treated separately in chapter 16, *infra*.
15 *Supra* n. 8

payment made in the previous year had been credited to his account, where-upon he sent the lessee a cheque for the equivalent amount. The attempted re-imbursement did not take place until some sixteen months after the original payment had been made.

The court refused to treat these events as creating any sort of waiver or estoppel. It noted that if any representation had been made by the lessors, presumably by retaining the payments, the lessee did not in any way alter its position. It had incurred no detriment, which is one of the tests that must be satisfied before estoppel will be invoked.

WAIVER IN ONTARIO

The principle of waiver seems to be on a somewhat different plane in Ontario than in the western provinces. In the early case of *Maple City Oil and Gas Co.* v *Charlton*[16] the lease contained an 'unless' clause and was attacked on a number of grounds. The court on its own initiative appears to have raised the issue as to a possible late payment. The Trial Judge on the assumption that it was a late payment was prepared to hold that the lessors had waived any forfeiture that might have resulted from failure to make payment within the proper time when the proceeds were actually withdrawn by the husband from the depository bank. In view of later decisions by higher courts, the authority of this case must be considered doubtful.

By the Gas and Oil Leases Act[17] the Province of Ontario has provided a procedure whereby a lessor or any other person with an interest in the land may apply to a judge of the county court for an order declaring the lease void. If it were not for this legislation, which is unique to Ontario, the lessor could only bring such an action before the provincial Supreme Court. Indeed, in view of the restrictions contained in the Act, a lessor would be well advised to ignore the route offered by the legislation and proceed in the normal course of litigation. The Gas and Oil Leases Act provides that an application may be made where a lessee has made default under the terms of a lease by failing to commence to drill and has failed to pay rentals in lieu thereof. Section 6 provides that the judge is not to take into account any rentals tendered after the making of the application unless such tender was accepted by the lessor. The legislation obviously treats the failure to drill or pay delay rentals as a 'default.'

The effect of the Ontario legislation has been reviewed at the Supreme Court of Canada level in *Modde* v *Dominion Glass Co. Ltd.*[18] where, under

16 (1912) 7 D.L.R. 345 (Ont.)
17 R.S.O. 1970, c 188   18 [1967] S.C.R. 567 (S.C.C.)

an 'unless' form of lease, two delay rental payments were late by several months. In the first instance, payment was made by cheque with an attached counterfoil and the lessor cashed the cheque, signed and returned the counterfoil. In the subsequent year the late payment was also made by cheque forwarded to the lessor. The lessor cashed the cheque, but did not sign or return the rental receipt acknowledgment attached to it. Subsequently, the lessor sought to have the lease set aside and, unfortunately for him, elected to follow the procedure under the Act. In the Supreme Court of Canada, Spence J noted that the jurisdiction of the county court judge was solely statutory and that the statute specifically refers to the failure to drill or pay rent as a default. If it was a default, then it could be waived. Section 6 of the Act specifically entitled the judge to take into account any payment accepted after the making of the application and the court agreed with the Ontario Court of Appeal that '*a fortiori* he is entitled to take into account one made before.'

Because the application was made under the statute, the many decisions holding that there was no duty upon the lessee to either drill or pay rental and therefore no breach to waive had no application.

Scholtens v *Sydenham Gas and Petroleum Co. Ltd.*[19] was a successful application made under the Ontario Gas and Oil Leases Act. In this case there had been a history of two tardy annual payments which had been accepted by the lessor. In the third year, however, the rental was not paid on the due date, July 29, and the application was made on July 31. Subsequently the lessees tendered a cheque for the rental but it was returned uncashed. Since the lessor had not accepted the payment made after the application was brought, Section 6 of the Act did not apply and the judge therefore was not required to take the act of tender into account. The ordinary law applied and the County Court Judge relied on both the *East Crest* and *Langlois* decisions to hold that the lease was void.

LACK OF GOOD FAITH BY LESSOR

A lessor cannot take advantage of a defective payment where he has actively thwarted the lessee's attempts to make proper payment. In *Imperial Oil Limited* v *Conroy and Berthiaume*[20] the defendant lessor had been successful in an action to have her surface title rectified to include minerals. Her predecessor in title had granted a lease to Imperial Oil Limited which she vigorously repudiated upon acquiring title to the minerals. She refused to

19 (1963), unreported but summarized in Lewis and Thompson, *Canadian Oil and Gas,* Vol. I, Dig. 211
20 (1954) 12 W.W.R. (N.S.) 569 (Alta.)

designate a depository and returned a delay rental cheque which had been tendered to her. Under these circumstances the court was unwilling to treat the lease as having lapsed through default in delay rental payment and held that the lessor could not take advantage of her own refusal to name a new depository and her rejection of the delay rental cheque. Nor could she be heard to complain of Imperial's acts following such a refusal and rejection. The judge was of the opinion that Imperial would not have been required to make a tender of the delay rental payment following the rejection, since any tender would have been 'a useless formality.'

EFFECT OF LITIGATION

There is an area of uncertainty as to the precise circumstances of a challenged lease while the litigation is in progress. What happens if, for example, the lessee fails to make a delay rental payment while the case is proceeding through the courts? The chances of this occurring are not negligible as the lessee's files will most likely be in the hands of the lawyers with some resulting confusion and disarray in the lessee's records. Is the fact that the issue is *sub judice* sufficient protection?

There is also the situation where the primary term of a lease may expire before the litigation is finalized. It would be of little comfort to a lessee to be assured by the Supreme Court of Canada that the lease had been valid at some previous point in time only to be met with a claim on the part of the lessor that it was now terminated by effluxion of time. The American case *Bingham* v *Stevenson*[21] affords the closest analogy. There the lessor had repudiated the lease, refused to accept rentals or to permit the lessee to drill for a period in excess of seven years. The primary term was held to have been extended by an equivalent period of time.

The safest course for the lessee to pursue under these conditions is to (a) insure that all delay rental payments are tendered during the litigation and (b) include in the relief sought a specific plea for an extension of the primary term, unless it is abundantly clear that a sufficient term will remain after the completion of all litigation.

CONCLUSIONS

Payment is a straightforward, simple act, and the volume of litigation on the subject is surprising. With one exception, that of mailing a payment, the level of authority in the 'unless' series of cases does not go beyond the

21 (1966) 420 P 2d 839

provincial appeal courts. It remains possible, therefore, that we may yet see some changes in what has been regarded for two decades as virtually settled law. The incontrovertible fact that the element of time is of great importance in the petroleum industry, however, will count heavily in support of the law as developed to date.

The areas of doubt and controversy, and their most probable judicial disposition are:

1   Time is of the essence; any gap, no matter how minute, between the expiration of the period and payment is fatal.
2   Although the result may be modified by the particular language used in the clause, the careful lessee should treat the delay rental period as ending on the day previous to the date of the lease.
3   If the lease provides for mailing or delivery, as most do, the act of mailing before the end of the critical day is sufficient compliance.
4   Payment must be in full; any deficiency, however insignificant, likely would be held to be an ineffective payment.[22] This result may not flow where the deficiency is caused by a legislative requirement, such as the obligation imposed by the Income Tax Act to withhold a designated percentage of certain type of payments to non-residents.[23]
5   The lessor is not required to give a notice of default as failure to pay is not an act of default on the part of the lessee.
6   Relief from forfeiture is not available to the lessee as termination of the lease for non-payment, or a defective or late payment, is not a forfeiture.
7   The depository bank or trust company can receive the payment only in accordance with the terms of the lease, and the act of the depository in crediting the amount to the lessor does not bind the lessor so as to constitute a waiver of the defective payment.
8   Even the retention of the funds by the lessor himself does not appear to be a waiver.
9   Ontario lessors should treat the Gas and Oil Leases Act with great caution. It is safe to use only when *absolutely nothing* has transpired since the act or omission that terminated the lease.

22 There is no Canadian authority directly on this issue but payment of the delay rental is regarded as an option and it is well settled law that an optionee must comply strictly with all requirements of the option. See generally discussion in chapter 9, *ante*
23 This question remains open, see *Paramount Petroleum and Minerals Corp. Ltd. and Bison Petroleum and Minerals Ltd.* v *Imperial Oil Ltd.* (1970) 73 w.w.r. 417 (Sask.), and discussion in chapter 9, *ante*

15
Termination of productive or potentially productive leases

When a lessee loses a lease through failure to make a timely commencement of drilling or payment of a delay rental, there may be some consolation in the fact that the true potential of the lands has been unexplored and un-determined. Also the lessee's out-of-pocket expenditures will be minimal since no costly drilling will have taken place.

It is otherwise with those leases which are terminated because the primary term has expired and the 'thereafter' provision has not been engaged success-fully. Here the lessee is faced with the loss of a valuable property and one, moreover, on which substantial expenditures are likely to have been made. Indeed, the lessee may be in the galling position of realizing that its estate inevitably must terminate and yet be helpless to avoid the oncoming end. Some of the decisions which have populated this judicial graveyard have already been analysed in those chapters dealing with the individual clauses in the lease. This was necessary in order to fully comprehend the evolution of the current form of the lease clauses. These may be referred to briefly in what follows, but only to the extent necessary to illumine those areas that can cause the involuntary termination of a lease.

OPERATIONS AT THE END OF THE PRIMARY TERM

The lessee who delays drilling until the primary term has nearly expired is flirting with disaster. The final year of the primary term is more fraught with hazard than the others. Subject to the effect of the third proviso to the *habendum*, which will be referred to later, the primary term of the lease can be extended only by something that amounts to production.

Canada-Cities Service Petroleum Corp. v *Kininmonth*[1] is a classic example of what happens when drilling operations have been commenced but not completed by the end of the primary term. In this case it will be remembered that the clause in the lease which might have permitted operations to be continued was interpreted as not applying until after the expiration of the primary term. Therefore it was as though the lease did not contain any provision extending the primary term while operations continued.

The lease was for a ten-year primary term commencing May 11, 1951. At the end of the primary term the lessee had drilled a well a total depth of 7200 feet and plugged it back to a shallower depth which was productive of oil. Before the well could be placed on production a process known as fracing was necessary. This was held in abeyance because of a road ban, so that by May 10, 1961, the well was incomplete and there were no operations on the wellsite. The lease was held to have expired on that date because it could not be said that any of the substances were 'being produced' at that time.

CLAUSE EXTENDING PRIMARY TERM

Most leases today contain a provision similar to the third proviso to the *habendum* in the standard lease discussed in chapter 6, *ante*, which purports to extend the primary term if certain operations, principally drilling, are taking place at the date on which the term would otherwise expire. While such clauses are generally given effect to, their operation is so restricted in the eyes of the court that the lessee cannot afford the slightest miscue. In *Canadian Superior Oil Ltd.* v *Paddon-Hughes Development Co. Ltd. and Hambly*[2] the lease was dated June 17, 1948, for a ten-year primary term and included this clause:

12. If Lessee shall commence to drill a well within the term of this Lease or any extension thereof, Lessee shall have the right to drill such well to completion with reasonable diligence and dispatch, and if oil or gas be found in paying quantities, this Lease shall continue and be in force with like effect as if such well had been completed within the term of years herein first mentioned.

Drilling operations commenced on June 10, 1958, and the well reached total depth on July 17, 1958. Drillstem tests were run and prospective formations

1 [1964] s.c.r. 439, 47 w.w.r. 437 (s.c.c.); (1961) 34 w.w.r. 392, 42 d.l.r. (2d) 56 (Alta. c.a.) See full discussion in chapter 6, *ante*
2 (1970) 74 w.w.r. 356 (s.c.c.); (1969) 67 w.w.r. 525, 3 d.l.r. (3d) 10 (c.a.); (1968) 65 w.w.r. 461 (Alta.) The same result was achieved in *Murdoch* v *Canadian Superior Oil Ltd.* (1969) 70 w.w.r. 768 (s.c.c.)

were perforated. The drilling rig was released on August 6, 1958, and subsequently the test lines were reconnected and gas flow testing was conducted on August 9 and 10, while well-site cleanup was done on August 11 and 12; the 'Christmas Tree' was painted on August 12, and chained and locked on August 13, 1958. The well was a gas well with no immediate market which brought the shut-in well royalty clause into operation. The lessee forwarded the shut-in royalty payment by letter dated August 13, 1958, which was received on August 14, 1958.

Under these circumstances the courts held that, while the clause did have the effect of extending the lease beyond its primary term, it did so only to that date upon which the well was drilled to completion and that the latest date on which completion could be said to have occurred was August 6, 1958. At that time there was no actual production and the shut-in royalty payment had not yet been made, so that there could be no constructive production. Under these conditions the lease must be considered as having terminated by its own terms.

If the well turns out to be an oil producer, the lessee must hustle to get it on production before the extended term expires. The difference between an oil and gas well was demonstrated in *Canadian Superior Oil Ltd.* v *Cull*.[3] Some lapse of time between actual completion of the well and commencement of production is permissible; it seems to be sufficient if the well's production allowable is met for the month in which the well is completed. The trial judge examined the various drilling operations with great care and concluded that the well was 'completed' on January 7, 1958 (beyond the primary term) when there was a 'Christmas Tree' in place and the well could have produced oil except that there was no separator or tank battery on the land. Sinclair J was prepared to hold that the lease terminated on that date. The lessee had proceeded with reasonable diligence to install the separator and tanks so that by January 11, all necessary facilities were ready. The higher courts refused to treat the lease as having come to an end on January 7 and rejected the idea that production at the very instant the well was completed was necessary in order to continue the lease in force. Under the facts of the case both the lessee and the lessor got the full benefits of production (because the well produced its monthly allowable) and this was sufficient.

CONCLUSIONS

Despite the fairly liberal construction adopted in the *Cull* case, the act of a lessee in placing itself in a position where it must rely upon this type of

---

3 [1971] 3 w.w.r. 28 (s.c.c.); (1970) 75 w.w.r. 606 (c.a.); (1970) 74 w.w.r. 334 (Alta.) See full discussion of this case in chapter 6, *ante*

extension of the primary term can only be described as foolhardy. If the property justifies the expense of drilling, it should be done in sufficient time so that the well can be completed and placed on production or the payment of shut-in royalty made prior to the expiration of the primary term.

POOLING AND SUSPENDED WELL ROYALTY PAYMENTS

Many a lease has perished in the treacherous ground of suspended well payments. These payments, if made properly and if the clause is worded correctly, amount to constructive production and activate the 'thereafter' extension. They are often used in conjunction with other provisions of the lease. In the foregoing discussion we have seen the suspended well payment used with the clause which extends the primary term while a well is being drilled to completion. Shut-in well royalties are also frequently encountered in a two-stage operation with pooling. The lands will be pooled with others on which there is a well, and then an attempt will be made to pay on a suspended well basis and thereby create constructive production.

POOLING

The concept of pooling is straightforward. If the lands covered by a lease are less than a spacing unit allocated under the applicable legislation for drilling or production purposes, they may be pooled with other lands to make up the necessary acreage. Virtually all leases contain a clause which empowers the lessee to pool the lands under such circumstances. It will be recalled, however, from our discussion on pooling in chapter 8 that many leases contain a pooling clause which is totally ineffective. In *Shell Oil Co.* v *Gibbard*[4] the Supreme Court of Canada held that the phrase 'when such pooling, or combining is necessary in order to conform with any regulations or orders of the Government of the Province of Alberta or any other authoritative body, which are now or may hereafter be in force in relation thereto' authorized pooling only where there was an affirmative requirement by the government to do so. Since there are no affirmative requirements that will activate the clause, many leases in effect today do not authorize the lessee to pool the lands.[5]

Sometimes the language used in the lease will not permit, in the view of the courts, the creation of constructive production through a combination of pooling and suspended well payments. In *Shell Oil Co.* v *Gunderson*[6] the

---

4 [1961] S.C.R. 725, 36 W.W.R. 529, 30 D.L.R. (2d) 386 (S.C.C.) See full discussion of this case in chapter 8, *ante*

5 As to compulsory pooling, see chapter 8, n. 17

6 [1960] S.C.R. 424, 23 D.L.R. (2d) 81 (S.C.C.) See also discussion in chapter 8, *ante*

habendum clause provided 'and so long thereafter as the leased substances or any of them are produced from the said lands.'

The suspended gas well royalty clause read:

3. Provided no royalties are otherwise paid hereunder, the Lessee shall pay to the Lessor each year as royalty the sum of Fifty Dollars ($50.00) for all wells on the said lands where gas only or primarily is found and the same is not used or sold, and while the said royalty is so paid each such well shall be deemed to be a producing well hereunder.

The last sentence of the pooling clause was 'Drilling operations on, or production of leased substances from, any land included in such unit shall have the same effect in continuing this lease in force and effect during the term hereby granted, or any extension thereof, as to all the said lands, as if such operation or production were upon or from the said lands or some portion thereof.'

The lease comprised a quarter section within the same section of land which also included the quarter section covered by the Gibbard lease. No well was drilled on the Gunderson quarter section but one was drilled on another quarter section and capped as a gas well. Prior to the expiration of the primary term a pooling notice was given under which the Gunderson quarter section was pooled with the balance of the section which included the capped gas well. The suspended gas well payment was also tendered which, the lessee contended, was sufficient to maintain the lease in force.

The court rejected this argument on the grounds that the *habendum* clause referred only to production 'from the said lands' which were defined as being the particular quarter section covered by the lease. Thus the well referred to in the suspended well clause could only be a well on the said lands. Nor could the last sentence of the pooling clause assist the lessee, because it referred only to 'drilling operations' or 'production.' The payment of the suspended well royalty could not amount to constructive production because that clause was limited to 'all wells on the said lands' and the well in question was not located on the said lands. Thus the lease was held to have terminated – a result which must have astounded and dismayed those who had prepared it.

Canadian Superior Oil of California Ltd. v *Kanstrup*[7] is another example where the language was not sufficiently precise to meet the exacting tests imposed by the court. The fact pattern in *Kanstrup* was the common situation where a lease covered a quarter section and a gas well had been drilled and capped on another quarter section within the one section spacing unit. The

---

7 [1965] S.C.R. 92, (1964) 49 W.W.R. 257, 47 D.L.R. (2d) 1 (S.C.C.)

original lease did not contain any provision for pooling, but by subsequent amendment the right to pool under certain conditions was granted. The pooling language appeared to have the same defect as in *Gibbard* inasmuch as it contained the reference to 'necessary in order to conform with any regulations or orders ... .' The amending letter, however, did recite the purpose of the pooling and that it was necessary because of the fact that the spacing unit for a gas well was 640 acres. Under these conditions the court was prepared to concede that pooling had been achieved, but this was of little assistance to the lessee. The amending letter also contained this language: 'Drilling operations on, or production of leased substances from any land included in such unit shall have the same effect in continuing this Lease in force and effect during the term hereby granted, or any extension thereof, as to all the said lands, as if such operation or production were upon or from the said lands, or some portion thereof.'

The original lease contained a capped gas well royalty which read in part as follows: 'Where gas from a well producing gas only is not sold or used, Lessee may pay as royalty $100.00 per well per year, and if such payment is made it will be considered that gas is being produced within the meaning of Paragraph 2 hereof' ... The lessee, of course, contended that the well drilled on another quarter section became a well within the meaning of the above clause and therefore payment of the capped gas well royalty continued the lease in force. Martland J analysed the portion of the amending letter, quoted above, which dealt with those items that were meant to continue the lease in force and effect. According to the view taken by the court, it was only drilling operations on or production of leased substances from any land other than the quarter section which would be effective to continue the lease. He pointed out that it did not say that a non-producing gas well not on the leased quarter section was to be equivalent to a non-producing gas well on the northwest quarter so as to entitle the lessee to rely upon the provision. The result is a clear example of the literalistic approach in action.

ABSENCE OF OR CESSATION OF PRODUCTION

It is axiomatic from the language of the lease itself that it will terminate if there is no production (actual or constructive) at the end of the primary term. In *Sohio Petroleum Company* v *Weyburn Security Company Limited*[8] the drilling operations did not commence until one week prior to the expiration of the ten-year primary term and the well was completed some ten days after that term had expired. The well went on production and royalty was paid to

8 (1970), 74 W.W.R. 626 (S.C.C.)

the lessor. The Supreme Court of Canada remarked, almost in passing, that the lease had terminated because there was no production within the primary term.

As to cessation of production after the primary term, the reader is referred to the discussion in chapter 6, *ante*, of *Krysa* v *Opalinski*.[9] The only open question appears to be the effect of interrupted or suspended production which was also discussed in chapter 6.

DUTY TO ACCOUNT FOR PAST PRODUCTION

The *Weyburn* decision is also useful as it is the only Canadian decision to date which deals with the question as to whether a lessee under a terminated lease has any obligation to account for past production. In the other cases that involved a termination of the lease, the issue either was resolved by private treaty between the parties or the lease was challenged and terminated prior to, or shortly after, going on production. In *Weyburn*, however, the well began to produce in November 1959 and the action to have the lease declared invalid was not taken until October 1966. Thus there was a very considerable volume of production at issue.

The Saskatchewan Court of Appeal took a broad brush approach to the problem, relying heavily on equitable principles and *bona fides*.

The court has jurisdiction to grant this relief on terms which will be just and equitable to all parties involved. The respondent, Sohio, proceeded under a mistake as to its rights, and did not knowingly take an unfair advantage of the appellant's lack of appreciation of its legal rights. The respondents were first aware that their position was challenged when the writ of summons was served upon them. At that time the revenue which they had received from the sale of the production exceeded the amount that they had expended. Under the circumstances, it would appear just and equitable to order the respondents to account for all benefits from production received by them after the date of service of the writ of summons upon them.[10]

This solution was expressly approved by the Supreme Court of Canada.

While neither the Court of Appeal nor the Supreme Court of Canada referred to any American decisions, the result is generally similar to what would have been achieved in the United States. There, the lessee under an invalid lease is treated as a trespasser. The courts then seek to determine whether the lessee is an innocent or wilful trespasser. This inquiry in turn

9 (1960) 32 w.w.r. 346 (Alta.)   10 (1969) **69** w.w.r. 680, 687 (Sask. c.a.)

narrows down to the *bona fides* or lack of same on the part of the lessee. If, for example, the lessee had cause to know that the validity of the lease was challenged or likely to be challenged and nonetheless proceeded to drill and take production, it would likely be classified as a wilful trespasser.

As in all subjective tests of this type the court is faced with determining the intent of the lessee. The Kentucky Court of Appeals defined the problem in this way:

The burden is always upon the offender to establish his status as an innocent or mistaken invader of another's property. To be sure the mere testimony of the person affected that he acted in good faith and honestly believed he was right in the position he assumed is not conclusive or, indeed, sufficient of itself to entitle him to the advantage of one occupying the place of innocence or good faith. The test to be applied is that of intent, but, being a state of mind, it can seldom be proved by direct evidence. The conditions and behavior are usually such that the court can determine whether the trespass was perpetrated in a spirit of wrong doing, with a knowledge that it was wrong or whether it was done under a bona fides mistake as where the circumstances were calculated to induce or justify the reasonably prudent man, acting with a proper sense of the rights of others, to go in and to continue along the way ... Among the factors to be considered as evidencing good faith are these:

There should be at least reasonable doubt of the other party's exclusive or dominant right. The trespasser acted upon the advice of reputable counsel, to whom all the facts had been fairly submitted, upon question of legal right concerning which a layman could hardly have knowledge, such as a disputed title, even though that advice proves to be bad. Of stronger influence, manifestly, is the fact that a court of competent jurisdiction has rendered a favourable judgement upon identical or similar issues. The test is not the trespasser's violation of the law in the light of the maxim that every man knows the law, but is his sincerity and his actual contention at the time.[11]

Some of the factors that determine whether a trespasser was acting in good or bad faith are listed in Williams and Meyers.[12] Among those that have been considered by the courts are: (a) honest belief by the lessee as to the validity of the title; (b) innocent mistake in the location of the boundary of the lands; (c) an ambiguous instrument in the chain of title and the trespasser makes an erroneous but good faith construction thereof; (d) operations conducted by the trespasser after a favourable judicial title determination which is later

11 *Swiss Oil Corp.* v *Hupp* 69 s.w. 2d 1037, 1041, 1042
12 Williams and Meyers, *Oil and Gas Law*, Vol. 1, 383–94

reversed; (e) whether or not there has been notice of the adverse claim before entry in drilling and the reasonableness of the trespasser's belief as to the right to drill; (f) the reliance by the trespasser on the advice of counsel; (g) any action by or other conduct of the owner which estops him from asserting that the trespasser was in good faith.

The classification of a lessee whose title ultimately fails has a profound effect upon the duty to account for past production. In both cases the lessee deprived of title must account for the minerals produced. The bad faith trespasser, however, is not entitled to set off against the proceeds from the sale of the minerals the costs of drilling and operating the well.[13] The good faith trespasser while required to account for past production is generally allowed to deduct the cost of producing and lifting the minerals.[14]

While not expressed in terms of trespass, the result in the *Weyburn* decision parallels the American compromise. Since a lessee under a terminated lease produced the minerals without any real title to them, a court could not adopt the position that there was no duty to account. Still, it seems prepared to ease the hardship by permitting a recovery of the expenses where the equities justify it.

13 *Supra* n. 11
14 *Marathon Oil Co.* v *Gulf Oil Corporation* 130 sw 2d 365; *Shell Oil Co.* v *Dye* 135 F 2d 365

16
Estoppel

On many occasions hard pressed counsel for the lessee, realizing that the language of the lease would fall short of the demands placed upon it by the courts, have fallen back on equitable defences outside the language of the document itself. Relief from forfeiture was summarily dismissed because the lessee had options not obligations. The doctrine of estoppel, however, seemed to have a potential if only the right fact pattern could be found.

The basic approach of estoppel is simply that the lessor by doing something, or neglecting to do something, has placed himself in a position where he is stopped from denying the existence of the lease. The argument runs that because the lessor has accepted a delay rental payment, a capped gas well royalty, production royalties, has allowed the lessee access to the wellsite, or has failed to treat the lease as cancelled, he can no longer deny the existence of an otherwise invalid lease. The underlying thrust of the doctrine of estoppel is simply that one party may be denied from establishing the true state of the legal relationship where it would be unjust or inequitable to allow him to do so. The basic principle of estoppel may be stated:

Where one has either by words or conduct made to another a representation of fact, either with knowledge of its falsehood, or with the intention that it should be acted upon, or has so conducted himself that another would, as a reasonable man, understand that a certain representation of fact was intended to be acted on, and that the other has acted on the representation and thereby altered his position to his prejudice, an estoppel arises against the party who made the representation, and he is not allowed to aver that the fact is otherwise than he represented it to be.[1]

1 *Halsbury's Laws of England* (3 ed) vol. 15, 169

The foregoing passage expresses the basic common law type of estoppel. Today there are a number of variations which are recognized and these may be subdivided into four main categories:

ESTOPPEL BY REPRESENTATION

This is the fundamental form and has been defined in the leading textbook on the subject as:

Where one person ('the representor') has made a representation to another person ('the representee') in words or by acts and conduct, or (being under a duty to the representee to speak or act) by silence or inaction, with the intention (actual or presumptive), and with the result, of inducing the representee on the faith of such representation to alter his position to his detriment, the representor, in any litigation which may afterwards take place between him and the representee, is estopped, as against the representee, from making or attempting to establish by evidence, any averment substantially at variance with his former representation, if the representee at the proper time, and in the proper manner, objects thereto.[2]

ESTOPPEL BY ACQUIESCENCE

This is really a refinement of estoppel by representation and deals with the situation where one party does nothing, and thereby lulls the other party into a sense of security. The difficult element here is that the acquiescing party may be required to have knowledge of the true position. Acquiescence combined with such knowledge gives rise to the implication of fraud:

It has been said that the acquiescence which will deprive a man of his legal rights must amount to fraud, and in my view that is an abbreviated statement of a very true proposition. A man is not to be deprived of his legal rights unless he has acted in such a way as would make it fraudulent for him to set up those rights. What, then, are the elements or requisites necessary to constitute fraud of that description? In the first place the plaintiff must have made a mistake as to his legal rights. Secondly, the plaintiff must have expended some money or must have done some act (not necessarily upon the defendant's land) on the faith of his mistaken belief. Thirdly, the defendant, the possessor of the legal right, must know of the existence of his own right which is inconsistent with the right claimed by the plaintiff. If he does not know of it he is in the same position as the plaintiff, and the doctrine of acquiescence is founded upon conduct with a knowledge of

2 Spencer Bower and Turner, *Estoppel by Representation* (2 ed) 1966, 4

your legal rights. Fourthly, the defendant the possessor of the legal right, must know of the plaintiff's mistaken belief of his rights. If he does not, there is nothing which calls upon him to assert his own rights. Lastly, the defendant, the possessor of the legal right, must have encouraged the plaintiff in his expenditure of money or in the other acts which he has done, either directly or by abstaining from asserting his legal right. Where all these elements exist, there is fraud of such a nature as will entitle the Court to restrain the possessor of the legal right from exercising it, but, in my judgement, nothing short of this will do.[3]

PROMISSORY ESTOPPEL

Equity is a constantly evolving process and the doctrine of estoppel has been no exception. The limitation of estoppel by representation or by acquiescence lay in the fact that the representation must relate to an already existing fact. If the representation was made with respect to the future, the doctrine permitted no remedy. This hiatus was covered by the now celebrated decision of Denning J in *Central London Property Trust Ltd.* v *High Trees House Ltd.*[4]

The *High Trees* case was a routine, unpretentious sort of dispute which involved the rent to be paid for a block of flats. The apartment block had been built in 1937 and at the outbreak of the war in 1939 few of the apartments had been let. The landlords agreed in writing in 1940 to reduce the rent but there was no consideration paid by the lessee. In an action by the landlords to recover the full rent the lessee attempted to set up estoppel by way of defence. Denning J noted that, under the current state of the law, estoppel could not have been maintained since the representation that the rent would be reduced was not a representation of existing fact but as to the future – a representation that the rent would not be enforced at the full rate but only at a reduced rate. The court observed that law could not afford to stand still and Denning J then struck off in a new direction:

There has been a series of decisions over the last fifty years which, although said to be cases of estoppel, are not really such. They are cases of promises which were intended to create legal relations and which, in the knowledge of the person making the promise, were going to be acted on by the party to whom the promise was made, and have in fact been so acted on. In such cases the courts have said these promises must be honoured. There are certain cases to which I particularly refer: *Fenner* v *Blake* (3) ([1900] 1 Q.B. 426), Re *Wickham* (4) ([1917] 34 T.L.R. 158), Re *William Porter & Co., Ltd.* (5) [1937] 2 All E.R. 361 and *Buttery* v

3 *Willmott* v *Barber* (1880) 15 Ch. D. 96, 105
4 [1956] 1 All E.R. 256; [1947] K.B. 130

Pickard (6) (1946) (174 L.T. 144). Although said by the learned judges who decided them to be cases of estoppel, all these cases are not estoppel in the strict sense. They are cases of promises which were intended to be binding, which the parties making them knew would be acted on and which the parties to whom they were made did act on. *Jorden* v *Money* (2) can be distinguished because there the promissor made it clear that she did not intend to be legally bound, whereas in the cases to which I refer the promisor did intend to be bound. In each case the court held the promise to be binding on the party making it, even though under the old common law it might be said to be difficult to find any consideration for it. The courts have not gone so far as to give a cause of action in damages for breach of such promises, but they have refused to allow the party making them to act inconsistently with them. It is in that sense, and in that sense only, that such a promise gives rise to an estoppel. The cases are a natural result of the fusion of law and equity; for the cases of *Hughes* v *Metropolitan Ry. Co.* (7) (1877) (2 App. Cas. 439), *Birmingham & District Land Co.* v *London & North Western Ry. Co.* (8) (1888) (40 Ch. D. 268), and *Salisbury* v *Gilmore* (9) ([1942] 1 All E.R. 457), show that a party will not be allowed in equity to go back on such a promise. The time has now come for the validity of such a promise to be recognized. The logical consequence, no doubt, is that a promise to accept a smaller sum in discharge of a larger sum, if acted on, is binding, notwithstanding the absence of consideration, and if the fusion of law and equity leads to that result, so much the better. At this time of day it is not helpful to try to draw a distinction between law and equity. They have been joined together now for over seventy years, and the problems have to be approached in a combined sense.[5]

The new or promissory estoppel has been summarized in Halsbury:

When one party has by his words or conduct made to the other party a promise or assurance which was intended to affect the legal relations between them and to be acted upon accordingly then once the other party has taken him at his word, and acted upon it the one who gave the promise or assurance cannot afterwards be allowed to revert to their previous legal relations as if no such promise or assurance had been made by him, but he must accept their legal relations subject to the qualifications which he himself has so introduced.[6]

ESTOPPEL BY DEED

The fourth branch of estoppel, and one which has attracted a good deal of notice in cases involving oil and gas leases has been that type of estoppel which arises when the parties have entered into some form of written agree-

5 Ibid, All E.R. 258, 259   6 Halsbury, *supra* n. 1, vol. 15, 175

ment. This is close to, but not quite, a contract in that there is no binding undertaking between the parties on the express point, but rather the document itself leads to the inescapable conclusion that the parties have agreed to act upon an assumed state of affairs. Having done so, they cannot thereafter challenge the situation. 'Estoppel by deed, then, arises where it appears from the formal writing of the parties that they have agreed to admit as true, or to assume the truth of, certain facts as the conventional basis upon which they have entered into contractual or other mutual relations.'[7]

While the underlying principle remains constant, each category of estoppel requires a different mixture of ingredients and must pass different tests.

ESTOPPEL IN OIL AND GAS LEASES

From the very beginning estoppel seemed to have more chance of success than any of the other equitable principles. While the courts found various reasons for not applying the doctrine under the facts of each case, they were careful to avoid rejecting its potential application. Then, in several provincial Supreme Court decisions, estoppel actually was applied to revive an otherwise defunct lease. It looked as though estoppel might succeed where all others had failed.[8]

The first occasion on which estoppel managed to revive a terminated lease was in *Canadian Superior Oil Ltd.* v *Murdoch*,[9] where the circumstances were such that the lease had terminated because there was no production, constructive or otherwise, at the end of the primary term. The automatic termination was unknown to both parties at the time it occurred, but there were other disputes between the mineral owners and the lessee. After the expiration of the primary term the lessor's husband commenced an action claiming title to the hydrocarbon substances underlying both railway grounds and a right-of-way which adjoined the farm. The lessee contended that these minerals really belonged to the lessor and thus were included under the original lease. This dispute led to legal proceedings under which the lessor filed a statement of claim which, among other things, stated: '(b) that in the further alternative, that said lease has expired due to the fact that ten (10) years has elapsed from the date of commencement of the lease and that Canadian Superior Oil of California Ltd. is not engaged in drilling said land or working operations but has drilled on said land and has "capped" wells on said land to the detriment of the plaintiff depriving her of oil royalties.'

---

7 Spencer Bower and Turner, *supra* n. 2, 146
8 On estoppel and leases generally see Ballem, 'The Continuing Adventures of the Oil and Gas Lease' (1972) 50 *Can. Bar Rev.* 423
9 (1968) 65 w.w.r. 473 (Alta.)

Eventually the various disputes were resolved and an agreement of settlement was entered into under which the lessor 'does hereby ratify and confirm that the said Lease is in good standing and of full force and effect.' Riley J defined the central issue of the case as that of estoppel. He found that the parties, although the lease had actually terminated, agreed to a different fact, namely, 'the lease is in good standing and of full force and effect.' There was nothing to prevent parties from agreeing that a certain fact is so and thereafter being bound by such agreement. This was equated by the trial judge to estoppel by contract, or estoppel by deed as above defined.

On appeal[10] the lease was maintained, but the fangs of estoppel were drawn. The Appellate Division, later affirmed by the Supreme Court, found that it was not necessary to resort to estoppel in order to give effect to the covenant contained in the settlement agreement. In fact the parties had agreed by contract that the lease was still in effect and it was not necessary to go beyond the simple fact of an existing and binding contract.

The Alberta Trial Division once again was prepared to use estoppel to revive an otherwise extinguished lease in *Canadian Superior Oil Ltd.* v *Cull*.[11] The fact pattern in this case was fully described in chapter 6 and it will be recalled that the trial judge held the lease to have terminated because of the time gap that existed between 'completion' of the well and the commencement of oil production. Having found that the lease had terminated on its own terms, Sinclair J went on to consider the effect of an agreement that had been entered into between the lessor and the lessee. There had been some dispute concerning that acreage underlying right-of-way lands; also the original lease was defective in that it did not contain a pooling clause. Negotiations took place and resulted in the execution of an agreement on July 11, 1958 (some months after the expiration of the primary term of the lease), but the agreement was made effective as of November 21, 1957 (prior to expiration of the primary term). The agreement amended the land description by including the right-of-way, added a pooling clause, and provided that 'all other terms, covenants and conditions contained in the said lease remain in full force and effect.'

It is noteworthy that at the time this amending agreement was entered into, there appeared to be no question in anyone's mind but that the lease was in full force and effect. Sinclair J applied the doctrine of estoppel by deed to the amending agreement and held that the fact that the lease was in effect was the conventional basis upon which the parties entered into the amending agreement.

10 (1969) 68 w.w.r. 390 (c.a.); (1969) 70 w.w.r. 768 (s.c.c.)
11 (1970) 74 w.w.r. 324 (Alta.)

As with the *Murdoch* decision, the higher courts upheld the lease but avoided the issue of estoppel[12] by holding that the requirements of the lease had been complied with. Thus it was unnecessary to consider the question of estoppel.

Although the reasoning was neither accepted nor rejected by higher courts, the Alberta Trial Division had twice utilized estoppel by contract or by deed to revive leases which it considered to have been extinguished. In short order, however, two other cases faced the higher courts with the doctrine of estoppel, and the result of this confrontation has virtually eliminated the doctrine as a means of reviving an otherwise terminated lease.

The cases were *Canadian Superior Oil Ltd.* v *Paddon Hughes Development Co. Ltd. and Hambly*[13] and *Weyburn Security Company Limited* v *Sohio Petroleum Company*.[14] They were heard back-to-back by the Supreme Court of Canada and, although the ingredients of estoppel were much less compelling in the *Paddon Hughes* case, that decision was delivered first and contains most of the reasoning of the court on the question of estoppel. It seems to have been used by the Supreme Court to make known its views on estoppel in oil and gas law. It must be borne in mind that in both cases there was no subsequent documentation which could have raised the issue of estoppel by deed or by contract. If estoppel existed, it did so only by reason of the conduct or acquiescence of the lessor. In both cases it was also conceded that the lease had terminated on its own terms so that estoppel was the only hope of the lessee.

The lease in the *Paddon Hughes* case had been – unknown to the parties at the time – terminated by a failure to make timely payment of the shut-in royalty. The acts and omissions which the lessee was able to muster were not very impressive from the point of view of establishing a representation on the part of the lessor that the lease remained in force. They were:

(a) The payment and receipt of shut-in royalties during the years 1958 to 1965. These payments went to a trust company by virtue of a royalty trust agreement that the lessor had entered into some years before. Under this agreement it was the duty of the trust company to receive all royalty income and distribute it among the royalty trust certificate holders. During the period

---

12 (1970) 75 w.w.r. 606 (c.a.); [1971] 3 w.w.r. 28 (s.c.c.)
13 (1970) 74 w.w.r. 356 (s.c.c.); (1969) 67 w.w.r. 525, 3 d.l.r. (3d) 10 (c.a.);
   65 w.w.r. 461 (Alta.)
14 (1970) 74 w.w.r. 626 (s.c.c.); (1969) 69 w.w.r. 680, 7 d.l.r. (3d) 277 (c.a.);
   66 w.w.r. 155 (Sask.) The *Paddon Hughes* and *Weyburn* cases are discussed in Currie, 'Recent Cases and Developments in Oil and Gas Law' (1971) 9
   Alta. L. Rev. 452

there were only two distributions made by the trust company and the lessor returned his share of the second one.

(b) Rental payments were received and retained by the lessor pursuant to a surface lease.

(c) When the lessee entered upon the lands to conduct operations such as to check or maintain the well, it sought and received consent from the lessor.

(d) In May 1960, the lessor happened to see a well pressure gauge that indicated the gas pressure was dangerously high and advised an employee of the lessee of this fact.

(e) The lessor had, as collateral security to a mortgage, executed an agreement which gave to the mortgage company 'all bonuses, rentals, delay rentals, and other considerations and benefits' payable under certain leases and surface leases, and one of the described leases was the one under attack.

The Appellate Division held that these events and happenings did not constitute representation by word or conduct on which a defence of estoppel could be founded.

The Supreme Court of Canada agreed that the evidence did not support a plea of estoppel, but also made some observations as to the applicability of estoppel to oil and gas leases which virtually closed the door on the possibility of estoppel ever reviving a terminated lease. The one possibility that now appears to remain open is estoppel by acquiescence which, as we shall see later, requires an element of fraud.

Dealing with estoppel in general, Martland J said:

Without attempting finally to determine the matter, I have serious doubt as to whether the issue of estoppel can properly be raised in the circumstances of this case. The appellants, as plaintiffs, seek a declaration that the lease is a good, valid and subsisting lease. For the reasons already given, it appears that the lease in question had terminated. It could not be revived thereafter except by agreement, for consideration, between the parties. To say that subsequent representations by Hambly could recreate the legal relations between the parties would be to say that such representations could create a new cause of action for Superior. But, subject to the equitable rule as to acquiescence, and to which I will refer later, a cause of action cannot be founded upon estoppel.[15]

Concerning estoppel by representation, Martland J said that the essential factors were: (1) a representation, or conduct amounting to a representation, intended to induce a course of conduct on the part of the person to whom

15 *Supra* n. 13, w.w.r. 360

the representation is made; (2) an act or omission resulting from the representation, whether actual or by conduct, by the person to whom the representation is made; (3) detriment to such person as a consequence of the act or omission. This branch of estoppel was disposed of because there was nothing that amounted to a representation by the lessor, Hambly.

The court's treatment of promissory estoppel is significant. Promissory estoppel was the branch of the doctrine which had been applied by Sinclair J in the earlier *Cull* decision to uphold the lease. It proceeds from the basis that, where the dealings between the parties lead one of them to suppose that the legal relations between them have a certain status, the other is estopped from denying that condition. Martland J, after quoting a well-known statement of the principle,[16] continued: 'This principle assumes the existence of a legal relationship between the parties when the representation is made. It applies where a party to a contract represents to the other party that the former will not enforce his strict legal rights under it. In the present case, however, the contractual relationship between the parties has come to an end before any representation is alleged to have been made. There is no allegation that Hambly, while the lease still subsisted, had ever represented that its provisions would not be enforced strictly.'

It appears that promissory estoppel is irrelevant to oil and gas lease cases. The whole purpose of the plea of estoppel is to revive a terminated lease. The normal acts of promissory estoppel that would be relied upon must occur after the termination of the lease which, in accordance with Martland J's reasoning, precludes the application of promissory estoppel.

Estoppel by acquiescence requires an additional ingredient, knowledge on the part of the representor that he has a right inconsistent with the right claimed by the other party. In other words, the acquiescing party is not bound unless he so acquiesces with knowledge of his own true legal position. Translated into oil and gas terms, it means that the lessor must know that the lease has terminated and, further that the lessee must not have this knowledge. The principle appears to require such a degree of knowledge on the part of the lessor and innocence on the part of the lessee that the continued acquiescence by the lessor amounts to a fraud. To say the least, the area in which this principle could operate with respect to leases is very limited, as it usually takes several levels of judicial examination to determine whether or not a lease has terminated at any given point in time. Furthermore, the lessee is almost always in a better position to be aware of the termination than is the lessor.

The *Weyburn* case[17] was as powerful a vehicle to advance the plea of

16 *Hughes* v *Metro Ry.* (1877) 2 App Cas 439, 448   17 *Supra* n. 14

estoppel as any counsel could desire. The lessee was able to parade a number of positive acts by the lessor pursuant to a lease which (unknown to both parties) had terminated for lack of production at the expiration of the primary term. This was the pattern insofar as it related to estoppel:

(1) The primary term expired on October 27, 1959 and production did not take place until some time in November of that year. This led to an automatic termination of the lease although the parties did not then appreciate that fact. Production continued to be taken from the well over a period of years and the lessor received the appropriate royalty thereon.

(2) The lessor by a letter dated April 5, 1960 demanded that the lessee drill an offset well pursuant to the offset drilling clause in the lease.

(3) The lessee complied with this demand and drilled the offset well.

(4) The lessor as surface owner granted a surface lease for the drilling of the offset well.

(5) The lessor demanded in each year (including a demand made during the very month of the trial) that the lessee reimburse the lessor for its seven-eighths share of the mineral taxes as required by the terms of the lease and the lessee did so.

The trial judge found that estoppel had been established; MacPherson J held the view that both estoppel by representation and promissory estoppel applied. He found that by demanding the drilling of the offset well and by granting the surface lease the plaintiff had conducted itself so as to represent to the defendant that the lease was subsisting. The same reasoning applied to the demands by the lessor plaintiff for reimbursement of the mineral taxes. These were regarded as positive acts by which the lessor made a demand of the lessee under the terms of the lease after the alleged termination.

The Supreme Court of Canada, however, found that estoppel had not been established since the actions of Sohio as lessee did not result from representations or conduct of the lessor but were taken because Sohio, as well as the lessor, was unaware of the fact that the lease had come to an end. Since Sohio believed that the lease had not terminated, its actions could not have been induced by any representation on the part of the lessor.

The Supreme Court also quoted with approval the Saskatchewan Court of Appeal's findings on promissory estoppel and, by so doing, introduced the requirement of knowledge into promissory estoppel.

In the instant case, if the conduct of the respondent could be said to amount to the type of promise, assurance or course of negotiation contemplated in the passages above set out, Sohio did not rely upon it to believe that the respondent would not contend that the lease had terminated.

The acts of Sohio which were found by the learned trial judge to be alterations of its position to its detriment, – drilling of the off-set well, entering into the surface lease, and payment of one-eighth [*sic*] of the mineral tax, – were performed because Sohio considered it was obligated to perform them under the terms of the lease. The respondent, in requesting or demanding that Sohio carry out the terms of the lease, and in allowing Sohio to proceed as it did, simply accepted the mistaken position that the lease had not terminated. Because the respondent was not aware of the true legal position, it is not now precluded from exercising its rights.[18]

Even more significant was the reiteration by Martland J of his doubt as to whether a lease could be revived by estoppel unless there was fraud: 'In *Can. Superior Oil Ltd.* v. *Hambly* (1970) 74 WWR 356, affirming (1969) WWR 525, 3 DLR (3d) 10, I expressed doubt as to whether a lease, which had terminated, could be subsequently enforced on the basis of representations or conduct occurring after its termination, unless, at least, they would amount to a fraud, of the kind defined by Fry, J. in *Wilmott* v. *Barber* (1880) 15 Ch D 96, at 105, 49 LJ Ch 792, ...'[19]

The defeat of estoppel leaves the lessee with the bare words of the lease itself; there can be no help or succour outside the document.

18 *Supra* n. 14, 14 W.W.R. 631
19 Ibid, 629

PART SIX

RECOMMENDED MODEL FORM OF LEASE AND
PRESENT FORM OF 'STANDARD' LEASE

17
Model lease

It would be idle to pretend that the hasty marriage of the Producers 88 form of lease with Canadian jurisprudence has been a happy and tranquil union. After more than two decades of uneasy cohabitation, the lease remains a minefield of potential hazards to the lessee, while remedial draftsmanship by the lessee has created areas of severe and often unexpected disadvantage to the lessor.

With the body of judicial decisions that have interpreted the lease and the experience accumulated since the late 1940s, it should be possible to devise a lease that strikes a balance of fairness between the two parties. Such a lease should recognize the right of the lessee to explore for and produce the minerals without interference from the lessor, and should also recognize the interest that the lessor has in the minerals and in their development. If the legal pitfalls that have plagued lessees over the years are removed, then the justification for the sophisticated and one-sided amendments to the form of lease will largely disappear. The model form of lease is therefore presented as a sort of balance between the rights and position of both parties; every attempt has been made to avoid weighting it in favour of one or the other.

Two general observations should be made. The 'unless' type of drilling clause has been abandoned in favour of the 'or' type. The continued insistence of the industry in using the suicidal 'unless' clause is difficult to understand. A survey of many of the leading corporate lessees indicated that the law departments were almost universally in favour of the 'or' clause, while most land departments preferred to continue with the 'unless' type. Apparently the reason behind the latter preference is that the land personnel feel they are familiar with the hazards of the 'unless' clause and, with proper rental records, can avoid its dangers. It would seem to follow that records could also be established to provide for a surrender at the required date just as easily as for the payment of a delay rental, and a miscue would not have the fatal consequences that occur with a faulty delay rental payment.

The power to unitize has been omitted, as is the case with the standard lease. Unitization is something separate and apart from a lease and should be by private treaty between the parties or by legislation where applicable. Additionally, there are so many hazards and uncertainties that surround such a power that any purported exercise of such a clause would be of very dubious value. These shortcomings and hazards are discussed in chapter 11 and, in our view, outweigh any possible advantages of such a clause.

The text of the model lease is accompanied by explanatory notes which attempt to highlight the main differences between it and the standard form and to describe the objectives which the changes are designed to achieve.

MODEL FORM   EXPLANATORY NOTES

MINERAL LEASE AND GRANT

THIS AGREEMENT made this .... day of
.... A.D. 19........
between .... of
the .... of ....
in the Province of .... (hereinafter called the 'Lessor'), and ....
.... a body corporate carrying on
business in the Province of ....
(hereinafter called the 'Lessee'), WITNESSETH
that the parties hereto have agreed as follows:

1 INTERPRETATION

1.1   In this Lease, unless there is something in the subject or context inconsistent therewith:

a) 'Anniversary date' means the date corresponding to the date above written in each year of the term of this Lease.
b) 'Commercial production' means the output from a well of such volume of the minerals

As a matter of arrangement, defined terms for the most part are described at the beginning of the lease.

By keying to a defined anniversary date, it should be possible to avoid confusion as to the precise date when a payment, or some other

or any of them after a production test of thirty (30) consecutive days that would commercially and economically warrant the drilling of a like well in the vicinity thereof, having regard to the cost of drilling and production operations and the price and quality of the minerals.

c) 'Deferment fee' means the sum of .... Dollars ($................) to be paid by the Lessee pursuant to clause 4 where the Lessee has not commenced operations.

d) 'Minerals' means all the petroleum, natural gas, and related hydrocarbons (except coal and valuable stone), all other gases and all other minerals and substances (whether in liquid, gaseous or solid form and whether hydrocarbons or non-hydrocarbons) that are produced in association with the aforesaid petroleum, natural gas, and related hydrocarbons, or are contained in any formation water produced with the foregoing substances.

e) 'Operations' means any one or more of the following: on-site preparation for drilling, drilling, testing, completing, reworking, recompleting, deepening, plugging back or repairing a well, production of the minerals, or work for or incidental to any of the foregoing, or a payment of the suspended operations fee pursuant to clause 3.3.

f) 'Pooled lands' means the said lands, together with any other lands or any zone or formation underlying such other lands, with which the said lands or any portion thereof may be pooled pursuant to clause 8 hereof.

act, is actually to be made or performed.

Referring to the payment to be made in lieu of drilling as a fee rather than a rental is closer to its real nature and avoids confusing it with a true rent.

The term 'minerals' has been selected as being more appropriate to a mineral grant than 'leased substances.' The actual definition closely parallels the standard lease.

The definition of operations recites all the things that will maintain the lease in force. The inclusion of 'on-site preparation' is designed to cover that murky area that occurs near the end of the primary term when something has been done but the well may not have been actually spudded. The specific inclusion of a suspended operations payment is meant to remove any doubt as to the effect of such a payment.

g) 'Said lands' means the ....
....
in Township .... Range ....,
West of the .... Meridian, as more
particularly described and set forth in Certi-
ficate(s) of Title No.(s) ....
....
of Record in the Land Titles Office for the
....
Land Registration District, including the
Lessor's interest, if any, in any lands excepted from, or roadways, lands or rights-
of-way adjoining the above-described lands,
or such portion or portions thereof as from
time to time remain subject to this Lease.

The definition of 'said lands' has been structured to land descriptions in Western Canada. Some modification will be required for Ontario leases.

h) 'Spacing unit' means the area normally
designated for drilling or production purposes for oil or gas wells, whichever shall be
applicable to any well or wells on the said
lands or pooled lands, or designated under
any special order, licence or other allocation
expressly made applicable to such well or
wells.

The definition has been expanded to clearly include general designations of spacing units, not just specific allocations.

i) 'Suspended operations fee' means any payment made pursuant to clause 3.3, which
payment shall be in an amount equal to the
deferment fee.

Ontario leases may substi-tute in the case of gas wells the table of suspended well payments that is related to the potential of the well in place of the deferment fee – see chapter 10.

1.2   Whenever required by the context, mascu-
line pronouns shall be deemed to include the
feminine and neuter genders, and the singular
shall be deemed to include the plural.

The interpretation prin-ciples are self-explanatory.

1.3   This Lease shall be interpreted in accordance with the laws of the Province of ....
1.4   Time shall be of the essence of this Lease.

Time has been held to be of the essence in oil and gas leases in countless cases.

2 THE GRANT

2.1 The Lessor, being registered as owner (or entitled to become so registered) of all the minerals within, upon or under the said lands, in consideration of the sum of .... Dollars ($...........................), paid to the Lessor by the Lessee (the receipt whereof is hereby acknowledged), and in the further consideration of the covenants of the Lessee herein contained, hereby GRANTS AND LEASES exclusively unto the Lessee the minerals within, upon or under the said lands, together with the right to explore for, drill for, take and dispose of same.

The grant clause contemplates that the full consideration will be paid when the Lessor executes the lease. This is the normal arrangement; any variation should be documented.

3 TERM

3.1 The Lessee may HOLD the minerals and the rights herein granted, unless earlier terminated under other provisions hereof, for the term of .... (................) years from the date hereof (hereinafter called the 'primary term'), and for so long thereafter as operations are conducted upon the said lands or the pooled lands with no cessation or interruption for more than ninety (90) consecutive days.

The grant is made exclusive. No surface rights are spelled out – in western Canada these are invariably acquired by separate document. In Ontario, where the mineral lease is frequently relied on for surface rights, the following should be added: 'and for the said purposes to enter upon, use and occupy the said lands or so much thereof and to such extent as may be necessary or convenient and to drill wells, lay pipelines and build and install such tanks, stations, structures and roadways and to fence any portion of the said lands used as a well site as may be necessary.'

3.2 If at any time or times during the primary term operations have been conducted on the said lands or the pooled lands but are discontinued, this Lease shall continue in force and the

Continuation of the lease is tied into the defined term 'operations.'

Lessee shall, on or before the anniversary date following the expiration of a ninety (90) day period during which operations remain discontinued, either resume operations or pay the deferment fee. If operations are discontinued during the final year of the primary term, this Lease shall continue in force until the expiration of either the primary term or a ninety (90) day period following the discontinuance of operations, whichever shall be the later date, and shall continue thereafter if operations are being conducted on such date, or if clause 3.3 applies.

Special provision is made for operations being suspended in the final year of the primary term.

3.3   If, at the expiration of the primary term, or any time or times thereafter, there is, or are, well or wells capable of producing the minerals or any of them on the said lands or the pooled lands, and all such wells are shut-in, this Lease shall continue in force. If no royalties have been paid or operations conducted during any year in which this Lease is so continued, the Lessee shall, on or before the anniversary date, pay a suspended operations fee. Operations shall be conclusively deemed to have been conducted during a year in which such fee is paid. When this Lease is being continued by operation of this clause 3.3, the Lessee will use reasonable diligence to produce and market or use the minerals capable of being produced, but in the exercise of such diligence the Lessee shall not be obligated to furnish or install facilities other than well equipment, separator, dehydrator, and such flowlines and tankage as may be necessary for the purpose of producing the well or wells in accordance with ordinary industry practice and custom.

The Lessee is placed under some obligation to attempt to produce when the lease is being prolonged through a suspended operations fee.

4   COMMENCEMENT OF OPERATIONS

4.1   The Lessee will, on or before the first anniversary date, either commence operations on the said lands or pay or tender the deferment

The drilling obligation has been removed from the *habendum* clause and

fee to the Lessor, and, during each successive year of the primary term until operations have been commenced on the said lands, the Lessee shall pay or tender the deferment fee on or before the anniversary date.

treated as an ordinary covenant. It is of the 'or' type and does not involve automatic termination.

5 ROYALTY

5.1 Subject to adjustment pursuant to the operation of clauses 6 and 8, the Lessee shall pay to the Lessor a royalty in an amount equal to the value at the well of .... per cent (...................%) of all the minerals produced, and sold, or used for purposes other than operations hereunder from the said lands or the pooled lands. No royalty shall be payable for any of the minerals produced from the said lands or pooled lands which are used for production or well-site or battery-site separation or treating of the minerals, or are unavoidably lost.

The royalty is related to the well. This is a more precise reference point than the 'said lands.'

The purposes for which minerals may be used free of royalty have been more precisely defined as including only production and simple separating and treating.

6 LESSER INTEREST

6.1 If the Lessor's interest in the minerals is less than the entire and undivided fee simple estate therein, then the royalty and deferment fee shall be paid to the Lessor only in the proportion which his interest bears to the whole and undivided fee.

7 OFFSET WELLS

7.1 If commercial production is encountered in any well on any spacing unit laterally adjoining the said lands and not owned by the Lessor, or if owned by the Lessor not under lease to the Lessee, and if no well has been or is being drilled to the same productive formation or formations on the spacing unit, within, or partly within, the said lands, laterally adjoining the spacing unit where commercial production was encountered, the Lessee shall, within six (6) months from the date on which such well is placed on regular production:

a) Commence drilling operations for an offset well on the spacing unit of the said lands laterally adjoining the spacing unit on which production is being obtained and thereafter drill the offset well to the same productive formation or formations; or

b) Surrender all or any portion of the said lands pursuant to clause 16, provided that the lands surrendered shall include at least that portion of the said lands comprised in the spacing unit laterally adjoining the spacing unit from which production is being taken; or

c) Where production is being taken from the said lands from a formation or formations other than the formation or formations from which production is being taken on the laterally adjoining spacing unit, surrender all formations comprised within the said lands except that formation or formations from which the Lessee is taking production.

7.2 Notwithstanding the foregoing, if the well drilled on the spacing unit laterally adjoining the said lands is productive primarily or only of natural gas, the Lessee shall not be obligated either to drill an offset well, or surrender all or any portion of the said lands unless an adequate and commercially profitable market for the natural gas which might be produced from the offset well is obtained.

8 POOLING

8.1 The Lessee shall have the right at any time and from time to time to pool the said lands, or any portion thereof, or any zone for formation underlying the same, but so that the lands so pooled shall not exceed one (1) spacing unit (the pooled spacing unit, limited as to zone or formation if applicable, is hereinafter called the 'unit').

8.2   The right to pool herein granted, if exercised, shall be by written notice from the Lessee describing the lands, and the formation or formations, if the pooling is so limited, that are comprised within the unit.

8.3   In the event of such pooling, there shall be allocated to that portion of the said lands included in the unit that proportion of the total production of the minerals from wells in the unit, after deducting any used in the manner permitted in clause 5 or unavoidably lost, which the area of that portion of the said land in the unit bears to the total area of lands comprised therein. The production so allocated shall be conclusively deemed for all purposes, including the payment of royalty, to be the entire production of the minerals from the portion of the said lands included in the unit in the same manner as though produced from the said lands under the terms of this Lease.

8.4   Any operations conducted on any lands included in the unit, whether conducted before, after, or during the exercise of the right to pool granted by this clause 8, shall have the same effect in continuing this Lease in force and effect as to all of the said lands, as if such operations were upon the said lands.

8.5   The Lessee may terminate any unit established hereunder by giving written notice thereof to the Lessor if at that time no operations are being conducted in the unit.

The Lessor must be given notice of the act of pooling.

De-pooling is expressly authorized.

9 OPERATIONS

9.1   The Lessee shall conduct all operations on the said lands in a diligent, careful and workmanlike manner and in compliance with the provisions of law applicable to the operations, and, where such provisions of law conflict or are at variance with the provisions of this Lease, the former shall prevail.

10 INFORMATION

10.1 The Lessee shall give written notice to the Lessor whenever a well is to be drilled on the said lands or the pooled lands, and within a reasonable time after drilling has ceased, shall advise the Lessor in writing of the status of the well, except where such information would not be available to the public from a governmental agency.

The Lessor at least is notified of the commencement of drilling and the ultimate fate of the well. There are too many imponderables, such as 'tight holes,' confidential status of wells and fields to require the Lessee to provide more information as a matter of right.

10.2 The Lessee shall provide with each royalty payment a statement showing the volume of the minerals produced from or allocated to the said lands during the applicable monthly period, the unit price received for same, and the deductions made.

The information to which the Lessor is entitled is considerably expanded.

10.3 The Lessee shall make available to the Lessor during normal business hours, at the Lessee's address hereinafter described, the Lessee's records relative to the minerals produced from the said lands, the price received therefor, and the deductions made.

11 INDEMNIFICATION

11.1 The Lessee indemnifies the Lessor against all actions, suits, claims and demands by any person or persons whomsoever in respect of any loss, injury, damage or obligation to compensate arising out of or connected with the work carried on by the Lessee on the said lands or in respect of any breach of any of the terms and conditions of this Lease insofar as the same relates to and affects the said lands.

12 COMPENSATION FOR SURFACE DAMAGE

12.1 The Lessee shall pay and be responsible for actual damages caused by its operations to the surface of, and growing crops and improvements on, the said lands.

13 DISCHARGE OF ENCUMBRANCES

13.1 The Lessee may at the Lessee's option pay or discharge the whole or any portion of any tax, charge, mortgage, lien or encumbrance of any kind or nature whatsoever incurred or created by the Lessor and/or the Lessor's predecessors or successors in title or interest which may now or hereafter exist on or against or in any way affect the said lands or the minerals, and the Lessee shall be subrogated to the rights of the holder or holders thereof and may, in addition thereto at the Lessee's option, reimburse itself by applying on the amount so paid by the Lessee the deferment fees, royalties, or other sums accruing to the Lessor under the terms of this Lease, and any deferment fees, royalties or other such sums so applied shall, for all purposes of this Lease, be conclusively deemed to have been paid to and received by the Lessor.

14 TAXES PAYABLE BY THE LESSEE

14.1 The Lessee shall pay all taxes, rates and assessments that may be assessed or levied in respect of the undertaking and operations of the Lessee on, in, over or under the said lands, and shall further pay all taxes, rates and assessments that may be assessed or levied directly or indirectly against the Lessee by reason of its interest in production of the said lands. The Lessee shall, on the written request of the Lessor, accompanied by such tax receipts, statements, or tax notices as the Lessee may require, reimburse the Lessor for seven-eighths (7/8) of any taxes assessed or imposed on the Lessor during the currency of this Lease by reason of the Lessor being the registered owner of the minerals or being entitled to become so registered.

15 TAXES PAYABLE BY THE LESSOR

15.1 The Lessor shall pay all taxes, rates and assessments that may be assessed or levied against the Lessor by reason of the Lessor's interest in production obtained from the said lands, or the Lessor's ownership of mineral rights in the said lands, and shall further pay all taxes, rates and assessments that may be assessed or levied against the surface of the said lands during the continuance of the term hereby granted or any extension thereof if and so long as the surface of the said lands is owned by the Lessor.

16 SURRENDER

16.1 The Lessee may, at any time, or from time to time, by written notice to the Lessor, surrender this Lease and term herein created as to the whole or any portion or portions of the minerals and/or the said lands, and this Lease and the term shall terminate as to the whole or any portion or portions thereof so surrendered, and the deferment fee, or royalty, shall be extinguished or correspondingly reduced as the case may be, but the Lessee shall not be entitled to a refund of any deferment fee previously paid.

17 REMOVAL FROM REGISTRY

17.1 If this Lease, or any caveat or any document in respect thereof, has been registered in the Land Titles Office or Registry Office for the area in which the said lands are situated, the Lessee shall withdraw or discharge the documents so registered, or register a notice of termination within a reasonable time after termination of this Lease.

18 REMOVAL OF EQUIPMENT

18.1   The Lessee shall, at all times during the term of this Lease and for a period of six (6) months from the termination thereof, have the right to remove any of its machinery, equipment, structures, pipelines, casing and materials from the said lands.

19 DEFAULT

19.1   If the Lessor considers that the Lessee has not complied with any obligation hereunder, the Lessor shall so notify the Lessee in writing, describing the alleged breach or breaches by the Lessee. The Lessee shall then have ninety (90) days after receipt of such notice within which to remedy or commence to remedy the breach or breaches alleged by the Lessor, and, having commenced to remedy such breach or breaches, the Lessee shall thereafter diligently continue to remedy same. The Lessor shall not commence any action for any alleged breach of this Lease until the expiration of the aforesaid ninety (90) day period. Neither the giving of the aforesaid notice nor the performance of any acts by the Lessee intended to remedy all or any of the alleged breaches shall be deemed an admission by the Lessee that it has failed to perform its obligations hereunder. If the Lessee fails to remedy or commence to remedy a breach or breaches within the ninety (90) day period (and having so commenced thereafter diligently proceed to remedy same), this Lease, except as hereinafter provided, shall thereupon terminate

The Lessor must describe the breach – which now includes the drilling provision.

and it shall be lawful for the Lessor to re-enter the said lands and the same to have again, repossess and enjoy; provided that this Lease shall not terminate nor be subject to forfeiture or cancellation if there is located on the said lands or the pooled lands a well capable of producing the minerals or any of them, and, in that event, the Lessor's remedy for any default hereunder shall be for damages only.

20 WARRANTY OF TITLE

20.1   The Lessor does not warrant his title to the minerals other than warranting that he has no knowledge of any charge or encumbrance other than those registered against the title or disclosed by the Lessor to the Lessee and that the Lessor has the right to enter into this Lease and that the Lessee, upon observing and performing the covenants and obligations on its part herein contained, shall and may peaceably possess and enjoy the same and the rights and privileges hereby granted during the said term and any extension thereof without any interruption or disturbance from or by the Lessor or anyone claiming under or through him.

The Lessor's warranty is limited.

The Lessor's obligations with respect to peaceful enjoyment are limited to himself and those claiming through him.

21 FURTHER ASSURANCE

21.1   The Lessor and the Lessee will each do and perform all such things and execute all such deeds, documents and writings and give all such assurance as may be necessary to give effect to this Lease.

22 MANNER OF PAYMENT

22.1   All payments to the Lessor provided for in this Lease shall, at the Lessee's option, be paid or tendered either to the Lessor or to the depository named in or pursuant to this clause, and all such payments or tenders may be made by cheque or draft of the Lessee either mailed or delivered to the Lessor or to said depository, which cheque or draft shall be payable in Canadian funds at par in the bank on which it is drawn. The Lessor does hereby appoint ....

....

at ....

....

as the depository for the receipt of all monies payable under this Lease, and the Lessor agrees that said depository and its successors shall be and continue as his agents for the receipt of any and all sums payable hereunder, regardless of changes of ownership (whether by assignment, succession or otherwise) of the said lands or the minerals or of the deferment fees or royalties to accrue hereunder. The Lessor may not cancel the appointment of a depository without designating a successor but may at any time designate a new depository by giving written notice to the Lessee specifying the name and address of such new depository; provided that only a bank or trust company in Canada may be designated as depository, that only one depository shall be designated at any one time as aforesaid, and that the Lessee shall not be required to recognize any change of depository until the expiration of forty-five (45) days from the receipt by it of the notice in writing. If any depository shall at any time resign or fail or refuse to act as depository and a successor depository shall not be designated within ten (10) days thereafter or if any monies payable hereunder become payable to more than one person and the persons to whom such monies are payable shall have failed to designate one depository hereunder, then the Lessee at its option may designate a bank or trust company in Canada as depository hereunder, which depository shall be entitled to charge its usual fees, and said bank or trust

Since either mailing or delivery before the required date constitutes compliance with the lease, it is not necessary to provide for a deemed receipt.

It is made clear that the Lessor cannot dismiss one depository without appointing a replacement.

company shall be the depository to all intents and purposes as if originally appointed by the Lessor.

23 FORCE MAJEURE

23.1 The performance of any of the obligations of the Lessee hereunder and the expiration of any time period, including those set forth in clause 3, shall be suspended while and so long as the Lessee is prevented from complying with such obligations or performing those acts set forth in clause 3, in part or in whole, by strikes, lockouts, acts of God, acts of the Queen's enemies, severe weather conditions and/or action of the elements, accidents, laws, rules and regulations of any governmental bodies or agencies, zoning or land use ordinances of any governmental agency, acts or requests of any governmental officer or agent purporting to act under authority, delays in transportation, inability to obtain necessary materials in the open market, inadequate facilities for the transportation of materials or for the disposition of production, or other matters beyond the reasonable control of the Lessee, whether similar to the matters herein specifically enumerated or not; provided that in no event shall lack of finances on the part of the Lessee be deemed to be a matter beyond its reasonable control.

The operation of the clause is expanded to include all aspects of the lease, not just the *habendum*, although that clause is specifically referred to. The acts of *force majeure* have been broadened to include a number of events that are of particular application to the industry.

23.2 The time periods specified in this Lease, including those in clause 3, shall be extended by a like period during which any of the aforesaid acts of *force majeure* obtain and continue.

This makes it clear that the relevant time periods are automatically extended.

24 ASSIGNMENT

24.1 The parties hereto may each delegate, assign, sublet or convey to any other person or persons, corporation or corporations, all or any of the property, powers, rights and interests hereunder, and may enter into all agreements, contracts and documents, and do all necessary acts and things to give effect to the provisions of this clause. The Lessee need not act upon any assignment of monies which are payable or which may be paid or become payable under this Lease until forty-five (45) days after the Lessee has been actually furnished with evidence satisfactory to it of such assignment and all payments made within the aforesaid period to the party or parties who would have been entitled to same in the absence of such assignment shall be conclusively deemed to have been made in accordance with the terms hereof; the foregoing shall not, however, prohibit the Lessee from acting upon the assignment prior to the expiration of the aforesaid forty-five (45) day period.

The Lessee has an option to either wait out the 45 day period or not.

The provision in the standard clause that divides the lease where the Lessee has made a multi-party assignment has been omitted. It could result in the Lessor being left with a fractional lease and is not necessary under the 'or' type of drilling clause.

25 NOTICES

25.1 All notices to be given hereunder may be given by postpaid letter addressed to the Lessee at .... and to the Lessor at .... or such other address as the Lessee or the Lessor may from time to time appoint in writing, and any such notice shall be conclusively deemed to have been received upon actual receipt by the other party or upon the expiration of seven (7) days after the mailing thereof, whichever shall first occur.

25.2 Nothing in this clause 25 shall in any way affect the payment of monies hereunder, which shall be governed solely by clause 22.

26 ENTIRE AGREEMENT

26.1 The terms of this Lease express and constitute the entire agreement between the parties, and no implied covenant or liability of any kind is created or shall arise by reason of this Lease or anything herein contained. The parties recognize that the terms of this Lease may be modified or affected by operation of legislation, regulation or orders made applicable thereto.

The reference to legislation is really for clarification only.

This Lease shall enure to the benefit of and be binding upon the parties hereto and each of them, their respective heirs, executors, administrators, successors and assigns.

...., the above-mentioned Lessee, does hereby accept this Lease of the above-described lands, to be held by it as tenant and subject to the conditions, restrictions and covenants above set forth.

The express acceptance of the lease by the Lessee is a compliance with legislation in Saskatchewan. It is not necessary in the other jurisdictions but does no harm.

This is the place where the Declaration of wife must be completed in Saskatchewan leases. In that province the Declaration must precede the execution signatures. The Declaration takes the following form: 'Declaration of Wife. I, ... wife of the within named

IN WITNESS WHEREOF the Lessor and the Lessee have executed and delivered this Lease the day and year first above written.

Signed, Sealed and Delivered in the presence of:

....
(Witness)   (Lessor)

(Name of Lessee Company)

....

.... do hereby declare that I have executed this Lease for the purpose of relinquishing all my rights in said homestead in favour of .... insofar as may be necessary to give effect to this Lease.'

....
(Signature of Wife)

NOTE: The lease should now be completed by inserting the proper form (as stipulated by the applicable provincial legislation) of two affidavits of execution: a dower or homestead affidavit; consent of spouse (except for Saskatchewan as above); and a certificate of acknowledgment by spouse.

While these affidavits and dower declarations may follow the actual signature, they must, nonetheless, form part of the document. The usual and best procedure is to print the lease, together with affidavits and declarations, on both sides of a double legal size sheet folded at the top. This allows easy insertion in a type-writer and enables all the required forms to be incorporated in the document itself.

18
The most common form of 'Standard' Lease*

THIS INDENTURE made the _____ day of _____ A.D. 19_____

BETWEEN: _____

(hereinafter referred to as the 'Lessor'), OF THE FIRST PART;

AND

_____,

a body corporate, having an office in the Province of Alberta
(hereinafter referred to as the 'Lessee'), OF THE SECOND PART

THE LESSOR, being registered as owner (or entitled to become registered as owner), subject, however, to such mortgages and encumbrances contained in the existing Certificate of Title, of, *inter alia*, the leased substances (as hereinafter defined) within, upon or under

in the Province of Alberta, as more particularly described and set forth in Certificate(s) of Title No(s) _____ of Record in the _____ Alberta Land Registration District, in consideration of the sum of _____ _____DOLLARS ($_____) paid to the Lessor by the Lessee (the receipt whereof is hereby acknowledged), and in consideration of the covenants of the Lessee hereinafter contained, DOTH HEREBY GRANT AND LEASE unto the Lessee all the petroleum, natural gas and related hydrocarbons (except coal and valuable stone), all other gases, and all minerals

*Used as the basis for discussion in Part Two

and substances (whether liquid or solid and whether hydrocarbons or not) produced in association with any of the foregoing or found in any water contained in any reservoir (all hereinafter referred to as the 'leased substances'), subject to the royalties hereinafter reserved, within, upon or under the lands hereinbefore described and all the right, title, estate, and interest, if any, of the Lessor in and to the leased substances or any of them within, upon or under any lands excepted from, or roadways, lanes or rights-of-way adjoining, the lands aforesaid, together with the exclusive right and privilege to explore, drill for, win, take, remove, store and dispose of the leased substances and for the said purposes to drill wells, lay pipe lines and build and install such tanks, stations, structures and roadways as may be necessary.

TO HAVE AND ENJOY the same for the term of Ten (10) years from the date hereof and so long thereafter as the leased substances or any of them are produced from the said lands or the pooled lands subject to the sooner termination of the said term and subject also to extension of the said term all as hereinafter provided.

PROVIDED that if operations for the drilling of a well are not commenced on the said lands or the pooled lands within one (1) year from the date hereof, this Lease shall terminate and be at an end on the first anniversary date, unless the Lessee shall have paid or tendered to the Lessor on or before said anniversary date the sum of _____ Dollars ($_____) (hereinafter called the 'delay rental'), which payment shall confer the privilege of deferring the commencement of drilling operations for a period of one (1) year from said anniversary date, and that, in like manner and upon like payments or tenders, the commencement of drilling operations and the termination of this Lease shall be further deferred for like periods successively;

PROVIDED FURTHER that if at any time during the said Ten (10) year term and prior to the discovery of production on the said lands or the pooled lands, the Lessee shall drill a dry well or wells thereon, or if at any time during such term and after the discovery of production on the said lands or the pooled lands such production shall cease and the well or wells from which such production was taken shall be abandoned, then this Lease shall terminate at the next ensuing anniversary date hereof unless operations for the drilling of a further well on the said lands or the pooled lands shall have been commenced or unless the Lessee shall have paid or tendered the delay rental, in which latter event the immediately preceding proviso hereof governing the payment of the delay rental and the effect thereof, shall be applicable thereto;

AND FURTHER ALWAYS PROVIDED that if at the end of the said Ten (10) year term the leased substances are not being produced from the said lands or the pooled lands (whether or not the leased substances have theretofore been produced therefrom) and the Lessee is then engaged in drilling or working operations thereon, or if at any time after the expiration of the said Ten (10) year term production of the leased substances has ceased and the Lessee shall have commenced further drilling or working operations within Ninety (90) days after the cessation of said production, then this Lease shall remain in force so long as any drilling or working operations are prosecuted with no cessation of more than Ninety (90) consecutive days, and, if they result in the production of the leased substances or any of them, so long thereafter as the leased substances or any of them are produced from the said lands or the pooled lands; provided that if drilling or working operations are interrupted or suspended as the result of any cause whatsoever beyond the Lessee's reasonable control, or if any well on the said lands or the pooled lands or on any spacing unit of which the said lands or any portion thereof form a part, is shut-in, suspended or otherwise not produced as the result of a lack of or an intermittent market, or any cause whatsoever beyond the Lessee's reasonable control, the time of such interruption or suspension or non-production shall not be counted against the Lessee, anything hereinbefore contained or implied to the contrary notwithstanding.

THE LESSOR AND THE LESSEE HEREBY COVENANT AND AGREE AS FOLLOWS:

1 Interpretation:
In this Lease, unless there is something in the subject or context inconsistent therewith, the expressions following shall have the following meanings, namely:
a) 'Commercial production' shall mean the output from a well of such quantity of the leased substances or any of them as, considering the cost of drilling and production operations and price and quality of the leased substances, after a production test of Thirty (30) days, would commercially and economically warrant the drilling of a like well in the vicinity thereof.
b) 'Spacing unit' shall mean the area allocated to a well for the purpose of drilling for and/or producing the leased substances or any of them, by or under any law of the Province of Alberta now or hereafter in effect governing the spacing of petroleum and/or natural gas wells.
c) 'Said lands' shall mean all the lands hereinbefore described or referred to, or such portion or portions thereof as shall not have been surrendered.
d) 'Pooled Lands' shall mean the said lands, together with any other lands or

any zone or formation underlying such other lands, which are pooled pursuant to the provisions of Clause 8 hereof.

2 Royalties:

The Lessor does hereby reserve unto himself a gross royalty of Twelve and one-half per cent (12½%) of the leased substances produced and marketed from the said lands. Any sale by the Lessee of any crude oil, crude naphtha, or gas produced from the said lands shall include the royalty share thereof reserved to the Lessor, and the Lessee shall account to the Lessor for his said royalty share in accordance with the following provisions namely:

The Lessee shall remit to the Lessor, on or before the 20th day of each month, (a) an amount equal to the current market value on the said lands of Twelve and one-half per cent (12½%) of the crude oil and crude naphtha produced, saved and marketed from the said lands during the preceding month, and (b) an amount equal to the current market value on the said lands of Twelve and one-half per cent (12½%) of all gas produced and marketed from the said lands during said preceding month.

Notwithstanding anything to the contrary herein contained or implied, the Lessee shall be entitled to use such part of the production of the leased substances from the said lands as may be required and used by the Lessee in its operations hereunder, and the Lessor shall not be entitled to any royalty with respect to said leased substances.

3 Shut-in Wells:

If all wells on the said lands or the pooled lands are shut-in, suspended or otherwise not produced during any year ending on an anniversary date as the result of a lack of or an intermittent market, or any cause whatsoever beyond the Lessee's reasonable control, the Lessee shall pay to the Lessor at the expiration of each said year a sum equal to the delay rental hereinbefore set forth, and each such well shall be deemed to be a producing well hereunder.

4 Lesser Interest:

If the Lessor's interest in the leased substances be less than the entire and undivided fee simple estate therein, then the royalties herein provided shall be paid to the Lessor only in the proportion which his interest bears to the whole and undivided fee.

5 Taxes Payable by the Lessor:

The Lessor shall promptly satisfy all taxes, rates and assessments that may be assessed or levied, directly or indirectly, against the Lessor by reason of the Lessor's interest in production obtained from the said lands, or the

Lessor's ownership of mineral rights in the said lands, and shall further pay all taxes, rates and assessments that may be assessed or levied against the surface of the said lands during the continuance of the term hereby granted or any extension thereof if and so long as the said surface of the said lands is or continues to be owned by the Lessor.

6 Taxes Payable by the Lessee:

The Lessee shall pay all taxes, rates and assessments that may be assessed or levied in respect of the undertaking and operations of the Lessee on, in, over or under the said lands, and shall further pay all taxes, rates and assessments that may be assessed or levied directly or indirectly against the Lessee by reason of the Lessee's interest in production from the said lands. The Lessee shall on the written request of the Lessor, accompanied by such tax receipts, statements or tax notices as the Lessee may require, reimburse the Lessor for seven-eighths (7/8ths) of any taxes assessed or imposed on the Lessor during the currency of this Lease by reason of the Lessor being the registered owner of the leased substances or being entitled to become such owner.

7 Offset Wells:

In the event of commercial production being obtained from any well drilled on any spacing unit laterally adjoining the said lands and not owned by the Lessor, or, if owned by the Lessor, not under lease to the Lessee, then unless a well has been or is being drilled on the spacing unit of the said lands laterally adjoining the said spacing unit on which production is being so obtained and to the horizon in the formation from which production is being so obtained, the Lessee shall, within Six (6) months from the date of said well being placed on regular production, either:

a) Commence or cause to be commenced within the Six (6) month period aforesaid operations for the drilling of an offset well on the spacing unit of the said lands laterally adjoining the said spacing unit on which production is being so obtained, and thereafter drill the same to the horizon in the formation from which production is being obtained from the said adjoining spacing unit; or

b) Surrender all or any portion of the said lands pursuant to the provisions of paragraph 14 hereof, provided that the lands surrendered shall include that portion of the said lands comprised in the said spacing unit laterally adjoining the said spacing unit on which production is being so obtained; or

c) Where production is being obtained from the said lands from a formation other than the formation from which commercial production is being obtained on the spacing unit laterally adjoining the said lands, surrender all formations which lie within the said lands except that formation within the said lands from which the Lessee is obtaining production.

PROVIDED, that if such well drilled on lands laterally adjoining the said lands is productive primarily or only of natural gas, the Lessee shall not be obligated either to drill an offset well or to surrender said spacing unit unless and until an adequate and commercially profitable market for natural gas which might be produced from the offset well can be previously arranged and provided.

8 Pooling:

The Lessee is hereby given the right and power at any time and from time to time to pool or combine the said lands, or any portion thereof, or any zone or formation underlying the said lands or any portion thereof, with any other lands or any zone or formation underlying the same, but so that the lands so pooled and combined (herein referred to as a 'unit') shall not exceed One (1) spacing unit as hereinbefore defined. In the event of such pooling or combining, the Lessor shall, in lieu of the royalties elsewhere herein specified, receive on production of the leased substances from the said unit, only such portion of the royalties stipulated herein as the surface area of the said lands placed in the unit bears to the total surface area of lands in such unit. Drilling operations on, or production of the leased substances from, or the presence of a shut-in or suspended well on, any land included in such unit shall have the same effect in continuing this Lease in force and effect as to all the said lands, as if such operations or production were upon or from the said lands, or some portion thereof, or as if said shut-in or suspended well were located on the said lands, or some portion thereof.

9 Operations:

The Lessee shall conduct all its operations on the said lands in a diligent, careful and workmanlike manner and in compliance with the provisions of law applicable to such operations, and where such provisions of law conflict or are at variance with the provisions of this Lease, such provisions of law shall prevail.

10 Records of Production:

The Lessee shall make available to the Lessor during normal business hours at the Lessee's address hereinafter mentioned the Lessee's records relative to the quantity of leased substances produced from the said lands.

11 Indemnification:

The Lessee shall indemnify the Lessor against all actions, suits, claims and demands by any person or persons whomsoever in respect of any loss, injury, damage or obligation to compensate arising out of or connected with the work carried on by the Lessee on the said lands or in respect of any breach of any of the terms and conditions of this Lease insofar as the same relates to and affects the said lands.

12 Compensation:

The Lessee shall pay and be responsible for actual damages caused by its operations to the surface of, and growing crops and improvements on, the said lands.

13 Discharge of Encumbrances:

The Lessee may at the Lessee's option pay or discharge the whole or any portion of any tax, charge, mortgage, lien or encumbrance of any kind or nature whatsoever incurred or created by the Lessor and/or the Lessor's predecessors or successors in title or interest which may now or hereafter exist on or against or in any way affect the said lands or the leased substances, in which event the Lessee shall be subrogated to the rights of the holder or holders thereof and may in addition thereto at the Lessee's option, reimburse itself by applying on the amount so paid by the Lessee the rentals, royalties, or other sums accruing to the Lessor under the terms of this Lease, and any rentals, royalties or such other sums so applied shall, for all purposes of this Lease, be deemed to have been paid to and received by the Lessor.

14 Surrender:

Notwithstanding anything herein contained, the Lessee may at any time or from time to time determine or surrender this Lease and the term hereby granted as to the whole or any part or parts of the leased substances and/or the said lands, upon giving the Lessor written notice to that effect, WHERE-UPON this Lease and the said term shall terminate as to the whole or any part or parts thereof so surrendered and the rental, royalty or otherwise, shall be extinguished or correspondingly reduced as the case may be, but the Lessee shall not be entitled to a refund of any such rent theretofore paid.

15 Removal of Caveat:

In the event of the Lessee having registered in the Land Titles Office for the area in which the said lands are situated this Lease or any caveat or other document in respect thereof, the Lessee shall withdraw or discharge the document so registered within a reasonable time after termination of this Lease.

16 Removal of Equipment:

The Lessee shall at all times during the currency of this Lease and for a period of Six (6) months from the termination thereof, have the right to remove all or any of its machinery, equipment, structures, pipe lines, casing and materials from off the said lands.

17 Default:

In the case of the breach or non-observance or non-performance on the part of the Lessee of any covenant, proviso, condition, restriction or stipulation herein contained which ought to be observed or performed by the Lessee and which has not been waived by the Lessor, the Lessor shall, before bringing any action with respect thereto or declaring any forfeiture, give to the Lessee written notice setting forth the particulars of and requiring it to remedy such default, and in the event that the Lessee shall fail to commence to remedy such default within a period of Ninety (90) days from receipt of such notice, and thereafter diligently proceed to remedy the same, then except as hereinafter provided, this Lease shall thereupon terminate and it shall be lawful for the Lessor into or upon the said lands (or any part thereof in the name of the whole) to re-enter and the same to have again, repossess and enjoy; PROVIDED that this Lease shall not terminate nor be subject to forfeiture or cancellation if there is located on the said lands a well capable of producing the leased substances or any of them, and in that event the Lessor's remedy for any default hereunder shall be for damages only.

18 Quiet Enjoyment:

The Lessor covenants and warrants that he has good title to the leased substances and the said lands as hereinbefore set forth, has good right and full power to grant and demise the same and the rights and privileges in manner aforesaid, and that the Lessee, upon observing and performing the covenants and conditions on the Lessee's part herein contained, shall and may peaceably possess and enjoy the same and the rights and privileges hereby granted during the said term and any extension thereof without any interruption or disturbance from or by the Lessor or any other person whomsoever.

19 Covenant for Further Assurance:

The Lessor and the Lessee hereby agree that they will each do and perform all such acts and things and execute all such deeds, documents and writings and give all such assurance as may be necessary to give effect to the Lease and all covenants herein contained.

20 Assignment:

The parties hereto may each or either of them delegate, assign, sub-let or convey to any other person or persons, corporation or corporations, all or any of the property, powers, rights and interests obtained by or conferred upon them respectively hereunder and may enter into all agreements, contracts and writings and do all necessary acts and things to give effect to the provisions of this clause; PROVIDED, that no assignment of royalties or other moneys payable hereunder shall be binding upon the Lessee, notwithstanding any actual or constructive notice or knowledge thereof, unless and except the same be for the entire interest of the Lessor in all of the said sums remaining to be paid or to accrue hereunder, nor then until Thirty (30) days after the Lessee has been actually furnished at its address hereinafter set forth with evidence satisfactory to the Lessee of such assignment of the entire interest of the Lessor in all the sums aforesaid, including, if effected by voluntary act, the original or a certified copy of the instrument effecting such assignment; PROVIDED FURTHER that in the event that the Lessee shall assign this Lease as to any part or parts of the said lands, then the delay rental shall be apportioned amongst the several leaseholders rateably according to the surface area of each, and should the Assignee or Assignees of any such part or parts fail to pay the proportionate part of the delay rental payable by him or them, such failure to pay shall not operate to terminate or affect this Lease insofar as it relates to and comprises the part or parts of the said lands in respect of which the Lessee or its Assignees shall make due payment of rental.

21 Manner of Payment:

All payments to the Lessor provided for in this Lease shall, at the Lessee's option, be paid or tendered either to the Lessor or to the depository named in or pursuant to this clause, and all such payments or tenders may be made by cheque or draft of the Lessee either mailed or delivered to the Lessor or to said depository, which cheque or draft shall be payable in Canadian funds at par in the bank on which it is drawn. A cheque or draft in payment of delay rentals which is mailed by deposit in one of Her Majesty's Mail Boxes or Post Offices at least Forty-eight (48) hours prior to each anniversary date, shall be deemed to have been received by the addressee in sufficient time to confer the privilege of deferring the commencement of drilling operations for a period of one (1) year from each such anniversary date. The Lessor does hereby appoint _____ at _____ as the depository for the receipt of all moneys payable under this Lease, and the Lessor agrees that said depository and its successors shall be and continue as his agents for the receipt of any and all sums payable hereunder regardless of changes of ownership (whether by assignment, succession or otherwise) of the said lands or of the leased substances or of the rentals or royalties to accrue hereunder. The Lessor may at any time designate a new depository by giving written notice to the Lessee specifying the name and address of such new depository; provided that only a bank or trust company in Canada may be designated as depository, that only one depository shall be designated at any one time as aforesaid, and that the Lessee shall not be required to recognize any change of depository until the expiration of Forty-five (45) days from the receipt by the Lessee of the notice in writing aforesaid. If any depository designated by the Lessor shall at any time resign or fail or refuse to act as depository and a successor depository shall not be designated as aforesaid within Ten (10) days thereafter, or if any moneys payable hereunder become payable to more than one person and the persons to whom said moneys are payable shall have failed to designate one depository hereunder, then the Lessee may at its option designate a bank or trust company in Canada as depository hereunder which depository shall be entitled to charge its usual fees, and said bank or trust company shall be the depository to all intents and purposes as if originally designated herein by the Lessor.

22 Entire Agreement:
The terms of this Lease express and constitute the entire agreement between the parties, and no implied covenant or liability of any kind is created or shall arise by reason of these presents or anything herein contained.

23 Notices:
All notices to be given hereunder may be given by registered letter addressed to the Lessee at _____
and to the Lessor at _____
or such other address as the Lessor and the Lessee may respectively from time to time appoint in writing, and any such notice shall be deemed to be given to and received by the addressee Seven (7) days after the mailing thereof, postage prepaid.

THIS LEASE shall enure to the benefit of and be binding upon the parties hereto and each of them, their respective heirs, executors, administrators, successors and assigns.

———,

the above mentioned Lessee, doth hereby accept this Lease, of the above described land, to be held by it as tenant, and subject to the conditions, restrictions and covenants above set forth.

IN WITNESS WHEREOF the Lessor and the Lessee have executed and delivered this Lease, the day and year first above written. SIGNED, SEALED AND DELIVERED.

Case index

Statute index

General index

acceptance of lease, by lessor in Saskatchewan 310; by lessee, in standard form, 322; *see also* contract

acquisition, of lease 23-4; procedure 72-3

ademption, granting of lease is not 11-12

agent, in obtaining a lease 111; lessee as, in pooling, *see* pooling; in unitizing, *see* unitization

agreement, to grant a lease 66-9; entire, standard clause 178, 321; model clause 309-10

amendment of lease, *see* top lease

American authorities, use of by Canadian courts 77-8

anniversary date, definition of, model clause 294

apportionment, *see* royalty

approach, of Canadian courts to lease 78-9, 245-6

assignment, right of parties to 169-72; standard clause 169-320; provisos to 169-72, 320; effect on payment of delay rentals 170-2; model clause 308-9

assurance, further, covenant for 168-9; standard clause 168, 319-20; applies only to parties 169; model clause 306

bonus consideration, payment of 23-4; a condition precedent 56-60; if condition subsequent 59n; standard clause 80, 312; tax treatment 80-1; model clause 297

capacity, to enter into lease, generally 24-46; age of majority 24-7; infants 13, 25-7; personal representatives 13-14, 15-18, 27; incapacitated persons, mental infirmity 28-9; married parties, *see* dower and curtesy

capped well royalty, *see* royalty

capture, rule of 82; *see also* unitization

category, legal, of lease 11-19; *see also* legal category of lease

caveat, removal of 163-4; standard clause 164, 318-19; model clause 304-5

commercial production, definition,